AIEL Series in Labour Economics

Floro Ernesto Caroleo
Sergio Destefanis
(Editors)

The European Labour Market

Regional Dimensions

With 43 Figures and 53 Tables

Physica-Verlag

A Springer Company

Professor Floro Ernesto Caroleo
Professor Sergio Destefanis

Università degli Studi di Salerno
Dipartimento di Scienze Economiche e Statistiche
Via Ponte Don Melillo
84084 Fisciano (SA)
Italy

caroleo@unisa.it
destefanis@unisa.it

ISBN-10   3-7908-1679-5 Physica-Verlag Heidelberg New York
ISBN-13   978-3-7908-1679-2 Physica-Verlag Heidelberg New York

Cataloging-in-Publication Data applied for
Library of Congress Control Number: 2006921280

Physica is a part of Springer Science+Business Media

springer.com

© Physica-Verlag Heidelberg 2006
Printed in Germany

Hard-Cover-Design: Erich Kirchner, Heidelberg

SPIN 11602552   88/3153-5 4 3 2 1 0 – Printed on acid-free and non-aging paper

Contents

Introduction and Overview[*]

Floro Ernesto Caroleo and Sergio Destefanis

University of Salerno, Italy

Some recent developments have crucially increased the regional dimension of European labour markets. The creation of a single currency prevents recourse to national monetary policies and stability clauses drastically reduce the autonomy of member countries, also in the field of fiscal policy. All this is happening when the enlargement of the European Union to Central and Eastern European countries has considerably extended the scope of issues concerning regional cohesion. These developments have already prompted considerable analytical efforts, among which are the papers presented at the Seventeenth AIEL Conference (University of Salerno, 2002) and now contained in this book. These papers constitute an up-to-date and stimulating body of findings, and we feel that there are ample grounds for bringing them together in a single volume.

A first block of papers provides a conceptual and empirical introduction to the main issues relating to interactions between the European economy and its regions. Particular attention is paid to the structure of the shocks affecting employment (regional, industrial, national), and the transition of Central and Eastern European countries to a market economy. The papers that follow are more specific and deal with such issues as:

1. the relationships between labour market efficiency and the regional distribution of unemployment. More specifically, what is the role of institutional factors in shaping the evolution of regional unemployment? Does skill mismatch matter?
2. the extent of labour market (and more particularly of wage) flexibility in EU member countries or in their regions. Is wage flexibility already at satisfactory levels in EU countries? Does labour market flexibility affect the transition of Central and Eastern European countries to a market economy?
3. The role of active labour market policies: are they able to affect the regional distribution of employment and unemployment?

The following brief presentation of the contents of the papers arranges them under the above headings. However, as will become clear, there are close interrelations and interactions among the papers.

---

[*] We gratefully acknowledge financial support from the Italian Ministry of Education, University and Research (PRIN 2003) and from the University of Salerno.

The main issues

Adalgiso Amendola, Floro E. Caroleo and Gianluigi Coppola analyse regional disparities in unemployment, employment and participation rates by means of STATIS. The latter is a dynamic multivariate analysis methodology allowing the calculation of latent factors for multidimensional phenomena that can be represented by variable-space-time matrices. The regional structure of the European labour market throughout the 1990s is represented using a set of ten economic variables. Some latent factors summarising the disparities and their dynamics in the period considered are successfully extracted. Very little convergence appears to have taken place across regions; instead, there is high regional variability. The authors find that flexibility in the labour market, as well as in the productive structure, has a role in determining labour market performance. On the other hand, the explanatory power of the New Economic Geography (Fujita et al. 1999) appears rather weak in this context.

Anna Maria Ferragina and Francesco Pastore survey the now ample theoretical and empirical literature on regional unemployment during transition in Central and Eastern Europe. Two main theoretical approaches are considered and discussed with reference to the available evidence: the neoclassical model of regional unemployment and the Aghion and Blanchard Optimal Speed of Transition model (Aghion and Blanchard 1994). In the first approach, slow-growth, high-unemployment regions are characterised by supply side constraints and institutional rigidities. Constraints on factors mobility contribute to the persistence of differences. The second approach explores the relationship between labour turnover and unemployment, suggesting that lower unemployment can be achieved by implementing transition more gradually. Moreover, international trade, foreign direct investment and agglomeration factors help explain the success of capital cities compared to peripheral towns and rural areas in achieving low unemployment.

The paper by Marelli considers the evolution of employment across 145 European regions (between 1983 and 1997) at a level of industrial disaggregation greater than that usually considered in the literature, using both shift-share and panel regression techniques. The results highlight the importance of both the regional and the industrial dimension. National boundaries are not particularly significant in singling out clusters of regions with similar levels of employment growth. What matters is industrial structure: manufacturing employment is correlated better across countries and regions than is aggregate employment, and the most dynamic regions are those in which the development of services is grafted on to a strong manufacturing sector. While the evidence confirms that there is growing integration among European regions, it does not corroborate the existence of a core of regions located in Northern Europe with more uniform employment dynamics.

Maggioni and Gambarotto conduct a critical survey of the recent empirical literature devoted to the analysis of local labour markets, with the Italian case being analysed in light of the experience of other European countries. The literature is organised according to a fourfold taxonomy: statistical-bureaucratic, where 'local' only means 'sub–national'; statistical-functional, with specific reference to travel-to-work areas and local labour systems; socio-economic, with the focus on the notion of 'industrial district'; economic-modelling, including empirical tests of results in the New Economic Geography literature. The authors also propose an encompassing approach where space is no longer a mere container of inputs but a relational asset.

These four papers provide a factual and Europe-wide background for the rest of the book. The next four papers in the book examine the relationships among labour market efficiency, institutions, and skill mismatch from a more country-based perspective.

Skills, institutions and unemployment across regions

Destefanis and Fonseca use frontier techniques to estimate a matching function (reformulated as a Beveridge curve) on data for the main Italian territorial areas (North, Centre, South) throughout the 1990s. The Southern labour market proves to be much less efficient than that in the rest of the country, especially in the case of unskilled labour. This approach is then utilised to assess the impact on the Italian labour market of the 1997 Treu Act, which greatly fostered the development of temporary work in Italy. This Act appears to have engendered an increase in labour demand, especially in the North and in the Centre. However, there is evidence of an outward shift of the Beveridge curve in the South, particularly as far as unskilled labour is concerned. As a consequence, the authors conclude that the Act reduced unemployment in the more developed regions of the country, but did not favourably affect the matching efficiency of the Italian labour market.

Domadenik and Vehovec report findings from a panel of Croatian and Slovenian firms throughout the period 1995–2000. Strictly speaking, Croatia and Slovenia are not regions, but scrutiny of them sheds light on regional issues, owing to their small size and because they were part of the same country until the early 1990s. The authors address the issue of defensive restructuring through dynamic labour demand analysis. The estimated short run elasticities of labour with respect to wages and output are very similar in the case of the two countries and confirm that firms in both economies adjusted employment gradually over time in response to exogenous shocks occurring at the beginning of transition. However, long-run wage elasticities are greater for Slovenian firms, suggesting that the extent and efficiency of strategic restructuring in Slovenia was a very significant factor in the differing economic performances of the two countries in the first decade of transition.

Building on the Layard and Nickell framework, Limosani proposes a simple model in order to analyse the relation among labour productivity, wages, and unemployment across the main territorial areas of Italy. Some panel data evidence is presented for the last four decades which strongly suggests that wage and productivity differentials are two of the main factors driving the dynamics of unemployment across Italian territorial areas.

In his paper, Newell investigates the extent to which the patterns of regional unemployment in Poland since the early 1990s can be explained by regional imbalances in the supply and demand for skilled labour. Indeed, massive changes in the relative demand for skilled labour are found to have taken place over this period, and by no means uniformly across Polish regions. Lower-skilled regional populations tend to generate higher rates of unemployment. Moreover, when controlling for population skill levels, higher levels of relative demand for skilled workers raise a region's rate of unemployment. Using a theoretical model in which regional labour supply mobility and relative wage flexibility are limited, the author interprets these findings as equilibrium and mismatch phenomena. They account for about half of the regional variation in Polish rates of unemployment.

Labour market flexibility across regions: theory and measurement

Whilst almost all the other contributions in the book are of a mainly empirical nature, Südekum uses some stylised facts concerning the EU-15 regions to build a theoretical model combining a wage curve with an increasing returns technology. Large 'core' regions have both higher equilibrium wages and lower unemployment rates than peripheral regions. Yet, New Economic Geography models usually abstract from unemployment. By contrast, wage curve models (Blanchflower and Oswald 1994) imply a negative correlation between regional unemployment and wages, but fail to account for agglomeration effects. Südekum's model combines features of both strands of theory: regional disparities can develop endogenously and labour mobility does not negate the wage curve mechanism, but rather strengthens it.

Despite the centrality of the issue of labour market flexibility in the literature, attempts to measure levels of flexibility consistently, either within or across countries, have been remarkably rare. Monastiriotis presents in his paper a complete set of labour market flexibility indicators for the UK and its regions. After discussing issues concerning the measurement of flexibility and the construction of the indexes, he examines the evolution of labour market flexibility and its various forms across the UK regions and over the period 1979–1998. Labour market flexibility is found to have increased throughout the period across all UK regions, but evidence of convergence in the regional levels of flexibility co-exists with a rather persistent pattern of a North-South dichotomy and regional specialisation in different forms of flexibility. If anything, labour market deregulation does not seem to have facilitated regional harmonisation in levels and forms of labour market flexibility.

Montuenga, García and Fernández analyse wage flexibility in five EU member states (France, Italy, Portugal, Spain and the UK) by estimating their respective wage curves. Different measures of labour slack (the rate of unemployment) are utilised in order to appraise the responsiveness of wages to it in various segments of the labour market. Drawing on information provided by a homogenous panel data set – the ECHP – the authors show that wage flexibility varies across countries and that the labour markets in the five countries in question are structurally different. A flexibility ranking can be constructed from the less flexible countries (Portugal and Italy) to the most flexible one (the UK), with France and Spain somewhere in between. Only in the UK does the labour market come sufficiently close to a spot market.

Active labour market policies across regions

Over the past two decades, large-scale restructuring in the labour market has occurred in many countries, requiring a substantial reallocation of labour across industries and causing high unemployment during the often prolonged adjustment period. Sena presents a simple theoretical framework which enables assessment of the government's role in industrial and regional labour reallocation. She then compares and appraises the experiences of East Germany and Poland in this regard. Her main conclusions are that a number of adverse incentive effects kept regional unemployment differentials high in those economies long after the initial transition shock. Active labour market policies (ALMPs) have apparently had little success.

Most evaluation studies of ALMPs focus on a microeconometric evaluation approach using individual data. However, since this approach usually ignores impacts on the non-participants, it should be regarded as a first step towards complete evaluation which includes a macroeconometric analysis. The papers by Altavilla and Caroleo and by Hujer, Blien, Caliendo and Zeiss pursue this aim. Moreover, both papers focus on the possibility that the impact of ALMPs varies according to the region in which they are implemented.

After discussing the theoretically expected effects of ALMPs, Hujer, Blien, Caliendo and Zeiss estimate the impacts of ALMPs in Germany for the 1999–2001 period, on regional data from 175 labour force districts. They also adopt a GMM estimator, paying particular attention to the inherent simultaneity problem of ALMPs. They find no significant effect for job creation schemes. Positive effects are detected for vocational training in West Germany, whereas in East Germany only structural adjustment schemes have a weak positive impact.

Altavilla and Caroleo assess the impact of ALMPs on unemployment and employment using a panel data set for the Italian regions in the period 1996–2002, with participants in various programmes used as a policy measure (the authors also include non-standard employment among the policy variables). They carry out both GMM and panel VAR estimates almost invariably finding stronger policy effects in the North of Italy. Only the GMM estimates for employment subsidies find stronger effects in the South.

Summing up

The evolution within the European Union of regional differences in GDP per capita, labour productivity, rates of participation, employment and unemployment, has passed through various phases (European Commission, various years). Theories of growth do not entirely fit the European experience of the past thirty to forty years, which displays alternating periods of convergence and divergence; while convergence across countries is sometimes manifest together with a widening of regional disparities. Moreover, in the last ten to fifteen years, unemployment has been growing in regions outside the so-called economic core of the EU. This phenomenon, well documented by several studies (see, for instance, Pench et al. 1999), stands in stark contrast to the experience of other industrialised countries, the USA in particular (evidence on the USA and Canada is provided in Obstfeld and Peri 1998), where no trend at all is apparent in the dispersion of regional rates of unemployment.

According to some seminal studies (Blanchard and Katz 1992; Decressin and Fatàs 1995), disparities in labour market performances stem from differing responses to exogenous shocks. Responsiveness may be reduced by supply-side factors: for instance, Mohlo (1995) emphasises the impact of a malfunctioning housing market on labour mobility, while Pench et al. (1999) stress the role of centralised wage bargaining. Elhorst (2003) does not deny the importance of supply-side factors, but stresses that the role of agglomeration effects and of industrial composition has often been neglected in the literature.

The papers contained in this book certainly furnish a weighty body of evidence (which mainly focuses on such significant country cases as Germany, Italy, and Poland, although there is interesting evidence on the UK, Croatia, Slovenia, as well as three cross-country studies). How do they relate to the literature? They do not (and they were not intended to) convey a unitary, monolithic, view. Generally speaking, some papers stress the importance of various forms of flexibility (Limosani, Montuenga et al., Sena), while others (Domadenik and Vehovec, Südekum) emphasise the influence of other mechanisms. The existence of skill mismatch is confirmed in various set-ups (chiefly Newell, but also Destefanis and Fonseca, and possibly Domadenik and Vehovec)

Considerable doubts are raised concerning the effectiveness of ALMPs (Altavilla and Caroleo, Hujer et al., Sena). However, neither do more market-oriented policy reforms appear to be particularly successful (both Altavilla and Caroleo, Destefanis and Fonseca, on Southern Italy). Monastiriotis also points out that labour market deregulation has brought about some convergence of labour market flexibility across UK regions. Yet, substantial regional differences in labour market performance still exist in the UK, particularly for low-skilled workers. The apparent convergence in regional rates of unemployment is somewhat misleading: as documented by Rowthorn (1999), there is little or no evidence of convergence when rates of non-employment are compared.

Hence, labour market policies have been changing in Europe since the mid-1990s, but there is no sign of decisive convergence among regional labour market performances (this is also the conclusion reached by the cross-country analyses in Amendola et al. and Marelli). The reasons appear to be numerous, and their relevance varies according to the situation: factors which should discourage policies based on a one-size-fit-for-all approach.

References

Aghion P, Blanchard OJ (1994) On the speed of transition in central Europe. In: Fischer S, Rotemberg JJ (eds) NBER Macroeconomics Annual, MIT Press, Cambridge (Mass.), pp 283–320.

Blanchard OJ., Katz LF (1992) Regional evolutions, Brooking Papers on Economic Activity, 1: 1–61.

Blanchflower D, Oswald A (1994) The wage curve. MIT Press, Cambridge (Mass.).

Decressin J, Fatàs A, (1995) Regional labor market dynamics in Europe, European Economic Review 3: 1627–1655.

Elhorst JP (2003) The mystery of regional unemployment differentials: theoretical and empirical explanations. Journal of Economic Surveys 17: 709–748.

European Commission (various years), Periodic report on the social and economic situation and development of regions in the European Union. European Commissioni, Brussels.

Fujita M, Krugman P, Venables AJ (1999) The spatial economy. Cities, regions, and international trade. MIT Press, Cambridge (Mass.).

Mohlo I (1995) Migrant inertia, accessibility and local unemployment. Economica 62: 123–132.

Obstfeld M, Peri G (1998) Regional non-adjustment and fiscal policy. Economic Policy 29: 207–59.

Pench LR, Sestito P, Frontini E (1999) Some unpleasant arithmetics of regional unemployment in the EU. Are there any lessons for EMU?. European Commission Economic Papers 134.

Rowthorn R (1999) The political economy of full employment in modern Britain. The Kalecki Memorial Lecture, Oxford.

1 Regional Disparities in Europe

Adalgiso Amendola, Floro Ernesto Caroleo and Gianluigi Coppola

University of Salerno, Italy

1.1 Introduction

In recent years, because the disparities among regions prove significantly greater than those among countries, analysis of the causes of the socio-economic differences among the European regions has attracted increasing interest.

This strand of analysis has been prompted mainly by the fact that the creation of the European Union was based on the belief that a broader area of free trade would be a necessary and sufficient condition for economic welfare to spread uniformly among countries. The first question that arises is why theoretical explanations of regional differences fail to account satisfactorily for the European case in recent decades. Indeed, if the three theories – the neoclassical theory in both its 'strong' and 'weak' versions, the theory of endogenous development, and the 'new geography' approach – are taken to their extreme consequences, they point to the conclusion that regional differences are either bound to converge on a single development path in the long period (the neoclassical theory) or that they will diverge permanently, with the creation of strong polarization processes.[1] As we have said, the regions of Europe display not only persistent differences but also a dynamics whereby periods of slow convergence alternate with others in which the tendency is towards divergence (Tondl 1999; Cuadrado-Roura 2001).

The second question concerns policy. That is, the problem arises as to which regional, national or European strategy is best able to accelerate the process of convergence among regions. Regional cohesion has always been a priority objective of the European Union, which has allocated huge amounts of economic resources (the European Social Fund and the Cohesion Fund) to its achievement. And regional cohesion has become even more topical as a result of recent developments in the process of European integration. The advent of the single currency and the financial stability constraints imposed by the Maastricht Treaty inhibit the pursuit of independent monetary policies and drastically reduce the autonomy of member-states as regards their fiscal policy: and this at a time when enlargement of the EU towards the East will soon radically extend the regional scope of the problems of economic and social cohesion. This European policy approach has been subject to widespread criticism (Boldrin and Canova 2001; De la Fuente 2002; Canova 2001; Davies and Hallet 2001 and 2002; Edervee and Gorter 2002;

---

[1] The literature on the subject is detailed and well known. Here we cite the valuable surveys by De la Fuente (2000) and the European Commission (2000).

Martin 1998) on the grounds that, as we have seen, it is not supported by the facts and that it is directed at regional contexts with extremely diverse socio-economic features.

Finally, analysis of convergence-divergence processes pays increasing attention to the institutional mechanisms that regulate the labour market, as well as to the characteristics of the labour supply and demand and their dependence on spatial factors (Niebhur 2002). The excessive rigidity and the scant mobility (Blanchard and Katz 1992; Decressin and Fatàs 1995; Obstfeld and Peri 1998) of the labour factor are judged to be the main causes of the intensification – or the persistence – of divergence among regions. In fact, as is well known, the variables used to assess convergence/divergence are measures generally tied to per capita GDP (Sala-i-Martin 1996; Barro and Sala-i-Martin 1991) and to its two components of employment rate and productivity. Econometric estimates unanimously agree that, in recent years in Europe, the convergence of per capita GDP has been very slow and has instead fostered the formation of clusters of homogeneous regions which are internally convergent but diverge with respect to each other, and this has been due exclusively to the trend in the employment rate and therefore to the characteristics of the labour market (Overman and Puga 2002; Combes and Overman 2004; Daniele 2002; Basile et al. 2003; Kostoris Padoa Schioppa and Basile 2002; Kostoris Padoa Schioppa 1999).

Examination has consequently been made of a series of regional factors connected with the labour market which are often complementary but sometimes concomitant, and which may potentially create, maintain or intensify divergence among regions (Erlhost 2003): the endowment of factors and 'fundamentals'; the structure of the labour market – natural growth and the age composition of the population, the composition of the labour force (Genre and Gòmez-Salvador 2002); migratory phenomena and commuting (Greenway et. al. 2002); the employment level, gross regional product, market potentials, the sectoral mix (Paci and Pigliaru 1999; Paci et al. 2002; Marelli, chap. 3 in this book); density and urbanization (Taylor and Bradley 1997); economic and social barriers, schooling levels – the institutional structure that regulates the goods and labour markets, or the composition of wages (Pench et. al. 1999; Hyclack and Johnes 1987).

The aim of this chapter is to apply a multivariate factorial analysis method (the STATIS method) which, we believe, lends itself well to verification of most of the phenomena just described. The STATIS method, in fact, enables the European regions to be 'read' on the basis of factors that sum up their main socio-economic characteristics, to group them into homogeneous clusters, and to examine their temporal dynamics. It can therefore be used to estimate whether structural features favour the formation of clusters of regions and whether these display a tendency to converge either to a single structure or instead to a multiplicity of socio-economic structures. On this basis, it is then possible to investigate a number of issues: among them, whether the criteria used by the European Union to identify the regions to be targeted by the Structural and Cohesion Funds refer to homogeneous or diversified realities, and therefore whether they require more appropriate instruments.

The second section provides a brief description of the STATIS method. In the third, the method is applied to the European regions and analysis is conducted of the characteristics of the main clusters of regions and of their dynamics over time. The concluding section provides a summary of the results.

1.2 Measuring disparities: three-way matrices

As we have seen, the disparities among regions (cases) can be studied on the basis of numerous indicators (variables) like per capita GDP, productivity and the employment rate, and they can also be measured in their temporal dynamics (time). The multidimensional nature of regional differences therefore lends itself well to analysis by means of multivariate analysis methods, and in particular by dynamic multivariate analysis.

We decided to apply the STATIS (*Structuration des Tables A Trois Indices de la Statistique*) method. This is a dynamic multivariate method which enables analysis of multidimensional (multiway) phenomena expressible in the form of three-way matrices: cases i, variables j, time t. The method has been developed by Escoufier (1985), and has found numerous applications in economics, in Italy as well (D'Ambra 1986; Fachin and Vichi 1993; Tassinari and Vichi 1994). Moreover, it has already been used to explain the dynamics of disparities among the Italian provinces (Amendola et al. 1997; Baffigi 1999).

This technique of exploratory analysis is based on study of a three-way data matrix $X_{I,JT}$ obtained from the temporal succession of data matrices $_tX_{i,j}$ of the same order, where i is the statistical unit and j the variable, both of them relative to the period t ($i = 1, 2...I; j = 1, 2...J; t = 1, 2...T$). The formula is:

$$X_{I,JT} = \left\| {}_1X \quad {}_2X \quad {}_TX \right\|$$

which can be presented as

$$X_{i,JT} = \left\|
\begin{array}{cccc|cccc|cccc}
{}_1x_{11} & {}_1x_{12} & \cdot\cdot & {}_1x_{1j} & {}_2x_{11} & {}_2x_{12} & \cdot\cdot & {}_2x_{1j} & {}_tx_{11} & {}_tx_{12} & \cdot\cdot & {}_tx_{1j} \\
{}_1x_{21} & {}_1x_{22} & & {}_1x_{2j} & {}_2x_{21} & {}_2x_{22} & & {}_2x_{2j} & {}_tx_{21} & {}_tx_{22} & & {}_tx_{2j} \\
\cdots & \cdots & \cdot\cdot & \cdots & \cdots & \cdots & \cdot\cdot & \cdots & \cdots & \cdots & \cdot\cdot & \cdots \\
{}_1x_{i1} & {}_1x_{i2} & \cdot\cdot & {}_1x_{ij} & {}_2x_{i1} & {}_2x_{i2} & \cdot\cdot & {}_2x_{ij} & {}_tx_{i1} & {}_tx_{i2} & \cdot\cdot & {}_tx_{ij}
\end{array}
\right\|$$

From the three-way matrix thus constructed it is possible to derive (Rizzi 1989):

1. The variance-covariance matrix

$$
\Sigma_{JT,JT} = \begin{Vmatrix}
{}_1\Sigma^2 & {}_{12}\Sigma & \cdots & {}_{1T}\Sigma \\
{}_{12}\Sigma & {}_2\Sigma^2 & \cdots & {}_{2T}\Sigma \\
\cdots & \cdots & \cdots & {}_{pq}\Sigma \\
{}_{1T}\Sigma & {}_{2T}\Sigma & {}_{pq}\Sigma & {}_T\Sigma^2
\end{Vmatrix}
$$

where ${}_{pq}\Sigma$ is the variance-covariance matrix between ${}_pX_{i,j}$ and ${}_qX_{i,j}$:

$$
{}_{pq}\Sigma = \left({}_p\hat{X}'_{i,j}, \,{}_q\hat{X}_{i,j} \right)\frac{1}{n}
$$

where $\hat{X}$ is the deviation matrix and $1 < p < T$, $1 < q < T$.

The matrices on the main diagonal represent the variance-covariance matrices of the matrix $X_{I,JT}$ at time t, while ${}_{pq}\Sigma$ measures the same relation between the variables relative to time q and time j.

2. The (TxT) square matrix $I_{T,T}$ where each generic element $I_{p,q} = tr({}_{pq}\Sigma)$ corresponds to the trace of the relative submatrix ${}_{pq}\Sigma$ of $\Sigma_{JT,JT}$

$$
I_{T,T} = \begin{Vmatrix}
tr({}_{11}\Sigma^2) & tr({}_{21}\Sigma) & \cdots & tr({}_{1T}\Sigma) \\
tr({}_{12}\Sigma) & tr({}_{22}\Sigma^2) & \cdots & tr({}_{2T}\Sigma) \\
\cdots & \cdots & \cdots & tr({}_{pq}\Sigma) \\
tr({}_{1T}\Sigma) & tr({}_{2T}\Sigma) & tr({}_{pq}\Sigma) & tr({}_{TT}\Sigma^2)
\end{Vmatrix}
$$

and is a measure of the dissimilarity between ${}_pX_{i,j}$ and ${}_qX_{i,j}$. The higher the value assumed by this index, the less the similarity between the structures of ${}_pX_{i,j}$ and ${}_qX_{i,j}$.

Alternatively, one may assume as the index of similarity Escoufier's (1976) coefficient:

$$
I^*_{p,q} = RV({}_pX_{i,j}, \,{}_qX_{i,j}) = \frac{tr({}_{pq}\Sigma \,{}_{pq}\Sigma)}{\sqrt{tr({}_p\Sigma^2)tr({}_q\Sigma^2)}}
$$

obtained by operating with matrices of deviations from the mean, and which have the characteristic of varying between 0 and 1. The coefficient, which can be considered a generalization of the Bravais correlation coefficient, is close to unity if the matrices have an almost identical structure.

1.3 The STATIS method

The STATIS method divides into three phases: *Interstructure*, *Compromise* and *Intrastructure*.

The purpose of the interstructure phase is to identify a suitable vectorial space smaller than T, where the T occasions can be represented.

To this end, examination is made of the matrix $I_{T,T}$ (also called the interstructure matrix), the column vectors of which are assumed as characteristic elements of each of the T occasions. Constructed from this is a factorial subspace $\mathfrak{R}^s$ with $s < t$ generated by the s eigenvectors corresponding to the s largest eigenvalues of $I_{T,T}$. The subspace thus constructed yields the best representation of the T occasions because it is demonstrated that the matrix Q, of rank $s < T$ – whose elements

$$Q_{(s)} = \sum_{a=1}^{s} \delta_a u_a u_a'$$

are linear combinations of the first δ_a eigenvalues and u_a eigenvectors of the matrix $I_{T,T}$ – has the characteristic of minimizing the square of the Euclidean norm $\| I - Q \|^2$.

A first result is thus obtained. The T occasions with coordinates equal to $\sqrt{\delta_1}u_1$, $\sqrt{\delta_2}u_2$, ... $\sqrt{\delta_h}u_h$ can be generated in the factorial subspace $\mathfrak{R}^s$ by the first eigenvectors u_a.

It is also possible to calculate indices relative to the quality of the representation, and also relative to the contribution made by each of the T occasions:

- the ratio between the sum of the first s eigenvalues and the total of all the eigenvalues is a measure of the percentage of total information contained in the space $\mathfrak{R}^s$;
- the ratio between the individual eigenvalue and the overall total measures the variability captured by the relative eigenvector;
- the square of the cosine of the angle formed by the factorial axis with the segment that joins the occasion-point with the origin is an index of the representation quality of the individual occasion from that axis;
- the proximity of two occasion-points in the space $\mathfrak{R}^s$ is an indicator of the similarity of the matrices.

In the compromise phase, a fictitious structure or synthesis matrix is identified which optimally summarizes the information contained in the T variance and covariance matrices. This structure, called 'compromise', is given by the matrix W obtained as a linear combination of the elements u_1 of the eigenvector of the matrix $I_{T,T}$ corresponding to the highest eigenvector and the matrices $\Gamma_t = {}_t\hat{X}_t\hat{X}'$:

$$W = \sum_{t=1}^{T} u_t \Gamma_t$$

In the space plotted by the s eigenvectors corresponding to the first s eigenvalues of the matrix W it is possible to represent both the j variables and the median positions of each individual. The latter are derived from the diagonalization of matrix W obtained by identifying a matrix M such that $W = MM\,D$ (where D is a diagonal matrix defined positive whose elements are the weights of the individuals, statistical units, $D = (1/L)I$, with L equal to the number of individuals, and where I is an identity matrix.

In other words, matrix W is the best compromise, in the sense defined above, among the various representations that can be associated with each of the T matrices taken separately for each unit of time.

If $s = 2$, the representation occurs in a two-dimensional space corresponding to the first two factors identified. Obviously, this projection will be better, the greater the incidence of the first two eigenvectors on the trace of W.

In the intrastructure phase it is then possible to represent the trajectories followed in time by each individual in the factorial space thus identified. If only the first two eigenvalues are considered, the representation of the trajectories may occur in a space where the system of Cartesian axes is constituted by the eigenvectors a_1 a_1 and a_2 a_2, and where the coordinates on the first axis of each individual are given by $(\delta_{1t}\Gamma a_1)^{-0.5}$ and on the second axis by $(\delta_{2t}\Gamma a_2)^{-0.5}$.

1.4 Analysis and results

The aim of this chapter, as said, is to analyse the medium-term dynamics of the performance of labour markets and economic structures in the European regions. Used for this purpose is the dynamic method for principal components analysis – the STATIS method – described in the previous section. This method enables identification of criteria with which to cluster regions in various years using a base information structure consisting, besides labour market variables, of indicators on income, composition of the population, and the sectoral structure of employment. It is thus possible to study the change over time in the territorial dimension of interactions between labour market and economic development, and to analyse how the various regional units in question relate to this evolution.

The variables used for this analysis are listed in Table 1.2. They are taken from the Eurostat REGIO database and the European regions database of Cambridge Econometrics Ltd. and they are, as said, indicators characteristic of the labour market and the production system (Wishlade and Yuill 1997). Labour demand is measured by the unemployment rate on the total working-age population (TOT), while the labour supply is measured by the labour-force participation rate (TAT). The percentage of the long-term unemployed (ULR) is used as a proxy for the structural gap between labour demand and supply. The percentage of part-time employment (PTT) is used as a measure of the flexibility of the regional labour market.

The production system is represented by four variables corresponding to the percentages of employed persons in agriculture (AGR), industry (IND), traditional services – commerce, hotels and non-market services (GHM) – and advanced services – transport, financial services and others (IJA). This grouping of production sectors was performed taking account of percentage variations in employment in individual sectors, and as regards services, of average labour productivity observed during the period examined. As Table 1.1 shows, between 1991 and 2001 in the European Union, the percentages of persons employed in agriculture and industry decreased, while they increased in the services sector. The latter divides sharply between advanced services, which recorded an average labour productivity above the European average, and traditional services, whose average productivity was instead below the European average.

The other variables considered are population density (DEN), as a proxy for the gravitational force of a region, and per capita income (PPS), which is the indicator most frequently used to represent regional disparities.

Table 1.1. Dynamics of employment and average labour productivity by production sector in the countries of the European Union. 1991–2000

Sector	Percentage change in employment	Labour productivity (period average thousands of euros 1995)
Agriculture, Forestry and Fishing	–23.33	22,520
Other Manufacturing Activities (DD–DK)	–13.03	39,910
Textiles and Clothing (DB–DC)	–18.73	22,070
Electronics (DL)	–13.61	40,930
Transport Equipment (DM)	–15.70	46,580
Mining and Energy Supply (C+E)	–16.27	94,090
Food, Beverages and Tobacco (DA)	–8.44	47,960
Construction	–2.90	31,390
Fuels, Chemicals, Rubber and Plastic Products (DF–DH)	–7.20	64,410
Financial Services (J)	6.12	65,710
Other Financial Services (K)	33.75	62,710
Transport and Communications (I)	5.02	42,650
Non-market Services	8.94	33,530
Wholesale and Retail (G)	11.44	29,070
Hotels and Restaurants (H)	20.59	25,730
TOTAL	4.48	39,760

Source: Cambridge Econometrics Ltd database

Table 1.2. Variables used in the STATIS analysis

N	Code	Variable	Index
1	DEN	population density	inhabitants /sq km
2	TAT	total activity rate	labour force/population aged over 15
3	TOT	employment rate	employed/population aged over 15
4	ULR	long-term unemployment rate	long-term unemployed/total unemployed
5	PTT	part-time employment rate	part-time employed/total employed
6	AGR	percentage employment in agriculture	employed in agriculture/ total employed
7	IND	percentage employment in industry	employed in industry/total employed
8	GHM	percentage employment in traditional services	employed in retail trade, hotels and non-market services /total employed
9	IJA	percentage employment in advanced services	employed in transport, financial and other services/total employed
10	PPS	per capita income	per capita GDP in Purchasing Power Standard

The European regions represent 130 cases. The level of territorial disaggregation of the European regions selected was intended to cover the entire territory and to provide the maximum disaggregation possible with the data available. This level corresponded to the Nuts 2 level for Greece, Spain, France, Italy, Austria and Portugal; Nuts 1 for Belgium, Germany, Holland, Finland, the United Kingdom; Nuts 0 for Denmark, Ireland, Luxembourg and Sweden, for which countries there are no Nuts 1 and Nuts 2 disaggregations (or data are not available with which to perform such disaggregations).[2] The time period was from 1991 to 2000.

The STATIS methodology, as said, consists in the analysis of the three-way matrix $(_tX_{ij})$, where t denotes the temporal observations, i the regions, and j the variables, obtained by the succession of T matrices of the same dimensions.

As explained in the previous section, the analysis moves through three phases: interstructure, compromise and infrastructure. The output from the interstructure phase describes the structure of the T matrices in a vectorial space smaller than T. This is reduced to two dimensions but still maintains a good similarity to the initial representation. The compromise phase consists in the estimation of a synthesis matrix which yields a representation, in the two-dimensional space identified, of the characteristic indicators and of the average positions of the regions in the time-span analysed (1991–2000). The result of this intrastructure phase is a representation of the trajectories followed by the individual regions in the same period of time.

---

[2] The complete list of the 130 regions is given in the Appendix.

In order to evaluate the goodness of the factorial representation yielded by construction of the compromise matrix, Table 1.3 shows the first three highest eigenvalues and the percentages of the total variance explained by the first three factorial axes.

Table 1.3. Eigenvalues and inertia percentages of the factorial axes

Axis	Eigenvalue	Variance explained	Cumulated variance explained
1	3.75547	36.76	36.76
2	1.99895	19.56	56.32
3	1.18853	11.63	67.95

To be noted first is that 36.8 per cent of the variance is explained by the first factor, and 19.6 per cent by the second, for a total of 56.3 per cent of the variance expressed by the set of all the variables. In other words, the first factor alone explains more than one-third of the total variability, while the first three factors jointly explain almost 68 per cent. Consequently, the reduction of the phenomenon's variability, obtained by representing it in a two-dimensional space, is a meaningful synthesis of the information considered.

Figures 1.1 and 1.2 show, respectively on the factorial plane generated by the first two and by the first and third principal components, the positions of the average annual value of each of the ten characteristic indicators considered.

In order to interpret the two figures, we may refer to Table 1.4, which shows the minimum and maximum period values of the correlations between the variables and the factorial axes. It will be seen that the variables most closely correlated with the first factor are, on the one hand (negative quadrant), the employment rate (TOT), the activity rate (TAT), the percentage of part-time employment (PTT), per capita income (PPS), and the percentage of employment in advanced services; and on the other (positive quadrant), the percentage of long-term unemployment (ULR), and the percentage of employment in agriculture (AGR). In other words, along the first axis one observes a clear polarization between the labour market indicators and those relative to the production structure.

Along the second axis one observes a close correlation among, on the one hand (positive quadrant), population density (DEB), per capita income (PPS), and the percentages of employment in traditional services (GHM) and advanced services (IJA), and on the other (negative quadrant), percentage of employment in industry (IND) and in agriculture (AGR), and the employment rate (TOT). In this case, we may state that the second axis identifies in marked manner only the phenomena representing variables located in the positive quadrant, namely those correlated with the territorial dimension. In fact, the indicators in this quadrant represent highly urbanized areas, or ones which contain rail or road infrastructures or sea ports, or with high levels of tourism. The negative quadrant, by contrast, comprises indicators which are more difficult to interpret and concern a mix of factors, such as low population density, the presence of agricultural employment, and high levels of industry.

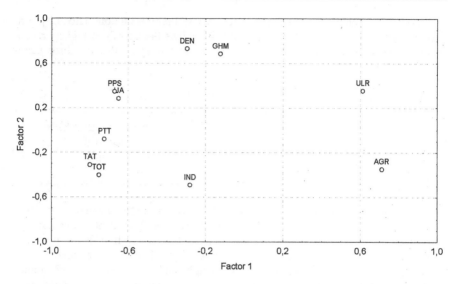

Fig. 1.1. Representation of the characteristic variables on the factorial axes. First and second factors

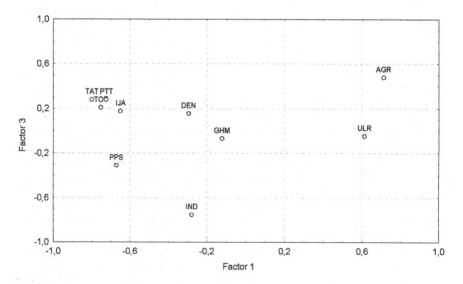

Fig. 1.2. Representation of the characteristic variables on the factorial axes. First and third factors

Table 1.4. Correlations between the variables and the factorial axes (minimum and maximum period values)

	Factor 1			Factor 2			Factor 3	
	Min	Max		Min	Max		Min	Max
TAT	−0.83	−0.75	IND	−0.51	−0.47	IND	−0.77	−0.71
TOT	−0.78	−0.72	TOT	−0.42	−0.37	PPS	−0.36	−0.27
PTT	−0.76	−0.69	AGR	−0.36	−0.34	ULR	−0.18	0.07
PPS	−0.69	−0.63	TAT	−0.34	−0.30	GHM	−0.09	−0.04
IJA	−0.66	−0.64	PTT	−0.11	−0.03	TOT	0.14	0.25
IND	−0.34	−0.22	IJA	0.27	0.30	IJA	0.14	0.20
DEN	−0.30	−0.29	ULR	0.30	0.38	DEN	0.15	0.16
GHM	−0.17	−0.07	PPS	0.33	0.36	TAT	0.19	0.32
ULR	0.58	0.64	GHM	0.64	0.73	PTT	0.21	0.33
AGR	0.70	0.72	DEN	0.73	0.73	AGR	0.47	0.49

The phenomenon of industrialization, however, is thrown in sharpest relief by the third factor. This latter, in fact, is closely correlated in the negative quadrant with the percentage of employment in industry (IND), while in the positive quadrant one finds, once again, a close correlation with variables denoting various characteristics: high percentage of employment in agriculture (AGR), but also a good labour market structure – high percentage of part-time employment (PTT), high employment rate (TOT), and high participation rate (TAT).

Figures 1.3. and 1.4 show the European regions on, respectively, the first two factorial axes and the first and the third. In this case, too, in order to interpret the results we may refer to Figs 1.5, 1.6 and 1.7, where the regions are given colours which diminish in intensity according to their position along the factorial axis from positive to negative. Moreover, in order to enable further comparison, the borders of the Objective 1 regions have been outlined in white. It will be seen from Fig. 1.5, which shows the positions of the regions along the first factor, that there is a marked contrast between the majority of the Objective 1 regions, which lie in the positive quadrant of the axis and are therefore characterized by high structural unemployment and/or a high percentage of employment in agriculture, and the central-northern regions of Europe and of central-southern England, which are characterized by dynamic labour markets producing high levels of employment and participation, and with pronounced institutional flexibility. Occupying an intermediate position are the majority of the French regions and those of northern Italy and north-western Germany, which may have both dynamic labour markets and a high proportion of employment in agriculture, or even high percentages of long-term unemployment. Also to be emphasised is that large part of these latter regions, together with those of East Germany and Ireland, and some Spanish regions, contribute to a minimal extent (< 0.09 per cent) to the formation of the first factor. We may therefore conclude that the Objective 1 regions, especially those of the Mediterranean basin and central-northern Europe, distinctively characterize the first factor.

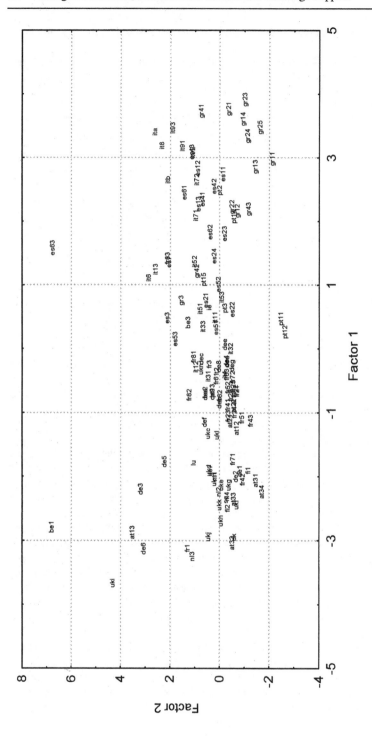

Fig. 1.3. Representation of the characteristic variables on the factorial axes. First and second factors

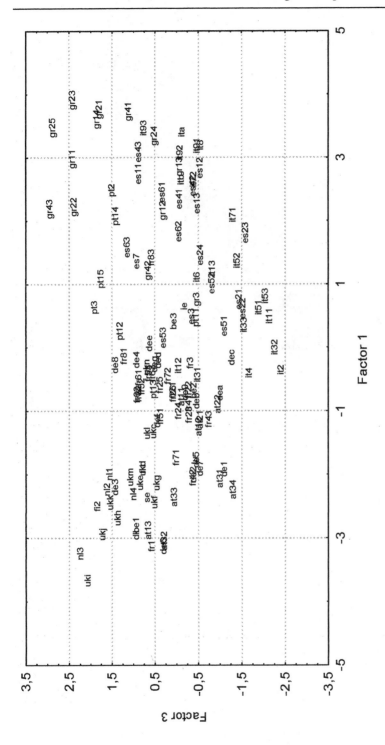

Fig. 1.4. Representation of the characteristic variables on the factorial axes. First and third factors

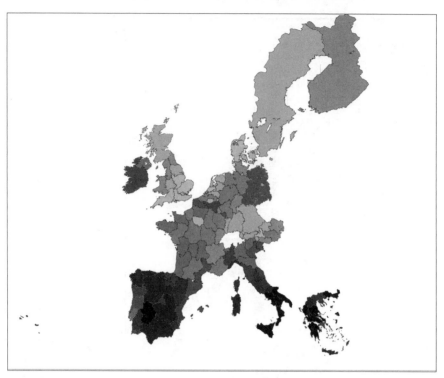

Fig. 1.5. Map of the First Factor

The borders of the Objective 1 regions are outlined in white

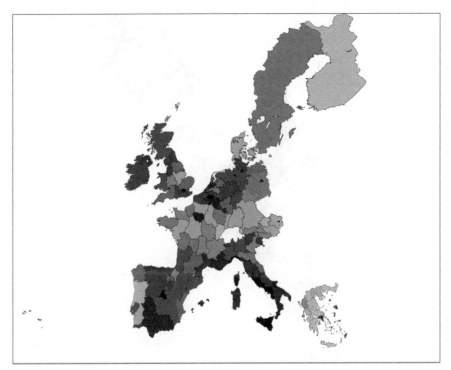

Fig. 1.6. Map of the Second Factor

The borders of the Objective 1 regions are outlined in white

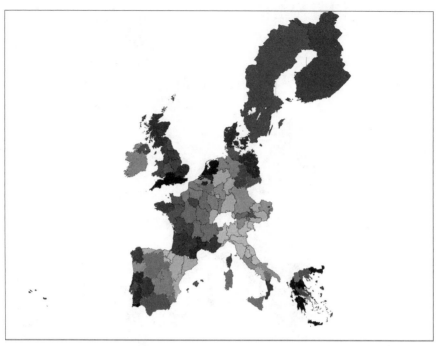

Fig. 1.7. Map of the Third Factor

The borders of the Objective 1 regions are outlined in white

The positions of the regions along the second factorial axis are much more diversified. As said, the regions lying in the positive quadrant are those associated
with localization factors (high population density, employment in services, and
high incomes), while the characterization of the regions in the negative quadrant is
less clear-cut. In fact, it will be seen in Fig. 1.6 that the regions with the darkest
colouring in the first quadrant are those which comprise the main European capital
cities, important transport infrastructures, or with particularly developed tourist
industries.

Also as regards the third factor, clear interpretation can only be made of the positions of the regions located in one of the two quadrants: in this case the negative
one, which is characterized by indices of high levels of industrialization. In fact,
the regions with the lightest colouring are those that can be associated with a high
percentage of industrial employment: the central and north-eastern regions of Italy, the regions of central Germany, Austria, and the north-eastern regions of
Spain.

A further result of the intrastructure phase analysis concerns the temporal trajectories followed by individual regions along the factorial axes and which highlight certain characteristics of the regional dynamics. A summary of these phenomena is provided by Tables 1.5 and 1.6, which show – for each year and only
for the first two factors – the sums of the square of the distances between the indi-

Table 1.5. Weighted average annual distances of the regions from the First Factorial Axis

Year	All the Regions	Index Number '91=100	Objective 1	Index Number '91=100	Core	Index Number '91=100	Periphery	Index Number '91=100
1991	6.86	100.00	4.31	100.00	2.36	100.00	4.50	100.00
1992	7.06	102.99	4.48	104.05	2.38	100.83	4.69	104.22
1993	7.74	112.85	4.91	114.13	2.59	109.80	5.15	114.44
1994	7.34	107.01	4.62	107.20	2.49	105.54	4.85	107.78
1995	7.64	111.41	4.73	109.75	2.54	107.80	5.10	113.33
1996	7.54	110.03	4.72	109.61	2.60	110.46	4.94	109.78
1997	8.11	118.22	5.07	117.69	2.86	121.31	5.25	116.67
1998	7.72	112.54	4.72	109.52	2.78	118.03	4.94	109.78
1999	7.77	113.36	4.83	112.05	2.72	115.48	5.05	112.22
2000	8.12	118.47	5.14	119.31	2.70	114.62	5.42	120.44

Table 1.6. Weighted average annual distances of the regions from the Second Factorial Axis

Year	All the Regions	Index Number '91=100	Objective 1	Index Number '91=100	Core	Index Number '91=100	Periphery	Index Number '91=100
1991	9.79	100.00	8.01	100.00	1.71	100.00	8.08	100.00
1992	9.70	99.06	7.83	97.67	1.80	105.30	7.90	97.74
1993	9.43	96.26	7.49	93.42	1.86	109.23	7.56	93.52
1994	9.23	94.28	7.38	92.13	1.76	103.37	7.47	92.36
1995	9.05	92.41	7.22	90.14	1.74	101.78	7.31	90.44
1996	8.65	88.37	6.79	84.78	1.79	104.87	6.86	84.89
1997	9.17	93.66	7.29	91.00	1.81	105.77	7.37	91.10
1998	8.97	91.64	7.23	90.28	1.65	96.81	7.32	90.55
1999	8.58	87.65	6.85	85.47	1.66	97.01	6.93	85.67
2000	7.69	78.57	6.04	75.35	1.60	93.64	6.10	75.39

vidual regions and the factorial axis, weighted for the region's contribution to formation of that axis. In this way greater importance is given to the paths followed by the regions making the greatest contribution to defining the factor. The distances have been separately calculated for all regions, for those considered to be the core regions, for those in the EU periphery (cf. Basile and Kostoris Padoa Schioppa 2002), and for the subgroup of the Objective 1 regions.

A first general phenomenon to be observed is that whilst for factor 1 the total distance increased during the decade for all the groups of regions considered, it diminished for factor 2. This seems to indicate that the regions gradually moved closer to the phenomena characterizing the second factor.

A second feature to be noted is that the distances of the core regions from both axes are much smaller than are those of the peripheral regions (and of the Objective 1 regions, to which category most of them belong). This means that the former are concentrated much more towards the centre of the axes, and therefore display a certain amount of homogeneity, while the latter lie more towards the extremes, and therefore display a greater structural characterization.

The third feature to stress is that the pattern of the distances is prevalently cyclical. The distances from the first factor are marked by shocks (1993, 1997, 2000) followed by slow and only partial recoveries in subsequent years, whereas as regards the second factor, the shocks are less pronounced and the dynamics is more constant. In the latter case, moreover, the core regions display a pattern opposite to that of the others: in fact their distances, with the exception of the final three years, tend to increase.

1.5 Summary and conclusions

The results of the analysis confirm the thesis of those who contend that the European economy is a diversified reality influenced by structural phenomena concerning labour market characteristics, sectoral composition, and localization factors which make it unlikely that integration processes – although accelerated by the enlargement of markets and their greater efficiency – will give rise to the hoped-for levelling of economic development in the near future. The main reason for regional differences still seems to be the composition and structure of labour markets. To be noted in particular is the marked contrast between the Mediterranean regions, most of which belong to the Objective 1 regions, and their high rates of structural unemployment, and the regions of central-northern Europe and central-southern England characterized by more flexible labour markets and high employment rates.

However, there are other phenomena responsible for regional disparities in Europe: localization factors (large conurbations, transport hubs, and tourism) which foster the development of connected service activities, and the presence of a solid industrial base accompanied by high levels of income and employment. These factors are associated with regions which are more territorially dispersed and therefore unlikely to form regional clusters, whilst, by contrast, industrialization phenomena are distributed across a transnational area formed by contiguous regions. This area stretches eastwards from the north-eastern regions of Spain along the Adriatic and through north-eastern Italy, and then northwards to the central regions of Europe, Austria and Germany. The dynamic analysis has shown not so much convergence as slow change in the structural characteristics that differentiate the regions of Europe, where localization factors and sectoral composition will probably be more influential in the future. Moreover, the peripheral regions seem to be more markedly characterized by structural differences than are the core regions.

Appendix

Table A.1. List of the 130 European regions used in the STATIS analysis. The country in which they are located and the corresponding NUTS level are indicated in bold

abbr.	Regions	abbr.	Regions
	Belgium – NUTS 1 – Regions		
be1	Région Bruxelles-capitale/Brussels hoofdstad gewest	be2	Vlaams Gewest
be3	Région Wallonne		
Dk	**Denmark – NUTS 0 – Nation**		
	Federal Republic of Germany (including ex-GDR from 1991) - NUTS 1 – Länder		
de1	Baden-Württemberg	de2	Bayern
de3	Berlin	de4	Brandenburg
de5	Bremen	de6	Hamburg
de7	Hessen	de8	Mecklenburg-Vorpommern
de9	Niedersachsen	dea	Nordrhein-Westfalen
deb	Rheinland-Pfalz	dec	Saarland
Ded	Sachsen	dee	Sachsen-Anhalt
Def	Schleswig-Holstein	deg	Thüringen
	Greece – NUTS 2 – Development regions		
gr11	Anatoliki Makedonia, Thraki	gr12	Kentriki Makedonia
gr13	Dytiki Makedonia	gr14	Thessalia
gr21	Ipeiros	gr22	Ionia Nisia
gr23	Dytiki Ellada	gr24	Sterea Ellada
gr25	Peloponnisos	gr3	Attiki
gr41	Voreio Aigaio	gr42	Notio Aigaio
gr43	Kriti		
	Spain – NUTS 2 – Comunidades autonomas		
es11	Galicia	es12	Principado de Asturias
es13	Cantabria	es21	Pais Vasco
es22	Comunidad Foral de Navarra	es23	La Rioja
es24	Aragón	es3	Comunidad de Madrid
es41	Castilla y León	es42	Castilla-la Mancha
es43	Extremadura	es51	Cataluña
es52	Comunidad Valenciana	es53	Baleares
es61	Andalucia	es62	Murcia
es63	Ceuta y Melilla (ES)	es7	Canarias (ES)
	France – NUTS 2 – Régions		
fr1	Île de France	fr21	Champagne-Ardenne
fr22	Picardie	fr23	Haute-Normandie
fr24	Centre	fr25	Basse-Normandie

abbr.	Regions	abbr.	Regions
fr26	Bourgogne	fr3	Nord - Pas-de-Calais
fr41	Lorraine	fr42	Alsace
fr43	Franche-Comté	fr51	Pays de la Loire
fr52	Bretagne	fr53	Poitou-Charentes
fr61	Aquitaine	fr62	Midi-Pyrénées
fr63	Limousin	fr71	Rhône-Alpes
fr72	Auvergne	fr81	Languedoc-Roussillon
fr82	Provence-Alpes-Côte d'Azur	fr83	Corse
Ie	**Ireland – NUTS 0 – Nation**		
	Italy – NUTS 2 – Regioni		
it11	Piemonte	it12	Valle d'Aosta
it13	Liguria	it2	Lombardia
it31	Trentino-Alto Adige	it32	Veneto
it33	Friuli-Venezia Giulia	it4	Emilia-Romagna
it51	Toscana	it52	Umbria
it53	Marche	it6	Lazio
it71	Abruzzo	it72	Molise
it8	Campania	it91	Puglia
it92	Basilicata	it93	Calabria
Ita	Sicilia	itb	Sardegna
Lu	**Luxembourg – NUTS 0 – Nation**		
	Netherlands – NUTS 2 – Provincies		
nl1	Noord-Nederland	nl2	Oost-Nederland
nl3	West-Nederland	nl4	Zuid-Nederland
	Austria – NUTS 2 – Bundesländer		
at11	Burgenland	at12	Niederösterreich
at13	Wien	at21	Kärnten
at22	Steiermark	at31	Oberösterreich
at32	Salzburg	at33	Tirol
at34	Vorarlberg		
	Portugal – NUTS 2 – Groupings		
pt11	Norte	pt12	Centro (P)
pt13	Lisboa e Vale do Tejo	pt14	Alentejo
pt15	Algarve	pt2	Açores (PT)
pt3	Madeira (PT)		
	Finland- NUTS 1 – Manner-Suomi/Ahvenanmaa		
fi1	Manner-Suomi	fi2	Åland
se	**Sweden- NUTS 0 – Nation**		
	United Kingdom –NUTS 1 – Government Office Regions		
ukc	North East	ukd	North West (including Merseyside)

abbr.	Regions	abbr.	Regions
uke	Yorkshire and The Humber	ukf	East Midlands
ukg	West Midlands	ukh	Eastern
uki	London	ukj	South East
ukk	South West	ukl	Wales
ukm	Scotland	ukn	Northern Ireland

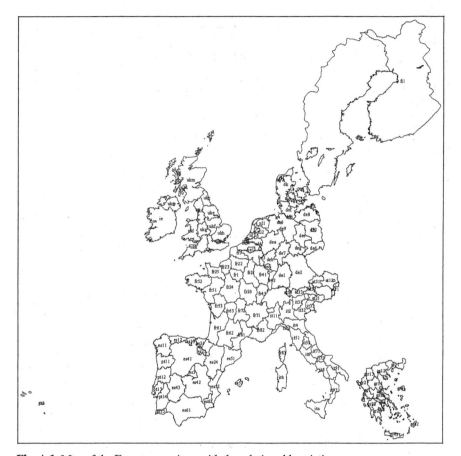

Fig. A.1. Map of the European regions with the relative abbreviations

References

Amendola A, Caroleo FE, Coppola G (1999) Differenziali territoriali nel mercato del lavoro e sviluppo in Italia. In: Biagioli M Caroleo FE Destefanis S (eds) Struttura della contrattazione differenziali salariali e occupazione in ambiti regionali, Collana AIEL, ESI, Napoli, pp 345–387.

Baffigi A (1999) I differenziali territoriali nella struttura dell'occupazione e della disoccupazione: un'analisi con dati a livello provinciale (1981–1995). In: Biagioli M, Caroleo FE, Destefanis S (eds) Struttura della contrattazione differenziali salariali e occupazione in ambiti regionali, Collana AIEL, ESI, Napoli, pp 319–344.

Barro RJ, Sala-i-Martin X (1991) Convergence across states and regions. Brookings Papers on Economic Activity 1:107–182.

Basile R, de Nardis S, Girardi A (2003) Dinamiche di sviluppo nel centro e nella periferia d'Europa: il ruolo delle politiche strutturali. Rivista di Politica Economica 3:89–134.

Blanchard OJ, Katz LF. (1992) Regional evolutions. Brooking Papers on Economic Activity 1:1–61.

Boldrin M, Canova F (2001) Inequality and convergence in Europe's regions: reconsidering European regional policies. Economic Policy, 32:207–253.

Canova F (2001) Are EU policies fostering growth and reducing regional inequalities?. Els opuscles del CREI 8.

Combes PP, Overman HG (2004) The spatial distribution of economic activities in the European Union. In: Henderson JV, Thisse J-F (eds) Handbook of urban and regional economics, vol 4, Elsevier, Amsterdam, pp 2845–2910.

Cuadrado-Roura JR, (2001) Regional convergence in the European Union: from hypothesis to the actual trends. Annals of Regional Science 35:333–356.

D'Ambra L (1985) Alcune estensioni dell'analisi in componenti principali per lo studio di sistemi evolutivi. Uno studio sul commercio internazionale dell'elettronica. Ricerche Economiche 2:233–260.

Daniele V (2002) Integrazione economica e monetaria e divari regionali nell'Unione Europea. Rivista Economica del Mezzogiorno, 3:513–550.

Davies S, Hallet M (2001) Policy responses to regional unemployment: lessons from Germany, Spain, Italy. European Commission Economic Paper 161.

Davies S, Hallet M (2002) Interactions between national and regional development. HWWA Discussion Paper 207.

De la Fuente A (2000) Convergence across countries and regions: theory and empirics. European Investment Bank Papers 5:25–45.

De la Fuente A (2002) The effect of Structural Fund spending on the Spanish regions: an assessment of the 1994–99 Objective 1 CSF. CEPR Discussion Paper 3673.

Decressin J, Fatàs A (1995) Regional labor market dynamics in Europe. European Economic Review 3:1627–1655.

Edervee S, Gorter J (2002) Does European cohesion policy reduce regional disparities? An empirical analysis. CPB Discussion Paper 15.

Elhorst JP (2003) The mystery of regional unemployment differentials. theoretical and empirical explanations. Journal of Economic Surveys 17:709–748.

Escoufier Y (1985) Statistique et analyse des données. Bulletin des Statisticiens Universitaires 10:1–71.

European Commission (2000) The EU economy: 2000 Review, European Commission, Brussels.

Fachin S, Vichi M (1994) Deindustrializzazione, specializzazione o ristrutturazione? Una analisi multiway in matrici fattoriali dell'evoluzione dell'industria manifatturiera italiana dal 1971 al 1983. Politica economica 10:373–404.

Genre V, Gòmez-Salvador R (2002) Labour force developments in the Euro area since the 1980s. ECB Occasional Paper Series 4.

Greenway D, Upward R, Wright P (2002) Structural adjustment and the sectoral and geographical mobility of labour. Leverhulme Centre for Research on Globalisation and Economic Policy Working Paper 3.

Hyclak T, Johnes G (1987) On the determinants of full employment unemployment rates in local labour markets. Applied Economics 19:615–645.

Kostoris Padoa Schioppa F (1999) Regional aspects of unemployment in Europe and in Italy. CEPR Discussion Paper 2108.

Kostoris Padoa Schioppa F, Basile R (2002) Dinamiche della disoccupazione nei "Mezzogiorni d'Europa": quali lezioni per il Mezzogiorno d'Italia?. Rivista di Politica Economica 92:83–124.

Martin P, (1998) Can regional policies affect growth and geography in Europe?. The World Economy 21:757–774.

Niebuhr A (2002) Spatial dependence of regional unemployment in the European Union. HWWA Discussion Paper 186.

Obstfeld M, Peri G (1998) Regional non-adjustment and fiscal policy. Economic Policy, 28:205–247.

Overman HG, Puga D (2002) Unemployment clusters across European regions and countries. Economic Policy, 34:117–147.

Paci R, Pigliaru F (1999) European regional growth: do sectors matter? In: Adams J, Pigliaru F (eds), Economic growth and change, national and regional patterns of convergence and divergence, Edward Elgar, Cheltenham, pp 213–235.

Paci R, Pigliaru F, Pugno M (2002) Le disparità nella crescita economica e nella disoccupazione tra le regioni europee: una prospettiva settoriale. In: Farina F, Tamborini R (eds), Da nazioni a regioni: mutamenti istituzionali e strutturali dopo l'Unione Monetaria Europea, Il Mulino, Bologna, pp 155–186.

Pench LR, Sestito P, Frontini E (1999) Some unpleasant arithmetics of regional unemployment in the EU. Are there any lessons for EMU?. European Commission Economic Paper 134.

Rizzi A (1989) Analisi dei dati, La Nuova Italia Scientifica, Roma.

Sala-i-Martin X (1996) Regional cohesion: evidence and theories of regional growth and convergence. European Economic Review 40:1325–1352.

Tassinari G, Vichi M (1994) La dinamica economica dei paesi avanzati negli anni ottanta: Riflessioni sulle traiettorie risultanti dalle analisi delle matrici a tre vie. Giornale degli Economisti e Annali di Economia, 53:101–134.

Taylor J, Bradley S (1997) Unemployment in Europe: a comparative analysis of regional disparities in Germany, Italy and the UK. Kyklos 50:221–245.

Tondl G (1999) The changing pattern of regional convergence in Europe. Jarbuch für Regionalwissenschaft 19:1–33.

Wishlade F, Yuill D (1997) Measuring disparities for area designation purposes: issues for the European Union, regional and industrial policy. University of Strathclyde Research Paper 24.

2 Regional Unemployment in the OST Literature

Anna Maria Ferragina[1] and Francesco Pastore[2]

[1] Università di Roma "Tor Vergata", Italy
[2] Seconda Università di Napoli, Italy

2.1 Introduction[*]

The aim of this chapter is to survey the now large body of theoretical and empirical literature on regional unemployment persistence in transition countries. This literature asks and answers the following questions: in what respect does regional unemployment differ from that in other mature market economies? Do we need a specific theoretical and methodological framework to understand such differences? Or, conversely, are the standard explanations sufficient for the purpose? The answers to these questions can be synthesised as follows. The determinants of regional unemployment in emerging market economies in the post-Soviet bloc differed from those in mature market economies especially in the early stages of transition. Massive and prolonged structural change, rarely experienced in mature capitalist economies, drove the process. A different pace of restructuring and the ability to attract foreign capital made some regions' economic transformation fast, successful and relatively painless, while less successful regions started to lag behind. These differences persisted over time for three main reasons: first, restructuring is still going on; second, foreign capital continued for many years to concentrate in successful regions; third, various forms of labour supply rigidity impeded the full process of adjustment.

The main focus of the analysis will be Central and Eastern Europe (CEE), rather than the republics of the CIS or the transition countries in Asia, though some reference to these last economies will be made.[1] Within the group of the CEECs, especial attention will be paid to Poland for two main reasons: first, this

---

[*] The material presented in this chapter has circulated widely in various forms and we are grateful to numerous colleagues for their helpful comments and suggestions, especially T Boeri, S Destefanis, B-Y Kim, H Lehmann, B Reilly, M Schaffer, M Socha and A Verashchagina. Pastore wishes especially to thank A Newell, with whom he discussed most of the issues dealt with in this chapter. Of course, the authors take responsibility for any errors that remain.
[1] For its very specific reform path, the case of East Germany is beyond the scope of this chapter. Unlike the CEECs, with the exception of the Czech Republic, the CIS republics have been able to keep unemployment at a very low level for a long time. For a survey of the evidence and explanations of differences between the labour markets of CEECs and CIS countries, see Pastore and Verashchagina (2003, 2004).

country is the largest and most populated one and displays dramatic and persistent spatial differences; second, the empirical literature has focused especially on Poland, also thanks to the availability of data sets of good quality.[2]

Mass unemployment erupted in most CEECs in 1990, soon after the beginning of the reform process intended to lead the centrally planned socialist system to a market driven capitalist one. In 1989, however unreliable they may have been, the official statistics had recorded sizeable numbers of excess vacancies. Kornai (1992) explained chronic labour shortage as a normal outcome of the socialist system and its emphasis on forced growth attained via extensive production methods used by the state to extract the entire available labour surplus.

Since 1990, Poland, the biggest country in CEE, has recorded the highest unemployment rate in the area, with a two-digit level already being reached in 1991, one year after the launch of the so-called 'Shock Therapy' implemented under the auspices of Balcerowicz's Big Bang programme. The first three years saw an astonishing increase in unemployment as about one million jobs per year were lost. The distribution of unemployment soon appeared to be dramatically uneven across regions, with some areas hit much harder than others. And it was persistent, given that many of the regions with the highest unemployment rates in 1990 maintain those levels still today. Newell and Pastore (2000) find that the correlation between *voivodship*[3] unemployment rates in 1992 and in 1997 was over 70 per cent, which refutes the hypothesis of a rapid series of localised unemployment explosions and a fast-changing geographical picture.[4]

For various reasons, this was not to be expected, and it is one of the most puzzling features of economic transition. In the early 1990s, unemployment was ex-

---

[2] For other CEECs, regional data, especially at an individual level, are simply not available or scarcely reliable. The Slovenian LFS does not contain a variable to identify the location of respondents. In the case of Hungary, Fazekas (2002, p. 177) note that the small sample size of the Hungarian Labour Force Survey is not suitable for a statistically meaningful analysis of labour market status at the NUTS3 level and even at a higher level of aggregation. Most information on Hungarian regions comes from unemployment register data and census data. Similar considerations apply to other CEECs.

[3] Wojewòdztwo is the Polish word for region. A new English word has been introduced to translate the Polish one: 'voivodship'. In fact, rather than regions, voivodships resemble English counties, considering that their number (49) is rather large compared to the country's size and population (38 million).

[4] The case of Poland is not unique, just the opposite. OCD (1995) and Boeri and Scarpetta (1996) document that this is the case also for Bulgaria, the Czech Republic, and Hungary during the years 1991–95. Bornhost and Commander (2004, pp. 3–5) provide evidence on the remarkable degree of regional unemployment persistence in six transition countries (Bulgaria, the Czech Republic, Hungary, Poland, Romania and Russia) for the years 1991 and 2001. The focus of their analysis is mainly the NUTS3 (Nomenclature of territorial units for Statistics) level, though they also consider the NUTS2 level. Evidence on specific countries is provided for Hungary by Fazekas (2002, pp. 177–185); for Poland by World Bank (2001, Tab. 3.9) for the years 1990–2000; and Rutkowski and Przybila (2002, pp. 157–160) for the years 1993-'01; for Romania by Kállai and Traistaru (2001, pp. 5–7) for the years 1992–95.

pected to be of short duration. Theoretical models of transition within the Optimal Speed of Transition (OST) literature, especially the so-called benchmark model (Aghion and Blanchard, 1994), predicted that continuous shifts of workers from the dismantling state to the emerging private sector would be the driving force behind economic transformation. Assuming a fixed labour supply, the benchmark OST model did indeed predict increasing unemployment at the outset of transition. Nonetheless, it foresaw that the growth of the private sector would be so rapid that in the medium run it would absorb the job losses due to the dismantling of the state sector. In other words, unemployment was expected to be a transitory – or "transitional" (Boeri 1994) – phenomenon bound to disappear as soon as employment shrank in the state and rose in private firms to 'normal' levels. However, as already noted, this theoretical prediction soon proved overly optimistic.

The standard explanation for regional unemployment in transition countries mirrors this theoretical framework. Unemployment reflects structural changes in labour demand. One needs to add arguments as to why unemployment might persist in order to reconcile a fairly stable pattern of unemployment with this explanation. Three main types of explanation are put forward. Firstly, to remain within the framework established by the first strand in the OST literature, there are many reasons why restructuring and privatisation may be gradual rather than immediate. Transition may generate a steady flow of mismatched workers into unemployment. In all CEECs, economic transition from a planned to a market economy happened concurrently with important (*between* and *within*) changes in the industrial structure due not only to domestic economic reforms but also to foreign direct investment, and shifts in the pattern of international trade.

A second explanation has been provided by a subsequent wave of the OST literature, which has discarded the hypothesis of a fixed labour supply typical of the early models (Boeri 2000). This strand in the literature points to the factors considered by the neoclassical models of regional unemployment (see e.g. Marston 1985). Allowing labour supply to play a role requires one to accept that shocks generating spatial unemployment may go unabsorbed because of the immobility of workers. High relocation costs and the insensitivity of wages to local labour market conditions are mainly responsible for this immobility. In many CEECs, a chronic lack of housing in potential destination areas has also been a major constraint on factor mobility (Boeri 2000). Moreover, high non-employment benefits at the outset of economic transition not only induced many workers to join the pool of the unemployed or the inactive; they also increased the reservation wage of non-employed workers, curbing their intention to seek new jobs in the private sector. Rutkowski and Przybila (2002) and Bornhorst and Commander (2004), among others, provide support to this last hypothesis.

A third, more traditional explanation for a stable regional pattern of unemployment is consistent with an equilibrium interpretation based on differences in tastes and technology across regions (Marston 1985). A mixture of these theories creates a convincing account in which gradual restructuring and supply-side rigidities combine to create persistence in the regional pattern of unemployment.

Regional unemployment in transition countries is particularly interesting for at least two reasons. First, transition countries provide an example of the sudden emergence of regional unemployment, as in a quasi-natural experiment. Consequently, part of the literature has focused not only on impediments to the adjustment process due, for instance, to supply side rigidities, these being the usual suspects for regional unemployment persistence in the neoclassical strand of the literature, but also on the causes of the emergence of regional unemployment differentials. This requires studying the process of structural change and the reasons why it may differ across regions.

Some applied studies seemingly confirm the theoretical predictions of the benchmark OST model that structural change largely explains regional unemployment in the 1990s. The relationship among industrial restructuring due to the reform process, a high level of labour turnover, and the local unemployment rate has been established empirically against the alternative hypothesis that unemployment differentials are due to differences in the job finding rate and in the duration of unemployment spells. As Newell and Pastore (2000) argue, when unemployment is positively related to workers' reallocation across regions, spatial unemployment differentials increase and the main reason is a different degree of industrial change; whereas when workers' reallocation is constant across regions with different unemployment rates, spatial unemployment differences are already persistent, and this is due to the slow process of job creation as well as to the sluggishness of the adjustment process. This test suggests the existence of an empirical law which distinguishes between the case when unemployment is due to a high degree of structural change and when it is due instead to labour market rigidities, which warrants further investigation in the case of non-transition countries.

For all these reasons, although the literature on supply side rigidities is large and important, the main focus of this survey will be on studies which assess the role of industrial change in shaping the regional distribution of unemployment. This seems to be the most innovative and interesting contribution of the OST literature to our understanding of the determinants of spatial unemployment.

The rest of this chapter is organised as follows. Section 2.2 outlines the neoclassical explanations of regional unemployment. Section 2.3 provides an overview of the benchmark OST model developed by Aghion and Blanchard (1994) and the successive model by Boeri (2000). Section 2.4 highlights some testable implications of the OST model on which the applied literature has focused and reviews the empirical literature and its attempts to test the validity of the OST model. Section 2.5 focuses on the impact of economic integration and capital flows from abroad on local labour markets. Some concluding remarks follow.

2.2 The neoclassical approach to regional unemployment

Hall (1970, 1972), Marston (1985), Topel (1986, 1994), Blanchard and Katz (1992) and Decressin and Fatàs (1995) are important examples of models of regional unemployment within the neoclassical strand of the literature.[5] All these

---

[5] Elhorst (2003) contains a detailed survey of the literature on regional unemployment differentials in western market economies.

models explain regional unemployment in terms of a failure of the adjustment process to absorb asymmetric shocks due to supply side rigidities, and they point to flexible labour markets as the solution enabling high unemployment regions to catch up with the rest of the country.

According to Marston (1985), who provides perhaps one of the clearest examples of a neoclassical model of regional unemployment, the factors behind local unemployment are "weak labour demand" and "economic and social barriers [that] may separate local labour markets". He suggests that regional unemployment may be either a dis-equilibrium or an equilibrium phenomenon.

Economic and social barriers may separate local labour markets. If these barriers restrict mobility severely, then weak labour demand in one geographic area will raise the unemployment rate there above its level in areas with stronger labour demand. On the other hand, if mobility is relatively free between areas, then strong labour demand elsewhere will leave workers away from a high unemployment area. Excess labour in the area will vanish quickly unless workers are compensated in some way that induces them to remain there voluntarily. Any persistent geographical unemployment differentials, then, are not evidence of uneven labour demand, but reflections of workers' underlying preferences for certain areas (Marston 1985, p. 57).

Hall (1970) claims that regional unemployment differences in the USA in the 1950s and 1960s were equilibrium phenomena due to the presence of higher-than-average wages in high unemployment regions. These high wages provided an incentive to remain in high unemployment areas, as in the equilibrium case. This finding is difficult to explain in a dis-equilibrium context, for if there were free labour mobility and wage flexibility, wages should adjust. However, flexibility may be so low and wage shifts so slow that it takes time for wages to adjust. Therefore, although the first explanation is unverified, it may also be valid, and the problem becomes that of establishing how long it takes before the adjustment process is complete. As Hall (1970) puts it: "The key question is the speed of equilibration: how long does a dis-equilibrium persists?"

Like Hall (1972), Marston (1985, p. 59) presents a model in which both wages and unemployment rates are determined by the preferences of firms and workers, given fixed endowments of land and amenities in the area. The model can be solved to give the wage rate, the unemployment rate and the labour force of each area in the economy. In particular, the equilibrium unemployment rate in each area will be some function of its amenities and land endowment.

The two factors stressed by Marston (ibid.) as the main causes of regional unemployment well summarise the neoclassical view of regional unemployment, its strength and weaknesses. Local unemployment is due to some unspecified shortage of labour demand and to barriers hindering the adjustment process which smoothes such differences. However, given that labour demand shortage is left essentially unexplained in the model, the entire focus is on the adjustment process.

Of course, failure of the adjustment process is itself an explanation for the existence over time of regional unemployment differentials and, presumably, of the way in which they change. However, while this theoretical setting is able to explain unemployment persistence, it seemingly fails to explain why such differences in productivity exist in the first place.

This view of regional unemployment is consequently not satisfactory. And it is especially unsatisfactory in the case of transition countries, where regional unemployment differences emerged from nothing at the outset of transition. Moreover, as argued in Bornhorst and Commander (2004), all the existing models of regional unemployment, including the synthesis by Blanchard and Katz (1992) have as basic assumption that of equilibrium, which is untenable for transition countries undergoing massive structural change. They note: "The first decade of transition was marked by profound structural adjustments not directly comparable to the demand shocks lying behind the dynamics outlined above [in the Blanchard and Katz model]. This makes identification of equilibrium conditions a largely futile exercise" (p. 3).

It is therefore not surprising that the literature of the early 1990s on regional unemployment in CEE focused more on the primary factors of uneven spatial unemployment, namely the factors weakening local labour demand, than on the factors hindering the adjustment process. Only at a later stage, particularly at the end of the 1990s, did the focus shift to study the supply constraints on the adjustment process.

2.3 Regional unemployment and the OST literature

The literature on regional unemployment in transition countries does not provide a specific theoretical framework to explain spatial unemployment differentials. However, as shown in this section, the OST literature does provide a framework in which to consider the reasons for the emergence of unemployment during transition. We suggest that such a framework can also be used to form predictions about regional unemployment. The first wave of the OST literature points to local labour demand shifts as factors responsible for high spatial unemployment. The second wave of the OST literature can be combined with the neoclassical tradition to provide insights into the factors hindering the adjustment to evenly distributed unemployment rates.

2.3.1 Economic transition as a process of structural change

There are various theoretical frameworks within which to consider economic transition from a centrally planned to a market economy (for surveys see Roland 2000; Boeri 2000; Havrylyshyn 2001; Pastore and Verashchagina 2003, 2004). However, the most widely used approach is the one based on the search for the Optimal Speed of Transition (OST) and introduced by Aghion and Blanchard (1994).[6]

---

[6] Given to its simplicity and clarity, the Aghion and Blanchard (1994) model has become very popular in the transition literature. Presentations of the model can be found in vari-

This model describes economic transition as essentially a regime change from an allocation system based on central planning to one based on market forces: a systemic process of liberalisation affecting the formation of prices, the rules of national and international trade and the private initiative drives this change. This definition is so general that it applies to all transition countries, from the CEECs to the CIS and other former communist countries.[7]

A well-known representation depicts transition as a move towards the production frontier from a point below it, say from point P to point E, in Fig. 2.1. This representation immediately conveys the idea that a centrally planned economy operates with a sizeable waste of resources and that the move to a decentralised decision-making process implies increasing productivity. Moreover, on the assumption that state firms only produce within a centrally planned economy, the liberalisation process implies a shift of resources allocation primarily from the state to the private sector, but also from agriculture and manufacturing to services and from large to small firms. In Fig. 2.1, this means a reallocation from the production of good x_1 to that of good x_2. Transition should therefore bring with it a sectoral reallocation as well as a substantial efficiency gain. In the long run, economic transition is supposedly able to push the production frontier upwards, favouring private initiative and investment. The long-run equilibrium would therefore be E_1.

Though very general, this definition is an excellent starting point for analysis. Within this general equilibrium framework, however, it is not possible to predict the time required for the process to come about, because transition is supposedly instantaneous. Nonetheless, particularly in the early stages of the transformation process, the speed of transition and of the ensuing reallocation process were widely debated issues. At what speed should the economy move from point P to point E_0 in Fig. 2.1?[8]

In the case of CEE transition, the eternal opposition in economics between advocates of free trade and interventionists took the form of debate on whether a *shock therapy* would be more effective than gradual transformation. According to Roland (2000, p. 1), three main positions were taken up on the issue. A first group of shock therapy advocates (Lipton and Sachs 1990; Åslund 1991; Sachs 1992; Balcerowicz 1994a, 1994b; Berg 1994) argued in favour of an immediate, fast

---

ous handbooks on economic transition (Blanchard 1997, Chap. 2; Roland 2000, Chap. 5), or in some recent studies (Boeri 2000, Chap. 1). Roland (2000) also describes alternative approaches to explanation of the transformation process. Discussion of these approaches, however, would be beyond the scope of this chapter.

[7] This definition also applies to China, where economic transition has not engendered any significant change in the political regime. It does not apply to Cuba, where reforms have not induced any significant change in the allocation system, which is still based on central planning.

[8] As noted in Roland (2000, p. 109): "this question of the optimal speed of transition applies to all situations of sectoral reallocation that involve innovations in capital equipment in some sectors and endogenous capital depreciation in others. Transition can then be defined as the time elapsed before the full replacement of the old equipment".

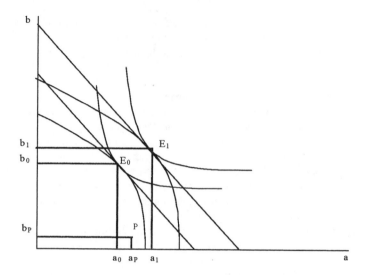

Fig. 2.1. Transition as a change of the allocation system

and comprehensive reform process which would engender a supposedly systemic regime change. For this strand in the literature there are no constraints on transition. It considers gradualism to be risky because it might render some individual measure ineffective, inducing the public to oppose reforms, so that transition eventually fails. A second group (Svejnar 1991; Portes 1990; Roland 1991; Dewatripont and Roland 1992; Aghion and Blanchard 1994; Murrell 1996) advocated gradualism with a different sequencing, or the reforms necessary to avert chaos and minimise the social costs of transition. Too rapid reform might give rise to permanently high levels of unemployment and thus produce a general desire to return to the old system. A third strand in the literature emphasised the need for rapid change along some dimensions, and for gradualism along others (see e.g. Kornai, 1992). As Roland (2000, p. 1) notes, this polarisation around three different positions was the most evident sign of the "unpreparedness of the economic profession for the task of transition".

Answering the question on the timing of transformation also requires examination of the frictions that may slow the transformation process down. Are these the same frictions as considered by any model of sectoral reallocation? Or are there specific transitional frictions to be taken into account? This issue is discussed further at the end of this section.

2.3.2 Transition through workers' reallocation

In the early stages of transition, there were two salient facts that theoreticians had to explain with their models: the dramatic fall in output, and burgeoning mass unemployment, which appeared to be at odds with the general equilibrium description of economic transition as a move to a more efficient allocation system.[9]

To explain these two features of transformation, Aghion and Blanchard (1994) chose a setting in which the dynamics is essentially driven by costly sectoral adjustment, and particular assumptions are made concerning the specificity of the event considered.[10] Aghion and Blanchard's model (henceforth ABM), also called the benchmark OST model, is analytically tractable and simple. The adjustment process is conceived as gradual rather than immediate.

Blanchard (1997, p. 25) describes transition as shaped by two main mechanisms: *reallocation* and *restructuring*. A reallocation of resources, especially labour, between the state and the private sector is the main driving force behind transition, and it well describes the nature of transition as a change in the allocation system. The cause of reallocation is restructuring and a two-sector framework is chosen to describe it. Production is essentially undertaken by a dominant but shrinking state sector (s) and by a buoyant new private sector (p). The production process is described by an identical constant returns production function using two factors, labour (N) and capital (K): $Y_i = F(N_i, K_i)$, where $i = s, p$. Labour productivity is higher in the private sector than in the state sector by a constant amount, θ, so that $y - x = \theta$. The analysis is carried out in continuous time, with the time indices omitted for simplicity's sake. Normalising the number of workers to one, the equilibrium condition of the labour market is as follows:

$$N_p + N_s + U = 1, \tag{2.1}$$

where U is the number of unemployed. Hence, there are only two labour market statuses, employment and unemployment, while flows in and out of non-participation and job-to-job transitions from the state to the private sector are excluded.[11]

The separation rate from the state sector can be thought of as exogenous (decided by the government)[12] and equal to s (like the *speed of restructuring*)

---

[9] The main question is "Under what circumstances will reallocation lead to a period of output decline and higher unemployment?" (Blanchard 1997, p. 26).

[10] In his discussion of the benchmark OST model, Kehoe (1994, p. 323) critically comments that "in essence, it is an adjustment cost story. Specifically, it is basically a simple model of sectoral adjustment with a few bells and whistles thrown in to make it more consistent with the micro realities of Poland. [...] while these extra bells and whistles look nice, they do not really affect the model's basic working or insight".

[11] Aghion and Blanchard (1994, p. 296) admit that, already in the early stages of transition, numerous hirings were made directly from state firms, rather than from unemployment. Nonetheless, they do not consider this simplification to be misleading. Conversely, according to Boeri (2000), assuming a fixed labour supply and no job-to-job moves is at odds with the empirical evidence. This would be a weakness of the benchmark model, which does not allow consideration of, for instance, the role of labour supply rigidities and their impact on labour reallocation. This point will be developed later.

[12] Aghion and Blanchard also consider endogenous separations (decided by the workers in the state sector), but this case is not considered here.

$$\hat{N}_s = \frac{dN_s}{dt} = -s \qquad (2.2)$$

Private job creation ($\hat{N}_P$, or H) is given by a function a of the profit firms make in the private sector. Profits equal the difference between labour productivity in the private sector and the cost of labour, including wages, w, and the tax levied on wages, essentially to pay unemployment benefits, z. Analytically, this can be written as:

$$\hat{N}_P = H = \frac{dN_P}{dt} = a\left[y - (w + z) \right] \qquad (2.3)$$

$\hat{N}_S$ is strictly negative and $\hat{N}_P$ is strictly positive. In other words, the state sector only destroys jobs and the private sector only creates jobs.[13]

Wages are determined according to efficiency wage considerations. Aghion and Blanchard (1994) adopt a simplified Shapiro and Stiglitz (1984) type of wage equation:

$$w = b + c\left(r + \frac{H}{U} \right) \qquad (2.4)$$

where wages in the private sector are set on the basis of labour market conditions at a level that equals the unemployment benefit plus a given share c of the sum of the interest rate and the probability of being hired in the private sector. Note that the hiring rate is simply given by the ratio between hiring and unemployment, because non-participation is not considered. Moreover, unemployment reduces wages, and thus fosters private sector growth (through Eq. 2.3). This result is obtained by assuming that firms fix the wage level in such a way that the value of being employed in the private sector, V_P, exceeds that of being unemployed, V_u, by some positive constant, c: $V_p - V_u = c$, where:[14]

$$rV_u = b + \left(\frac{H}{U} \right)(V_P - V) + \frac{dV_U}{dt} \qquad (2.5)$$

and

$$rV_P = w + \frac{dV_P}{dt} \qquad (2.6)$$

---

[13] In fact, the high degree of job and worker turnover typical of private activities is well documented in the transition literature (see e.g. Adamchick and King 1999), which suggest that the private sector found it extremely difficult to emerge during the transition period.

[14] Also the variations must be equal for the equality to be maintained over time: $dV_U / dt = dV_P / dt$.

In addition, the overall expenditure on benefits, given by a time-invariant per capita level of unemployment benefits times the stock of the unemployed should equal the tax levied on wages times the number of workers employed in the state and in the private sector, or:

$$bU = z(1-U) \tag{2.7}$$

It is apparent from (2.7) that unemployment also has adverse effects on private job creation, because it increases the level of taxes per worker, z, thus reducing the level of profits, the only source of financing for private firms. To sum up, unemployment has both a positive *and* a negative effect on private job creation. On the one hand, through (2.4), it reduces the wage per worker, therefore increasing the profits on which the hiring decisions of firms are assumed to depend. On the other hand, through (2.7) it increases the taxes per worker and therefore reduces profits and private job creation. As discussed later in more detail, this non-linearity is essential to the model (it shows that there is only one level of unemployment for which the hiring rate is highest).[15]

Before showing the dynamics of the model, we consider the labour market. Assuming that there is non-zero employment in the private sector, the before-transition equilibrium can be described as point A in Figure 2.2. The real wage is measured on the vertical axis. On the horizontal axis, employment in the state sector is measured from left to right and employment in the private sector from right to left. Equilibrium implies that there is no unemployment and that the real wage equals w^*.

One way of describing the beginning of transition is to imagine that the private sector expands by a small amount because small private firms open in the trade sector and in small services. This happens almost 'naturally', with no need of capital.[16] The immediate effect of transition is simply a leftward shift of labour demand in the state sector due to price liberalisation and the removal of subsidies to state employment. As shown in Fig. 2.2, this leads to point B, namely to unemployment, assuming that the private sector is initially unable to hire the labour shed by the state sector. At a later stage, the expansion of new private employment is a function of the profit per worker, as shown in (2.3). As such it is bound to encounter two main constraints: (a) limited access to external finance; (b) high adjustment costs, not only in terms of availability of physical capital but also in

---

[15] Aghion and Blanchard (1994, p. 297) argue that the negative effect of unemployment on job creation through unemployment benefits and taxes is actually a proxy of various burdens on the state budget, such as the pensions to pay for early retirements, the lack of state funds to finance public investment, the introduction of political uncertainty which reduces the contribution of direct investment from abroad: all factors that cannot be explicitly considered in the model's setup. However, it could be argued that the impact of unemployment benefits on the tax rate is limited, thereby suggesting that this second negative effect of unemployment on job creation is irrelevant. This hypothesis would require consideration only of the positive slope of the H curve in Fig. 2.3.

[16] Rostowski (1993) provides statistical evidence for these initial mechanisms in the case of Poland.

terms of the time required by the learning-by-doing process that private firms must undergo. Only with the removal of these constraints will unemployment be absorbed.

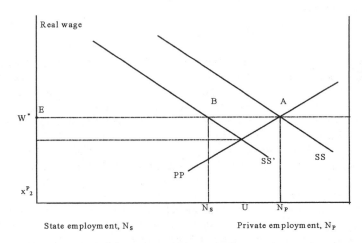

Fig. 2.2. The before and after transition equilibrium in the labour market

Consider again the dynamics of the model. The main objective is to define the conditions under which the optimal speed of transition can be obtained. If at any time restructuring generates a separation rate higher than the maximum hiring rate in the private sector, then unemployment increases indefinitely. The obvious implication of this line of reasoning is that transition must be gradual.

If separations are below the maximum hiring rate in the private sector, economic transition may either succeed, if unemployment is kept at a sufficiently low level, or fail, if unemployment increases too much. To demonstrate this result, we consider the rate of change of unemployment over time, $\hat{U}$. Unemployment is increasing (decreasing) if the inflow into it exceeds (is lower than) the outflows out of it. The inflow to unemployment is a given share, s, of state employment and the outflow from unemployment is private job creation. Analytically:

$$\hat{U} = \frac{dU}{dt} = s(1-\lambda) - H , \text{ with } U_0 = 1 - N_S - N_P \tag{2.8}$$

In turn, as already noted, private job creation is affected by unemployment through two main channels: wages and taxes. Increasing unemployment exerts a downward pressure on wages, thus increasing profits and pushing up private job creation. However, increasing unemployment is bound to raise the fiscal component of labour costs, thus reducing profits and private job creation. This effect is obtained by substituting the values of wages from (2.4) and the value of the per worker tax (2.7) into the equation for the hiring rate, (2.3):

$$H = \frac{aU}{U+ac}\left[y - rc - \left(\frac{1}{1-U}\right)b\right] \qquad (2.9)$$

Equation (2.9) summarises the double effect of unemployment on the hiring rate. In the first term on the right hand side, increasing unemployment augments job creation, because the numerator increases by a multiple of unemployment, whereas the denominator increases only by the absolute value of unemployment. In the second term on the right hand side, increasing unemployment reduces private job creation, because it increases the coefficient of b, thus reducing profits and investments.

Figure 2.3 plots the hiring rate as a bell-shaped function of unemployment. Notice that unemployment ensues from the fact that state restructuring precedes the establishment of private firms both logically and chronologically. H equals zero in two cases, namely when U equals zero and when U is sufficiently high to reduce the second term of (2.9) to zero. This latter case happens when the unemployment rate has become so high that the private sector entirely disappears. For intermediate values, as unemployment increases, its downward pressure on wages dominates the negative effects through increasing taxes for firms, so that profits and private job creation increase. However, as unemployment becomes sufficiently large, the negative effect through taxes dominates the positive effect through wages, and private job creation declines. The evolution of unemployment depends, in turn, on the separation rate: when this is above (below) the hiring rate, unemployment increases (shrinks).

When the speed of restructuring is too fast, actual separations exceed the maximum hiring rate ($\hat{N}_S \rangle \hat{N}_P$) and private job creation is unable to absorb the workers laid off by the state sector. Unemployment increases steadily. Wages initially tend to fall, increasing the hiring rate, but the latter never increases to the extent that is necessary to hinder the increase in unemployment. Eventually, unemployment reaches such a high level that the fiscal burden it generates causes the reforms to fail.

According to the ABM, the most common case is when $\hat{N}_S \langle \hat{N}_P$. In this case, which is depicted in Fig. 2.3, two equilibrium unemployment levels are possible, of which only A is stable. For any level of unemployment lower (higher) than U_A, the separation rate exceeds (is lower than) the hiring rate and unemployment increases (shrinks). Unemployment is steady when it reaches the level U_A, where the flows in and out of unemployment equal each other. In U_A, unemployment is stable until transition has been achieved. Conversely, if unemployment reaches the level U_B, the negative effect on taxes offsets the positive effect on wages, which causes the reforms to fail.

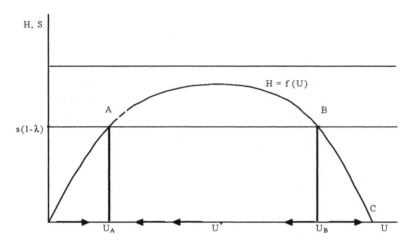

Fig. 2.3. The OST under exogenous separations

2.3.3 The predictions of the ABM

To our knowledge, there is no explicit modelling of regional unemployment in transition countries available in the literature. The aim of this section is to speculate on the implications of the benchmark OST model to find possible explanations for regional unemployment differentials.

As shown in the previous section, the ABM predicts unemployment in terms of labour turnover. Assuming that the ABM model applies also at a regional level, there seem to be two possibilities. According to a first hypothesis high unemployment regions are those regions that reach the second unstable equilibrium, namely point B in Fig. 2.4. In this case, high unemployment regions can be conceived as experiencing an unsuccessful transition process, with a too high separation rate at the beginning of transition, so that the unemployment rate exceeds its equilibrium level. The fact that the country is posited on point A at a national level weakens the feedback mechanisms, which would lead the reforms to fail, since the speed of reforms is decided centrally. As a consequence, the regional dispersion of unemployment remains and is steady, with some tensions from the periphery to the centre being absorbed over time.

A testable hypothesis with which to verify whether this is the case assumes that the separation and hiring rates are constant across regions with different unemployment rates. We shall call this 'Hypothesis One' or H_1. As a consequence, also labour turnover should be constant across the spatial distribution of unemployment. Only in the early stages of transition was the separation rate higher in the high unemployment regions. Subsequently, however, persistent unemployment can be considered the consequence of a low job creation rate, rather than of a high separation rate. As shown later, this hypothesis is at odds with the fact that the separation rate is persistently different across regions (and countries).

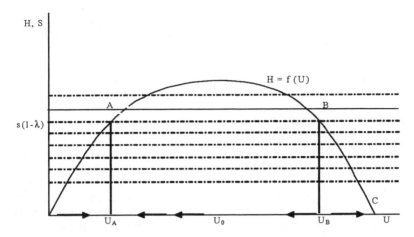

Fig. 2.4. The benchmark OST model and regional unemployment

An alternative hypothesis – which we shall call 'Hypothesis Two' or H_2 – is that the regional dispersion of unemployment is shaped by a different degree of restructuring across regions. In other words, there is no national separation rate, but rather persistently different rates of separation and hence of unemployment across regions. Figure 2.4 illustrates this idea as well. Each region has a different equilibrium rate of separation and hiring. In this case, therefore, regional unemployment can be conceived as an equilibrium phenomenon which disappears only when transition comes to an end. Once the separation rate has reached a given level, it tends to persist, and also determines the rate of unemployment. Hypothesis Two therefore implies that the rate of labour turnover differs across the spatial distribution of unemployment: that is, it should increase with the unemployment rate.

In both cases, one must explain why transition happens at a different speed at a local level. Under H_1, the separation rate in some regions is high only at the beginning of the transformation process, whereas under H_2 it is persistently high. This is an issue of interest not only in the OST literature but also in the theory of regional unemployment, where it is still unresolved.

Excluding the possibility that the policy-maker wishes to implement reforms at different speeds across regions, the most likely possibility is that the policy-maker is in fact unable to affect the actual rapidity of transition at a local level. This implies that there are factors that make transition proceed at a different pace across regions. According to the OST literature, one possibility is that the strength of the trade unions varies across regions. Union power is a function of various observed and unobserved differences across sectors: the stronger the power of the unions, the lower the separation rate in the area. Unfortunately, information on union power is lacking in all transition countries, so that this hypothesis is difficult to test.

Another possibility is to be found outside the ABM in the economic geography literature. Location factors may play an important role in determining the success of restructuring, with the most urbanised and most closely-linked regions exploiting the advantages of economic integration and therefore reducing the effect of re-structuring on unemployment (see e.g. Newell et al. 2000, 2002). This hypothesis has been long discussed in the transition literature and is considered in more detail in the last section of this chapter.

Our conclusion on the benchmark OST model's predictions regarding regional unemployment seems to be in line with those made by authoritative economists. Blanchard et al. (1994) argued during the early stages of economic transition that unemployment in transition countries may be due to two main factors within the flow approach to labour market analysis: (a) an increasing share of long-term un-employment generating low outflow from unemployment into jobs; (b) or a persis-tently high inflow from employment to unemployment. The policy implications of these alternatives are partly different. Whilst a low job finding rate essentially in-dicates the need for supply side policies in favour of the long-term unemployed, namely increasing labour market flexibility and/or educational reforms and active labour market policy on a large scale, Hypothesis Two also requires interventions on the demand side. For instance, assuming that the government is able to do so, it should reduce the rate of separation and/or increase the life expectancy of private businesses in the high unemployment regions.

Before we proceed, two issues require brief discussion. First, the ABM implies that the primary factor in (regional) unemployment in transition countries is indus-trial restructuring and the ensuing process of workers' reallocation from the state to the private sector. This factor is more influential than, as claimed instead by – among others – Dewatripont and Roland (1992), aggregate disturbances. This as-sumption finds considerable support also in the applied literature: for instance, us-ing different empirical strategies, Barbone et al. (1999), Newell and Pastore (2000) show that a large part of Polish unemployment is due to industrial turbu-lence. However, the role of supply side factors and constraints on the adjustment process are not clear in the ABM. [17]

Second, the OST literature comprises further developments of the ABM. Two waves of theoretical models subsequent to the ABM can be distinguished. Blanch-ard and Kremer (1997) initiated the second wave of the OST literature by focusing on the specific forces driving the process of transformation in the CIS, a region beyond the scope of this chapter. Boeri's (2000, Chap. 2) model (henceforth BM) marked the beginning of the third wave, which includes other important studies (see e.g. Commander and Tolstopiatenko 1998; Rutkowski and Przybila 2002; Bornhorst and Commander 2004). These recent contributions all underline factors of importance in explaining regional unemployment in transition countries. In the terms of the two hypotheses defined above, one may say that the BM develops H_1, while also putting forward arguments related to labour supply rigidities as factors

---

[17] Roland (2000) surveys various models in which transition is driven by an aggregate de-mand shock. This debate is reminiscent of the debate on Lilien's (1982) hypothesis that sectoral shifts drive aggregate unemployment. Abraham and Katz (1986) objected that it is hard to disentangle sectoral shifts from aggregate disturbances. See Elhorst (2003) for a discussion of the recent debate on the role of sectoral shifts and aggregate disturbance in causing unemployment.

liable to hinder adjustment to the equalisation of unemployment differentials. The following sections describe the BM and its predictions concerning regional unemployment during transition.

2.3.4 The predictions of the BM

Boeri (2000) points out what he perceives as the main shortcoming of the ABM: its overly simplistic assumptions concerning the way in which the labour market works. Only slightly more than 10 per cent of the labour market transitions in Poland during the early 1990s would be accounted for by the benchmark OST model, which would ignore two important facts in particular: (a) the high flow to inactivity; (b) state-to-private and private-to-state sector transitions. However, these two factors explain the most distinctive features of transitional labour markets: (a) the reduction in labour market participation, especially among the male population; (b) the reduction in employment. They both imply an inward shift in labour supply, which would explain, in turn, increasing unemployment rates.

Boeri (2000, Chap. 2) claims that two myths influenced the debate on transition in the early 1990s and misled theoreticians seeking to explain transition. The first was the supposedly abundant supply of human capital. At the outset, it was a widely held belief that the previous system had developed a highly qualified labour force (CEPR 1990). "Contrary to such belief, the Communists over invested in narrowly based vocational training, forcing most of those entering secondary education to invest in skills that were not 'fungible', i.e. non-transferable across different jobs" (Boeri 2000, p. 54).[18] The second myth was the supposedly complex production system: in fact, the socialist production system was characterised by a formidable lack of product variety.

Why are these two points important? According to Boeri, the lack of product variety suggests that at the outset of transition there was high potential for the development of numerous small-scale activities which would fill the gaps in the supply of varieties to consumers. However, private activities had a relatively high failure rate because workers could not easily move across occupations and industries, and because of the inherited specificity of their skills.

Boeri attempts to assemble all the evidence just discussed in a model based on an aggregate matching function whose arguments are vacancies and job-seekers. The structure of the model is similar to the ABM, although the existence of various types of labour market transitions makes graphical representation difficult. For this reason, no attempt is made here to reproduce the structure of the BM.

The assumptions of the model are as follows (Boeri 2000, p. 71). First, restructuring means not only downsizing but also changing the product specialisation of firms. In the pre-transition period, all firms produced few goods. Transition obliged numerous firms to change their production. There are two sectors in Boeri's model: an old sector and a new one, which are not to be confused with the

---

[18] On the role of human capital depreciation in transition countries, see also Ferragina and Pastore (2005) and the literature cited therein.

state and the private sector, in that state firms could restructure and produce new goods. In this model, it makes sense to say that the old sector is bound to disappear. Second, unlike in the ABM, separations may be not only to unemployment but also to employment in the new sector and to inactivity. Third, employers offering jobs in the new sector can recruit either from among the non-employed or from among workers employed in the old sector. Employed and non-employed workers have the same productivity, but employers are not indifferent between the two types of workers, as the non-employed have a higher reservation utility and hence are less likely to accept a job in the new sector owing to the availability of generous non-employment benefits. As a consequence, once a worker has opted for non-employment (unemployment and inactivity), s/he finds it difficult to find a job in the new sector.

At each point in time the model generates the following transitions: (a) workers employed in the old sector can flow either to non-employment or to employment in the new sector; (b) workers employed in the new sector can only flow to non-employment; (c) non-employed workers can only flow to employment in the new sector. The only types of flow excluded by the model are ones to the old sector: which means that transition is bound to come to an end.

The model is calibrated against real transition data, and different scenarios are presented on the basis of specific assumptions which essentially concern the evolution of the level of unemployment benefits over time. The results in Boeri (2000, p. 78) are presented in relation to two scenarios: one of low and one of high unemployment benefits at the outset of transition. The results of the model are the following: (i) the length of transition depends on the generosity of non-employment benefits at the outset of transition: low (high) non-employment benefits bring transition to an end in eight years (over ten years); (ii) the output fall observed at the outset of transition is the consequence of the large drop in employment in the old sector, which is not counterbalanced by equal growth in the new sector, because workers flow to inactivity; (iii) the only way to shorten the reform process and reduce the non-employment pool and hence unemployment is to increase the fungibility of non-employed workers by reducing their reservation utility; (iv) however, a reduction in the non-employment benefit system is effective only when the non-employment pool is very small: when the non-employment pool is large, reform of the benefit system is ineffective and non-employment becomes persistent.

The main conclusions of the model are: (a) unemployment is persistent because the unemployed are crowded out by employed job-seekers; b) the initial stages of transition crucially determine the degree of persistence of transitional unemployment.

The BM initiated the third wave in the OST literature, which is essentially an attempt to incorporate supply side explanations of unemployment persistence into the analysis of economic transition. This theoretical and empirical literature commonly assumes that unemployment is due to rigid labour markets supposedly like those of the transition countries.

The novel features of this approach compared to the ABM are as follows. First, the BM expands the analysis with some important facts concerning transition, such as the dramatic downward shift of employment and participation in the

CEECs and the CIS republics. Second, the BM also provides an explanation for the high turnover of private activities, especially small businesses.

Third, the benchmark OST model had wrong policy implications. Neglecting labour supply has meant that much emphasis has been placed on the issue of gradualism *versus* the big-bang approach to reforms. This emphasis was ill-placed, because it amounted to assuming that the government was able to control the pace of closure of state enterprises. However, if quits due to voluntary choices are the main cause of separations, the latter should be considered an endogenous variable. Also, subsidies to state firms were supposedly not a control variable (Boeri 2000, Chap. 2). As a consequence, the implication of the ABM and of the early transition literature that the resistance of insiders to restructuring should be overcome by 'buying them off' with generous non-employment benefits may have given rise to wrong policy prescriptions. If separations are endogenous and workers tend to move to new jobs or to non-employment, high unemployment benefits tend to increase the flow to non-employment and reduce the flow to new jobs. This may be one of the main factors responsible for the underdevelopment of the private sector in transition countries.

According to Boeri (2000, p. 43), the key policy variable during transition is unemployment benefit, but not in the sense with which the early transition models considered it. Boeri maintains that all transition countries made the wrong choice in regard to the timing of unemployment benefits. They made overgenerous non-employment benefits available from the outset, thereby creating the conditions for stagnant unemployment pools throughout transition. In its turn, "long-duration unemployment made the premises of high non-employment benefits unsustainable because such benefits had been conceived for unemployment of a shorter duration. Moreover, this tightening has not been found to reduce significantly the duration of unemployment. Rather than starting with generous non-employment benefits and then subsequently cutting them down, our framework suggests that the right sequence should have been the other way around" (Boeri 2000, p. 56).

Fourth, the third strand in the OST literature has the merit of anticipating the problems of economic transition typical of the late 1990s and early 2000s, when the old sector has almost disappeared and the reform process is close to conclusion. The BM is thus a bridge between the OST literature and the neoclassical explanation of regional unemployment differentials in terms of frictions which impede the adjustment process, as discussed in Section 2.1. In addition, although still sizeable in some countries in the late 1990s, such as Poland (World Bank 2001; Newell 2001), the leftward shift of labour demand experienced in the immediate aftermath of economic transition as a consequence of heavy industrial restructuring has, with the passage of time, become as important as the ability of labour supply to adjust to it. The stress on the labour supply, and on the political economy of institutional upgrading as one possible instrument to fight unemployment, has been general in recent years.

It seems clear that the BM adopts the aforementioned hypothesis H_1: labour turnover is constant across regions and a low job finding rate contributes to explaining long unemployment spells in high unemployment regions. Within the BM, regional unemployment persistence can also be conceived as the consequence of different average durations of unemployment across the country. Labour market institutions are bound to play a decisive role in affecting the degree of persistence of regional unemployment differentials in this theoretical setting. A policy of generous non-employment benefits in the highest unemployment regions may contribute to regional unemployment differentials by reducing the incentive for new (private) firms to hire workers from the non-employment pool, rather than from the ranks of the workers employed in the old (state) sector. This would contribute to making the non-employment pool stagnant. In fact, if in high (low) unemployment areas wages are not lower (higher) than the average, the reservation wage of non-employed workers will be relatively higher (lower) in high (low) unemployment regions. Moreover, low wage differentials and insufficient labour mobility may affect the degree of persistence of regional unemployment.

Boeri (2000, Chap. 3) argues that long-term unemployment is an important factor in explaining the regional unemployment distribution in Poland, doing so by means of a complex line of reasoning. In his view, the rural/urban gap in unemployment rates[19] depends mainly on the low degree of mobility of unemployed workers from rural to urban areas. He finds evidence that: (a) the distribution of the reservation wage by levels of education is much flatter in rural areas, suggesting that highly educated workers expect a very low wage premium in those areas; and (b) it is higher for low-educated workers in rural rather than in urban areas, suggesting that low-skilled workers are better off in rural areas. They prefer to be involved in home production or family-run businesses, often in the informal sector, rather than move or commute to urban areas. For the same reasons, in rural areas the low-skilled unemployed tend to flow to non-participation, rather than to unemployment, as is instead the case in urban areas.

2.4 Testing the OST literature

2.4.1 The hypotheses

The most direct test of the ABM adopted in the applied literature has involved inspection of labour market dynamics across countries, sectors and regions. The focus has been on the distribution of gross and net job flows (see e.g. Faggio and Konings 2003; Walsh 2003) as well as on gross and net worker flows (see e.g. Bellman et al. 1995; Cazes and Scarpetta 1998; Newell and Pastore 1999, 2000; Boeri 2000; Cazes and Nesporova 2001; World Bank 2001; Vodopivec 2002). It has been possible to use this approach because of the ready availability of longitudinal data at the firm (for job flows) or individual level (for worker flows), as well as administrative data on job finding by the registered unemployed. The conclusions reached in this literature are somewhat ambiguous, because they reflect differences in the periods covered and the data source used (administrative or sur-

---

[19] Boeri (2000) assumes that urban/rural differentials largely overlap with regional differentials.

vey). The following predictions by the ABM and the BM have been subjected to applied analysis:

a) If transition is considered to be essentially a process of structural change on a large scale and therefore of workers' reallocation across sectors, the flow out of employment to unemployment in particular, and the level of labour turnover in general, should be higher in transition than they are in mature capitalist economies, where structural change is a minor feature;

b) On this line of reasoning, as shown in the previous sections, two hypotheses can be formulated regarding the relationship between the unemployment rate and the degree of labour turnover. According to H_1, the degree of labour turnover is the same across regions with different unemployment rates. This would suggest that the main cause of unemployment is a greater share of long-term unemployment in high unemployment regions. According to H_2, the degree of labour turnover increases together with the unemployment rate. This would suggest that the main cause of unemployment is a greater degree of industrial restructuring in high unemployment regions;

c) If H_2 holds true, one should also find a closer correlation between the degree of industrial restructuring, on the one hand, and the amount of labour turnover and regional unemployment on the other. The argument is that put forward in Lilien (1982): that sectoral shifts that do not simultaneously alter the aggregate level of the demand for labour will have no impact on unemployment only if workers are perfectly mobile and substitutable. However, if workers are not perfectly mobile and substitutable, shifts in the sectoral composition of labour demand will have an impact on the local unemployment rate.

Vice versa, if H_1 holds true, there should be no correlation among the degree of industrial restructuring, the amount of labour turnover, and the unemployment rate. Figure 2.5 gives a graphical representation of H_1 and H_2.

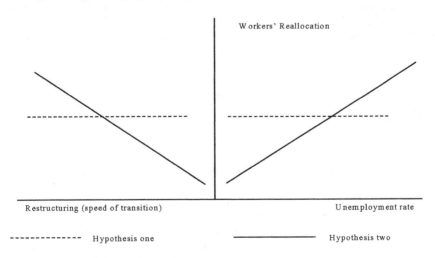

Fig. 2.5. Restructuring, workers' reallocation and unemployment

As noted in Newell et al. (2002), where unemployment depends on a high degree of industrial restructuring and job separation, one should observe a considerable difference in labour turnover across regions with different unemployment rates. In contrast, where unemployment depends on low job finding and therefore on a large share of long-term unemployment, one should observe no difference in labour turnover across regions with different unemployment rates. This empirical law appears to be one of the most interesting results of the debate on regional unemployment in transition countries, and it could also be fruitfully applied to regional unemployment in other OECD countries.

Relating to point c) is the issue of finding an indicator of industrial restructuring which is independent of aggregate negative shocks and exogenous with respect to labour turnover;

d) one would expect high (low) unemployment countries and regions to be more (less) developed and close to (far from) successful completion of the reform process. This conclusion has sometimes been used to justify the claim that the unemployment rate is the best indicator of the speed of restructuring and transition;

e) several studies have estimated the determinants of job separations and/or job finding at a regional level;

f) according to the BM and the neoclassical tradition, regional unemployment persistence during transition is related to several labour supply constraints.

The rest of this section surveys the empirical literature on the above issues.

2.4.2 Workers' reallocation across countries

The evidence for the ABM-based predictions concerning the degree of workers' reallocation in transition countries – point (a) in the previous section – is ambiguous. On the one hand, several observers (e.g. Boeri 1994; Boeri and Scarpetta 1995, 1996; Boeri 2000; World Bank 2001; Boeri and Terrell 2002), find that transition countries initially experienced a low degree of labour turnover, below that of the low turnover European countries, and also of the USA. They explain this apparently surprising finding arguing that: (a) job-to-job moves from the state to the private sector accounted for a substantial share of workers' reallocation; (b) unemployment was the consequence of a low job finding rate due, in its turn, to the inability of the private sector to emerge because of a shortage of skills suitable for the market economy.

Other scholars (Konings et al. 1996; Cazes and Nesporova 2001), however, find that workers' reallocation was sizeable in transition countries. Previous studies were induced to stress a supposedly low degree of labour turnover in transition countries by the data source used, which gave a false impression of low labour turnover which later studies maintained. The early analyses used monthly flow measures based on unemployment register data, rather than annual flow measures based on labour force survey data, which have become widespread only since the mid-1990s. Compared to transitions computed on longer periods, monthly transitions tend to reflect institutional rather than structural factors. They also increase the right censoring problem,[20] although they are less affected by measurement errors, attrition and unrecorded spells. Institutional arrangements, especially entitlement to non-employment benefits, may affect the decision to register at the employment office. If workers register for reasons other than job search, they may remain on the register even after they have found a job, which may give rise to an underestimation of the extent of transitions into jobs. Moreover, as noted by Kiefer (1988), monthly transition rates tend generally to be lower than annual ones.

Table 2.1, which summarises transition rates for a number of CEECs, CIS republics and mature market economies, confirms this result. The inflow to unemployment and the outflow from unemployment are both very high in all the countries considered. Admittedly, the degree of turnover in the USA is much higher.

Table 2.1. Changes in labour market status in international comparison (annual percentage flow rates)

	Unemployment to Employment	Employment to Unemployment
Bulgaria, 1994–95	32.3	5.9
The Czech Republic, 1994–95	49.6	1.3
East Germany, 1990–91	35.0	9.3
Estonia, 1992	23.7	2.3
Poland, 1992–93	36.1	4.0
Poland, low unemployment voivodships, 1995–96	36.3	2.5
Poland, high unemployment voivodships, 1995–96	31.5	4.4
Russia, 1992–93	65.9	2.8
Russia, 1994–95	40.8	3.7
Russia, 1995–96	39.5	5.6
Slovakia, 1990–91	23.7	2.3
Italy, 1994–95	13.1	1.6
United States, 1992–93	65.9	2.8
UK, 1989–90	38.4	2.4
UK, 1999–90	35.6	2.1
Germany, 1992–97 (average)	25.4	
France, 1990–97 (average)	32.2	
EU-13	28.7	

Note: EU-13 does not include the Netherlands and Luxembourg.

Sources: Poland, Tables 7 and 8; Italy, own calculations based on data from the Rilevazione Trimestrale delle Forze di Lavoro; United States and Russia, Boeri (1997); UK, Schmitt and Wadsworth (2004, Table 8); Germany, France and EU-13, IDB (2004, Table 2.2); Bulgaria, Slovakia and the United States, Boeri (1998); for the Czech Republic, Sorm and Terrell (2000); for East Germany, Bellmann et al. (1995); for Poland, Góra and Lehmann (1995); for Estonia, Vodopivec (2002); for Russia, Foley (1997).

---

[20] By right censoring problem, we mean the fact that employment and unemployment spells are observed only until a given date. The shorter is the period of observation the lower is the probability to observe the end of a spell.

However, comparison with the USA should be made with caution: it is well known that the high level of labour turnover in the USA is due to a much more flexible labour market with few restrictions on the hiring and firing decisions of firms and a relatively high share of workers on temporary contracts. On the other hand, Italy, a country with a traditionally very rigid labour market, has a much lower degree of labour turnover compared to transition countries. Of course, also comparison with Italy should be hedged about with caveats, but it nevertheless proves that turnover was not low in transition countries: quite the opposite.

The average duration of unemployment computed using LFS data was around 12.2 months in Poland in 1997. The average share of long-term unemployment was 38.5 in Poland over the years from 1992 to 1997, which compares well with the figures for EU countries – France (39.5 per cent), Germany (37 per cent), Spain (51.5 per cent) and the UK (42.2 per cent) – although it is much higher than that for the USA (12.7 per cent) in 1987 (Alogoskufis et al., 1994, Table 1.2).

2.4.3 Testing H_1 against H_2

The next step in the analysis – point (b) in Section 2.4.1 – is to consider the results of applied research which tests H_1 against H_2. This amounts to testing whether in equilibrium the regional distribution of unemployment exploded all at once and was persistent because of low outflows and long-term unemployment in high unemployment regions or, alternatively, whether it was nourished by a persistently high separation rate in the high unemployment regions. In the former case, labour turnover – meaning the sum of separations and hiring – is constant across regions, whereas, in the latter case, it increases with the local unemployment rate. Once the regional pattern of unemployment is shaped, a reduction (an increase) in regional unemployment is achieved either through a reduction (increase) in the separation rate in high unemployment regions or an increase (a reduction) in the hiring rate in low unemployment regions.

As already noted in the previous sections, Boeri and Scarpetta (1996) and Boeri (2000) are the best examples of advocates of hypothesis H_1. Boeri and Scarpetta (1996, p. 253) find evidence of slowdown of industrial restructuring in high unemployment regions already in the early 1990s. The stabilisation of unemployment differentials occurred therefore at the cost of increasing differences in non-employment rates across regions. Finally, wage moderation and labour mobility offered a limited contribution to the reduction of labour market imbalances. Boeri and Scarpetta (1996, p. 239) build a classification of regions in five CEECs (Bulgaria, the Czech Republic, Hungary, Poland and the Slovak Republic), based on their structural characteristics. The taxonomy uses a sequential selection process. In the first step, three broad groups were identified, namely regions with a marked specialisation in agriculture, those dominated by industrial activities and a residual group of more diversified regions. In the second step, each of these three groups was split into more developed and less developed regions on the basis of various structural indicators, including the level of infrastructure development (proxied by the number of telephone lines), the presence of tourism and trade activities in agricultural regions, the share of private firms and the size of industrialised plants in industrialised regions and the share of the working-age population with higher education, together with the previous indicators in diversified regions. They also find a low degree of labour turnover in low unemployment regions – with a developed diversified economic structure – in all the countries considered, except for the Czech Republic, and argue that it was achieved through sizeable direct job-to-job shifts, with relatively less intermediate unemployment spells. Labour turnover was measured as monthly inflow and outflow from unemployment as obtained by unemployment register data.

Newell and Pastore (2000) have compared average transitions from employment to unemployment, and vice versa, with regional unemployment rates, in 49 Polish voivodships during the period 1994–97, which was before the reform that reduced the number of administrative units to 16. They use Labour Force survey data to compute gross worker flows and find a correlation coefficient between the job separation rate and the unemployment rate of 0.76, significant at the one-per cent level. Not surprisingly, also the job finding rate displays a similar degree of correlation to the unemployment rate. Overall, high unemployment voivodships tend to be regions of large-scale transitions from employment to unemployment. This is as one would expect if industrial turbulence is a major cause of the regional pattern of unemployment. This suggests that higher rates of separations derive from the higher-than-average speeds of transition of some regions. In turn, high unemployment regions have higher inflow rates to unemployment, rather than longer unemployment duration. Hence, high unemployment is related to high rates of destruction of job-worker matches and low unemployment is related to greater job stability, which seems to contradict the received wisdom according to which the greater the degree of flexibility in local labour markets, the lower the level of unemployment.

This finding seems only partly confirmed, however, by data on gross job flows computed on the Amadeus data base and covering large-sized firms (more than 100 employees), mainly in the manufacturing sector. Plotting gross job flows over the period 1994-'97 as reported in Faggio and Konings (2003, Tab. 5) against voivodship unemployment rates in 1994 and in 1997 gives invariably a flat line, supporting the hypothesis H_1. The difference from previous studies may be attributed to the different nature of the data: restructuring at the level of large-sized state-owned enterprises might not represent well the overall level of labour turnover, which is decisively affected also by the difficulty to survive of newly established small-sized private enterprises. There is large evidence supporting the idea that job destruction and creation has been sizeable in the private sector all over the 1990s.

Lehmann and Walsh (1999) support hypothesis H_2 by attributing a decisive role to the human capital level of the population inherited from the past. They develop a theoretical model very similar to the ABM, but where separations are endogenously determined by the quality level of human capital in the region. Where human capital is fungible, workers do not oppose restructuring, which takes place generating unemployment, but also fast output recovery. Like in the ABM, unemployment benefits play an important role, that of a temporary pit-stop in the reallocation process. The authors build a classification of Polish regions by level of economic development and find that the low unemployment regions are those regions where the restructuring process was very slow. These are the regions on the Eastern border, where the economic structure is less diversified and human capital is hard to adapt to the needs of the market economy.

Walsh (2003) develops the work by Góra and Lehmann (1995) and Lehmann and Walsh (1999). He builds a classification of regions by the level of inherited public infrastructure, as measured by the number of telephone, of fax machines, of railways, of public roads, of employment in services and of urbanisation. He ends up with six groups of regions and finds a non-linear relationship between the degree of job reallocation (as measured again with firm level data drawn from the Amadeus data base) and the average local unemployment rates in these groups of regions: low local unemployment is achieved either via high unemployment inflows with short unemployment spells or with low inflows with long durations (Walsh 2003, Tab. 1). The former group of regions includes some of the most developed voivodships and the latter some of the least developed regions on the Eastern border with Belarus. Walsh (2003) concludes that the ABM is right in considering unemployment benefits useful to speed up the process of reallocation and that job-to-job moves had not the important impact on local unemployment rates as assumed in the BM.

In fact, the conclusions of Walsh (2003) are not in contrast with those of Newell and Pastore (2000). Also the latter find that low unemployment rates are either in very developed (Western and urbanised) or in depressed (Eastern) regions in Poland. However, labour turnover, as measured using individual level data, is found to be lower than average also in booming regions.

2.4.4 An empirical law about regional unemployment?

The aim of this section – point (c) in Section 2.4.1 – is to survey the attempts to test for the causality chain from restructuring to workers' reallocation to unemployment hypothesised in Fig. 2.5. As already noted, this exercise requires one to find an exogenous measure of the degree of industrial restructuring, which is independent of aggregate shocks. Newell and Pastore (2000) propose the index of industrial turbulence suggested in Layard et al. (1991, Chap. 6). This measures the fraction of all jobs in the economy that have changed sector of industry.[21] The authors calculated this index for Poland using the May 1994 and November 1997 Labour Force Surveys, these being the earliest and latest available surveys using a consistent 32-industry classification.[22] Similar indices for other dimensions of the transition were also calculated: by ownership in order to capture privatisation, and by firm size. The percentage figures are sizeable. The share of workers changing

---

[21] The index typically used is: $I = 0.5\left(\left|S_{i,t} - S_{i,0}\right|\right)$, where $S_{i,t}$ is the share of employment in industry i at time t and $i = 1, 2, ..., n$.

[22] The degree of aggregation is extremely important, because a sizeable part of worker reallocation may occur within industries in a way not necessarily correlated to changes between industries. Using 32 industries does not ensure that aggregation issues are completely controlled for.

their sector of industry was 19.6 in low unemployment regions and 25.1 per cent in high ones.[23]

Moreover, the authors present the correlations across voivodships between these restructuring indices and unemployment rates. Clearly, there is a strong relationship between industrial change and change in ownership, on the one hand, and unemployment rates on the other.[24] The correlation with the degree of restructuring by firm size is much lower, owing to the small number of cases considered: the Polish labour force survey includes only five classes of firm's size. However, as also noted by Blanchard (1994) and Barbone et al. (1999), it is likely that most changes have occurred within, rather than among, the size groups considered.

Finally, Newell and Pastore (2000) compute correlations among inflow rates, outflow rates, unemployment rates and the aforementioned index of industrial change. Inflow rates and industrial change are strongly correlated, and so too are inflow rates and unemployment rates. As we have already seen, unemployment and structural change are also significantly correlated. Lastly, unemployment and outflow rates are significantly correlated, although outflow rates are uncorrelated with inflow rates and industrial change. Regressions of the unemployment rate data on the inflow rate and outflow rate data show that inflow rates account for over 60 per cent of the regional variance of unemployment rates, and that adding the outflow rates adds only 7 percentage points.

This research confirms the impression that the force driving regional unemployment during transition is a continuous structural change and the ensuing destruction of jobs. The transition process has not happened in one single year, but over a long period of time and is in many CEECs still in place. Moreover, there is evidence that structural change and job destruction are dispersed unevenly across regions, and dispersed in a persistent fashion. The aim of the following sections is to understand why this was the case. Different demand and supply side factors are considered.

2.4.5 Sources of shifts in labour demand

This sections deals with the relation between regional unemployment differentials and the sources of structural change during transition – point (e) in Section 2.4.1.

---

[23] Layard et al. (1991) calculated average annual percentage rates for a number of countries over the decades from the 1950s to the 1980s. On average, on the basis of eight sectors of industry, these rates were 1 per cent, and none of them was higher than 2.2 per cent. Part of the difference is due to the degree of aggregation and to the length of time on which changes in shares were computed. However, this finding confirms the high degree of industrial turbulence in Poland.

[24] Krajnyàk and Sommer (2004) find a strong correlation between the same index of industrial turbulence used by Newell and Pastore (2000) and the unemployment rate at a regional level in the Czech Republic over the years 1998-1999, when restructuring actually started.

In the meantime, the section discusses also the relationship between fast restructuring and unemployment, namely point (d) in Section 2.4.1.

A. The initial conditions (Góra and Lehmann 1995; Scarpetta 1995; Gorzelak 1996; Lehmann and Walsh 1999). The communist legacy is not a constant across regions. Historical differences affect the development of regions during transition in various ways.[25]

First, important differences existed in the model of socialism adopted in each country: in Yugoslavia cooperative enterprises operated in a quasi-market environment, while in Poland, for instance, agriculture was never entirely collectivised. Only in Northern Poland was state agriculture common, and this, according to many authors, explains the high local rate of unemployment in the 1990s. Some countries, such as Hungary and the Czech Republic, started the reform process already in the 1980s, though blandly.

Second, in the absence of market mechanisms, the communist planner sought to define artificial models of product specialisation, allocating to some regions the task of producing only certain goods for the entire country, with the consequence that several areas were heavily industrialised, while others remained agricultural. Regional development was conceived as forced industrialisation and consisted of locating large plants in remote rural areas. The one-industry town was also a typical outcome, with some towns being developed around one individual manufacture employing almost all the inhabitants.

Amongst others, Scarpetta (1995) assumes that transition hit hardest the regions in which the former socialist planner had concentrated the largest part of economic activities, especially in the manufacturing sector. The abolition of the state subsidisation system and increasing internal and external market competition pushed those activities out of market, generating unemployment. The argument is again that of Lilien (1982), mentioned previously.

Linked to Lilien's argument that structural change has spatially asymmetric effects is the argument of Simon (1988) and Simon and Nardinelli (1992). They found evidence of a *portfolio effect* in the labour market using the Herindhal index to measure the degree of industry concentration in estimates of the determinants of unemployment across US states over time. The hypothesis is that the higher is the degree of industry diversification, the lower is the impact on the local production structure of a sectoral shift and the higher is the probability for dismissed workers to find employment in other sectors.[26]

In the case of Poland, several authors (see e.g. Gorzelak 1996; Rutkowski and Przybila 2002; Fazekas 2002; Pastore 2004) have noted that all the least diversified regions were hit by high unemployment rates. In the case of Poland, high un-

---

[25] The discussion in this section refers to regions, although some Central and Eastern European countries, e.g. the Czech and Slovak republics and Slovenia, are so small that they have only a few regions.

[26] Elhorst (2003) reports that some, if not all the studies using various indices of industry concentration found a significant positive effect on local unemployment in mature market economies.

employment concentrated in the northern regions (dominated by large state-owned farms), Gdanskie (by the steel industry), Lódzskie (by the textiles and clothing industry), and Walbrzyskie (by coal mining). Using micro-data drawn from labour force surveys, Cazes and Scarpetta (1998) find evidence of localised unemployment effects of past industrialisation policy in some regions of Bulgaria and in Poland. Fazekas (2002) supports this view for some Hungarian regions.

Conversely, other regions had more diversified production structures, so that they were able to minimise the risk of aggregate shocks. This was especially the case of the most urbanised areas, such as, in the case of Poland, Warszawskie, Bielskie, Katowickie, Krakovskie, Poznanskie, Skiemewickie.

However, whether the degree of industry diversification inherited from the communist era had an impact overall in the country is difficult to prove by means of econometric analysis. Boeri and Scarpetta (1996) notice that there is no correlation between unemployment rates and the economic structure of the regions in five CEECs. Góra and Lehmann (1995) for Poland and other studies in Scarpetta and Wörgötter (1995) for other countries were unable to find clear evidence for such an impact. They used micro-data and tested whether the probability of job finding, estimated either by multinomial logit or survival analysis, in the early 1990s was affected by industry diversification and the level of development, proxied either by indices of industrial concentration (the Herfindhal index) or by classifications of regions according to the level of development and of industrial diversification. A similar conclusion was reached by Lehmann and Walsh (1998). Newell and Pastore (2000) noted that the classifications used in such studies tended to consider the level of development, rather than the pace of economic development. Also Newell et al. (2002) did not find econometric evidence for such a correlation using the same index of industrial concentration and the same classifications of regions in a later period (1996–97). They analysed labour force survey data relative to Poland and estimated the probability of job separation (rather than of job finding) by means of survival analysis. Using aggregate cross-regional data and multiple regression analysis, Rutkowski and Przybila (2002) instead found a positive *ceteris paribus* relation between the hiring rate of a Polish *voivodship* and the share of services, taken as a measure of the degree of industry diversification. They argue that the independent contribution of variables related to economic growth is limited, because they are correlated with variables representing the economic structure of the region. In turn, these last explain about 80 per cent of the variation in job finding rates.

Third, some countries and regions are closer than others to the core of Europe. In almost all CEECs, the capital city, the most urbanised regions and those close to the Western border have lower unemployment rates, while unemployment concentrates in rural areas on the Eastern border, with the exception, perhaps of the Eastern regions of Poland, where the reform process has progressed very slowly and so has also unemployment (Gorzelak 1996; Fazekas 2002, p. 178). This may have triggered direct and indirect capital flow from abroad. The ability to attract new foreign investment depended not only on geographical proximity to Western countries but also on other factors, such as ease of market access (presence of good transportation systems at low cost), the size of local markets (as measured, for instance, by per capita GDP), and so forth. The role of distance and its impact on economic integration will be considered also in the last section of this chapter.

The problem with the initial conditions and the communist legacy is that, as a multifaceted fact, it did not always affect unemployment in the same way, so that it is difficult to assess its overall impact.

B. The reform path followed (Góra and Lehmann 1995; Scarpetta 1995; Lehmann and Walsh 1998; Svejnar 2002a). This is also a multifaceted fact. Various dimensions of the reform process have been discussed in the literature as factors able to affect the economic outcome. We mention only some of them: (i) gradualism *versus* shock therapy; (ii) different models of privatisation; (iii) different solutions to the problem of establishing financial markets and institutions. While these factors are important determinants of unemployment differentials across countries, they are, in principle, less important at a regional level. Nonetheless, it seems evident that, as noted in the previous sections, the degree of dispersion of the regional unemployment rate also reflects the depth and speed of the reform process, in as much as it affects the degree of restructuring. In general, when restructuring is high and fast, regional growth and unemployment differentials are wider. This depends also on the agglomeration effects discussed above: economic integration tends to concentrate in some more developed and better-connected areas, which may grow faster when markets liberalise, widening the gap with the rest of the country.

C. Technological upgrading. Economic transition and the opening up of the economy imply a process of technological upgrading, also fostered by investment from abroad. This is a specific factor of economic change which in itself is able to affect unemployment differentials via shifts in labour demand away from low-skilled and towards high-skill labourers. Technological upgrading may favour the more developed regions endowed with a higher level of human capital, on the one hand. On the other hand, a high concentration of human capital in some regions may trigger economic growth and employment, while reducing the average risk of long-term unemployment, since high-skill workers are more mobile and fungible. In addition, a high concentration of human capital in the local labour market may favour further technological upgrading, thus generating a virtuous circle.

In the already-mentioned study, Rutkowski and Przybila (2002) find a positive correlation between the voivodship's hiring rate and the share of workers with secondary or higher educations. Moreover, they show that a higher level of development, a more diversified economic structure, better infrastructures, especially related to communication, flexible wages also correlate with higher than average regional hiring rates. A similar conclusion, again for Poland, is reached in Newell's chapter in this book.

In turn, this is evidence in favour of agglomeration factors. In other words, job opportunities tend to concentrate in urbanised, "central" regions, as one would expect if returns to scale and social externalities of human capital and technology were at work.

D. Economic integration with Western countries (see e.g. Landesmann and Burgstaller 1998). Some authors have stressed the labour market impact of the adjustment process triggered by the massive trade diversion and trade creation following the opening up of Central and Eastern European countries (CEECs) to international trade after the collapse of the COMECON. Economic integration was an important source of industrial restructuring in the country. From a theoretical point of view it had a similar impact on the speed of reforms. However, economic integration has potentially different distributional consequences. While economic transition should favour the most skilled workers, as evidenced by the literature on returns to education (Newell and Reilly 1999; Brainerd 2000), the most important effect of this process is instead the specialisation of CEECs in industries using unskilled labour and physical capital. Economic integration may combine with agglomeration factors in favour of urbanised areas where the demand for unskilled labour may increase. This feature will be discussed further in the final section of this chapter.

2.4.6 Supply side factors

The massive shifts in labour demand caused by the economic reforms, technological change, and economic integration discussed in previous sections have had different impacts across regions also according to the reaction by the labour supply and the labour market institutions. As already noted, given the debate's belief in low labour turnover, it has consequently stressed the characteristics of unemployed workers, especially the long-term unemployed, and supply side rigidities such as wage rigidities imposed by national wage-fixing agreements, too generous unemployment benefits, barriers to labour mobility, especially the high cost of housing, and so on. From time to time, especially in recent years, reducing supply side rigidities has been advocated by many observers, who argue that this is an essential means to foster job creation and reduce the high rate of unemployment. The discussion that follows will be organised around the following issues: (i) insufficient wage differentials; (ii) the insufficient sensitivity of wages to local labour market conditions (wage curve hypothesis); (iii) low interregional labour mobility; (iv) the minimum wage. The role of unemployment benefits has already been discussed in previous sections.

(i) Wage differentials. As noted in Section 2.2, low wage differentials and insufficient labour mobility may be factors able to generate persistent regional unemployment. Conversely, sufficiently large wage differentials may help absorb negative shocks. In fact, if wages adequately reflect local unemployment rates, depressed high-unemployment regions may be favoured if the unemployed move to low-unemployment but high-wage regions, and if capital moves to high-unemployment regions, being attracted to them by the low cost of labour. The consequence will be the equalisation of unemployment differentials. This type of adjustment mechanism seems to work in different ways in the USA and in the EU, producing different outcomes in terms of employment and inactivity rates. In the USA, as Blanchard and Katz (1992) find, the speed at which labour moves out of high-unemployment regions is much greater than that at which capital moves into them. The consequence is that employment and output levels will be permanently lower in depressed regions. In the EU, as Decressin and Fatàs (1995) find, regional unemployment rates also tend to converge, but at the cost of reducing activity rates in high unemployment areas, rather than employment, since workers are scarcely mobile.

Scarpetta (1995) was the first study to point out the role of insufficient wage differentials (and low labour mobility) as possible determinants of regional unemployment persistence. Various sources of wage rigidity were considered. Several Central and Eastern European transition countries were already implementing tight wage policies in the early 1990s in order to curb two- or even three-digit inflation. Wage policy is a potential source of wage rigidity if wages are fixed at national level without considering spatial differences in productivity growth. The fear that wages were becoming rigid caused, in its turn, the withdrawal of wage policies in most transition countries in the second half of the 1990s. Moreover, the wedge between the cost of labour and the net wage actually earned by workers was higher than in other EU countries also because of the burden that unemployment benefits represented for the state budget.[27]

Despite these potential sources of wage rigidity, according to Bornhorst and Commander (2004), wages in transition countries are not inflexible: quite the opposite. In fact, regions that have experienced larger adverse shocks have been characterised by lower relative rates of wage increase, but also by lower employment increases. Bornhorst and Commander's conclusion is that wages do depend on local labour market conditions, but the actual degree of wage flexibility is insufficient to absorb negative shocks. Fazekas (2000) reaches a similar conclusion when examining the Hungarian case.

Rutkowski and Przybila (2002) instead find a positive correlation between the job finding rate and the degree of wage flexibility across Polish regions. Wages are considered flexible when the productivity is higher relative to wages and the wage structure is less compressed. Landesmann (2002), however, notes that causality may operate the other way around, since booming regions may have higher productivity growth and wage dispersion is higher in more diversified economies. Sibley and Walsh (2002) find, in fact, that in Poland wage dispersion is higher in regions that experience a higher degree of restructuring, are more advanced, and are open to international trade.

(ii) Sensitivity of wages to local labour market conditions (the wage curve hypothesis). One way to measure the degree of flexibility and efficient functioning of the labour market is to estimate the sensitivity of wages to local labour market conditions. Blanchflower and Oswald (1994) suggested using the so-called wage

---

[27] For a more systematic assessment of labour market rigidity/flexibility in CEECs, see Riboud et al. (2002), Svejnar (2002b). The World Bank ranks 145 countries by various indices of labour market flexibility. The results are available at: http://rru.worldbank.org/DoingBusiness/. They show that CEECs are not greatly dissimilar from EU countries in this respect.

curve to ascertain whether wage differentials follow any unemployment pattern. The method consists of testing the coefficient of regional unemployment rates (in natural logarithm) for statistical significance in Mincerian-types of earnings equations. The expected sign is negative. The main idea behind the wage curve is that wages should react to increased unemployment at a local level, after controlling for human capital levels and other determinants of individual earnings.

There are various theories able to explain why this may be the case. Blanchflower and Oswald (1994) assume that in non-competitive labour markets, an increase in the unemployment rate implies a reduction in the power of workers to make upward wage claims. A non-union interpretation of the wage curve is given within the efficiency wage framework: with the local unemployment rate increasing, employers are able to reduce the wage that ensures the maximum productivity of workers. In any case, the greater the sensitivity of wages to local labour market conditions, the faster the adjustment process to adverse asymmetric shocks becomes. Blanchflower and Oswald (1994) find a coefficient of around –0.1, which is remarkably stable in the case of mature market economies. [28]

Blanchflower (2001, Table 7) provides a first survey of the evidence until 2001, which at that time was still scarce and inconclusive. He also estimates a wage curve for several CEE and CIS transition economies using different types of data sets and definitions of wages. The International Social Survey Programme data base relative to the period 1991–97 suggests a wide variation of coefficients: several countries (the Czech Republic, Hungary, the Slovak Republic) had a lower wage curve effect; the GDR had a similar coefficient; and other countries showed coefficients generally much higher than those found previously. The unemployment elasticity of pay ranged from –0.15 for Poland, to –0.24 for Bulgaria and –0.46 for Latvia, implying that doubling the local unemployment rate causes wage to reduce by 15 per cent in Poland, by 24 per cent in Bulgaria and by 46 per cent in Latvia. No wage curve effect is found for Slovenia, confirming the results of other studies on the high degree of labour market rigidity.

Blanchflower (2001, Table 7) presents similar estimates carried out on the World Bank HEIDE data base relative to the period 1993-95. These estimates yield a very different picture: all CEECs in the sample exhibit a high wage curve effect, including Hungary (–0.36) and Slovakia (–0.19). [29]

Svejnar (2002b, p. 14) reports that attempts to find evidence of a wage curve in several transition countries based on firm-level data have failed.

---

[28] See also Card (1995) for discussion of the possible theoretical interpretations of the wage curve.

[29] In the case of Russia, while the ISSP data suggest a very low unemployment elasticity of pay, other data sets seem to show a sizeable wage curve effect, higher in absolute value than –0.25 (Blanchflower 2001, Table 7). Using household survey data, Pastore and Verashchagina (2005) find a wage curve effect for Belarus, a slow transition country. The effect (of –0.23 in 1996 and of –0.36 in 2001) is similar in size to that of several transition countries with a high degree of wage flexibility, and much higher than in market economies.

To sum up, research efforts on the wage curve have produced mixed evidence: (a) contrary to what has previously been found for mature market economies, different data sources produce different results; (b) nonetheless, the available evidence suggests that "The unemployed serve to bid down the wages of those in work in both East and West and to an approximately similar degree. The basic structure of East Europe's wage curve is apparently like that of other nations" (Blanchflower, 2001, p. 15); (c) and, finally, wage flexibility seems to be much higher in some transition countries than in others.

(iii) Interregional labour mobility. Another mechanism through which geographical differences in unemployment rate can be absorbed is interregional labour mobility. Blanchard and Katz (1992) find that labour mobility, more than any other factor, including capital mobility, is decisive in achieving regional convergence in unemployment rates across the United States. They also find that labour mobility is driven more by the need to escape from unemployment in depressed areas than by the attraction of higher wages in booming regions.

Already in the early 1990s, Scarpetta (1995) noted that, despite being neither abundant nor fully reliable, the available information on labour mobility pointed to very low interregional flows. Bornhorst and Commander (2004, Table 7 and Fig. 4) show that, though reacting to economic incentives, internal migration flows remained persistently low in several transition countries throughout the 1990s. Gross migration rates of several transition countries were much lower than those in the USA and similar to those typical of low mobility EU countries, such as Spain and Italy. As a consequence, net migration flows were positive in low unemployment regions, as one would expect, but the correlation was weak, sometimes statistically insignificant. The net negative flow from high unemployment areas was considered insufficient to compensate for large unemployment differentials. Similar conclusions have been reached by Rutkowski and Przybila (2002) for Poland, and by Kertesi (2000) for Hungary.

The debate has also addressed the issue of the factors hindering internal migration. The research on the wage curve surveyed in the previous section suggests that wages do respond to local labour market conditions in transition countries. What, then, is the reason for low interregional mobility? A first possible answer is that wages are not flexible enough, or alternatively, that although wages are flexible, other factors affecting the cost of moving hinder labour mobility. In the early 1990s, the high cost of housing and a poorly functioning rentals market were considered decisive factors in low internal labour mobility. These factors were in their turn the consequence of various others, such as the dominance of owner-occupying housing, the lack of clarity over property rights and the absence of long-term housing finance. Nonetheless, no systematic analysis of these factors is available in the literature.

In addition, Boeri (2000) and Rutkowski and Przybila (2002, p. 159) ascribe low labour mobility also to differences in reservation wages by skill, and to a mismatch between the unskilled workers residing in high unemployment regions and the demand for skilled labour in low unemployment areas. They argue that long-term unemployment performs an important role in explaining regional unemployment distribution in Poland. In rural areas, the low-skilled unemployed tend to flow to non-participation, rather than to unemployment, as instead happens in urban areas. Moreover, they prefer to remain in high unemployment areas and be involved in home production, family-run businesses, often in the informal sector, rather than move or commute to urban areas.[30]

This argument would also explain Bornhorst and Commander's (2004, Table 2) finding that regions with high unemployment had high non participation rates in 2000 in all the transition countries considered, the only exception being Romania. They explain this finding in terms of a discouraged worker effect: workers in high unemployment regions tend not to participate to the labour market because they feel that they have a low probability of finding jobs. In their turn, low participation rates may be the way in which transition countries absorb negative shocks in the long run, as in the EU case depicted by Decressin and Fatàs (1995).

(iv) The minimum wage. The aim of research in this field has been to show that a nationwide arrangement like the minimum wage may produce different effects across regions with different levels of development. As well as increasing the overall degree of wage rigidity, thus hindering the adjustment process, the introduction of minimum wage arrangements may cause low job creation for the low-skill unemployed especially in high unemployment regions. In fact, the minimum wage represents an important share of the wage of low-skill workers and thus dramatically reduces their likelihood of finding jobs by truncating the earnings distribution.

Brainerd (2000) claims that, since the early 1990s, the labour markets in CEECs have been much more rigid than in the CIS, among other reasons because of the introduction of minimum wage arrangements in almost all CEECs.

In the case of Poland, Rutkowski and Przybila (2002, pp 166–169) note that the minimum wage is set around 40 per cent of the average (mean) wage. However, its "bite" (real effect) depends on the ratio to the average wage of low-skill workers in each region. The first step is to compare the minimum wage against the average wage by region. One thus finds that, while in Warsaw the minimum wage is 36 per cent of the average wage, in other regions it increases, up to 58 per cent in the voivodship of Cechanowskie. The second step is to contrast the minimum wage with the wages in different quantiles of the wage distribution. The result is that the bite is 48 per cent for a median worker, but 65 per cent for young workers, 72 per cent for workers in elementary occupations, and as much as 82 per cent for bottom-quintile workers. These figures suggest that the minimum wage truncates the wage distribution for less productive workers and is thus likely to exclude them from employment. The situation worsens when one looks at the bite of the minimum wage in the depressed regions, such as Slupskie, Wloclawskie and Ciechanowskie, where the minimum wage represents over 90 per cent of the median wage for bottom-quintile workers. The authors argue that these figures provide a strong indication that the seemingly low minimum wage may cost a non negligible number of jobs in the depressed regions of Poland. Moreover, they cor-

---

[30] Rutkowski and Przybila (2002, p. 159) note that special subsidies are paid to farmers in Poland.

roborate this indication with econometric analysis, regressing the regional unemployment rate on the bite of the minimum wage (the ratio of the minimum wage to the region's bottom decile wage) and a set of other variables representing the region's level of development (per capita GDP, investment, level of human capital, employment structure, and infrastructure). They find a positive significant coefficient, at the 10 per cent significance level when all the variables are included, and at the 1 per cent level when per capita GDP, investment and the proxy for the level of infrastructure are dropped. According to Rutkowski and Przybila (2002), these results suggest that a 10 per cent nationwide increase in the minimum wage would result in a 3.1 per cent increase in the unemployment rate of depressed regions, other things held constant. Nonetheless, they warn that this pattern, found using cross-section analysis, may not hold in a dynamic framework. Besides the problem of causality, this type of estimate may suffer from omitted variable bias and multicollinearity.

Summary remarks on supply side factors. Overall, the literature surveyed in this section suggests that wage flexibility is not a major factor of regional unemployment in most CEECs, with the exception, perhaps, of Slovenia. This conclusion is confirmed by concurring evidence on the reaction of wages to changes in employment and on wage elasticity to local unemployment rates. Which does not mean that wage flexibility is high, rather that it is not lower than in EU countries.

More important is the low degree of labour mobility. But this in turn seems to depend on the rigidity of other markets, such as the housing market, and the weakness of the transportation infrastructure. In his assessment of the labour market flexibility in CEECs, Svejnar (2002b) points to the rigidity of capital markets, of corporate governance regulations and of the business environment as factors no less important than labour market rigidity in fostering job creation and labour mobility.

Finally, there is circumstantial evidence that a minimum wage fixed at national level may affect the job opportunities of low-skill workers in high unemployment regions or at least push them towards informal work. However, the available research on this topic is still tentative and needs to be confirmed by more detailed analysis.

2.5 The role of economic integration and convergence

As noted in the introduction, regional differences in unemployment rates in transition countries depend on various demand side factors. Restructuring destroys old jobs and generates new ones. The consequent job reallocation may be higher in some areas than others, which amounts to say that some areas may have been more successful than others in implementing the transition process. Two types of low unemployment regions have been detected. Some backward peripheral regions have attained low labour reallocation and, therefore, low unemployment by postponing the transformation. Other more developed and central regions have managed to attain low labour turnover and greater job stability, because they have been able to attract sizeable flows of foreign direct investment and exploit the advantages of specialisation following the opening up of the economy. In the least successful regions, the cost of restructuring may have been particularly high, since fast restructuring was coupled with a backward economic structure and a substantial inability to exploit the advantages of economic integration.

This section aims to discuss in more detail the role of economic integration with the EU and, more generally, with the world economy in shaping the regional pattern of unemployment. This issue was already touched on in a previous section, but this section provides a more systematic treatment. It first discusses different theories of the labour market impact of international trade and then provides evidence on the nature of trade flows among Central and Eastern European transition countries especially with EU countries, which remain the main trading partners. This enables us to add another important group of studies to the general explanation of regional unemployment persistence in transition countries.

2.5.1 The theoretical predictions on regional convergence in CEE

Each step of economic integration among nations raises concerns about its impact on the location of production activities within the area concerned. The question is whether industrial agglomeration processes in an integrated area will be stronger than dispersion and diversification forces among participating nations. The degree of convergence of regions towards a common level of development and unemployment will crucially depend on the relative magnitude of those forces (for surveys of the debate on regional convergence and the EU enlargement process, see Funck and Pizzati 2003; Ferragina and Pastore 2004).

We shall discuss two opposing scenarios of the future economic geography of the recently enlarged European Union, paying especial attention to the economies of the new EU member states. According to the first scenario, there will be a predominance of horizontal intra-industry trade among Eastern and Western European nations, resulting in weak specialisation in terms of production and employment. By 'horizontal intra-industry trade' (HIIT) we mean two-way trade in goods and commodities classified within the same industrial sector and of the same quality level. According to the traditional models of horizontal IIT (Krugman 1980; Helpman 1981; Helpman and Krugman 1985), this kind of competition typically arises among advanced countries with similar specialisation and factor intensities and generates the reciprocal rationalisation of productions, scale economies, more variety, and lower costs. If this IIT scenario of integration comes about, as argued in Frankel and Rose (1998), support will be provided for an optimistic view of overall economic convergence among EU member states and regions: asymmetric shocks and increasing spatial disparities resulting from the strong relocation of activities will be smaller than sometimes feared.

It is important to bear in mind that the labour adjustment costs generally associated with horizontal intra-industry specialisation are much less disruptive than those arising from inter-industry trade, from vertical intra-industry trade, and from outward processing trade. By 'inter-industry trade' is meant a kind of trade in goods and commodities classified in different industrial sectors and based on factor endowment differentials, whereas still meant by 'vertical intra-industry trade' is a two-way trade in goods and commodities classified within the same industrial sector but of different quality level. Outward processing trade involves the exchange of raw materials and intermediate products against final products within the same broad industrial classification, and it is linked to the relocation of the production phases of firms from more advanced economies in less advanced ones.

The most common argument is that, since in the former case – horizontal intra-industry trade – factor input ratios in export and import sectors exhibit greater similarity than they do in the latter – inter-industry trade, vertical intra-industry trade and outward processing trade – the factor price differential should be narrower in the first case and, as a result, the adjustment to trade opening should be less dramatic in terms of factor prices and also in terms of employment. The reason for this would be that if factor intensities between sectors are similar, we should expect labour to transfer from one sector to another with relative ease. In fact, the skills acquired by working in the import substitute sector can be redeployed in the export sector with minimal retraining costs. To adopt the conclusion reached by Krugman (1981), each country gains from trade, paying much lower employment and redistribution costs than those associated with inter-industry trade, provided that the countries have similar capital-labour ratios and skill levels, and that trade takes place in productions with strong economies to scale and high product differentiation.

A less optimistic scenario of integration envisages increased specialisation based on comparative advantages and increasing trade of inter-industry type or of vertical intra-industry type. This latter type of trade has been explained by the so-called neo-Heckscher-Olin (H-O) literature (Falvey 1981; Falvey and Kierzkowski 1987), which shows how intra-industry trade may result from a quality competition and is not necessarily associated with identical endowments and technologies. The adjustment effects of this trade in terms of wage and employment are as dramatic as they are in the traditional H-O type of inter-industry trade.

The two scenarios sketched above explain why most of the research on economic integration of CEECs within EU markets has focused on whether they are more likely to follow an intra-industry specialisation path or one of deeper specialisation according to comparative advantages. In the former case, with increasing horizontal intra-industry trade, the CEECs would experience more industrial diversification; while in the latter case, with increasing inter-industry trade or vertical intra-industry trade, the risk of asymmetric shocks and of falling into development traps would be greater, because these countries develop trade relations with the EU based on their specialisation in traditional and unskilled labour intensive industries. Instead of creating conditions that would enable them to compete in global markets, some countries may attempt to exploit their own static comparative advantages, which would lock them in traditional sectors and reduce the opportunity to upgrade for a long period of time.

There are also important implications in terms of the spatial distribution of economic activities to consider. Under the hypotheses of the so-called New Economic Geography (NEG) literature, economic integration gives rise to a spatial core/periphery schema resulting in higher agglomeration which is especially detrimental to peripheral countries and regions. Dispersion and agglomeration forces depend on the interaction between imperfect competition, economies of scale and agglomeration externalities. Regional integration reduces transaction costs and encourages firms to concentrate so that they can benefit from economies of scale. Increasing return-intensive sectors will tend to concentrate in regions with good market access and better backward and forward linkages, while traditional activities with constant returns to scale will concentrate in peripheral regions. Moreover, the market size increases as manufacturing agglomerates and as cumulative causation occurs (underdevelopment traps). These models argue that closer integration would give rise to increased polarisation and specialisation. However, this relation is non-monotonic. Industrial agglomeration generates a regional wage differential. The immobility of the workforce cannot equal the regional remuneration, and wage competition becomes a centrifugal force. At low trade costs, firms become more sensitive to costs differentials, which induces the modern sector to spread into peripheral regions (Krugman and Venables 1995; Venables 1996; Puga 1999).

Such models have considerable implications for the integrated Europe. Further integration may increase the probability that industry spreads as a result of wage differentials among nations: Eastern European regions would attract low-skilled intensive activities, while the high-skilled intensive activities would remain in the core.

The different scenarios of integration outlined above have already been tested and contrasted in light of the integration of the old EU members during the past two decades. This research (see e.g. Fontagné et al. 1998) has found that intra-European trade is mainly of intra-industry type. However, traded goods are predominantly vertically differentiated. Therefore, EU countries already face structural and technological asymmetries which, according to the H-O and neo-H-O models, lead to higher specialisation and dramatic labour market adjustments, and according to the NEG models, to more aggregated production structures. However, polarisation is found to occur not so much across nations where production structures are roughly homogeneous as across regions, which are diverging within all European nations (Boldrin and Canova 2001, 2003). This is rather obvious if we consider that labour is much more mobile across regions.

We expect different sets of behaviour to be displayed by the various groups of countries and regions that can be formed among the CEECs according to their production structures, factor endowments, trade openness, and FDI flows. Only Central European countries tend to develop intra-industry trade, while the more peripheral countries in Eastern Europe still exhibit high levels of specialisation in traditional sectors. As a result, reasoning based on the economic geography approach suggests a persistent core/periphery structure.

2.5.2 Contrasting theories and evidence

This section reviews the main stylised facts on specialisation and FDI dynamics put forward in the applied literature on economic integration of CEECs into the EU.

EU-CEE trade potential. Gravity models have been widely used over the past decade or so to evaluate EU-CEE trade potential, and to compare it with the actual level of trade. More specifically, gravity equations have been estimated relative to the already integrated EU-15 to obtain the coefficients of the main determinants of bilateral trade, namely national income and population size of the two countries involved, distance, common land border and common language. These coefficients have been used in similar equations, but with variables relative to EU-CEECs, in order to assess trade potential. The aim of these exercises has been to determine whether the integration process was already completed before accession, or whether one can expect further trade integration, which may continue to affect the labour markets in the two areas concerned.

The results of such exercises available in the literature are mixed, and they depend closely on the period considered, specification and estimator, as well as on the computation method used to calculate trade potential. Wang and Winters (1992) find that East-East trade was large in 1985, while East-West trade was only a fraction of what it would have been in an integrated Europe. Hamilton and Winters (1992) adopt a similar approach, finding that trade within the former Soviet Union and the Eastern Europe bloc (SUEE) was static or falling, while trade with Western Europe may increase by up to five times. Baldwin (1994) finds that potential EU12-CEE exports and imports are twice the actual 1989 exports and imports.

All the studies which have used data on the early transition period in order to estimate trade potential support a different conclusion. Most of them suggest that a level of integration between Eastern and Western countries which is high and above the potential level has long since been reached. This indicates that adjustment is complete and that there is no need for special protection in Western countries (Gros and Gonciarz 1996; Brenton and Di Mauro 1999; Nilsson 2000). For instance, Gros and Gonciarz (1996) correct Baldwin's estimates on the grounds that he used a GDP which was overvalued because it was calculated on pre-transition data (the per capita GDP used by Baldwin was much higher than the 1992 GDP for CEECs). Combining the parameters from Baldwin (1994) with the 1992 data on GDP, Gros and Gonciarz end up with a downward revision of Baldwin's projections of CEEC-EU trade, and their results suggest that the adjustment is complete.

Two recent studies on trade integration measured by gravity models (Egger 2000, 2002) have cast doubt on the results of the above-cited literature. They make three main criticisms: 1) most of these results are based on cross-section gravity models which are mis-specified because they do not take account of exporter and importer effects, while only few authors make use of panel econometrics; 2) those authors who do use panel analysis to compute potential trade adopt a random effect model (the exception is Egger) which may be affected by the problem of correlation between the explanatory variables and the unobserved time invariant effects; 3) most analyses obtain information on trade potentials using the 'in-sample' prediction approach; that is, the residuals of the estimated equation are interpreted as the difference between potential and actual bilateral trade relations, but this is in contrast with the fact that, in the case of proper specification, the estimators are consistent and efficient and therefore should exhibit white-noise residuals, rather than identifying large systematic differences between observed and in-sample predicted values among country groups.

This criticism undermines most previous analyses and policy conclusions which have used coefficients obtained from cross-section estimates to determine the under-trading or over-trading of countries or areas. As shown above, apart from Baldwin (1994), early empirical studies used cross-section data to estimate gravity models. Ferragina and Giovannetti (2004), Ferragina et al. (2004) calculate trade potential based on panel data analysis and the out-of-sample method. They obtain different panel estimates of intra-EU15 trade relative to the period 1995–2002 and provide out-of-sample estimates of potential to actual trade of five EU countries. Interestingly, they find evidence for the existence of an important potential for trade which has not yet been exploited. This was 1.7 to 2.5 times higher in the case of CEECs, depending on the countries considered.[31] The differences between these results and those of previous studies depend on the period and method used. The authors employ out-of-sample predictions and concentrate on a period when GDP was much higher, in most CEECs.

Inter-industry trade. Inter-industry trade is a sizeable component of total EU-CEE trade, ranging between 50 (Czech Republic) and 95 per cent (Baltic Republics) circa in 1996, and amounting on average to 55 per cent in 2000 (Caétano et al. 2002).

Moreover, studies based on the analysis of revealed comparative advantages have shown that CEE specialisation mainly concerns productions based on labour and natural resources and, though less markedly, physical capital intensive sectors; whereas exports of goods embodying high R&D content lag behind.

There are wide differences among trade specialisations in the new EU, with obviously different patterns displayed by core and peripheral countries. Geographic distance from the European core seems to matter, in that the most peripheral countries are also the most specialised ones.

If we apply the Krugman index of relative specialisation to the candidate countries and to EU members (using sectoral export data for 72 products), we observe that the core and the largest countries are the least specialized; while the peripheral countries are more specialised than the EU average. Huge disparities exist among the candidate countries. The Czech Republic, Hungary, Slovenia and Poland are more diversified than such peripheral countries as Portugal and Greece, while the Balkan and Baltic countries exhibit the highest values for the specialisation index (Dupuch et al. 2004).

New EU members are generally specialised in resource-intensive industries (metals, wood, and wood products) and labour-intensive industries (textiles and clothing), while they continue to suffer comparative disadvantages in capital-intensive industries such as machinery, equipment goods, and chemical products (Freudenberg Lemoine, 1999). However, there are wide divergences among these

---

[31] Ferragina et al. (2004) tested the robustness of these results by computing indices of trade potential based on different panel estimation methods. The results were remarkably stable across different specifications.

countries, and some of them are undergoing great changes in their trade specialisation. The most advanced CEECs are achieving some new advantages in technology and capital-intensive sectors while maintaining their comparative advantages in low-tech sectors. For instance, Hungary has achieved new specialisation in the electronic and computer industries, and Estonia in telecommunications, although they still have comparative advantages in the food and wood products industries respectively. By contrast, other Baltic states, Bulgaria and Romania, and Poland to a lesser extent, still exhibit a high share of traditional activities (food, products, metals, textiles) in their export structure (Caétano et al. 2002; Ferragina 2004).

Although wage growth rates are higher in the candidate countries than in the EU, productivity gains enable them to maintain a strong competitive advantage in terms of unit labour costs. According to this index, all the CEECs are advantaged relative to the EU countries, especially in sectors sensitive to price competitiveness. Only Slovenia has an index close to Greece, while Bulgaria, Romania and Slovakia, where labour costs are only 10 per cent of the EU average, still rank bottom (Eurostat 2002a).

However, if we consider similarity in export structures between the CEECs and the EU members by using a Finger-Kreinin similarity index, we find that the Central CEECs – Hungary, Czech Republic and also, to a lesser extent, Poland and Slovenia – have very similar export structures relative to the EU, and especially relative to Spain and Portugal. They should therefore not be subject to the risks associated with strong specialisation in traditional sectors. By contrast, this optimistic view cannot be held concerning the more peripheral countries, which appear to be only similar to Greece, particularly in the case of Bulgaria. It is worth noting that the CEECs are especially distant from Ireland, which has experienced strong technological catch-up – with the marked exception of Hungary, which suggests a catch-up by high technology industries in that country (Dupuch et al. 2004).

Intra-industry trade. Analysis of trade patterns between the EU and the candidate countries shows that inter-industry trade prevails. However, since the beginning of transition, IIT has undergone rapid growth, and some countries, such as Hungary (35 per cent), Slovenia (35 per cent) and the Czech Republic (48 per cent), achieve the highest shares of IIT among all the internal and external EU partners (Aturupane et al. 1999; Caétano et al. 2002).

Three different groups can be identified in 2000: first, the Central European countries (Hungary, Slovenia and the Czech Republic) exhibit a high share of intra-industry trade which outweighs that of Portugal and Greece; Poland and Slovakia stand at an intermediate level (30 per cent and 38 per cent); while inter-industry trade still greatly predominates in both the Balkans and the Baltic countries (from 85 per cent to 95 per cent).

As anticipated, existing IIT is not necessarily an indicator of similarity of trade between East and West Europe: as noted by Freudeberg and Lemoine (1999), the bulk of total IIT, between 80 and 90 per cent, is of vertical kind involving the exchange of goods belonging to the same industry but of different quality. This again demonstrates a certain specialisation by CEECs in low-value added segments. Vertical IIT has undergone significant decline in favour of horizontal IIT in the past decade only in those countries which initially exhibited higher levels of intra-industry trade. The shift signifies increasing disparities among the new EU members, and that catching-up is still slow for the entire region.

The role of human capital. As regards skill levels, there is mixed evidence for the candidate countries relative to the EU. Human capital measures are complex and unsatisfactory, because they only take account of educational attainment and exclude generic and job-specific work experience, as well as the skills acquired while at work. Barro and Lee's (2001) human capital measures referred to 1996 are mainly indicators of educational attainment. The CEECs are rather homogeneous with the OECD average from this point of view. Except for Slovenia, they often benefit from educational levels higher than in other developed countries.

However, according to Landesmann (2003), when the educational levels of the active population alone are considered, around 30 per cent of workers have not reached a secondary school level, and the share increases to more than 40 per cent in the case of Bulgaria and Romania. Moreover, the EU members have a share of high-skilled workers (share of active population with a tertiary education level) amounting to around 20 per cent, whereas it is no more than 14 per cent in the CEECs.

Finally to be considered are R&D expenditures as a measure of economic catching up. The index is appreciably lower in the CEECs than in the EU, and only in Slovenia and the Czech Republic does it converge to EU standards, which themselves are not the highest in the world. In 2000, if we exclude Slovenia (1.52), which was very close to the EU-15 figure (1.93) and the Czech Republic (1.33), R&D expenditure as a percentage of GDP for the remaining CEECs ranged between 0.37 (Romania) and 0.7 (Poland) (Eurostat, 2002b). The index has remained stable, and even decreased in some cases, because of transition. There is also evidence of the 'crowding out' of existing human capital by the process of economic transition, which helps explain the CEE specialisation in low-quality exports to EU markets found by recent empirical investigations (Greenaway and Torstensson 2000; Ferragina and Pastore 2005).

The role of FDIs. Some transition countries were already industrialised at the beginning of integration and they were well endowed with physical capital, infrastructure, although their productive systems were in need of modernisation. Some firms anticipated formal integration by setting up production units or joint venture agreements with firms in EU countries in order to benefit from first-mover advantages in regard to expansion of foreign capital on local goods and labour markets.

Two distinct strategies regarding FDIs can be associated with these two specialisation patterns. Vertical multinational strategies predominate in the context of deeper inter-industry specialisation. Multinational firms locate the more labour-intensive stages of the production process, such as assembly, in countries with cheaper labour. Given that these FDIs are motivated by differences in factor endowment, the international division of labour that they support reinforces inter-industry specialisation patterns.

In contrast, FDI is horizontal when multinational firms are attracted mainly by expansion on local markets. This type of FDI is more likely to occur between countries whose preferences are similar (Markusen 1995). It depends on market access considerations and is more likely to come about in technology intensive industries, both increasing the number and improving the quality of products, and therefore reinforcing intra-industry trade patterns in goods of similar quality (Fontagné et al. 1998).

Within candidate countries, FDI is not evenly distributed by country, by industrial sector, or by region. In 2002, three countries (the Czech Republic, Poland and Hungary) accounted for more than three-quarters of total FDI in the region (UNCTAD 2003), while the Baltic Republics and Bulgaria accounted for less than 10 per cent.

In 1995, FDI appeared to be mainly directed to tertiary activities in the most advanced CEECs (the Czech Republic, Hungary and Slovenia), but more to manufacturing sectors and traditional activities in Poland and Romania. In the former case, FDI performs a potentially positive role in changing the specialisation patterns of those economies; in the latter, the concentration of FDI in comparative advantage industries is likely to have reinforced specialisation in traditional industries (UNCTAD 1997).

Eurostat (2002b) data on stocks of FDI in 1999 confirms this picture. There are marked disparities among countries, and the existence of three distinct patterns is confirmed. The first pattern is typical of Bulgaria, which is a special case in that manufacturing industries predominate over tertiary activities as FDI recipients, with traditional sectors such as food and metals being the main beneficiaries. Poland, Slovenia, Slovakia, and the Czech Republic belong to the second group of countries, where FDI is more balanced across sectors: here services account for the large majority of the total stock of FDI, and slightly more than half of it (53 per cent) concentrates in trade and financial activities. However, some countries still exhibit a large proportion of FDI in traditional sectors (food in Poland, metals in Slovakia) while the chemicals industry is the most attractive sector in Slovenia, and machinery and equipment goods receive the largest share in Slovakia. Finally, tertiary activities are dominant (two-thirds of the total stock of FDI) in the Baltic Republics (trade and distribution, financial activities, transport and telecommunications).

In Poland, 90 per cent of FDI was concentrated in Warsaw and a few other large central cities. Fazekas (2002) provide evidence that also in Hungary most FDI was concentrated in Budapest and other urban regions. Nonetheless, a share of FDI in low-technology industries located also in some rural areas. Traistaru and Pauna (2003) report that over 50 per cent of the FDI located in Bucharest.

To sum up, foreign investments in medium-high technology industries with high growth potential are already substantial. Since FDI favour the emergence of competitive firms, they also influence patterns of comparative advantage and therefore perform a key role in transforming the productive systems of some CEECs. However, this process is coming about unevenly across countries, and across regions within each country.

The evidence on trade and FDI trends suggests that the sectoral divergence resulting from agglomeration economies is likely to persist through a high-skilled core, attracting increasingly technology-intensive activities and a low skilled periphery. The outcome seemingly reflects the core/periphery model. However, two different scenarios emerge in terms of international specialisation, production allocation and employment outcomes. The Central European countries are likely to follow a 'Spanish model' based on catching up, industrial diversification and intra-industry trade, while the Eastern countries may lag further behind, increasing their comparative advantages in low-tech and labour-intensive sectors.

The role of FDI in this context is crucial. In some CEECs it has already caused an important shift towards intra-industry specialisation. In fact, foreign firms are bringing with them technology, know–how and management structures that affect the transition process by favouring a more competitive and market-based economy.

The picture of a diversified Europe in which some nations keep the bulk of activities should be maintained. The core/periphery pattern is likely to persist with a larger core consisting of Slovenia, a few urban and border Hungarian and Polish regions, the Czech Republic and Slovakia, and a EU periphery enlarged to include the Eastern countries.

2.5.3 Estimating the impact of economic integration on regional unemployment

How the forces of economic integration affected labour markets, in general, and the regional distribution of unemployment in transition countries, in particular, is difficult to say. The literature on the impact of international trade on unemployment is still scarce and the OST literature is no exception under this respect. On the one hand, several studies point to economic integration, also in terms of ability to attract investment from abroad to explain the relative success of urban regions and of regions on the Western border. On the other hand, with few exceptions, research on this issue provides only circumstantial evidence.

One reason of the little attention of applied research is the methodological difficulty of the object under analysis, which would require a general equilibrium framework to catch the impact across different sectors. Moreover, as noted, among others, by Landesmann (2002), analysis of the labour market impact of FDIs requires careful consideration of the indirect effects on growth and economic performance. Focusing only on the direct impact in specific sectors would miss the point. In addition, the implementation of the methodologies necessary for the analysis is hard especially in the case of transition countries for the lack of suitable data at a regional level.

Until now, the research in this field has focused on different issues: (a) explaining the actual pattern of location of FDIs; (b) explaining the impact on local labour market of FDIs; and of (c) international trade.

Fazekas (2000) finds that in the case of Hungary a sizeable flow of FDI has concentrated in the most urbanised regions where there is a strong concentration of a skilled work force. Moreover, capital inflow is negatively correlated with distance. An interesting finding is that rural regions on the Eastern border with Ukraine and the Slovak Republic attracted comparatively high levels of FDIs, other things held constant. This is attributed by Fazekas to the nature of the capital flow in different areas. Urban areas attract FDIs in skill-intensive industries, whereas rural areas attract capital flows in low-skill productions. These results confirm some of the conclusions of Lehmann and Walsh (1999) and Walsh (2003) mentioned in a previous section regarding the role of human capital.

However, Fazekas (2000) also finds that despite the magnitude of the inflow of capital, its direct impact on local unemployment in Hungary seems to be weak. This may be explained by the relatively high share of takeovers as opposed to "green-field" investment during transition, the relatively low labour intensity of foreign investments (compared to domestic enterprises), as well as the practice of hiring from the ranks of employed workers rather than from the pool of unemployed persons.

Newell et al. (2002) furnish circumstantial evidence on how Poland's international comparative advantages in labour-intensive manufacturing combine with the economic advantages of urbanised regions to play a significant role in shaping the regional distribution of the country's unemployment. They estimate hazard functions of the probability of moving from employment to unemployment using individual level LFS data relative to the years 1994–97 and find that the manufacturing sector, especially highly labour-intensive industries, provide their employees with particularly secure jobs in low unemployment regions, but not in high unemployment ones. They detect the factor intensity of industrial sectors applying the Neven (1995) taxonomy. They interpret this as reflecting a combination of comparative advantages in terms of factor intensities and agglomeration effects. A variable measuring the magnitude of capital flows at a vovodship level in the same econometric setting turns out insignificant, perhaps because of the high concentration in Warsaw.

A recent strand of literature, is addressing the question why urbanised regions have been able to exploit the advantages of trade integration and of capital flow from abroad. The answer is that human capital concentration in urbanised regions is an important factor to attract FDI in advanced sectors and reduce the cost of restructuring. As already noted, this hypothesis is at the core of Lehmann and Walsh (1999) model. World Bank (2004, pp 29–31) note a strong negative correlation between regional unemployment and the share of workers with a high level of education in Poland. In fact, individuals with a high level of human capital have shorter unemployment spells. Chapter 8 in this book develops the analysis of Newell et al. (2002), focusing on the role of human capital in generating economic development in urbanised regions. Complementarity between high technology industries and human capital generate persistence in unemployment differentials with respect to rural, depressed areas.

2.6 Concluding remarks

This chapter has surveyed the explanations set out in the OST literature for the dramatic and persistent regional unemployment experienced by all transition countries after the beginning of the reform process. Two theoretical models have been considered: the Aghion and Blanchard (1994) model and the Boeri (2000) model. The former stresses the role of demand side factors, essentially the process of structural change experienced in all countries of Central and Eastern Europe, whereas the latter points to supply side factors, such as wage rigidity and labour immobility. Whilst the former seems better suited to explaining the onset of regional unemployment in the early 1990s and its persistence during the rest of the decade, the latter addresses the more recent argument that removal of various forms of labour market rigidities is an important condition for the adjustment process to reach completion.

The ABM suggests that industrial restructuring and workers' reallocation explains the rise in unemployment. Two hypotheses have been found in the literature. Hypothesis One assumes that the cause of regional unemployment in transition countries is the low job finding rates of high unemployment regions and, therefore, the concentration in them of a large share of long-term unemployed. Hypothesis Two assumes that unemployment is higher in regions where the rate of separation of workers from their jobs is greater. The empirical literature provides circumstantial evidence in favour of hypothesis Two. For the ABM, this correlation signals different speeds of reform across regions.

Relating to this test is what can be considered an empirical law: when local unemployment is associated with a high degree of labour turnover, the reason for it is the extent of structural change caused by industrial restructuring. The opposite case is when there is no positive relationship among industrial restructuring, labour turnover and unemployment. In this case a low job finding rate and, consequently, a high share of long-term unemployment shapes the geographical distribution of unemployment.

The available evidence suggests that regional differences in the separation rate arose because of various factors: the concentration under the previous regime of certain economic activities in certain regions, and the ability of the most urbanised areas to exploit the advantages of trade integration and to attract direct investment from abroad. Among the advantages of the low unemployment regions, ease of market access, the size of local goods markets, and the labour force's level of educational attainment were important.

However, the ABM model does not provide a framework in which to consider supply side constraints on the adjustment process. But the BM stresses the role of such factors. Regional unemployment patterns may also depend on the different effect exerted by national-level labour market institutions on local labour markets. High non-employment benefits at the outset of transition pushed many low-skill workers towards unemployment or inactivity by increasing their reservation wage. In its turn, this had an asymmetric effect across regions, inducing low skill workers to remain in rural areas and be involved in home production or family-run businesses, often in the informal sector, rather than move or commute to urban areas.

The policy suggestions of those observers who stress the role of demand side factors are only slightly different from those indicated by other authors who have stressed the role of labour supply factors. The recommendations to introduce effective educational and training policies in order to help the population cope with increased labour turnover and find re-employment as rapidly as possible are important for both. In addition, those observers who stress the role of industrial restructuring also suggest that the restructuring process in high unemployment regions should be slowed down so that they can absorb the existing pool of unemployed (Lehmann and Walsh 1999). Investment in the infrastructural endowment of peripheral regions may help attract new investment from large domestic or foreign firms.

The OST literature on regional unemployment has grown rapidly, reaching high levels of elaboration and generally providing a convincing explanation for the phenomenon under scrutiny. Moreover, it has made interesting contributions to the development of the general analysis of regional unemployment differentials. The most innovative contributions seem to be those which underline the relationship among industrial restructuring, labour turnover and spatial unemployment differentials. This relationship has been previously studied in the case of mature market economies. However, the availability of longitudinal data has enabled the study of transitions among different labour market statuses across regions, and this is a new development.

The main shortcoming of the literature considered seems to be its lack of a clear and unified theoretical framework. The BM can be taken to represent this type of model, although it is not designed to explain regional unemployment persistence directly. However, this conclusion amounts to saying that the literature on transition countries shares a problem typical of the general literature as well. Regional unemployment differentials remain a "mystery", to quote the title of Elhorst's (2003) survey.

Many questions posed in the literature remain on the agenda. For theoreticians, the challenge is to provide a general theoretical framework in which to analyse the different factors responsible for regional unemployment persistence.

For applied economists, there are numerous topics still to be analysed. First, some studies should be updated so that they cover the more recent years. With the focus of the debate now shifting to more traditional supply side factors and to the adjustment process, demand side factors seem to receive increasingly less attention. However, with few exceptions, such as Slovenia, transformation seems far from complete, especially in the peripheral areas. Moreover, EU accession is likely to generate further tensions on local labour markets. Second, there are many areas in which analysis still seems to be incomplete, unsystematic and circumstantial. The availability of new data, especially of longer time series covering longer periods will probably help remedy this shortcoming.

References

Abraham KG, Katz LF (1986) Cyclical unemployment: sectoral shifts or aggregate disturbances?. Journal of Political Economy 94: 507–522.
Adamchik V, King AE (1999) The impact of the private sector on labour market flows in Poland. Lehigh University, mimeo.
Aghion P, Blanchard OJ (1994) On the speed of transition in central Europe. In: Fischer S, Rotemberg JJ (eds) NBER Macroeconomics Annual. MIT Press, Cambridge (Mass.), pp 283–320.
Alogoskoufis G, Bean C, Bertola G, Cohen D, Dolado J, Saint–Paul G (1994) Unemployment: choices for Europe. CEPR, London.

Åslund A (2001) The myth of output collapse after communism. Carnegie Endowment for International Peace Working Paper 18.

Aturupane C, Djankov S, Hoekman B (1999) Horizontal and vertical intra–industry trade between Eastern Europe and the European Union. Weltwirtschaftliches Archiv 135:62–81.

Balcerowicz L (1994a) Common fallacies in the debate on the economic transition in Central and Eastern Europe. Economic Policy 19 Supplement:17–50

Balcerowicz L (1994b) Transition to a market economy: Poland, 1989–1993 in comparative perspective. Economic Policy 19 Supplement:71–97.

Baldwin RE (1994) Towards an integrated Europe. CEPR, London.

Barbone L, Marchetti DJ, Paternostro S (1999) The early stages of reform in Polish manufacturing. Structural adjustment, ownership and size. Economics of Transition 7:157–177.

Barro R, Lee JW (2001) International data on educational attainment: updates and implications. Oxford Economic Papers 53:541–563.

Bellman L, Estrin S, Lehmann H, Wadsworth J (1995) East German labour market in transition: gross flow estimates from panel data. Journal of Comparative Economics 20:139–170.

Berg A (1994) Does macroeconomic reform cause structural adjustment? Lessons from Poland. Journal of Comparative Economics 18:376–409.

Blanchard OJ (1997) The economics of post–communist transition. Clarendon Press, Oxford.

Blanchard OJ, Katz LF (1992) Regional evolutions. Brookings Papers on Economic Activity 1:1–75.

Blanchard OJ, Kremer M (1997) Disorganisation. Quarterly Journal of Economics 112:1091–1126.

Blanchard OJ, Commander S, Coricelli F (1994) Unemployment and the labour market in Eastern Europe. In: Boeri T (ed) Unemployment in Transition Countries: Transient or Persistent?. OECD, Paris, pp 59–79.

Blanchflower, DG, Oswald AJ (1994) The wage curve. Cambridge (Mass.), MIT Press.

Blanchflower DG (2001) Unemploymemt, well–being and wage curves in Eastern and Central Europe. Journal of the Japanese and International Economies 15:364–402.

Boeri T (1994) 'Transitional' unemployment. Economics of Transition 2:1–25.

Boeri T (1997) Labour market reforms in transition economies. Oxford Review of Economic Policy 13:126–140.

Boeri T (1998) Labour market flows in the midst of structural change. In: Commander S (ed.) Enterprise restructuring and unemployment in models of transition. World Bank, Washington (D.C.), pp 143–167.

Boeri T (2000) Structural change, welfare systems, and labour reallocation. Lessons from the transition of formerly planned economies. Oxford University Press, Oxford.

Boeri T, Scarpetta S (1995) Dealing with a stagnant pool: policies for coping with long–term unemployment in Central and Eastern Europe. In: Dobrinsky R, Landesmann M (eds) Transforming economies and European integration. Edward Elgar, Aldershot, pp 231–262.

Boeri T, Scarpetta S (1996) Regional mismatch and the transition to a market economy. Labour Economics 3:233–254.

Boeri T, Terrell K (2002) Institutional determinants of labour reallocation in transition. Journal of Economic Perspectives 16:51–76.

Boldrin M., Canova F (2001) Inequality and convergence in Europe's regions. Reconsidering European regional policy. Economic Policy 32: 207–253.

Boldrin M, Canova F (2003) Regional policies and EU enlargement. In: Funck B and Pizzati L (eds) European integration, regional policy, and growth. World Bank, Washington (D.C.), pp 33–94.

Bornhorst F, Commander S (2004) Regional unemployment and its persistence in transition countries. IZA Discussion Paper 1074.

Brainerd E (2000) Women in transition: change in gender wage differentials in Eastern Europe and FSU. Industrial and Labour Relations Review 54:139–162.

Brenton P, Di Mauro F (1999) The potential magnitude and impact of FDI flows to CEECs. Journal of Economic Integration 14:59–74.

Caétano J, Galero A, Vaz E, Vieira C, Vieira I (2002) The eastward enlargement of the Eurozone trade and FDI. Ezoneplus Working Paper 7.

Card D (1995) The wage curve: a review. Journal of Economic Literature 33:785–799.

Cazes S, Nesporova A (2001) Labour market flexibility in the transition countries. How much is too much?. International Labour Review 140:293–325.

Cazes S, Scarpetta S (1998) Labour market transitions and unemployment duration: evidence from Bulgarian and Polish micro–data. Economics of Transition 6:113–144.

CEPR (1990) Monitoring European integration. The impact of Eastern Europe. CEPR, London.

Commander S (ed.) (1998) Enterprise restructuring and unemployment in models of transition. World Bank, Washington (D.C.).

Commander S, Tolstopiatenko A (1998) Role of unemployment and restructuring in the transition. In: Commander S (ed.) Enterprise restructuring and unemployment in models of transition. World Bank, Washington (D.C.), pp 169–192.

Decressin J, Fatàs A (1995) Regional labor market dynamics in Europe. European Economic Review 39:1627–1655.

Dewatripont M, Roland G (1992) The virtues of gradualism and legitimacy in the transition to a market economy. Economic Journal 102:291–300.

Dupuch S, Jennequin H, Mouhoud EM (2004) EU enlargement: what does it changes for the European economic geography. Revue de l'OFCE 89 Special Issue:241–274.

Egger P (2000) A note on the proper econometric specification of gravity equation. Economics Letters 66:25–31.

Egger P (2002) An econometric view on estimation of gravity models and the calculation of trade potential. The World Economy 25:297–312.

Elhorst JP (2003) The mystery of regional unemployment differentials. Theoretical and empirical explanations. Journal of Economic Surveys 17:709–748.

Eurostat (2002a) A survey on training throughout professional life in the accession countries. Statistics in Focus, Theme 3, 2/2002.

Eurostat (2002b) Foreign direct investment within the candidate countries. Statistics in Focus, Theme 2, 55/2002.

Faggio G, Konings J (2003) Job creation, job destruction and employment growth in transition countries. Economic Systems 27:129–154.

Falvey R (1981) Commercial policy and intra–industry trade. Journal of International Economics 11:495–511.

Falvey R, Kierzkowski H (1987) Product quality, intra–industry trade and im(perfect) competition. In: Kierzkowski H (ed.) Protection and competition in international trade, Blackwell, Oxford, pp 143–161.

Fazekas K (2000) Impact of foreign direct investment on the performance of local labour markets. The case of Hungary. Budapest Working Paper 2003/3.

Fazekas K (2002) Regional disparities in unemployment in Central and Eastern Europe: the case of Hungary. In: Funck B and Pizzati L (eds) (2002) Labour, employment and social policy in the EU enlargement process. Changing perspectives and policy options, World Bank, Washington (D.C.), pp 176–196.

Ferragina AM (2004) Catching up of candidate countries: factors, skills and quality. University of Rome Tor Vergata, mimeo.

Ferragina AM, Giovannetti G (2004) Integrazione commerciale dell'Europa con i paesi del Partenariato euro–mediterraneo?. In: L'Italia nell'economia internazionale, Rapporto ICE 2003–2004. ICE, Rome, pp 91–120.

Ferragina AM, Giovannetti G, Pastore F (2004) EU integration with Mediterranean partner countries vis-à-vis CEE–10. A gravity study. Università Commerciale Luigi Bocconi, CNR Study Group on International Economics and Development, Milan, November.

Ferragina AM, Pastore F (2004) Regional policy in an integrated Europe. Insights from the literature. In: Benc V (ed.) Readiness of candidate countries for the EU regional policy, PHARE, Bratislava, pp 23–42.

Ferragina AM, Pastore F (2005) Factor endowment and market size in EU–CEE trade. Would human capital change the actual quality trade patterns?. Eastern European Economics 43:3–36.

Foley M (1997) Labour market dynamics in Russia. Yale University, Economic Growth Center Discussion Paper 780.

Fontagné L, Freudenberg M, Peridy N (1998) Intra–industry trade and the single market: quality matters. CEPR Discussion Paper 1953.

Frankel J, Rose A (1998) The endogeneity of optimum currency criteria. Economic Journal 108:1009–1025.

Freudenberg M, Lemoine F (1999) Central and Eastern European countries in the international division of labour in Europe. CEPII Working Paper 5.

Funck B, Pizzati L (eds) (2002) Labour, employment and social policy in the EU enlargement process. Changing perspectives and policy options. World Bank, Washington (D.C.).

Funck B, Pizzati L (eds) (2003) European integration, regional policy, and growth, World Bank, Washington (D.C.).

Góra M, Lehmann H (1995) How divergent is regional labour market adjustment in Poland?. In: Scarpetta S, Wörgötter A (eds) The regional dimension of unemployment in transition countries: A challenge for labour market and social policies. OECD, Paris, pp 126–163.

Gorzelak G (1996) The regional dimension of transformation in Central Europe. Jessica Kingsley Publishers, London.

Greenaway D, Torstensson J (2000) Economic geography, comparative advantage and trade within industries: evidence from the OECD. Journal of Economic Integration 15:260–180.

Gros D, Gonciarz A (1996) A note on the trade potential of Central and Eastern Europe. European Journal of Political Economy 12:709–721.

Hall RE (1970) Why is the unemployment rate so high at full employment?. Brookings Papers on Economic Activity 3:369–402.

Hall RE (1972) Turnover in the labour force. Brookings Papers on Economic Activity 3:709–764.

Hamilton CB, Winters AL (1992) Opening up international trade with Eastern Europe. Economic Policy 14:77–104.

Havrylyshyn O (2001) Recovery and growth in transition: a decade of evidence. IMF Staff Papers, 48 Special Issue:53–87.

Helpman E (1981) International trade in the presence of product differentiation, economies of scale and monopolistic competition. A Chamberlin–Heckscher–Ohlin approach. Journal of International Economics 11:305–340.

Helpman E, Krugman P (1985) Market structure and foreign trade. Cambridge (MA), MIT Press.

IDB (2004) Good jobs wanted: labour markets in Latin America. Inter-American Development Bank, Washington.

Kállai E, Traistaru I (2001) Characteristics and trends of regional labour markets in transition economies: empirical evidence for Romania. LICOS Discussion Paper 72.

Kehoe PJ (1994) Comment to "On the Speed of Transition in Central Europe". In: Fischer S, Rotemberg JJ (eds) NBER Macroeconomics Annual, MIT Press, Cambridge (Mass.), pp 320–328.

Kertesi G (2000) Migration and commuting: two potential forces reducing regional inequalities in economic opportunities?. SOCO Project Paper 77a, Institute for Human Sciences, Vienna.

Kiefer N (1988) Economic duration data and hazard functions. Journal of Economic Literature 26:646–679.

Konings J, Lehmann H, Schaffer M (1996) Job creation and job destruction in a transition economy: ownership, firm size, and gross job flows in Polish manufacturing 1988–1991. Labour Economics 3:299–317.

Kornai J (1992) The socialist system. The political economy of communism. Oxford, Oxford University Press.

Krajnyàk K, Sommer M (2004) Czech Republic. IMF Country Report 4/265.

Krugman PR (1980) Scale economies, product differentiation and the pattern of trade. American Economic Review 70:950–959.

Krugman PR, Venables T (1995) Globalisation and the inequality of nations. Quarterly Journal of Economics 110:857–880.

Landesmann M (2002) Spatial disparities and labour mobility. Discussant notes. In: Funck B, Pizzati L (eds) (2002) Labour, employment and social policy in the EU enlargement process. Changing perspectives and policy options, World Bank, Washington (D.C.), pp 232–234.

Landesmann M (2003) Structural features of economic integration in an enlarged Europe: patterns of catching–up and industrial specialization. European Commission Economic Paper 181.

Landesmann M, Burgstaller J (1998) Vertical product differentiation in EU markets: the relative position of East European producers. Russian and Eastern European Finance and Trade 34:32–78.

Layard R, Nickell S, Jackman R (1991) Unemployment. Macroeconomic performance and the labour market. Oxford University Press, Oxford.

Lehmann H, Walsh PP (1999) Gradual restructuring and structural unemployment in Poland: a legacy of central planning. LICOS Discussion Paper 78.

Lilien DM (1982) Sectoral shifts and cyclical unemployment. Journal of Political Economy 90:777–793.

Lipton D, Sachs J (1990) Creating a market economy in Eastern Europe: the case of Poland. Brookings Papers on Economic Activity 1:75–147.

Markusen JR (1995) The boundaries of multinational enterprises and the theory of international trade. Journal of Economic Perspectives 9:169–189.

Marston ST (1985) Two views of the geographic distribution of unemployment. The Quarterly Journal of Economics 100:57–79.

Murrell P (1996) How far has the transition progressed?. Journal of Economic Perspectives 10:25–44.

Neven D (1995) Trade liberalisation with eastern nations: how sensitive?. In: Faini R and Portes R (eds) European union trade with Eastern Europe: adjustment and opportunities. CEPR, London, pp 19–60.

Newell A (2001) Why have a Million more Polish workers become unemployed in the midst of an economic boom?. Tripartite Conference on Unemployment and Employment Policy in Poland, Warsaw, 2–3 July.

Newell A, Pastore F (1999) Structural change and structural unemployment in Poland. Studi Economici 69:81–100.

Newell A, Pastore F (2000) Regional unemployment and industrial restructuring in Poland. IZA Discussion Paper 194.

Newell A, Reilly B (1999) Rates of return to education in the transitional economies. Education Economics 7:67–84.

Newell A, Pastore F, Socha M (2000) Niektóre czynniki Kształtujące regionalną strukturę bezrobocia w Polsce. Ekonomista 6:789–808.

Newell A, Pastore F, Socha M (2002) Comparative advantages, job destruction and the regional pattern of Polish unemployment. Acta Oeconomica 52:187–204.

Nilsson L (2000) Trade integration and the EU economic membership criteria. European Journal of Political Economy 16:807–27.

Pastore F (2004) Regional unemployment persistence in Poland. A survey of the evidence and some insights from the literature. Current Politics and Economics of Russia, Eastern and Central Europe 16:97–116.

Pastore F, Verashchagina A (2003) Patterns of economic transition in the CIS, EMERGO. The Journal of Transforming Economies and Societies 10:30–50.

Pastore F, Verashchagina A (2004) Slow and steady wins the race? An appraisal of ten years of economic transition. Economia Politica 21:437–458.

Pastore F, Verashchagina A (2005) The distribution of wages in Belarus. Comparative Economic Studies, forthcoming.

Portes R (ed.) (1990) Economic transformation in Hungary and Poland. European Economy 43 Special Issue.

Puga D (1999) The rise and fall of regional inequalities. European Economic Review 43:303–334.

Riboud M, Sánchez–Páramo C, Silva–Jáuregui C (2002) Does eurosclerosis matter? Institutional reform and labour market performance in Central and Eastern European Countries in the 1990s. in: Funck B, Pizzati L (eds) Labour, employment and social policy in the EU enlargement process. Changing perspectives and policy options. World Bank, Washington (D.C.), pp 315–338.

Roland G (1991) Political economy of sequencing tactics in the transition period. In: Csaba L. (ed.) Systemic change and stabilisation in Eastern Europe, Dartmouth Press, Aldershot, pp 45–64.

Roland G (2000) Transition and economics. Politics, markets and firms. MIT Press, Cambridge (Mass.).

Rostowski J (1993) The implications of rapid private sector growth in Poland, CEP Discussion Paper 159.

Rutkowski J, Przybila M (2002) Poland: regional dimensions of unemployment. In: Funck B, Pizzati L (eds) (2002) Labour, employment and social policy in the EU enlargement process. Changing perspectives and policy options, World Bank, Washington (D.C.), pp 157–175.

Sachs J (1992) The economic transformation of Eastern Europe: the case of Poland. Economics of Planning 25:15–19.

Scarpetta S (1995) Spatial variations in unemployment in Central and Eastern Europe. Underlying reasons and labour market policy optimum. In: Scarpetta S, Wörgötter A (eds) The regional dimension of unemployment in transition countries: A challenge for labour market and social policies. OECD, Paris, pp 27–74.

Scarpetta S, Wörgötter A (eds) (1995) The regional dimension of unemployment in transition countries: A challenge for labour market and social policies. OECD, Paris.

Schmitt J, Wadsworth J (2002) Is the OECD jobs strategy behind us and British employment and unemployment success in the 1990s?. In: Howell D (ed.) Fighting unemployment: the limit of free market orthodoxy. Oxford University Press, Oxford, pp 167–204.

Shapiro C, Stiglitz JE (1984) Equilibrium unemployment as a worker discipline device. American Economic Review 74:433–44.

Sibley CW, Walsh PP (2002) Earnings inequality and transition: a regional analysis of Poland, IZA Discussion Paper 441.

Simon CJ (1988) Frictional unemployment and the role of industrial diversity. Quarterly Journal of Economics 103:715–728.

Simon CJ, Nardinelli C (1992) Does unemployment diversity always reduce unemployment? Evidence from the great depression and after. Economic Enquiry 30:384–397.

Sorm V, Terrell K (2000) Sectoral restructuring and labour mobility: a comparative look at the Czech Republic. Journal of Comparative Economics 28:431–455.

Svejnar J (1991) A framework for the economic transformation of Czechoslovakia. Eastern European Economics 29:5–28.

Svejnar J (2002a) Transition economies: performance and challenge. Journal of Economic Perspectives 16:3–28.

Svejnar J (2002b) Labour market flexibility in Central and Eastern Europe. WDI Discussion Paper 496.

Topel RH (1986) Local labour markets. Journal of Political Economy 94:111–143.

Topel RH (1994) Wage inequality and regional labour market performance in the US. In: Tachibanaki T (ed.) Labour market and economic performance, St. Martin Press, New york, pp 23–127.

Traistaru I, Pauna C (2003) The emerging geography in Romania. In: Traistaru I, Nijkamp P, Resmini L (eds) The economic geography in EU accession countries, Ashgate, Aldershot, pp 242–284.

UNCTAD (1997) World investment report, Geneva.

UNCTAD (2003) World investment report, Geneva.

Venables T (1996) Equilibrium locations of vertically linked industries. International Economic Review 37:341–359.

Vodopivec M (2002) Worker reallocation during Estonian transition to market. International Journal of Manpower 23:77–97.

Walsh PP (2003) The cyclical pattern of regional unemployment flows in Poland. Economic Systems 27:155–169.

Wang Z, Winters AL (1992) The trading potential of Eastern Europe. Journal of Economic Integration 7:113–136.

World Bank (2001) Poland's labor market: the challenge of job creation. World Bank Country Study 23033, Washington.

World Bank (2004) Growth, employment and living standards in pre–accession Poland, Report 28233, Washington.

3 Regional Employment Dynamics in the EU: Structural Outlook, Co-Movements, Clusters and Common Shocks

Enrico Marelli

University of Brescia, Italy

3.1 Introduction[*]

In the past two decades, European employment dynamics have attracted the attention of economists, researchers and policymakers. The prolonged arrest of employment growth, the rise in unemployment, and labour market rigidities – affecting many countries in continental Europe (in contrast to the Anglo-Saxon ones) – have shaped not only the theoretical discussion, especially concerning the 'eurosclerosis' hypothesis, but also recent economic policy proposals and labour market reforms. Indeed, in many European countries labour and employment policies have changed – at least since the mid-1990s – and in some of them to a significant extent. Moreover, labour market performances are now noticeably different from those that prevailed some years ago.

A second point to be stressed is that the adoption of a single currency by twelve European countries has abolished the use of such instruments of economic policy as the national exchange rate and monetary policies, and it has made the operation of some others more difficult, particularly the fiscal policies governed by the Maastricht and Stability Pact criteria. Hence, market adjustment mechanisms, including labour market adjustments, have now become more important. The starting of an Economic and Monetary Union (EMU) in Europe has also reinforced the regional dimension of economic issues.

As regards employment dynamics, therefore, their determinants should be investigated at different territorial levels: regional, national, European. This study emphasises not only the regional dimension but also the role of the *economic structure*, which is of importance in distinguishing between types of shocks (e.g. symmetric versus asymmetric) and the different ways in which they affect economic systems.

In view of data limitations, the subsequent empirical analysis will proxy the economic structure with the sectoral composition of employment, distinguishing

---

[*] This is a slightly modified version of the paper originally prepared with the title *La crescita occupazionale nell'UE: andamenti comuni, specificità regionali e settoriali* for the 17th Congress of AIEL and presented at the International Conference of the Regional Studies Association, Pisa, 12–15 April 2003.

among the main productive sectors. This approach, which emphasises structural determinants, does not necessarily imply neglect of institutional aspects and of the role of economic policies.

The review of the literature (Section 2) begins with discussion of the links between employment dynamics and institutional regimes. It then analyses the issue of regional convergence in the EMU and subsequently investigates the sectoral and regional dimensions. The empirical research is described in Section 3, which explains the working hypothesis and the data set employed.

Section 4 sets out some preliminary results with reference to employment growth in twelve European countries, i.e. the EU12 area prior to the 1995 enlargement, and the related interregional dispersion coefficients. The importance of the sectoral (industrial) structure in employment dynamics is supported by shift-share analysis; furthermore, within the complete set of 145 regions, groups of regions with similar structural characteristics are identified by means of cluster analysis.

Section 5 then shows several correlation coefficients between the employment growth of individual countries and EU12 growth, and also between individual regions and both the EU12 and national mean growths, although in the latter case only the national averages are given in the tables. Panel regressions are also used to estimate the elasticity of regional employment growth to European growth. A number of comparisons are made with previous empirical results, especially those of Decuessin and Fatàs (1995) and Fatàs (1997), but this study makes use of an up-to-date data set, employs a finer regional disaggregation, and distinguishes among the main productive sectors, instead of considering total employment alone; in fact, there are many good reasons for considering at least the manufacturing sector separately.

The main results of the empirical investigation are that it is not only national boundaries that are matter from the point of view of structural determinants: for, as shown by cluster analysis, the regional dimension may be even more important. The sectoral breakdown, too, seems to be important, since industrial (manufacturing) employment is more closely correlated across countries and regions than is total employment. The increasing international integration of the European regions is also confirmed, whilst the existence of a core group of countries in central Europe with a greater degree of integration is disputed. These results are summarised in Section 6, which concludes with some policy implications for the operation of EMU, and with a specific proposal for a new role of the Structural Funds.

3.2 A review of the literature on employment dynamics and regional convergence in Europe

3.2.1 Employment dynamics and institutional models

European employment dynamics have been analysed by many studies, especially in the past ten years. Research has focused on performances and trends at the national and European levels, while studies at a sub-national level have been less numerous.

Most of the studies conducted in the 1980s and 1990s made comparisons not only among different national evolutions but also with performance and trends in the USA. The Eurosclerosis literature stresses the limited capacity of European labour markets – in contrast to the American one – to create an adequate number of jobs compatible with full employment, even during economic upswings: a great amount of European unemployment is believed to be structural. This literature[1] identifies the main causes of Europe's poor performance in labour market rigidities and high levels of taxation, especially on labour. However, this mainstream interpretation disregards the links between slow employment growth and poor aggregate demand evolution.

The literature mentioned is not solely empirical; it is based on specific theoretical hypotheses concerning the institutional models best able to generate jobs, reduce unemployment to frictional levels, and facilitate labour market adjustments. However, it would be beyond the scope of this chapter to analyse the various institutional models either proposed or existing in the European countries.[2]

The 'dichotomy' between the Old and the New continents underlying the Eurosclerosis interpretation has substantially lessened, doing so with reference not only to Britain or certain other countries like Ireland, the Netherlands or Spain, but also to the majority of European countries, at least in the past five years. The EU and the USA are less distant than they used to be because important labour market reforms – following recommendations by international bodies such as the OECD and the European Commission itself – have been undertaken. Labour market policies have been increasingly oriented toward the liberalisation, decentralisation and 'flexibilisation' of the market, despite the persisting variety of institutional models and social and historical arenas.[3]

As a consequence, the performances of the labour markets on the two sides of the Atlantic have also grown more similar in the past five years. The gap between unemployment rates has narrowed – they now stand at around 8 per cent in the EU and 6 per cent in the USA (compared to 4 per cent before the recession of 2001) – and so too has the gap between the elasticities of employment to output or GDP, despite the fact that real growth continues to be ignominiously low in Europe. This change in employment dynamics is not the consequence of cyclical factors; rather, it is the effect of labour market reforms undertaken in the European countries:[4]

---

[1] See for example Bean (1994).

[2] The literature abounds, but see Nickell and Layard (1999) as well as Caroleo (2000) as general references, and Eichengreen and Iversen (1999) for an historical approach.

[3] A variety of models is probably an asset, also because not all Europeans are willing to adopt the 'American' model by renouncing the goals of social equity and the benefits of welfare systems, which must be reformed but certainly not eliminated altogether.

[4] This point is stressed in the recent analysis by Garibaldi and Mauro (2002).

more flexible wage agreements,[5] reduced taxes on labour, weaker employment protection laws, more active labour market policies, etc.

3.2.2 Regional convergence in the EMU

Another institutional factor which has conditioned the performance of European labour markets in the past ten years is convergence towards the macroeconomic and financial stability required by the Maastricht Treaty for the euro-candidate countries.

High degrees of nominal convergence – inflation, interest rates, public deficit and debt – have been achieved by the 12 members of the euro-zone, although at the cost of slowing economic and employment growth. The formerly deviating countries have been 'punished' for their vices of the past (undisciplined public finances, inflation-prone behaviour, etc.); but they have also been rewarded by the benefits of the EMU itself, some of which have already been reaped (lower interest rates and debt service). Once it has been determined that public finances are really set on sustainable paths, with medium-run balanced budgets as required by the Stability Pact, and once the European Central Bank has acquired a good anti-inflation reputation, then more expansionary macroeconomic policies will probably be adopted to accompany and reinforce the labour market reforms.

According to EU policymakers,[6] nominal convergence gradually leads to real convergence, owing to the benefits of macroeconomic stability, the removal of exchange-rate uncertainty, the reduction of uncertainty concerning inflation and interest rates (as well as the levels of the latter variables in the formerly deviating countries), the spur of investments and international trade, and finally the strengthening of economic growth, which may even become permanent thanks to dynamic scale effects.

If we consider, however, the degree of real convergence existing at present within the euro-zone, then it does not seem that the economic systems of the various countries are already very similar, as regards either economic structures or the outcomes of economic activities in terms of output, employment, income, and so on. Note that convergence in outcomes is fostered by the process by which economic structures grow increasingly similar.

This has been demonstrated by various lines of economic inquiry. In the long run, conditional convergence models in the economic growth literature[7] show that when the structural conditions of economic systems become progressively similar,

---

[5] The diffusion of 'atypical contracts' has given greater flexibility even to those labour markets traditionally considered the most rigid, such as Italy's (see Marelli and Porro 2000).

[6] See Buti and Sapir (1998).

[7] If we refer to the growth rates in the long run, rather than to the levels of output or income, it is true that endogenous growth models normally produce diverging paths for different economic systems, but it has been shown that in some cases convergence is still possible (Pigliaru 2001).

then also the steady states will be equalised, e.g. with reference to per-capita output. Moreover, in the short (and medium) run, real convergence makes economic shocks more symmetric, thus producing more similar outcomes, i.e. responses by the real variables: product, employment, unemployment, etc.

Focusing here on the second approach, which has also been studied in the optimum currency area literature, we point out that an asymmetric shock may raise output and employment in some countries and lower them in others belonging to the same monetary union, also because the traditional macroeconomic instruments (exchange rate and monetary policy) are lacking.

The customary distinction between symmetric and asymmetric shocks has been recently challenged. At the aggregate level, it has been shown that a shock which is initially asymmetric because it hits only one country may soon affect all the countries in the currency area because of the direct and indirect connections among economic systems: trade links, financial and macroeconomic relationships, including the various types of externalities and spillovers analysed in the literature.[8] Furthermore, from a sectoral point of view, idiosyncratic shocks hitting individual sectors but many countries at one time may give rise to different national outcomes, at least in terms of the intensity of the responses. Hence, sector-specific shocks may automatically become nation- or region-specific, given the extent to which countries and, especially, regions are specialised.

3.2.3 Productive specialisation

Diverging sectoral specialisations make economic shocks more asymmetric and consequently raise the costs of a monetary union which comprises heterogeneous countries. Moreover, according to some studies (for example Krugman 1993) it is the process itself of economic integration that may give rise – owing to scale economies, externalities, and some other reasons – to growing sectoral specialisations, diverging economic structures, and widening gaps among the economic growth rates of countries and, more probably, regions. The theoretical base is provided by *endogenous growth* models with many sectors and international trade,[9] or by the spatial models of the *new economic geography*.

Conversely, a more optimistic view maintains that convergence may result from trade and economic links with the other economic systems. In fact, if we look at the past, the similarity of economic systems seems to have increased, also by virtue of the coordination of macroeconomic policies induced by the workings of the European Monetary System[10] and the attainment of the Single Market in the 1980s and early 1990s.

---

[8] See Farina and Tamborini (2002).

[9] Divergence is the normal outcome of these models, but minor changes to the basic models – e.g. introducing intersectoral and international technology spillovers – may give rise to convergence (Pigliaru 2001).

[10] A better synchronisation of the business cycles of the EMS countries is shown by Artis and Zhang (1999).

Furthermore, even a possible exacerbation of asymmetric shocks, in the EMU's initial period of operation, may be offset by the greater flexibility of markets, by appropriate reforms of the goods, capital and labour markets, and at the community level (as the European Commission itself asserts), by the appropriate use of structural and cohesion funds.

The degree of sectoral disaggregation is of course relevant to measurement of productive specialisation. In any case, Clark's well-known 'three stages' law of economic development may also be pertinent: it is true that in the long run this law states that economic structures will converge, but the timing of the transition from one stage of development to the next is quite different from country to country, and from region to region as well. Many areas in Southern Europe still have large primary sectors;[11] whilst in some regions of Europe the tertiarisation process has been ongoing for decades, and in some others the peak of industrialisation has not yet been reached.[12]

Structural convergence and diversification of production are found to be important forces behind the dynamics of employment, output and productivity. In the case of employment growth, and with reference to European regions,[13] it seems that 80 per cent of total variance in the long run is due to sectoral effects, while national effects explain the remaining 20 per cent. Moreover, sectoral factors account for more than half of the short-run fluctuations.

Structural change seemingly also plays a prime role in labour productivity. In about 100 European regions, productivity convergence in the 1980s can be associated with structural change to a large extent, which explains about three-quarters of total variance.[14] More specific studies have produced similar results. In the Spanish regions, productivity convergence is substantially explained by structural convergence – even if three sectors alone are examined – rather than by the oft-cited mechanisms of scale economies and technological spillovers.[15]

Other types of empirical study reach the same conclusions. Shift-share analysis finds that the initial structure (share component) is important in determining the productivity advantage of the richest regions of Central Europe, while the peripheral regions instead take advantage of the dynamic (shift) component. But if structural change is included in the analysis, the narrowing disparities in productivity are accounted for – to a large extent – by labour shifts from low-productivity sectors to high-productivity ones. Structural convergence has been generally found

---

[11] A recent empirical work by Boldrin and Canova (2001) shows that the share of agriculture in production is one of the three most important factors in explanation of income disparities across the European regions (the other two are employment rates and total factor productivity).

[12] For a descriptive analysis of the structure of employment, in three sectors and 145 European regions for the period 1983–97, see Marelli (2004).

[13] Regions in ten European countries have been considered in this case (see Marimon and Zilibotti 1998). For a more complete analysis of regional employment evolutions in the EU, which stresses some other elements, see Martin and Tyler (2000).

[14] See Pigliaru (2001).

[15] See Cuadrado Roura et al. (1999).

both within and between countries; although if consideration is made of very disaggregated industrial activities within the manufacturing sector, regional structures do not seem to converge.[16]

The point to be stressed is that even a structural analysis based on the three broad economic sectors may produce interesting results. Since most of the studies on the international propagation of shocks are based on aggregate models, better understanding can be obtained by considering, at least, the manufacturing sector separately from the total economy: in fact, manufacturing (and also the industrial sector as a whole) is the tradable sector by definition, and it is therefore more affected – compared to services – by trade and economic integration processes in Europe. Hence, the impact of exogenous shocks is normally greater in manufacturing.[17]

In a long-run perspective, moreover, Kaldor's hypothesis that the manufacturing sector is the 'engine of growth' has been borne out by recent empirical studies, which – even on considering a simple dichotomic structural disaggregation, e.g. agriculture versus non-agricultural sectors – have been able to explain a large amount of convergence among the European regions until the 1990s.[18]

3.2.4 The regional dimension

Regional economies are, as we know, much more open than national ones. Consequently, they are more likely than national economic systems to be specialised in certain sectors or activities. Even when the average productive structures of two countries appear similar, regional specialisations may be very different.

As a consequence, the probability that sector-specific shocks are asymmetric is much higher at the regional level. From this point of view, and also in regard to policy implications, the regional dimension is certainly more important than the national one. Many economists are willing to concede that Krugman's hypothesis of a growing sectoral specialisation is more realistic at the regional level than at the national one.

But what is a region in the present-day European setting? The distinction between national and regional economies has been blurred by the supra-national integration within EMU now transforming the countries in certain large regions, on the one hand, and the administrative decentralisation or devolution experiences in some countries on the other.

We have just seen that the degree of sectoral breakdown may be important: the same applies to spatial disaggregation. The smaller the spatial units analysed, the more specialised they become, with asynchronous movements. Many empirical studies have revealed that asymmetric shocks are more common at the regional

---

[16] See Molle (1997).

[17] In comparison with aggregate indicators such as the unemployment rate (Belke and Gros, 1999).

[18] See Paci and Pigliaru (1999).

level than at the national one.[19] Moreover, persistence in specialisation is more likely in small territorial units, and in its turn affects the persistence of income disparities.

According to many empirical studies, interregional disparities in per capita income or productivity are wider in the EU than in the USA. They decreased from the 1950s to the mid-1970s, but they did so quite slowly: 2 per cent was the annual reduction in the β-convergence estimations; an unsatisfactory pace given the goal of economic and social cohesion set by the EU's institutions. Thereafter, the trends have become even more unclear, with convergence limited to certain subgroups of countries (club convergence) and specific time intervals, and, in any case, still weaker.[20]

Interregional disparities seem to be substantial with reference to other economic variables as well: the unemployment rate is a clear example. This has considerable policy implications, for if unemployment is mainly a regional problem, then structural policies or labour market reforms planned at the national level are bound to fail.

3.3 Working assumptions and data set

Before the empirical investigation is described, its main working assumptions should be specified. The first is that the analysis of past trends, in particular those of the 1980s and 1990s, is not only interesting in terms of historical trends; it may also provide insights into the probable future working of EMU. As a matter of fact, a certain degree of trade and macroeconomic convergence, although less marked if compared with the EMU experience, was achieved already during the EMS period.

The second assumption is that the spatial unit best suited to our empirical analysis is the region. Besides theoretical considerations (Section 3.2.4), the importance of the regional dimension compared to the national one will be apparent from the empirical results themselves. A fine disaggregation has been chosen: Eurostat's NUTS-2 level, which the European Commission has defined as the most appropriate territorial level at which to judge the persistence or reduction of interregional disparities. Although this level unfortunately includes regions of different sizes, it has been chosen not only to draw a significant distinction between regions and countries but also in view of policy aspects, with particular regard to community regional policy.

Another assumption is that the outcomes – employment dynamics in our case – depend on the shocks that may hit economic systems as well as the economic and

---

[19] See for example De Nardis et al. (1996).

[20] Among the most recent studies, see Tondl (1999), Boldrin and Canova (2001). According to the latter study, the European regions manifested in 1980–96 neither convergence nor divergence in per capita income (the apparent convergence in growth rates left disparities in income levels unchanged).

institutional structure (see Section 3.2.2 above): this approach has been adopted in the most recent literature.[21] However, rather than the institutional framework,[22] emphasised here are the productive structure and sectoral specialisation. The three broad productive sectors – agriculture, industry, services – are considered, although a finer breakdown would be advisable for some investigations. Nevertheless, as already explained (Section 3.2.3) also a three-way disaggregation, with a distinction of the industrial (manufacturing) sector, would be fruitful.[23]

The fourth assumption concerns the choice of the basic variable for the empirical investigations that follow: this variable is *employment*, and more precisely, employment change over time. It is well-known that employment, together with unemployment, is an important economic policy objective; moreover, macroeconomic studies on the effects of shocks have emphasised labour market adjustments. There are also practical reasons for choosing employment: first, international comparisons are easier with employment data, unlike output or income data, for which additional assumptions about exchange rates are needed; second, the definition of employment is less ambiguous, across countries, compared to the alternative measure (unemployment); finally, a sectorally disaggregated analysis can be carried out with employment data but not with unemployment data.

The last assumption is that a synthetic measure is required to identify the shocks and their effects on regions and countries. We have already seen that distinguishing between symmetric and asymmetric shocks is not always straightforward (Section 3.2.2), and that in any case, whatever the initial shock may be, its spatial propagation and the *intensity of response* – in countries and regions – is what really matters. Thus, a good synthetic index is the degree of correlation of shocks, which in our case is computed by means of employment growth (linear) correlations.

Previous studies on similarity and convergence among productive structures have made use of output or production data; while studies on interregional disparities in Europe have generally focused on income or productivity data. Hence, the use of employment data is somewhat novel.[24]

Besides the use of employment data and of a sectoral disaggregation, another original aspect of this study is its fine regional breakdown: 145 regions of Eurostat's NUTS-2 classification, and the twelve countries of the EU before 1995; the

[21] See Blanchard and Wolfers (2000).

[22] As said (Section 3.2.1), employment dynamics depend strictly on labour market institutions and employment policies. However, since policymakers, international agencies and individual researchers (see Garibaldi and Mauro 2002, as a recent example) have constantly stressed institutional elements, we have preferred to follow a different and more innovative approach, if compared with the literature of the last decade; an approach based on structural determinants.

[23] Moreover, when choosing the data set, a trade-off arises between the degrees of spatial and sectoral disaggregations: hereinafter we have opted for the former.

[24] Notable exceptions are Fatàs (1997), Decressin and Fatàs (1995).

period is 1983–97.[25] For three countries (Luxembourg, Ireland, Denmark) no regional breakdown is provided.

The time span 1983–97 is divided, for certain analyses, into three sub-periods: 1983–87, 1988–92, 1993–97. This enables account to be taken of cyclical and medium-run evolutions. As to the most recent sub-period, note that 1993 is the year of the deepest recession in many European countries, with lasting effects on employment in the following years as well; and in that same year nominal convergence initiate as a consequence of the Maastricht Treaty.

3.4 Employment growth and economic structure of the European regions

3.4.1 Employment growth in EU12 countries and regional dispersion

Average employment growth in 1983–97 in the EU12 area was about 1 per cent per year (Fig. 3.1.A). Higher than average rates of growth were recorded by the Netherlands (NL), Ireland (IE), Spain (ES) and the United Kingdom (UK); and the only negative change, for the entire period, by Italy (IT). Italy and Ireland perhaps represent the two opposite 'models' of economic growth: productivity growth has been similar in the two countries, but in the former it has been achieved at the expense of employment, whilst in the latter it has favoured the expansion of production, income, and employment.

Average national growth rates are incomplete, however. Given the difficulty of presenting the growth rates of fully 145 regions, an easy way to give some idea about interregional dispersion is to compute, at the national level, the standard deviations (S.D.) of the regional employment growth rates. The highest dispersion-coefficients are those for the countries of Southern Europe[26]; the lowest are for Germany (DE) and the United Kingdom (UK).

When focusing separately on employment growth in the *industrial* sector,[27] one finds that growth in 1983–97 was on average negative (see again Figure 3.1.A). The only exceptions, i.e. positive changes, were IE, ES, NL and DK (Denmark); the biggest falls in industrial employment were instead recorded by FR (France), UK and IT. Interregional dispersions were even greater in the case of industry than for the total economy, with peaks in PT (Portugal), NL, IT and ES.

---

[25] For some regions, especially in Southern Europe, the data set begins in 1986 or 1988. East Germany Landers are not included.

[26] The Italian regional dispersion is not the highest, in contrast to unemployment, employment rates, activity rates, productivity or per-capita income levels. Note that this concerns employment *growth* rates: if growth rates are more or less similar among the Italian regions, this means that the initial wide gaps remain unchanged over time.

[27] This sector includes manufacturing, energy and construction.

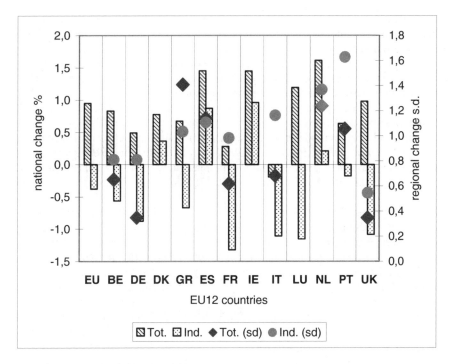

Fig. 3.1.A Employment growth 1983–97

The three sub-periods display the following distinctive features:
- in the mid-1980s (1983–87), there was a slight increase in total employment and a substantial fall in industry in most countries, following the recession of the early 1980s and the restructuring stage of industrial activities, which in some countries and regions for the first time gave rise to a de-industrialisation process. However, international and interregional dispersions were already significant in this period (Fig. 3.1.B);
- in the second sub-period (1988–92), there was an unequivocal upturn in employment growth: the annual growth rates of total employment were above 2 per cent, and growth rates were positive in industry as well. Total employment was stagnant in only one country (IT), and industrial employment fell in two countries (UK, DK) (Fig. 3.1.C);
- in the most recent sub-period (1993–97), total employment stagnated in the EU12 area, and industrial employment shrank rapidly – about –2 per cent per year on average – because of the lagged effects of the 1992–93 recession and the consequent restructuring, especially in industry. Industrial employment still grew in IE alone, and total employment exhibited positive growth rates in UK and GR (Greece) too (Fig. 3.1.D).

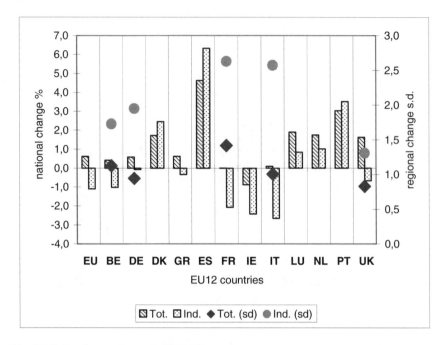

Fig. 3.1.B. Employment growth 1983–87

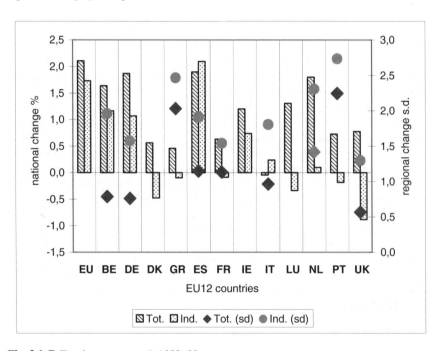

Fig. 3.1.C. Employment growth 1988–92

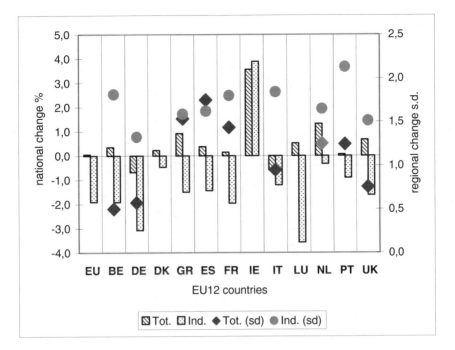

Fig. 3.1.D. Employment growth 1993–97

As a general comment, to be noted is that dispersion in industrial employment growth rates is greater, in all sub-periods, than the corresponding total employment dispersion: this is the case both across countries and among the regions of each country. The distinctive nature of the industrial sector – hence the need to keep it separate from the economy as a whole – emerges in yet another way.

Although the persistence over time of regional employment growth is rather low for the economy as a whole – as shown by Fig. 3.2.A where the regional growth rates of the 1993–97 sub-period are correlated with those of 1983–92 – the intertemporal correlation becomes definitely negative, though at a low significance level, in the industrial sector (Fig. 3.2.B): that is to say, the most dynamic regions as regards industrial employment growth in the 1983–92 period were the ones hardest hit by the 1993–97 crisis.

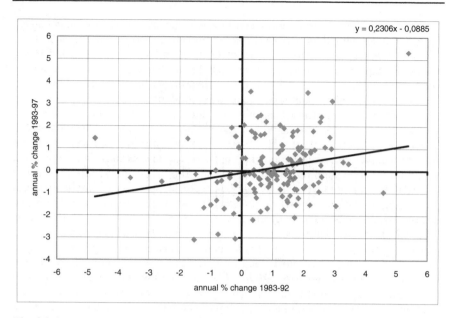

Fig. 3.2.A. Regional employment growth: all sectors

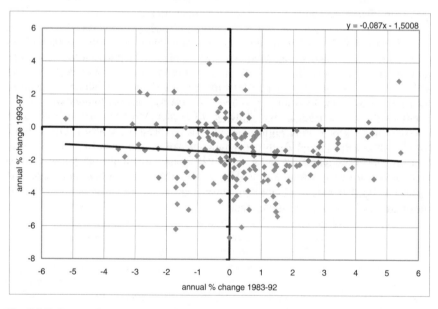

Fig. 3.2.B. Regional employment growth: industry

3.4.2 The importance of the sectoral mix

The previous empirical results have already shown that employment dynamics should be analysed in a sectorally disaggregated way, at least by distinguishing the industrial sector. Previous studies have obtained general results by means of a three-sector classification (see Section 3.2.3). A similar approach will now be adopted here by employing the well-known shift-share analysis.

This technique allows us to determine, within the employment growth of countries or regions, the effects engendered by the sectoral structure (or industry mix). This is the *share* or *mix* component, which may induce higher or smaller growth rates relative to some 'average' value, in our case the EU12 average. At the present stage of development, the mix effect benefits tertiarised regions and penalises those still specialised in agriculture or also in industrial activities. On the other hand, if after employment growth has been corrected for structural differences, a region or a country exhibits higher-than-average or lower-than-average growth, this is due to a *shift* effect caused by different competitive conditions or 'comparative advantages' of regions (for example, because of localisation and agglomeration scale economies) or countries (including in this case institutional regimes and economic policy effects).

If $N_{i,r,0}$ is employment in sector i, region r at time 0; $a_{i,r,0}$ the initial share of sector i in total regional employment $\left(=N_{i,r,0}/\sum_i N_{i,r,0}\right)$; $a_{i,0}^*$ the corresponding share for all regions $\left(=\sum_r N_{i,r,0}/\sum_r \sum_i N_{i,r,0}\right)$; $g_{i,r}$ the employment growth rate in sector i, region r $\left(\Delta N_{i,r}/N_{i,r,0}\right)$; g_r the employment growth rate in region r $\left(=\sum_i \Delta N_{i,r}/\sum_i N_{i,r,0}\right)$; g_i^* the employment growth rate in sector i $\left(=\sum_r \Delta N_{i,r}/\sum_r N_{i,r,0}\right)$; then it is possible to introduce the following variables:

- $_c g_{i,r} = \Delta N_{i,r}/\sum_i N_{i,r,0} = a_{i,r,0}g_{i,r}$ is the contribution of sector i to total employment growth in region r;

- $g_r = \sum_i a_{i,r,0}g_{i,r}$ is total employment growth in region r;

- $_m g_r = \sum_i a_{i,0}^* g_{i,r}$ is a virtual *mix-adjusted* growth, where the sectoral growth rates are averaged by using EU12 initial shares, instead of the region's initial shares;

- $_s g_r = \sum_i a_{i,r,0}g_i^*$ is a virtual *shift-adjusted* growth, where sectors are assumed to grow at the average EU12 growth rate, but these rates are weighted by the initial shares of region r.

Computation of the above variables for the twelve EU12 countries and the period 1987–97 yields numerical values for the 'virtual' growths ($_m g_r$ and $_s g_r$) that differ from the actual growth rates (g_r) (Fig. 3.3). The differences are even greater in the case of the regions. For example, in the countries of Southern Europe (SP,

PT, GR)[28] and in Ireland, growth rates would have been greater than the real ones (g_r) had they had a common sectoral structure ($_mg_r$).

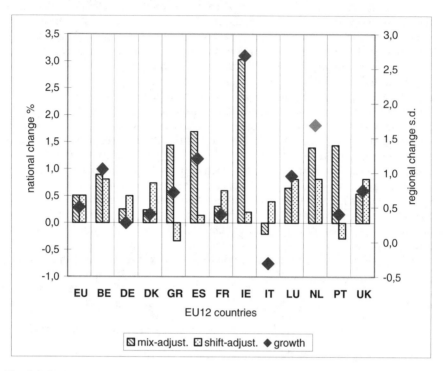

Fig. 3.3. Shift-share employment growth

The rankings of the countries in terms of employment growth rates also change if we move from real to virtual (mix-adjusted $_mg_r$) growth rates (Table 3.1): the above-mentioned countries, especially GR and PT, would have grown much faster if their sectoral structures had been the same as the European average.

---

[28] In the case of Italy, significant differences between virtual and real growth rates do not emerge in the country as a whole, owing to its heterogeneous regional production structures. In fact, the fall of total employment in the *Mezzogiorno* regions, close to −1 per cent per year, is due to a large extent (about half) to the initial sectoral mix.

Table 3.1. Shift-share employment growth – EU12 country ranks (1987–97)

	Employment growth	Mix-adjusted	Shift-adjusted
BE	4	6	4
DK	9	11	5
DE	11	10	7
GR	7	3	12
ES	3	2	10
FR	10	9	6
IE	1	1	9
IT	12	12	8
LU	5	7	3
NL	2	5	2
PT	8	4	11
UK	6	8	1

Source: Elaboration on Eurostat data

3.4.3 Regional clusters

Given the importance of the sectoral employment structure, it is of interest to group the European regions according to their structural characteristics.[29] A *cluster analysis* over the 145 European regions was carried out by first considering the regional sectoral shares in total employment: $\lambda_{A,r}$, $\lambda_{M,r}$, $\lambda_{S,r}$, corresponding respectively to agriculture, industry, services; and then also the regional per capita income (y_r) specified as an index number in purchasing power parities with EU12 = 100. The clustering procedure[30] was repeated for an initial period (1983–86) and for a final one (1994–97).

---

[29] Similar clustering techniques have been employed in the past: for a study complementary to this one, because it deals with to regional specialisations within manufacturing, see De Nardis et al. (1996). Note that the results of cluster analysis generally confirm the 'convergence clubs' hypothesis: see Boldrin and Canova (2001) for a recent empirical study.

[30] This was the 'K-means cluster', which yields an optimal solution conditional on an exogenously fixed number of clusters. The latter were set equal to alternative values between 2 and 6. For more details on the cluster analysis, see my previous work: in fact, subsection 3.4.3 in this chapter substantially replicates the treatment in Marelli (2004), pp. 44–45.

The results, for a number of clusters equal to 4, are presented in Table 3.2, which includes the number of regions in each cluster and the mean values of the above-mentioned variables. In qualitative terms, the composition and characteristics of the four clusters can be summarised as follows.

A. The first cluster is a small one (7 regions) and includes the richest European regions, with a per capita income 70 per cent above the European average, corresponding to the service-oriented capital-city regions (in BE, FR, NL) and the most developed German Landers.
B. This cluster comprises about 20 regions specialised in agriculture in GR, SP and PT, with a per-capita income slightly more than half the European average but reaching 60 per cent at the end of the period. The catching-up of these regions is associated with a shrinking of agriculture and a tertiarisation process, yet not at the expense of the industrial sector.
C. The third cluster is the largest one and includes about 70 regions in Northern and Central Europe and also some regions of North and Central Italy. Per capita income is above the European average and increasing over time, 14 per cent higher in the final period. The industrial sector still employs one-third of workers, despite steady tertiarisation.
D. The final cluster is relatively large as well. It comprises around 50 regions, especially in Italy's *Mezzogiorno*, in Spain, but also in Central Europe (FR, NL); in these regions, agriculture still has some weight, services have now become the leading sector, while industry has never attained a crucial role.

Table 3.2. Regional clusters: 1983–86 e 1994–97

	Initial (1983–86)					Final (1994–97)			
	n	y_r^1	$\lambda_{A,r}^1$	$\lambda_{M,r}^1$	$\lambda_{S,r}^1$	n	y_r^2	$\lambda_{A,r}^2$	$\lambda_{M,r}^2$	$\lambda_{S,r}^2$
A	7	168.8	2.4	30.6	67	7	169.2	1.5	25.6	72.9
B	22	53.7	35.5	24.9	39.6	23	59.8	24.6	24.3	51.1
C	72	106	6.9	37.4	55.7	50	113.8	4	33.8	62.2
D	44	77.6	12.3	28.8	58.9	65	86.7	6.6	27.3	66.1
Tot	145	100	8.3	33.7	58	145	100	5.2	29.4	65.4

Source: Elaboration on Eurostat data

The mean per capita income has risen in the latter group of regions from 77 per cent to 87 per cent of the European average. However, this does not correspond to a real catching up process since the composition of the cluster has changed over time and now contains many more regions (of UK, BE, DE), mostly originating from cluster C, whose per capita income was higher. A possible explanation is that cluster C initially included two sub-groups of regions: a majority of solidly industrialised regions, which over time began their tertiarisation process anyway, with increasing per capita income; another sub-group of regions, about 20, which, following incipient industrialisation, have shifted to more rapid tertiarisation and whose per capita income, though higher than cluster D's average, has grown more slowly than that of the regions remaining in cluster C.

A more general conclusion is that, apart from the top regions strongly specialised in services,[31] higher-than-average per capita income is more frequent in industrialised regions than in tertiarising regions which have not yet completed their industrialisation stage.[32] This finding once again corroborates the role of the industrial sector in development processes, in accordance with Kaldor's 'engine of growth' hypothesis.

Another primary conclusion is that national boundaries are not significant for regional classifications based on structural characteristics: structurally similar regions can be found in several (not necessarily contiguous) countries. When conducting our clustering analysis, we did not impose the spatial proximity condition, because we were more interested in the structural characteristics of regions, rather than in localisation and agglomerative factors. These are nevertheless important because they indubitably give rise to a spatial concentration of employment.[33]

Of course, national boundaries may be significant for other reasons, concerning institutional regimes and economic policies, for instance. But from the point of view of structural characteristics, regions are analytically more useful spatial units than nations.

3.5 Regional employment growth correlations

3.5.1 Correlations between countries

The previous section discussed the general evolution of employment in Europe in the period 1983–97, and it stressed the importance of both the regional and the sectoral dimensions. We now examine the co-movements of employment over time across countries and regions. The degree of *similarity* of employment dynamics may reflect the degree of symmetry or asymmetry of shocks, as well as homogeneity in responses (adjustments) to the shocks themselves.[34] This assumption is today widespread in the empirical literature also with reference to other macro-

---

[31] The service specialisation of the 'top' European regions can be evaluated in terms of both quantitative and qualitative aspects.

[32] Labour re-allocation from agriculture to sectors less likely to foster economic growth, such as services and especially the more traditional service activities, is a possible cause of the slow-down of growth and convergence processes, as established by many empirical studies (see for example Pigliaru 2001).

[33] This type of cluster has recently been retrieved by Overman and Puga (2002).

[34] In the case of annual data — as opposed to multi-annual data — it is likely that the correlations will more intensely reflect the degree of symmetry of shocks, although some adjustment may take place within the one-year time span as well; the speed of adjustment may also be influenced, as we have seen, by the institutional regimes.

economic variables: for instance, the dispersion in regional unemployment rates has been used to assess the importance of both asymmetric shocks and the ensuing speed of adjustment. It was explained in Section 3.3, however, why employment growth data are better than unemployment data.

The best-known previous study making use of employment growth data is that by Fatàs (1997), who found that the correlations between regional employment growth rates and the European average have increased over time, while the correlations between the regional data and the national means have decreased: also from this point of view, national boundaries have become less significant.

We used our data set first to compute the simultaneous correlation coefficients – over the period 1983–97 – at the *national* level, i.e. between the national employment growth rates and the EU12 average. In the case of total employment (all sectors), the highest correlations with EU12 were found for the following countries (see Table 3.3 for details): Germany, then Italy and Portugal; central European countries (BE, NL, FR) and also Spain are in the middle range; negative correlations were found for GR, IE, and the UK.[35] According to these results,[36] although some peripheral countries do indeed exhibit asynchronous movements, the existence of a *core* of countries in central Europe,[37] more closely interconnected, more structurally similar, and thus the best candidates for an optimum currency area, would seem to be confuted.

A second important result, although it is a preliminary one,[38] is that correlations of national employment variations with EU12 have increased over time, reaching the highest values in the 1993–93 sub-period. It seems paradoxical that the dynamics of employment became more homogenous in Europe precisely in the years of employment stagnation, but it is likely that the shocks became more symmetric, or that they met with a more homogenous policy response: suffice it to consider the cautious macroeconomic policies that followed the Maastricht Treaty.

---

[35] However, the correlation of UK with EU12 becomes positive and large (0.65) if we exclude the 1991 observation, this being the year of deepest recession for the British economy, while Germany and the 'continental' countries were still following an upward trend.

[36] Fatàs's (1997) results were somewhat different: the highest correlations were obtained in the case of northern and central European countries (UK, IE, BE, FR, NL), in addition to Germany. Differences in the data set and in the time interval can explain the differing results: in fact, Fatàs's second interval (1979–92) partly overlaps but does not coincide with the one used here.

[37] This hypothesis was formulated at the beginning of the 1990s (see for example Bayoumi and Eichengreen, 1993) jointly with the proposal of a two-speed monetary union. Later studies, however, have gradually extended the core: Forni and Reichlin (1997) include the northern Italian regions and some regions of Spain in it.

[38] We computed the correlation coefficients for the three sub-periods: the unweighted average for the twelve countries increases from 0.21 for 1983–87 to 0.58 for 1993–97. Correlations for all countries and the most recent sub-period are shown in Fig. 3.4.A.

Table 3.3. Employment growth correlations (1983–97)

	Countries vs. EU12		Regions vs. EU12	Regions vs. country
	All sectors	Industry	All sectors	All sectors
BE	0.49	0.47	0.23	0.52
DE	0.83	0.85	0.28	0.58
DK	0.08	0.27		
GR	−0.58	0.16	−0.31	0.36
ES	0.39	0.52	0.23	0.72
FR	0.45	0.62	0.09	0.21
IE	−0.12	0.15		
IT	0.70	0.66	0.43	0.59
LU	0.29	0.16		
NL	0.37	0.34	0.25	0.62
PT	0.73	0.57	0.49	0.69
UK	−0.10	0.19	−0.02	0.70
mean	0.29	0.41	0.19	0.56

Source: Elaboration on Eurostat data

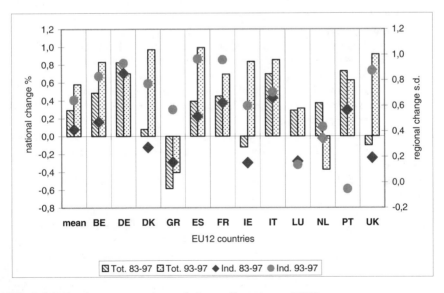

Fig. 3.4.A. Employment growth correlations – Countries vs. EU12

A third and more innovative result concerns the correlations computed for the three branches of activity. Presented here is only the outcome for the industrial sector, which – compared to the economy as a whole – is more closely integrated with foreign economies, open to international competition, and sensitive to asymmetric shocks. The correlation coefficient rises, on average for the twelve countries, to 0.41 compared to the 0.29 value for the total economy: in almost all countries the correlations are now larger, significant gains are achieved in FR and ES, and the negative correlation coefficients previously found for some countries disappear (see Table 3.3).

3.5.2 Correlations between regions

The correlation analysis based on country-level data has yielded some significant results, as just indicated. But the nation is not always the most interesting territorial dimension, the regional one may be more effective and stimulating, as shown by the theoretical discussion (Section 3.2.4) and by our preliminary empirical results (Section 3.4.3).[39]

We have thus computed the correlation coefficients between, on the one hand, regional employment growth rates and, on the other, two alternative 'reference' data:

- European (EU12) growth rates,
- national growth rates (for all regions of the same country).

For both types of correlations, the unweighted national averages of the regional correlation coefficients are presented in Table 3.3. As regards the first type (correlations with EU12), the overall average for the nine countries with regional breakdown is now equal to 0.19, which is of course lower than the one obtained for the national correlations (0.29). Indeed, the smaller the territorial unit, the more likely it is that shocks will be asymmetric and idiosyncratic. This also explains why our mean correlation coefficients are much lower than those found by Fatàs (1997), where use is made of a regional classification less disaggregated than ours.[40]

The previous findings concerning the country-level correlations are supported also by the regional correlations:

a. the absence of a core of more similar regions located in central Europe: many regions in Southern Europe exhibit employment evolutions similar to the EU12 average;
b. growing correlations over time, i.e. the increasing integration of European regions;

---

[39] A further finding relevant to the present discussion is that in the European regions about 75 per cent of output variance is explained either by global (European) or local (regional) factors, with the national component being non-significant (see again Forni and Reichlin 1997).

[40] Some other differences in the two data sets consist in Fatàs's consideration of the four largest European countries only, compared to our nine, and of a distinct time span, as already stated.

c. higher correlations in industry relative to the total economy: considerable improvements are exhibited by the German, French and Spanish regions (see Fig. 3.4.B).

It is also interesting to note that the averages of the regional correlations computed for the four clusters of regions, obtained in Section 3.4.3, are relatively large in the case of cluster A, the top European regions, and cluster C, the industrialised regions (see Fig. 3.4.D).

Turning to the second type of regional correlations, i.e. those relative to the national averages, the correlation coefficients are undoubtedly higher: some of the factors behind employment evolutions are clearly national, e.g. institutional or economic policy factors. Within countries, employment dynamics are fairly homogenous, with few exceptions (GR and surprisingly FR). However, there is no evidence of rising coefficients over time, i.e. convergence in regional employment dynamics[41] (see Fig. 3.4.C), as already found by previous studies.[42] Moreover, the regional correlations versus the national averages are no larger in the industrial sector than in the economy as whole, in contrast to the case of the regional correlations versus the EU12 area: this implies that non-manufacturing sectors, including services, are still much more integrated nationally than internationally.

A country example is illuminating. In Italy, employment dynamics have recently been rather similar across regions:[43] this is confirmed by the close regional correlations with the national averages computed for the four territorial areas (see Table 3.4). On the other hand, regional correlations with EU12 are on the whole rather large, but they exhibit greater territorial variability: the lowest value is found for the *Mezzogiorno* regions and the highest one for the north-eastern regions: in the latter area, correlations with EU12 are even larger than are correlations with the national averages. For these regions, the European business cycle, and European evolutions more generally, are today more relevant than national ones.

---

[41] The regional correlation coefficients (with the national averages) diminish in the 1993–97 sub-period, especially in DE and IT.

[42] Fatàs (1997), over a different time horizon, detected a decrease in the regional correlations relative to national employment dynamics (from 0.73 for 1966–79 to 0.57 for 1979–92); this contrasts with the rising regional correlations with EU12 (from 0.43 to 0.48 in the two sub-periods): the latter increase has been larger in the regions of the EMS countries.

[43] Remember that we are discussing dynamics, not levels, as already stated in Section 3.4.1.

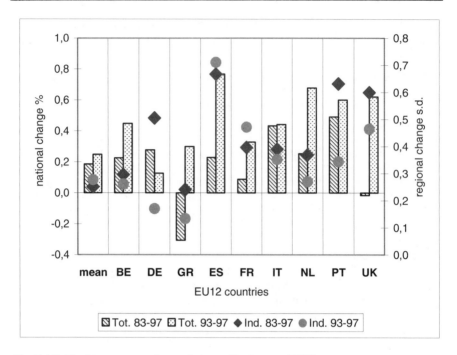

Fig. 3.4.B. Employment growth correlations – Regions vs. EU12

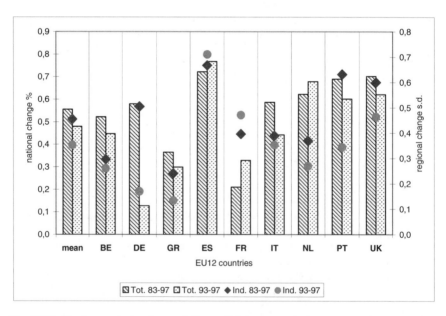

Fig. 3.4.C. Employment growth correlations – Regions vs. country

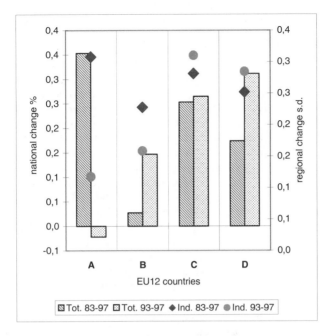

Fig. 3.4.D. Employment growth correlations – Regional clusters vs. EU12

Table 3.4. Employment growth correlations: Italian regions (all sectors 1983–97)

	Regions vs. EU12	Regions vs. Italy
North West	0.51	0.60
North East	0.62	0.59
Centre	0.46	0.61
Mezzogiorno	0.29	0.56
All regions	0.43	0.59

Source: Elaboration on Eurostat data

3.5.3 Panel regressions

A final type of empirical investigation seeks to exploit time-series and cross-section information jointly in order to assess whether employment shocks are distributed symmetrically, or vice-versa asymmetrically, across the European regions. First estimated were several OLS regressions, one for each of the 145 regions in the data set:

$$\Delta \log\left(N_{r,t}\right) = \alpha r + \beta r \; \Delta \log\left(N_t^{EU}\right) + \varepsilon_{r,t} \tag{3.1}$$

where $N_{r,t}$ is employment in region r and year t, N_t^{EU} is total employment in EU12, $\Delta\log$ is the logarithmic difference.

The estimated coefficients $\overline{\beta}_r$ represent the elasticities of regional employment relative to the European one: these coefficients turned out to be equal to or greater than one, at a significance level of 5 per cent, in 58 regions out of 145. The degree of explained variance was low, however: less than in similar regressions estimated by Decressin and Fatàs (1995). To be stressed again is that our regions are smaller than those examined in their study, so that common factors are consequently less important in our research, while idiosyncratic (local) elements are more significant: for example, if the territorial unit is small, it is more likely to be specialised in particular productions, and hence more sensitive to sectoral shocks.

Taking the 20 per cent of explained variance – obtained by Decressin and Fatàs on average for the European countries and compared by them with the 60 per cent achieved in the USA – as a benchmark, only in four countries was it possible to obtain similar values in our estimations: adj.–R^2 equal to 18.4 per cent for Italy, 25.1 per cent for Spain, 22.4 per cent for Portugal, and 23.7 per cent for the UK.[44] In the remaining countries, the adj.–R^2 were rather low, equal to 11 per cent even in Germany, and in some cases close to zero or negative.

This problem can be solved, again following Decressin and Fatàs, by considering national factors as well: for example, the effects of national fiscal and monetary policies. This can be done by introducing time dummies in panel data regressions with fixed effects. Such regressions can be estimated for each country (c) subdivided into regions (r), by letting the coefficients β_r vary across regions, while the coefficients γ_t^c are equal for all regions of the same country in a given year:

$$\Delta\log\left(N_{r,t}^c\right) = \alpha_r + \beta_r\Delta\log\left(N_t^{EU}\right) + \gamma_t^c T_t + \varepsilon_{r,t} \qquad (3.2)$$

where $N_{r,t}^c$ is total employment in region r belonging to country c in year t, T_t is the time dummy.

Table 3.5 presents the results for each regression (each country). Similar regressions were run for the twelve countries, for the 145 regions (altogether), and for the four clusters of regions obtained in Section 3.4.3. The table shows, for each regression, the number of cross-sections, the number of panel observations, the number of regions with an estimated coefficient $\overline{\beta}_r$ significant at least at 10 per cent, the adj.–R^2 and the adj.–R^2 obtained by excluding the time dummies.

Even with this specification, the average adj.–R^2 in our estimates is lower than the one obtained by Decressin and Fatàs, which was between 0.4 and 0.6 for most countries, enabling them to conclude that about half of total variance of employment dynamics in the European regions is explained by the model, i.e. by common European or national factors. In our estimates, adj.–R^2 of similar magnitudes were obtained for five or six countries only. It is also interesting to note in regard to the

---

[44] But excluding the 1991 observation for this country.

Table 3.5. Regressions: regional employment growth vs. EU12 (1983–97)

spatial unit	n. cross section	n. panel obs.	n. regions ß significant at 10%	n. time-dummies significant at 10%	R^2–adj.	R^2-adj. (no time-dummies)
Countries	12	152	0	0	0.28	0.33
All regions*	145	1749	55	3	0.27	0.21
Spain	17	187	5	7	0.66	0.35
Portugal	7	74	0	4	0.57	0.25
United Kingdom	8	104	1	3	0.55	0.22
Netherlands	12	119	0	11	0.44	–0.05
West Germany	31	403	6	2	0.43	0.10
Italy	20	260	0	0	0.38	0.23
Belgium	11	143	11	9	0.29	–0.03
Greece	13	125	0	0	0.08	0.03
France	21	273	6	1	0.02	0.01
cluster A	7	88	0	0	0.24	0.00
cluster B	22	229	0	0	0.18	0.14
cluster C	72	914	0	0	0.17	0.12
cluster D	42	496	0	0	0.26	0.25

* AR(1)'s coefficient is –0.24 (s.e. 0.03).

Source: elaboration on Eurostat data

last three columns of the table that, in some cases, the time dummies do not explain a significant fraction of the variance: this is the case of Italy, France, the ensemble of all countries and all regions, and of three clusters.[45]

The main conclusion of this section thus far is that – despite the increasing integration of European regions as confirmed by the results of the previous sections – a small fraction of the variance of regional employment dynamics is explained by common, national or continental, factors. Local, region-specific, elements are still most relevant: but what are their characteristics? Here only brief discussion is possible concerning the persistence of local shocks, which can be recovered from the residuals $\varepsilon_{r,t}$ of Eq. (3.1).

Consider the univariate process:

---

[45] In the case of the clusters and of the aggregate estimations (all countries and all regions), the obvious explanation is that the time-dummies cannot capture the national factors.

$$\varepsilon_{r,t} = \alpha_1 + \alpha_2 \varepsilon_{r,t-1} + \alpha_3 \varepsilon_{r,t-2} + \eta_{r,t} \tag{3.3}$$

and put all the regions in the same *pool* of 145 cross-sections by introducing regional fixed effects. We obtain estimated values of α_2 and α_3 equal respectively to –0.23 and –0.06, with standard errors of 0.02 for each parameter.

It thus seems that local shocks decline rapidly over time. A similar conclusion was reached by Decressin and Fatàs (1995), who obtained a slightly higher degree of persistence in the USA than in Europe, although in both areas local shocks did not seem to be very persistent in the long run.[46] The explanation for the differing results in the two areas is based on consideration of typical labour market adjustments in the two areas, which are brought about by labour mobility in the USA and by changes in labour force participation in Europe.

To return to our estimations, even when local shocks are obtained by excluding both community and national shocks, their degree of persistence remains low. For proof, add a first-order auto-regressive process in the pool of all 145 regions (Eq. (3.2) above): the AR(1) estimated coefficient in Table 3.5 confirms our statement.

3.6 Policy implications and conclusions

The foregoing empirical investigation of employment dynamics in 12 countries and 145 regions in Europe for the period 1983–97 allows us to highlight some *common* elements, principally the great transformations induced by long-run structural change and the international business cycle. The latter is, for example, the main cause of the widespread employment stagnation that affected the European countries after the 1992–93 recession. There were few exceptions, most notably Ireland. Another common element concerns more similar labour market reforms and more homogenous employment policies, which have already had noticeable effects on labour market performances in the most recent period. This issue has been only marginally discussed (also because of the limitations of our data set) in the introductory sections.

A first distinctive feature of national and regional employment evolutions is the sectoral composition. Indeed, even if we consider a three-sector disaggregation some specific characteristics of the main branches of activity emerge from the data. The cluster analysis has revealed that, apart from the top regions, the most dynamic European areas are the regions which began their tertiarisation process only after they had achieved a solid industrial position. The correlation analysis has shown that industrial employment is more closely correlated across countries and regions than is total employment.

The second feature highlighted by our investigations is the regional dimension. Another important conclusion of the cluster analysis is that national borders are

---

[46] By using two samples of 51 regions for both areas, in the period 1966–87, they obtained estimated values of α_2 and α_3 equal to –0.002 and +0.05 for Europe, +0.65 and –0.08 for the USA.

not always important as structural determinants, although they may be so in regard to institutional aspects and economic policies: in fact, structurally similar regions are to be found in different countries which are not necessarily spatially adjacent.

The correlation analysis seems also to reject the hypothesis of a core of more integrated countries or regions located in Central Europe: some Southern countries (Greece is a notable exception) and many regions of Southern Europe exhibit high correlation coefficients between their employment dynamics and the European (EU12) average.

It is true that a large amount, half or more than half, of the variance in regional employment changes is explained by neither European factors nor national ones, as confirmed by our panel data regressions; it is also true that, in general, regional correlations of employment dynamics with the European average are lower than national ones, since idiosyncratic shocks are more likely in smaller territorial units. Nevertheless, the international economic integration of most European regions is increasing over time, and some European regions, for example those of north-eastern Italy, are today more closely integrated with the rest of Europe than with the rest of the country.

There are several policy implications to be discussed. The first is that the decision to start with a large Monetary Union in Europe comprising 12 countries, including those of Southern Europe, has been not only a courageous political choice but is to some extent justified by the economic fundamentals.

The second implication is, however, that the weight of the idiosyncratic elements, i.e. the purely regional component of employment dynamics, points up the inadequacy of a common monetary policy in counteracting local shocks. The present institutional framework of EMU[47] – according to which the ECB's common monetary policy is assigned to stabilisation following symmetric or common shocks, while decentralised fiscal policies together with the other economic policy instruments should respond to specific national or local shocks – is fragile, owing to the difficulty of distinguishing between symmetric and asymmetric shocks (see Section 3.2.2).

Now, even if we are willing to admit that a differentiation of non-monetary policies, either fiscal or structural, is beneficial, it is important to stress that national differentiation is not always the most appropriate strategy. Our empirical results establish that, although spatial distinction is sometimes beneficial, regional differentiation is to be preferred to national differentiation in many circumstances. To be noted in passing is that, in the pre-EMU European setting, the exchange rate was not always an appropriate policy instrument, owing to differences in the productive specialisations within countries; hence the abolition of the exchange rate instrument within the EMU is not a great loss from this point of view.

Since structurally similar regions are not necessarily located within national borders but can be found in several countries, as we have shown, common Euro-

---

[47] See Buti and Sapir (1998). Note that this institutional framework has been defended on the basis of some theoretical arguments: for example that the centralisation of the monetary policy alone facilitates fulfilment of the objectives of monetary stabilisation and fiscal discipline.

pean policies could be designed to tackle the problems of 'similar' regions starting from sectoral characteristics (i.e. relative to sectoral specialisation), but possibly including many other aspects not analysed in this chapter: innovation, urbanisation, demographic evolutions, migratory flows, etc. For example, common policies might be devised for agricultural regions, industrialising zones, those marked by industrial decline, service-oriented metropolitan areas, etc.

One could argue that this approach already underpins EC Structural Funds in their present form. But this is only partially true, even without considering the problems of budget limitations and of reforms of the Funds made necessary by EU enlargement. The real issue is how to combine the long-run distributive goals of present-day Structural Funds, aimed at the convergence of less developed regions, with macroeconomic stabilisation goals by devising measures to foster the adjustment of the Euro-zone or some parts of it following exogenous shocks.

At the national level, these measures would compensate countries for their consent to removal of the exchange rate instrument and independent monetary policies; at the regional level. These funds would also counterbalance the costs of the increasing specialisation and regional concentration of production: if we agree with Krugman, at least for the first period of EMU, such costs could indeed be significant for the weakest peripheral regions of the EU.

The recent literature on monetary unions has suggested, on the one hand, the adoption of private-insurance or risk-sharing schemes to counteract idiosyncratic shocks, although such schemes sometimes produce distortions and are difficult to implement; on the other hand, automatic fiscal transfers have also been advocated, possibly together with centralisation of fiscal policy at the European level. However, such transfers are virtually absent not only in the present but also in the foreseeable future EMU setting. The 5–7 per cent threshold of the community's GDP to accommodate fiscal transfers for both equalisation and stabilisation purposes envisaged in 1977 by the well-known MacDougall Report seems almost nonsensical today.

Our proposal falls between the two solutions put forward in the literature: reform the Structural Funds in order to introduce some stabilisation elements, also by abating some other structural interventions, e.g. in the common agricultural policy. This idea is also less exposed to criticism than the schemes where equalisation prevails over insurance goals. In fact, some authors[48] have criticised fiscal transfers because they are inefficient: even at the national level – it is argued – they reduce labour mobility and hence engender a permanent 'non-adjustment' of regions hit by shocks. One could respond that distributive considerations cannot be ignored and that labour mobility itself is not always an efficient adjustment mechanism, especially if the shock is transitory and if account is taken of relocation costs; and in any case, labour mobility among European regions will remain at low levels in the immediate future.

It could be added that, from a 'political economy' perspective, an increase in the community budget allocated to these new types of funds, unlike the 'old' ones, should not encounter the outright opposition of the richest regions and countries.

---

[48] See Obstfeld and Peri (1998).

The new funds should be granted conditionally on the appearance of a shock affecting a given group of regions. They should be temporary in their duration, at least as far as the stabilisation component is concerned, and furnished having regard of the efficiency conditions.[49]

In contrast to the automatic fiscal transfers made at the national level, these new funds would have the advantage of supporting the adjustment of individual regions hit by shocks. They should consequently be preferred to a relaxation of Maastricht and Stability Pact criteria:[50] a loosening of such constraints on national budgets would be favourable if it concerned the national automatic stabilizers; less so if it induced discretionary fiscal policies not necessarily aimed at correcting unfavourable shocks affecting specific sectors or regions.

If the Structural Funds could be reformed, for example along these lines where the stabilisation purpose would accompany the redistributive one, their survival could be economically justified beyond the historical and political reasons of the 'acquis communitaire'.[51] Otherwise, in the opinion of many experts,[52] the only alternative would be the scaling down or abolition of such funds, also with a view to making room for the centralised provision of new public goods: defence, foreign policy, immigration policy and border patrol, etc.

In the event that, on the contrary, the subsidiarity principle is 'literally' followed in the future EMU setting and that structural policies, together with fiscal ones, continue to be assigned to the national level, then some European policy guidelines would be appropriate in this case as well, and likewise the existing macroeconomic stability and convergence plans. Such structural policy guidelines would provide operative recommendations – or possibly would establish behavioural rules for national governments – in the case of shocks or problems of structurally similar regions; thereafter the actual implementation would be more properly regional than national.

Other indications for future economic policies, with particular reference to regional policies, can be derived from our empirical results. But we prefer to return, in conclusion, to some analytical aspects of the chapter. An obvious extension of this study is investigation of a sectoral breakdown more disaggregated than the one used here, in order to assess the main evolutions within the manufacturing sector, even at the cost of losing detail in the regional disaggregation. A second extension – as soon as new data sets become available – is scrutiny of a longer time span which includes the five years following 1997, a period when important reforms were made to labour markets, and employment dynamics in Europe began to change.

---

[49] This to forestall the claim by public opinion and also some distinguished economists that 'much of the money spent on structural funds is wasted' (see Blanchard's comment on Obstelfd and Peri's paper, p. 250).

[50] A relaxation for this reason was suggested by Obstfeld and Peri (1998). Of course, some other justifications for loosening of the Stability Pact constraints, e.g. concerning public investment expenditures, may be more wise.

[51] European Commission (2002).

[52] See Tabellini (2003).

References

Artis MJ, Zhang W (1999) Further evidence on the international business cycle and the ERM: is there a European business cycle?. Oxford Economic Papers 51:120–32.

Bayoumi T, Eichengreen B (1993) Shocking aspects of European monetary integration. In: Torres F, Giavazzi F (eds), Adjustment and growth in the European Monetary Union, Cambridge University Press, Cambridge, pp 193–229.

Bean CR (1994), European unemployment: a survey. Journal of Economic Literature 32: 573–619.

Belke A, Gros D (1999) Estimating the cost and benefits of EMU: the impact of external shocks on labour markets. Weltwirtschaftliches Archiv 135:1–47.

Blanchard O, Wolfers J (2000) The role of shocks and institutions in the rise of European unemployment: the aggregate evidence. Economic Journal 110:C1–C33.

Boldrin M, Canova F (2001) Inequality and convergence in Europe's regions: reconsidering European regional policies. Economic Policy 32:205–45.

Buti M, Sapir A (eds) (1998) Economic policy in EMU, Clarendon Press, Oxford.

Caroleo FE (2000), Le politiche per l'occupazione in Europa: una tassonomia istituzionale. Studi Economici 55:115–152.

Cuadrado-Roura JR, Garcìa-Greciano B, Raymond JL (1999) Regional convergence in productivity and productive structure: the Spanish case. International Regional Science Review 22:35–53.

Decressin J, Fatàs A (1995) Regional labor market dynamics in Europe. European Economic Review 39:1627–1655.

De Grauwe P (2000), The economics of monetary union, Oxford University Press, Oxford.

De Nardis S, Goglio A, Malgarini M (1996) Regional specialization and shocks in Europe : some evidence from regional data. Weltwirtschaftliches Archiv 132:197–214.

Eichengreen B, Iversen T (1999) Institutions and economic performance: evidence from the labour market. Oxford Review of Economic Policy 15:121–138.

European Commission (2002) First progress report on economic and social cohesion. European Commission, Brussels.

Farina F, Tamborini R (2002) Le politiche macroeconomiche di stabilizzazione in Europa nel nuove regime di "unione monetaria". In: Farina F, Tamborini R (eds) Da nazioni a regioni: mutamenti istituzionali e strutturali dopo l'Unione Monetaria Europea, Il Mulino, Bologna.

Fatàs A (1997) EMU: countries or regions? Lessons from the EMS experience. European Economic Review, 41:743–751.

Forni M, Reichlin L (1997) National policies and local economies: Europe and the United States. CEPR Discussion Paper 1632.

Garibaldi P, Mauro P (2002) Anatomy of employment growth. Economic Policy 34:69–113.

Krugman P (1993) Lessons of Massachusetts for EMU. In: Torres F and Giavazzi F (eds), Adjustment and growth in the European Monetary Union, Cambridge University Press, Cambridge, pp 241–269.

Marelli E (2000a) Convergence and asymmetries in the dynamics of employment: the case of the European regions. Jahrbuch für Regionalwissenschaft/Review of Regional Research 20:173–200.

Marelli E (2000b) Istituzioni e politiche del lavoro: le tendenze in Italia ed in Europa. In: Marelli E, Porro G (eds) Il lavoro tra flessibilità e innovazione, F. Angeli, Milano, pp 287–340.

Marelli E (2004) Evolution of employment structures and regional specialisation in the EU. Economic Systems 28:35–59.

Marelli E, Porro G (eds) (2000) Il lavoro tra flessibilità e innovazione, F. Angeli, Milano

Marimon R, Zilibotti M (1998) Actual versus virtual employment in Europe: is Spain different?. European Economic Review 42:123–153.

Martin R, Tyler P (2000) Regional employment evolutions in the European Union: a preliminary analysis. Regional Studies 34:601–16.

Molle W (1997) The regional economic structure of the European Union: an analysis of long term developments. In: Peschel K (ed) Regional growth and regional policy within the framework of European integration. Physica, Heidelberg, pp 66–86.

Nickell S (1997) Unemployment and labor market rigidities: Europe versus North America. Journal of Economic Perspectives 11:55–74.

Nickell S, Layard R (1999) Labour market institutions and economic performance. In: Ashenfelter O, Card D (eds) Handbook of labor economics, vol 3. Elsevier, Amsterdam, pp 3029–3085.

Obstfeld M, Peri G (1998) Asymmetric shocks: regional non-adjustment and fiscal policy. Economic Policy 28:205–47.

Overman HG, Puga D (2002) Unemployment clusters across Europe's regions and countries. Economic Policy 34:115–147.

Paci R, Pigliaru F (1999) European regional growth: do sectors matter?. In: Adams J and Pigliaru F (eds) Economic growth and change. National and regional patterns of convergence and divergence, Elgar, Cheltenham, pp 213–235.

Pigliaru F (2001) Analisi della convergenza regionale: troppa o troppo poca?. In: Mazzola F, Maggioni MA (eds) Crescita regionale ed urbana nel mercato globale. F. Angeli, Milano, pp 86–129.

Tabellini G (2002) Principles of policymaking in the European Union: an economic perspective. CESifo Economic Studies 49:75–102.

Tondl G (1999) The changing pattern of regional convergence in Europe. Jahrbuch für Regionalwissenschaft 19:1–33.

4 Does Space Matter for Labour Markets and How? A Critical Survey of the Recent Italian Empirical Evidence

Mario A. Maggioni[1] and Francesca Gambarotto[2]

[1] Catholic University of Milan, Italy
[2] University of Padua, Italy

4.1 Introduction[*]

As the cultural and political focus shifts from the nation state to sub-national (e.g. provinces and regions) and supranational aggregations (e.g. the EU), numerous theoretical and empirical studies have shown that spatial clustering heavily influences the efficiency and effectiveness of labour market policies and interventions. This can be explained by a series of local economic and institutional factors that hinder or assist the achievement of particular policy goals.

The local clustering of economic activities can be a competitive advantage for an economic system, since collective wage bargaining procedures, firms' training processes, activity rate and unemployment levels (to name just a few) are affected by local customary informal norms. Moreover, some major market distortions (adverse selection and moral hazard) can be resolved, or at least reduced, by institutional collective mechanisms such as trust, diffused cooperative habits, and social capital. Agglomeration economies may also play a negative role, however, for entrenched cliques of local firms may adopt path-dependent behaviour which gives rise to rent-seeking: in this case the existence of local institutional mechanisms may prevent the achievement of specific policy targets.

The aim of the chapter is accordingly to disentangle the relationship between firms' location decisions and labour market functioning, the purpose being to evaluate how spatial variables affect the expected impact of labour policies.

---

[*] This chapter draws on a previous paper by the same authors (Gambarotto, Maggioni 2003) where the emphasis was more on empirical than on policy analysis. Thanks are due to G Brunello, M Nosvelli, P Pini and to the participants at the Aiel Conference in Salerno (September, 2002) and the Aisre conference in Reggio Calabria (October, 2002) for their useful comments and observations. Financial support from Cofin Miur 2003 project (no. 2003131274) 'Dinamica strutturale: imprese, organizzazioni, istituzioni' and from the bilateral project "integrated actions" funded by the Science, Research and Technology ministries of Italy and Spain is gratefully acknowledged.

We believe that the large body of literature on regional science and industrial economics, with its particular focus on the Italian case and the industrial district, is a good starting point for identifying the characteristics of local labour markets.

The chapter identifies a major divide in the literature between the functional (endogenous) and standard (exogenous) definitions of the object of inquiry (namely the area termed the 'local labour market'). This twofold taxonomy can be used to distinguish between two bodies of analysis. On the one hand are studies on 'travel to work areas' and other functional partitions of the territory identified in light of the commuting behaviour of workers and the functional specialisation of firms (as in the classical tradition of Italian industrial districts). On the other hand are studies which take for granted the standard division of sub-national units of land (regions, provinces, counties, boroughs, etc.) and either measure a series of indicators of labour market performance – looking for some convergent or divergent behaviour of lower level territorial units belonging to a common upper level (whether national or European) – or examine the effects of centripetal and centrifugal forces of firms' location on local employment and wages (as in the new economic geography tradition).

The advantages and drawbacks of the two approaches will be identified both from a purely academic perspective (i.e. the advantages of in-depth single case study-analysis versus cross-sectional econometric studies of large transnational datasets) and from that of the policy-maker.

A section showing the existence of a strict causality relation between a given analytical framework and the consequent economic policy instruments implemented by the public authority (with some examples of current practices of local labour policies) concludes the chapter.

4.2 Firms' location and the labour market

The locational choices of firms are crucial for economic growth because they shape the geographical distribution of economic activities: that is, they determine the concentration or dispersion of production, and the process of regional integration or separation. Theoretically, three main factors affect firms' location choices and the geographical organisation of economic activities: agglomeration economies, market size, and transportation costs.

Agglomeration economies produce economic advantages via knowledge and pecuniary externalities. The clustering process is such that production is organised through the territorial coordination of firms, frequent interactions, and technological diffusion. At the same time, pecuniary advantages stemming from local backward and forward connections among firms spur investments and cooperation, as well as complementary productions. The spatial density of firms locally affects the characteristics of the labour market (skills, competence accumulation, educational levels, training investments). At the same time, it affects the job expectations of workers, their mobility, and labour-market participation by the active population.

Besides agglomeration economies, also market size, increasing returns, and economies of scale play a crucial role in the functioning of local labour markets.

When firms become larger, because of economies of scale, they become more efficient. Due to the increased productivity they are able to produce a larger output and enlarge their market by increasing their exports. This Kaldorian growth mechanism, produces the spatial concentration of firms, an increase in the labour demand and, consequently the population growth in the region thanks to migration inflows. In this way, the regional economic base expands and regional GDP rapidly grows. The result of these spatial dynamics of economic variables is a core/periphery pattern of regional growth divergence between favoured and less-favoured regions.

Transportation costs may also affect the locational choice of firms. Theoretically, when transportation costs are high, firms tend to cluster because proximity reduces the transportation of inputs/outputs. Of course, there is an upper limit to agglomeration economies above which congestion and diseconomies arise. In the opposite case – low transportation costs – firms located far from business centres suffer a low marginal effect of distance on profit. In this case a dispersed industrial geographical pattern dominates the economic landscape. However, is there empirical evidence for a different geographical pattern? when transportation is taken into account: industrial agglomerations take place even with low transportation costs, because of path-dependencies and agglomeration advantages. Transportation costs affect migrations and commuting behaviour within local labour markets, even if the commuting behaviour depends upon a set of worker characteristics such as gender, job types, and educational levels.

Finally, agglomeration is the spatial outcome of both market enlargement and product differentiation. A higher demand level and increasing opportunities for outsourcing and subcontracting on a scale larger than the regional one boost economic efficiency and competitiveness. Moreover, specialisation and product differentiation attract particular skills and competencies, giving rise to pooling and poaching processes in the local labour market.

Agglomeration is not the only source of advantages, however. The polarisation of economic activities and inputs (capital and labour) entails geographical inequalities, given that poor economic areas are extraneous to the concentration process. This means that the European integration process may have the unintended outcome of increasing regional differences instead of reducing them. The European geographical distribution of economic activities displays this unbalanced growth pattern along a core-periphery trend. According to some observers, this calls for policy solutions intended to achieve more convergent development, especially since monetary union and market enlargement. Policy-makers rely on the creation of economic opportunities to produce competitiveness and social cohesion via a policy of regional integration. Which means that attention must focus on the transmission of knowledge, the production of innovation, and the exploitation of local comparative advantages within the European market. Moreover, regional inequalities depend on the geographical concentration or dispersion of production, i.e. on the spatial organisation of economic activities largely dependent on firms' capacity to exploit internal a/o external economies of scale.

The geographical pattern of economic activities arising from firms' location decisions shapes the features of regional labour markets. The specialisation/diversification and agglomeration/dispersion of production affect regional labour market dynamics because they require the development of specific characteristics: for example, the accumulation of certain technological competencies, the educational level of workers, the presence of atypical labour contracts, and the relevance of informal recruitment channels. In other words, factors such as: firms' propensity to adopt technological innovations, their cooperative/competitive attitude, the local endowment of social capital, and the existence of relational goods, have crucial effects on the regulation mechanisms of the local labour market.

As a consequence, location features can act either as mechanisms which reinforce labour policies geared to fostering local development and reducing regional divergences, or as mechanisms which weaken them because they hamper organisational and technological innovations. Policies addressed to local labour markets mismatch must take account the existence of path-dependence phenomena and of specific local mechanisms for coordinating economic activities. The labour market is thus location-specific and its flexibility depends partly on the spatial characteristics embedded in the institutional context. Social norms, conventions and relational endowments contribute to the endogenous development of every region, doing so either positively or negatively.

4.3 The importance of the definition of the territorial unit

The definition of the basic unit is not as straightforward in territorial empirical analyses as it is in other areas of economic inquiry. Regions are irregular in terms of population, economic size, and geographical extension, and their choice as the territorial unit? may have various policy implications. This becomes evident if the focus of the analysis centres on disparities, for spatial inequalities have been shown to be sensitive to the definition given to 'region' (Brülhart and Traeger 2003).

This problem is often referred to as the 'modifiable areal unit problem' (MAUP). This concerns the arbitrariness of the geographical partition used and implies that the results of statistical analysis for territorial areas vary according to the boundaries used. Arbia (1989a) shows that contrasting and paradoxical results can be obtained when using statistical measures that neglect the consequences to which the MAUP gives rise. The MAUP can introduce a bias into any statistical measure, a bias which will depend on the units selected whenever they are? modifiable (which is the case in territorial analyses).

The problem is twofold: on the one hand, the best aggregation scale must be chosen (scale problem); on the other, units must be correctly assigned to the right area (aggregation problem).

As regards the scale problem, the same data set may produce different results according to whether it is grouped at the individual, NUTS 3, NUTS 2, NUTS 1, etc., level. When a single variable is examined across regions, the conclusions will depend on the territorial scale selected; furthermore, when the correlation between two or more variables is studied, its value will depend crucially on the territorial scale adopted. This spatial dependence diminishes as larger areas are chosen.

As far as the aggregation problem is concerned, statistical results are sensitive to the shape of the chosen territorial unit. Given the number of territorial units that it is decided to use, the conclusions will depend on the shape of their borders. Again, the value of a single variable or of the correlation between variables will depend crucially on the way in which regions are defined.

In real life, far from the theoretical abstractions of optimal spatial partitions, there is a great deal of evidence for the validity of the 'first law of geography' (Tobler 1970), which states that nearby areas are more similar than distant ones, with the corollary that raising the geographical level of analysis (from the local to the regional; from the regional to the national) inevitably reduces variance and increases the correlation between any pair of variables.

Consequently, the basic territorial unit can be fixed either exogenously or by the dynamics of economic relationships. The regional partitioning which organises the national territory at different administrative levels may be unsatisfactory when it segments the territorial coherence of an economic phenomenon. Normally, administrative data sets collect population and industry census information and other macroeconomic variables (GDP, unemployment, education, and so on) in order to describe a region's economic performance and its economic structure. However, a partition with unchanging regional boundaries may miss information on the territorial dimension of firms' and workers' behaviour and its variability during time. Statisticians have sought to remedy this shortcoming by using a territorial partition endogenously defined on the basis of commuting behaviour.[1] They are thus able to observe the dynamics of spatial and economic behaviour and obtain a finer-gauge description of the distribution of economic activities.

In such conditions, conclusions based on the standard statistical measures are not absolute; they are only relative to the particular administrative partition used, and they may vary significantly. From an operational point of view, this requires the researcher to have the most disaggregated level of source data possible, so that the analysis take account of variations in the results due to the different geographical partitions used.

4.4 Endogenous perspectives on local labour markets

The analyses of local labour markets and their dynamics now discussed adopt an endogenous territorial partition: that is, they define the spatial dimension according to firms' and workers' location behaviour. Two statistical perspectives can be distinguished within the endogenous approach: the 'institutional-economic' approach developed by Italian scholars of Marshallian industrial districts, and the statistical-functional approach originating from Anglo-Saxon geographical studies.

The **institutional-economic** approach is often associated with the industrial district (ID) perspective. It addresses the competitiveness of SME agglomeration

---

[1] As described in some detail in Section 4.4.

by focusing on the coordination of competencies and knowledge, and on the efficiency of the local division of labour. The spatial boundaries of the ID are plotted on the basis of firms' interaction dynamics and proximity. Agglomeration economies stemming from firms' networking and labour market pooling are crucial for an industrial cluster's competitiveness, and they depend on two basic cognitive factors: the alignment of absorptive capacity of individual perceptions, and the sharing of a common environment (Cohen and Levinthal 1990). Together with social capital, these elements foster innovation diffusion, cooperation on production and distribution, and spin-offs. The population of firms in the ID is able to withstand exogenous shocks by virtue of the ID's flexible division of labour arising from the variety of contractual forms and the widespread use of temporary and part-time work arrangements, home working and, in particular, subcontracting. The negative side-effect of this division of labour is the instability of jobs and the more uncertain temporal horizon that it produces for individuals (Storper and Walker 1989; Scott 1988; Storper and Scott 1990). However, these negative outcomes are more than off-set by the social embeddedness of economic relationships: as Becattini (1987, 1989) puts it, IDs are bounded economic units wherein social norms and rules substitute for the formal guarantees normally required by large firms for worker recruitment. As a consequence, economic relationships differ from place to place because regulation mechanisms arise from local formal and informal institutional routines: hence, history matters for the coordination and implementation of the local institutional set-up (Digiovanna 1996).

Traditional ID scholars state that it is impossible to describe the operation of IDs using statistical indexes and econometric estimates, given that local factors are bound up to such a large extent in economic performance that they give rise to a distinctive production function. This implies that the observation of empirical facts involves qualitative description rather than formal tests and quantitative measures. This, however, is a 'theoretical weakness' because on the one hand it is difficult to identify general rules or common features, while on the other, it is difficult to refine and/or improve the plethora of definitions, concepts and new theoretical categories by means of robustness analyses (Plummer and Taylor 2001; Signorini 2000). Besides the numerous case-studies describing the economic geography of IDs, a more recent statistical stream of research led by Banca d'Italia takes a different approach and grounds the study of IDs on quantitative methods. The aim of these studies is to measure the *district effect*, that is, the impact of agglomeration economies on an individual firm's efficiency, on labour cost, on production specialisation, and on cluster entry and exit options (Signorini 2000; Fabiani et al. 1998; Pellegrini and Fabiani 1998).

Using different information sources,[2] these studies estimate, for each firm, a parametric production function with capital and labour factors and two independent causal variables, one of which captures the district effect, i.e. the technical ineffi-

---

[2]   The Istat (1996) LLS dataset was used and the IDs were extrapolated from the 1991 partition. A sample of firms producing in thirteen manufacturing sectors and belonging to IDs was extrapolated from the Centrale dei Bilanci dataset (1991–1995). Pellegrini and Fabiani (1998) additionally crossed this information with the Cerved and Inps datasets.

ciency level with respect to the production frontier of the manufacturing sector. Econometric analysis reveals that the Becattini hypothesis is fairly robust: on average, firms belonging to an ID have an efficiency level 2–4 per cent higher than firms producing in the same sector but not located in an industrial cluster. A less straightforward result has been obtained using labour cost analysis: on the one hand, the per capita labour cost is lower for ID workers, which contradicts the theoretical hypothesis, while on the other, the average wage for blue collars is higher, which confirms it. This result can be easily explained by the fact that ID firms recruit workers with flexible contractual forms.

The regression reveals three further labour features: female labour-market participation is particularly high in IDs and displays high tenure levels even though it is associated with lower wages. Young people, too, have easier access to the ID labour market. Job turnover is high and a shift from worker to entrepreneur status is also observed, especially at mature working stages.

Whilst these stylised facts corroborate the theory on industrial districts, numerous scholars are sceptical that the district effect can be considered a residual factor. These empirical analyses say nothing about socio-economic factors such as social capital, reputation, local formal institutions, which are of crucial importance for the economic performance of IDs and play a key role in industrial organisation. Moreover, case-studies concentrate on the stock-flow process of institutional and economic variables but neglect to determine whether the same elements do not perform the same role in other territorial areas.

The second empirical approach – the **statistical-functional** one – includes analyses adopting the travel-to-work-areas (TTWA) method. The attractive feature of this regionalisation method is that it is a bottom-up procedure based on an economic function. The TTWA regionalisation method stems from the interest of many scholars – economists, geographers, statisticians – in spatial phenomena as constitutive properties of local labour markets (Brown and Holmes 1971; Bellacicco 1992; Coombes 2000; Martini 1993; Erba 1998; Erba and Capelloni 1994, Arbia 1989a, 1989b, 1993). The latter are usually defined on the basis of three factors: the spatial self-containment of the local population's dwellings and jobs, the spatial contiguity of areas affected by commuting flows, and a gravitational principle. Whilst this kind of partition is attractive because it defines a functional area, it nevertheless has an number of shortcomings because the regional identification depends on subjective criteria like the minimum threshold of commuting.[3]

Operationally, a geographical area is defined as a TTWA if 75 per cent of the local population lives and works within the same territory. This implies that the spatial dimension of the economic organisation changes over time because the area's economic performance, planning decisions by local policy-makers, and variation in the local infrastructure stock affect the commuting behaviour of residents. The administrative partition, on the other hand, is defined by a top-down

---

[3] This statistical definition has been criticised for lacking a microeconomic analysis of local labour markets and for excluding technological innovation effects on physical mobility (see King 1972).

procedure and is non-modifiable even when a change in the spatial dimension of economic activities is observed.

There are two statistical methods that enable definition of homogenous areas: the single and the multi-step procedures. The former adopts a single criterion of partition and may be limited by a lack of aggregations or an excess of multiple aggregations. The latter procedure requires a contiguity constraint for spatial partition. This assumption introduces a statistical distortion into the partition technique because it is already included in the self-containment function in order to guarantee the area's compactness.

Widely used in American and English territorial analyses, the TTWAs is also employed for labour market analyses. Coombes et al. (1988) use functional areas of this kind to examine differences in commuting behaviour among different socio-economic groups of workers, observing that workers do not compete for the same labour market. The commuting gradient produced by their analysis shows that at one extreme managers and professionals display long-distance commuting behaviour, while at the other extreme, low-skilled workers prefer to commute over short distances in order to reduce their transportation costs. However, the mobility patterns emerging from the study may partly depend on planning and on local transportation infrastructures. TTWAs have also been used to estimate local 'job shortfalls', that is, the difference between the expected change in the active population and the real change in the employment level (Owen and Green 1989; Owen et al. 1984; Green and Owen 1991; O'Donoghue 2000). The labour market 'accounts' technique is adopted to estimate the 'employment deficit', which is a measure of the mismatch between employment change and labour supply increase. This measure, calculated for each TTWA and for the period 1971–1981, synthesises (i) demographic change (in the active population, migrations), (ii) economic change (increasing participation by the active population), and (iii) employment change (changes in the number of employed and unemployed residents, structural change in unemployment) with respect to the imbalance between changes in labour supply and demand. The emerging spatial patterns of labour market variations vary considerably, from fast economic growth with both employment surplus and increasing unemployment (due to in-migration) to patterns characterised by economic decline, the extent of which depends on workers' reactions: in some cases the unemployed population prefers to maintain unemployed status instead of migrating, either for social reasons (social embeddedness) or because they have positive expectations of sectoral growth.

TTWAs have also been used to observe differences in American workers' spatial patterns on the basis of their educational level, labour market experience, gender and race (Bound and Holzer 2000). The authors show that during the 1980s workers adjusted spatially to demand shocks taking into account their job expectations and the cost of migration. Given that migration costs and expectations vary among groups with different skills, it follows that demand shocks affect the relative supply of different local jobs but not the structure of local labour demand.

Istat (1997) introduced the TTWA spatial partition for Italy in 1997. The new functional regions have been called *Italian local labour systems* (LLS), and stylised facts have been identified and interpreted by reorganising the national census data (Sforzi 1987, 1997; Istat-Irpet 1989; Istat 1997, Frey et al. 1998). Moreover, given that industrial districts (IDs) are a subset of LLSs, this partition can be used for comparative analyses between IDs or between industrial districts and other local systems without ID features.[4]

The LLSs used by Italian economic geographers corroborate the existence of a North-South path-dependency: the divergence in growth rates persists although the geographical partition exhibits a marked spatial heterogeneity in both sector and employment dynamics (Pellegrini 2001). Comparison between the two census datasets and the corresponding LLS partitions shows that they expanded and numerically decreased during the ten years observed. More precisely, the re-aggregation process reduced the number of LLSs (from 955 in 1981 to 784 in 1991) located in the central-southern regions (Marche, Lazio, Abruzzo, Molise, Campania and Sicily), and in the North-eastern ones (Veneto, Friuli).

This process depends partly on a reorganisation of manufacturing which has led to less labour-intensive production for large firms and growing labour demand by SMEs. In fact, those LLSs also defined as IDs record high employment growth, especially in the business services industry (80.4 per cent) (see Table 4.1), while in the case of local systems comprising large firms, the increase in business services is below the national mean (44.3 per cent), and the employment level in manufacturing is decreasing (–29.5 per cent) rapidly.

Table 4.1. LLS employment changes in industry and services, 1981–1991 (percentages)

Local system	Industry					Services		
	Agriculture and fishing	Construction	Mining	Manufacturing	Producer	Consumer	Social	Traditional
small firm	18.05	34.3	16.03	17.06	80.4	50.5	45.1	31.6
small-medium firm	–6	16	–13.8	1.02	51	24.3	19.4	6
large firm	23.04	5.02	10.04	–29.5	32	10.6	3.3	–5.3
other local system	17.01	7.09	–26.4	–10.6	42.4	9.2	13.2	3.9
Italy	**–7.1**	**11.08**	**–15.6**	**–10.6**	**44.3**	**15.2**	**14.6**	**4.6**

Source: Istat (1997)

---

[4] Istat (1996) identified ID areas according to the following criteria (i) local specialization: the employment level in the manufacturing sector with respect to total non-agricultural employment must be above the national mean; (ii) SME system: the proportion of manufacturing employment in firms with fewer than 250 workers must be greater than the national mean; (iii) industrial concentration: employment in a particular manufacturing sector must be higher than the national mean; (iv) the local system is an industrial district: for locally concentrated sectors, employment in small firms must be above the national mean.

Geographically, these SMEs are clustered in regions ranging from the North-East through the central regions and the Adriatic corridor to the Puglia region. This new spatial pattern highlights a new distribution of employment and economic activities where a larger economic-geographical area participates in GDP.

On the basis of this geographical partition, Paniccia (2002) selects twenty-four Italian IDs by combining demographic and economic census data with qualitative information collected by means of interviews. She shows that ID features vary over time in terms of both territory and division of labour. Consequently, IDs cannot be reduced to a simple set of characteristics. Industrial districts are evolving production organisations where agglomeration economies and labour relationships change over time in order to ensure the ID's dynamic stability. Three crucial factors emerge when variance is analysed: the level of agglomeration, the degree of integration between specialised manufacturing and local services, the extent of the division of labour with respect to firms' size. Proxies for these factors are the indexes of concentration and specialisation, and the local division of labour. In order to measure ID performance, Paniccia adds a competitiveness measure, turnover, employment change in the local dominant sector, the local community's level of well-being, and infrastructure endowment. Four categories of IDs emerge from the statistical exercise: *integrated industrial districts* where the number of white collars exceeds the number of blue collars, there is a low rate of home working, a low level of education, few subcontracting relationships, and a propensity to substitute informal labour relationships with subcontracting ones; *service-oriented industrial districts* with a high concentration of the production and distribution of business services: here the unemployment rate is very low; *canonical industrial districts* with a low level of tertiary and white collar workers: the production system consists of a large number of small and micro-firms, and large families predominate demographically; *embryonic industrial districts*, mainly concentrated in the central-southern area of the country: their characteristics are: high unemployment rates, low population participation, and a low educational level; firms are of small size and are linked with enterprises located in the North of the country.

Bruni and Ceccarelli (1995) and Nosvelli (1999) identify local labour markets on the basis of local labour markets behavioural homogeneity, rather than the production specialisation. They describe ID performance by measuring labour flows between three different worker conditions: employed, unemployed, and not in labour force.

The 'geography' of local labour markets is applied to the Lombardy labour markets during the period 1989–1996. The following ID taxonomy resulted from the labour market analysis: ID with an *active* labour market (there is both a growing labour force and a relevant job searching activity); ID with a *mixed* labour market (the employment level and the non labour force increase as well as the unemployment level); ID with a *growing* labour market (the employment level increases more than the other flows), ID with an *inactive* labour market (where only the non labour force increases), ID with a *crisis* labour market (the labour force increases only due to the increase in the unemployment level); ID with a *depressed* labour market (both the unemployed and the individuals not in the labour force increase).

Volpe (2001) focuses on labour mobility in conducting an empirical investigation of IDs located in the provinces of Treviso and Vicenza within the Veneto region. Compared to the previous study, this one is more concerned to depict the intra-area features of mobility, showing that ID areas do not display the greater labour mobility claimed by the theory. Moreover, labour market features differ between the core and ring areas of the ID: younger workers, women, and a high turnover predominate in the ring, while more highly skilled workers with longer tenure are located in the core.

The structural heterogeneity of LLSs has been organised by Pacinelli (1998) into five clusters using the 1991 Istat partition and 41 indicators from the industrial census. The first cluster comprises 30 per cent of the LLSs with self-containment of the labour market greater than 80 per cent, most of them located in the North and Centre of the country; the second comprises 11 per cent of the LLSs producing for the primary sector, all located in the South; the third has 22 per cent of the LLSs comprising urban and tourist agglomerations: these are mainly located in the North and central areas, with very few of them in the South; the fourth has 10 per cent of LLSs, located in the North macro-region and with few jobs; the fifth one comprises 27 per cent of the LLSs, mainly distributed in the mountains and hills with very restricted labour markets.

4.5 Exogenous perspectives on local labour markets

The term 'exogenous' in the title to this section refers to a perspective (or a set of approaches) which examines local labour markets in terms of exogenously given criteria. Two main approaches (namely the statistical-bureaucratic approach and the economic modelling approach) analyse labour market dynamics within territorial units, which they take for granted, and then compare their relative performances cross-sectionally without questioning the existence and position of their borders.

According to the older of the two approaches, the **statistical-bureaucratic** approach, 'local' means solely 'sub-national'. Thus, by 'local labour markets' is meant the labour markets of territorial administrative units (such as provinces, regions etc.) which exist below the national level. The approach is widely used by European-level macroeconomic analyses of employment and unemployment disparities among the various European regions, which are defined according to either national rules or Eurostat's 'artificial regions': the NUTS (Nomenclature of Territorial Units for Statistics) which divides the economic territory of the European Union (EU 15) into a hierarchically defined system consisting of 72 regions at NUTS 1 level, 213 regions at NUTS 2 level and 1091 regions at NUTS 3 level.

Most empirical analyses of Italian local labour markets which use this approach focus on regional disparities in unemployment, and with special regard to the wide gap between the country's North and South (the '*Mezzogiorno*').

Two studies published at the beginning of the 1990s (Attanasio and Padoa Schioppa 1991; Bodo and Sestito 1991) emphasise the significance of the North-South divide and highlight the role played by limited internal migration flows in the persisting disequilibrium among local labour markets and the pro-cyclical evolution of the divide. More recently, Faini et al. (1997) have identified several causes for the relative labour immobility which characterises Italy: high mobility costs (with especial reference to the housing market), information asymmetries and imperfections in the labour market, the existence of skill mismatch, and the level of public income transfers to the *Mezzogiorno*.

Although it is indisputable that the (large and increasing) North-South divide is the prime feature of the Italian labour market – indeed, it is described as its most important 'stylised fact' by the IMF (Prasad and Utili 1998) – this prominent feature often conceals the existence of more complex and multifaceted scenario which should be analysed at a lower territorial level such as the regional or the provincial ones.

Amendola et al. (1999) examine the historical evolution (1960–1994) of several indicators of labour market performance at different territorial levels. They analyse in particular the index of relative unemployment (calculated as the ratio between the unemployment rates at the regional and national levels) of four macro-regional areas: North-West, North-East, centre and *Mezzogiorno*, finding that whilst the North-West and centre display a pro-cyclical trend, the North-East and Mezzogiorno shows a similar but opposite acyclical one (unemployment steadily decreases in the North-East owing to the economic development of the area and the growth of local production systems,[5] and it steadily increases in the *Mezzogiorno* owing to the scarcity of production investments (lack of firms locating in the area). Amendola et al. therefore suggest that the unemployment behaviour of these areas has little to do with the supply side of the labour market (namely, population dynamics and labour supply); rather, it depends heavily on the demand side, i.e. changes in the production structure of the macro-regions driven by the simultaneous existence of a widening gap in productivity levels and a convergence of wage levels. Their analysis is completed with a dynamic principle component analysis (Statis technique) at the provincial level which confirms that the dualistic performance of the Italian labour market is due to the different production structures of different provinces (with specific regard to the share of manufacturing and services and to the level of economic development). A similar conclusion is reached by the IDSE 'Structural Change Report' (Idse-Cnr 1999), which – on the basis of a long-term empirical analysis (1951–91) – states that 'a balanced industrial composition and the spatial diffusion of SMEs' produces both good firms' performance and growing employment.

Taylor and Bradley (1997) compare the evolution of regional disparities in the 1983–94 period in three major European countries (Italy, Germany and the UK) with dualistic national labour markets. Their analysis, conducted at the NUTS 2 level, shows the importance of the economic structure in determining the employment performances of the three countries examined, but with significant country-specific differences. For example, relative specialization in manufacturing is correlated with good regional employment performance in Italy but with bad regional performances in Germany and the UK. Moreover, analysis of the top five

---

[5] Mainly consisting of SMEs and often referred to as 'industrial districts'.

and bottom five regions shows that regional disparities in labour costs and in the industry-mix are of greatest importance in explaining the employment performances of the Italian regions.

This conclusion has been partly contradicted by Martin and Tyler (2000), who examine a large number of European countries for the period 1976–1998, and by the OECD's 'Employment Outlook' (OECD 2000). Both of these studies conduct a shift-share analysis and conclude that the influence of the production structure on the behaviour of local labour markets is no less important than other institutional factors.

Brunello et al. (2001) use a database for the period 1960–94 to examine unemployment dynamics in Italian regions and to identify the causes of unemployment divergences between northern and southern Italy. They conduct three distinct analyses looking at the role played by, respectively, asymmetric shocks, wage determination mechanisms at the regional level, and workers' and firms' mobility. The results of the first analysis show that public transfers to southern households have a double negative effect of reducing the incentive to migrate and increasing the reservation wage. The second analysis finds empirical evidence for the leading-area hypothesis in that it demonstrates that the relationship between regional unemployment and wage level becomes insignificant for the South once the unemployment level of the leading region (the North-Centre) has been controlled for. The results of the third analysis show that labour mobility is explained by the following factors (with the elasticity values in brackets): the wage gap between North and South (2.78), the extent of public transfers (0.35) and the increase in the southern level of unemployment (0.19). By means of a beta convergence analysis, Brunello et al. show that, between 1985 and 1993, whilst regional unemployment levels increasingly diverged, the firms' location process displayed significant convergence, thus demonstrating that southern Italian unemployment cannot be explained mainly in terms of labour demand conditions.

Baffigi (1999) uses a mixed system of analysis which (for the period 1981–1995) clusters exogenously defined spatial areas (such as the Italian provinces) into seven groups endogenously defined by the average level and long-term trend of each local labour market.[6] This analysis is able to show that, besides the oft-cited North-South divide, there is a variety of local labour market patterns (ranging from the crisis in Liguria to the relative success of Benevento, Lecce, Siracusa, and a significant part of Sardinia).

The **economic modelling** approach,[7] regards the dynamics of local labour markets as being strictly interconnected with the location choices of firms. Whilst the geographical distribution of goods demand and labour supply is one of the main

---

[6] Thus the taxonomy ranges from progressive and high-performance provinces (such as Pesaro, Arezzo, Ferrara, Padua, Rovigo, Treviso, Venice and Verona), mainly located in the North-east, to regressive and low-performance provinces (such as Imperia, L'Aquila, Potenza, Cosenza, Naples, Foggia, Taranto, Agrigento, Catania, Enna, Messina, Palermo and Trapani), mainly located in the south.

[7] This can be considered an empirical spin-off of the New Economic Geography (mostly theoretical) approach.

drivers of firms' location decisions, the geographical distribution of labour demand and goods supply is correspondingly one of the main drivers of household location decisions. Thus, although this approach has the advantage that joint consideration is made of location factors of importance to the firm (transport costs, scale economies, market demand) and location factors which are of importance to the worker (mainly wage levels and vacancy characteristics), and does so in a general equilibrium perspective, it nevertheless still considers the geographical units to be exogenously given (and often characterised by very different production structures). Workers and firms are free to locate and relocate in an exogenously given and abstract geographical space.

In 1990, just before the advent of the 'New Economic Geography' approach,[8] Fujita proposes a fourfold taxonomy of all theoretical attempts to fit space into economic theory (with special reference to the problem of firms' and workers' location). Fujita (1990) classifies the economic literature on the spatial issue into four main groups: comparative advantage, oligopolistic interaction, non-price interactions, and monopolistic competition. The first group, of clear Ricardian origin,[9] comprises studies on the non-uniform ex-ante distribution of resources which derive the location decisions of economic agents from transport cost minimisation algorithms. The second group[10] examines the location strategic decisions of a limited number of large-sized economic agents which take as given the spatial distribution of demand (i.e. of consumers). The remaining two groups of studies can be seen as the origins of the 'new economic geography' approach, for which both non-price interaction and (above all) monopolistic competition explain the location decisions of firms and workers.

In its simplest version (set out in Krugman 1991a) the core/periphery model works as follows. The location pattern of economic activity (which includes both firms and workers) is the product of three forces, two centripetal and one centrifugal, the first two being the desire of firms to locate close to the largest possible market and of workers to have access to the largest number of goods, and the third one being the desire of firms to serve the peripheral agricultural market.[11] The existence and persistence of the geographical concentration of industrial activity therefore depends crucially on the interaction among three parameters describing the share of manufactured goods in total expenditure,[12] the level of transportation costs, and the extent of scale economies.

Unlike the well developed theoretical models of the 'new economic geography' approach, its empirical side is still in its early stages. This applies all the more to

---

[8] Which is commonly regarded as being the publication date of the two seminal studies by Krugman (1991a, 1991b).

[9] With explicit references to the *least cost* approach of the location theory literature (from Weber 1929 to Hoover 1948; from Palander 1935 to Isard 1956).

[10] Which expressly draws on the demand side approach to location theory (from Fetter 1924 to Lösch 1954, via Hotelling 1929).

[11] This is an analytical device used by Krugman to deal elegantly with congestion and competition on immobile resources.

[12] As opposed to the share of locally produced and consumed agricultural goods.

such analysis of the Italian production structure as to be found in the domestic and international economic literature. Mancini (2000), Barbieri et al. (2001), Maggioni (2002) and Maggioni and Bramanti (2001) focus on the clustering patterns of economic activity, while Decressin and Fatàs (1995), Puhani (2001) and Murat and Paba (2001) concentrate on the causes and effects of migration patterns.

Mancini (2000) conducts a simple exercise in which the (employment-based) concentration index proposed by Krugman (1991a) is calculated for a series of sub-sectors within two traditionally-known clustered industries (textiles and non-metallic minerals), some of the so-called 'Made in Italy' industries selected for the differing impacts of transport costs on the prices of final goods and the extent of scale economies. The analysis yields results compatible with the prediction of Krugman's model: several industries in the textile sector (such as the spinning, weaving and finishing industries) display a high degree of geographic concentration which is explained in terms of a low effect of transport cost on the unit price. In the non-metallic minerals industry, various activities (such as glass, ceramics, bricks) also display significant clustering due to the existence of high fixed costs in production which give rise to important economies of scale.

Barbieri et al. (2001) argue that the use of concentration indexes as empirical tests of the core-periphery model suffers from several serious drawbacks: the heavy dependence of these indexes on the selected territorial unit of analysis,[13] the intrinsic limitation of a static analysis, and the ambiguous interpretation of results which may be compatible with alternative theoretical explanations. As a partial solution to the second problem, Barbieri et al. propose the joint use of a concentration, or inequality, index (the Gini index) and an agglomeration index (Moran's I index) according to Table 4.2.

Table 4.2. Different evolution patterns of an industry and development models

		Changes in agglomeration	
		+	−
Changes in concentration	+	(1) core/periphery	(2) natural and non-mobile resources
	−	(3) growth pole	(4) diffusion and de-glomeration

The analysis is based on changes for the period 1991–1996 in forty-seven industries measured at the level of local labour systems, and it shows that most Italian manufacturing industries evolve towards higher agglomeration and lower concentration, a finding compatible with Perroux's growth pole theory. Three traditional sectors (leather, footwear and clothing) display an evolutionary pattern compatible with Krugman's core/periphery model, whilst two sectors (the same

---

[13] This issue is discussed above under the heading of 'MAUP' (the modifiable area unit problem).

industries analysed by Mancini 2000) record a slight decrease in both the agglomeration and concentration indexes.[14]

Maggioni (2002) focuses on the clustering patterns of five high-tech industries[15] in four OECD countries (Italy, France, the UK, the USA) and uses two 'middle/low-tech' industries (motor vehicles and textiles) as benchmarks. His analysis, based on census data for both employment and local units and performed on two different variables (employment and number of firms) and two different levels of territorial aggregation,[16] shows that concentration, inequality and specialisation measures depend heavily on the level of data aggregation and the variable chosen. Moreover, Maggioni uses an OLS cross-section estimation to show that, in general, scale and agglomeration economies (as suggested by Krugman, 1991) work together in determining the industrial specialisation of a region and that scale economies usually prevail over agglomeration economies.

Maggioni and Bramanti (2001) draw on Hallet (2000) to analyse the effects of EU financial and economic integration, using a perspective complementary to that of Barbieri et al. (2001). They focus on two orthogonal perspectives dealing with the clustering phenomenon: the first concerns industries, the second concerns regions; so that it is possible to inspect the effects of EU integration on changes in the industrial specialisation of the European regions, or alternatively on changes in the regional concentration of European industries. The resulting fourfold taxonomy is set out in Table 4.3.

Table 4.3. Different evolutions of the EU integration process

		Changes in industrial concentration	
		+	−
Changes in	+	(1) Industrial district Europe	(2) Natural resources and rural Europe
regional specialisation	−	(3) Core-periphery Europe	(4) 'Backyard capitalism' autarkic Europe

When Hallet's results (2000) are interpreted using the framework set out in Table 4.3, one finds that, whilst most European regions (between 1980 and 1995) have increased their specialisation, different industries have evolved in radically

[14] Services also evolve in a composite manner: production services exhibit a 'core/periphery' pattern while financial services exhibit a 'growth pole' one.

[15] Aerospace, Computers and office machinery, Electronic components, Pharmaceuticals, and Scientific instruments.

[16] Termed FLAs (First Level Areas, viz.: county in the UK, *département* in France, *provincia* in Italy, state in the US) and SLAs (Second Level Areas, viz.: region in the UK, *région* in France, *regione* in Italy, census division in the US).

different ways (with increasing, decreasing, non-monotonic and even random patterns).

Decressin and Fatàs (1995), Puhani (2001) and Murat and Paba (2001) examine how migration flows react to changes in the production structure. Decressin and Fatàs (1995) concentrate on local labour markets (NUTS 3) and show that idiosyncratic shocks are absorbed in Europe through changes in the participation rate, while similar shocks in the US are absorbed through interregional labour flows. The same results are obtained by Bentivogli and Pagano (1999). Puhani (2001) uses a different level of analysis (NUTS 2) and studies the behaviour of regional labour markets in three large European countries (Italy, France, Germany) for the period 1980–1996. His results show that, given an increase in the unemployment rate, after one and a half years, 30 per cent of it is off-set by labour force migration in Germany, 8 per cent in France, and only 4 per cent in Italy.

An alternative viewpoint on labour migration is offered by Murat and Paba (2001), who consider the consequences on labour migration flows of the structural changes which affected the Italian economy between 1951 and 1991. These authors show that – besides the traditional explanation in terms of wage gaps and the existence of family networks, accounting for many of the inefficiencies in labour mobility as an mechanism adjusting local labour market imbalances in contemporary Italy –one must take into account the role played by major structural changes such as the change from Fordism to post-Fordism, or the change from large corporations of the North-western 'industrial triangle' to the system of SMEs which constitute thi industrial districts: the fabric of the 'Third Italy'.

4.6 Policy implications and conclusions

Location and agglomeration factors play an increasingly crucial role in labour policies, especially in Europe. Regional disparities due to local deficits and different social capital endowments influence the effectiveness of local bargaining and local development (Maggioni and Nosvelli 2003).

Even though empirical studies on local labour markets are heterogeneous and lack robustness, one observes that area bargaining (territorial agreements or negotiated programming at local level) is a device to foster economic development that has become part of the public actor's 'tool box'. The principle that the efficacy of an economic policy is associated with the sub-national (regional and local) territorial dimension is now widely accepted, and it is also supported by the European Union. The Structural Fund policy and local labour market policies are devices designed to support economic development and employment: they act via the establishment of economic conditions able to contain and reduce local negative occupational phenomena, such as low active population participation, high unemployment rates, a marked mismatch between labour demand and supply, strong unemployment hysteresis, and so on. The European Union's recommendations concerning the territorial dimension have been reiterated by the *Libro bianco sul mercato del lavoro in Italia,*[17] which urges regions and local institutions to draw up regional and local employment plans. Besides the usual passive employment policies (unemployment benefits and other social security 'shock absorbers'), these institutions encourage the devising of local active employment policies aimed at creating worker 'employability' via the promotion and development of vocational training (Campbell 2000; Antonelli and Paganetto 1999; Antonelli and Nosvelli 2002).

However, if the aim is to make labour allocation more efficient and to reduce the social costs of unemployment, it must be borne in mind that industrial policy can also play a major role in the process. Policies are required that can both improve the competitiveness of local systems and increase labour demand. The goal of workfare therefore depends also on behaviour of employers, which in these days may often be confined to monitoring financial market trends and pays relatively little attention to the potentially negative effects exerted on final demand by cost reduction strategies centred on wage flexibility (Lunghini 2001; Sestito 2001). As there are marked structural and cycle differences between geographical areas in terms of employment and employability, it is of crucial importance to measure local sensitivity to economic policy interventions (Campbell 2000; Casavola and Utili 2002) in order to identify the most efficacious mix.

The four approaches used here to outline various perspectives on the structure and dynamics of labour markets can be arranged in a taxonomic table (Table 4.4), the purpose of which is to highlight the different goals pursued by the intervention instruments available to public decision makers willing to design and implement a series of relevant labour policies. Although Table 4.4 is not intended to be comprehensive, it highlights various properties of labour policy interventions: their main ingredients, strengths and weaknesses, implications in terms of efficacy/efficiency/fairness, and clarity/contradictions.

The functional-statistical approach sets out to describe local labour market characteristics on the basis of workers' commuting behaviour and the gravitational level of labour demand in relation to the professional figures demanded. This approach seeks the maximum level of local spatial interactions in order to identify the boundaries of an area comprising most of the relationships between labour supply and demand. For this reason, it views labour policy instruments from a microeconomic perspective focused on demand – that is, on internal dynamics – and aimed at removing the obstacles against the free circulation and mobility of individuals and information within the restricted, but functionally identified, area of the local labour market.

The institutional-economic approach emphasises the positive role of agglomerative externalities and social capital in the local dynamics of district labour markets. It consequently considers labour policies in close connection with policies supporting social and relational capital growth, and with shared technological and productive knowledge and abilities. Moreover, because industrial districts are

---

[17] White paper on the labour market in Italy (Ministero del Lavoro e delle Politiche Sociali 2001)

Table 4.4. Instruments and targets of active labour policies at local level

Instruments	Approaches			
	Statistical-bureaucratic	Statistical-functional	Institutional economic	Economic modelling
	Key factors unemployment rate regional competitiveness	Key factors commuting gravitational principle	Key factors Local labour market Industrial District's effect Social capital	Key factors transport costs factors mobility/immobility scale economies/increasing returns
Infrastructural and mobility policies	aimed at reducing regional disparities in unemployment rate	aimed at improving the internal transport and logistic infrastructure	aimed at improving the external transport and logistic infrastructure of the industrial district	aimed at changing workers mobility and at reducing transport costs
Educational and training policies	aimed at reducing structural unemployment and deskilling		aimed at maintaining a local pool of tacit knowledge and specific competences a/o at creating new industrial specialisation	aimed at changing workers mobility
Information and access to work policies	aimed at managing/controlling interregional migration flows	*inter-area mobility* aimed at reducing information asymmetries and mismatches in the labour market	*intra-area mobility* aimed at reducing information asymmetries and mismatches in the local labour market	
Entrepreneurship and local development policies	aimed at fostering the development of local entrepreneurship in order to increase the level of labour demand and self-employment rate (concentration vs. dispersion)		aimed at fostering the development of local entrepreneurship in order to strengten the ID structure (specialisation) or at developing a competitive advantage based on labour costs	aimed at fostering the development of local entrepreneurship and at increasing the level of agglomeration economies
Equal opportunities policies	aimed at reducing dualism, segregation and discrimination within provinces and regions	aimed at reducing dualism, segregation and discrimination in the LLM	aimed at reducing dualism, segregation and discrimination in the Industrial Districts	

mostly export-based, the policies proposed by this approach are intended to strengthen infrastructural connections and to improve/maintain local competitiveness by means of greater labour contract flexibility.

The statistical-administrative approach studies the non-homogeneous territorial distribution of national and European unemployment levels. It offers a macroeconomic and geographical description of the structure and dynamics of labour relationships in Italy and emphasises the role that local bodies and institutions – with a fair balance between decisional autonomy and horizontal and vertical coordination (i.e. the subsidiarity principle) – must play in planning, implementing and evaluating economic labour policy interventions. For these reasons, this approach views the goals of local labour policies as being essentially the management and control of macroeconomic variables within an unresolved dilemma between efficiency and equity often converted into a plurality of contradictory interventions which support the competitiveness of the advanced regions while at the same time attempting to reduce the gap between core and periphery (Overman and Puga 2002).

The economic-modelling approach seeks to explain the structure and dynamics of local systems and their labour markets by means of a microeconomic analysis of workers' and firms' behaviour. It consequently views local labour policies as interventions able to modify (successfully or otherwise) certain key features of the economic system and of actors' behaviour (transport expenses, trend towards mobility, urbanisation-regionalisation economies).

Each approach offers a mix of explanatory variables of the relationship between spatial phenomena and employment dynamics. None of them can be defined as better than the others, not even in terms of policy. Methodological plurality is after all a guarantee, and especially so when the aim is to manage, to adopt and adapt, both in different economic contexts and different territories, a set of active labour policy instruments able simultaneously to ensure economic development, employment creation while maintaining (a/o improving) labour quality.

References

Amendola A, Caroleo FE, Coppola G (1999) Differenziali territoriali nel mercato del lavoro e sviluppo in Italia. In: Biagioli M, Caroleo FE, Destefanis S (eds) Struttura della contrattazione. Differenziali salariali e occupazione in ambiti regionali. ESI, Napoli, pp 345–387.

Antonelli G, Paganetto L (1999) Disoccupazione e basso livello di attività in Italia. Il Mulino, Bologna.

Antonelli G, Guidetti G, Leoncini R, Novelli M, Pombeni L, Zamparini L (1998) Apertura dei mercati locali del lavoro e fabbisogno di risorse umane da parte delle imprese. F. Angeli, Milano.

Antonelli G, Nosvelli M (eds) (2002) Monitoraggio e valutazione delle politiche del lavoro per una 'nuova economica'. Il Mulino, Bologna.

Arbia G (1989a) Spatial data configuration in statistical analysis of regional economics and related problems. Kluwer, Dordrecht.

Arbia G (1989b) Diseguaglianze territoriali. Rassegna Economica 3:569–595.

Arbia G (1993) Recenti sviluppi nella modellistica spaziale. In: Zani S (ed.) Metodi statistici per le analisi territoriali. F. Angeli, Milano, pp 193–217.

Attanasio O, Padoa Schioppa F (1991) Regional inequalities, migration and mismatch in Italy, 1960–1986. In: Padoa Schioppa F (ed.) Mismatch and labour mobility. Cambridge University Press, Cambridge, pp 237–324.

Baffigi A (1999) I differenziali territoriali nella struttura dell'occupazione e della disoccupazione: un'analisi con dati a livello provinciale (1981–1995). In: Biagioli M, Caroleo FE, Destefanis S (eds) Struttura della contrattazione differenziali salariali e occupazione in ambiti regionali. Collana AIEL. ESI, Napoli, pp 319–344.

Barbieri G, Pellegrini G, Paradisi F (2000) Diffusion and concentration of growth in Italy. Journal of Cities and Regions, Urban Development Special Issue:11–20.

Becattini G (1989) Modelli locali di sviluppo, Il Mulino, Bologna.

Becattini G (ed.) (1987) Mercato e forze locali: il distretto industriale, Il Mulino, Bologna.

Bellacicco A (1992) Local labour markets identification: a unified point of view. Labour 6:127–149.

Bentivogli C, Pagano P (1999) Regional disparities and labour mobility: the Euro-11 versus the USA. Labour 13:737–760.

Bodo G, Sestito P (1991) Le vie dello sviluppo. Il Mulino, Bologna.

Bound J, Holzer HJ (2000) Demand shifts, population adjustments, and labour market outcomes during the 1980s. Journal of Labour Economics 18:20–54.

Brown LA, Holmes J (1971) The delimitation of functional areas, nodal regions and hierarchies by functional distance approaches. Journal of Regional Science 11:58–61.

Brülhart M, Traeger R (2003) An account of geographic concentration in Europe. University of Lausanne, mimeo.

Brunello G, Lupi C, Ordine P (2001) Widening differences in Italian regional employment. Labor Economics 8:103–129.

Bruni M, Ceccarelli D (1995) I mercati locali del lavoro: un modello per l'analisi congiunturale. F. Angeli, Milano.

Campbell M (2000) Reconnecting the long term unemployed to labour market opportunity: The case for a 'local active labour market policy'. Regional Studies 34:655–668.

Casavola P, Utili F (2001) Promozione di partnerships locali per incoraggiare lo sviluppo locale: una valutazione preliminare dei patti territoriali. Sviluppo Locale 9:3–30.

Cohen WM, Levinthal DA (1990) Absorptive capacity: A new perspective on learning and innovation. Administration Science Quarterly 35:128–152.

Coombes MG (2000) Defining locality boundaries with synthetic data. Environment and Planning A 32:1499–1518.

Coombes MG, Green AE, Owen DW (1988) Substantive issues in the definition of 'Localities': Evidence from sub-group local labour market areas in the West Midlands. Regional Studies 22:303–318.

Decressin J, Fatàs A (1995) Regional labour market dynamics in Europe. European Economic Review 39:1627–1655.

Digiovanna S (1996) Industrial districts and regional economic development: a regulation approach. Regional Studies 30:373–86.

Erba A (1998) Definizione di aree e di indicatori per la misurazione della dotazione di infrastrutture. Parte I: la definizione delle aree. In: Istituto Tagliacarne, Statistica e territorio. F. Angeli, Milano, pp 245–259.

Erba A, Capelloni L (1994) L'individuazione dei mercati del lavoro locale. In: Documenti CNEL, Norme e metodi sul mercato del lavoro 41:49–80.

Fabiani S, Pellegrini G, Romagnano E, Signorini LF (1998) L' efficienza delle imprese nei distretti industriali italiani. Sviluppo Locale 9:42–73.

Faini R, Galli G, Gennari P, Rossi F (1997) An empirical puzzle: falling migration and growing unemployment differential among Italian regions. European Economic Review 41:571–579.

Fetter FA (1924) The economic law of market areas. Quarterly Journal of Economics 39:520–529.

Frey L, Croce G, Tagliaferri T (eds) (1998) Mercati del lavoro locali e politiche dell'occupazione e del lavoro. Quaderni di economia del lavoro 60. F. Angeli, Milano.

Fujita M (1990) Spatial interactions and agglomeration in urban economics. In: Chatterji M, Kuenne RE (eds) New frontiers of regional science. Macmillan, London, pp 184 – 221.

Green AE, Owen DW (1991) Local labour supply and demand interactions in Britain during the 1980s. Regional Studies 25:295–314.

Hallet M (2000) Regional specialisation and concentration in the EU. European Commission Economic Paper 141.

Hoover EM (1948) The location of economic activities. McGraw-Hill, New York.

Hotelling H (1929) Stability in competition. Economic Journal 39:41–57.

Idse-Cnr (1999) Trasformazioni strutturali e competitività dei sistemi locali di produzione. Rapporto sul cambiamento strutturale dell'economia italiana. F. Angeli, Milano.

Isard W (1956) Location and space-economy. MIT Press, Cambridge (Mass.).

Istat–Irpet (1989) I mercati locali del lavoro in Italia. F. Angeli, Milano.

Istat (1996) Rapporto annuale. La situazione del Paese nel 1995. ISTAT, Roma.

Istat (1997) I mercati locali del lavoro. ISTAT, Roma.

King JE (1972) Labour economics. The Macmillan Press, London.

Krugman P (1991a) Geography and trade. MIT Press, Cambridge (Mass.).

Krugman P (1991b) Increasing returns and economic geography. Journal of Political Economy 99:483–499.

Lösch A (1954) The economics of location. Yale University Press, New Haven.

Lunghini G (2001) Politiche eretiche per l'occupazione. In: Lunghini G, Silva F, Targetti Lenti R (eds) Politiche pubbliche per il lavoro. Il Mulino, Bologna, pp 35–44.

Maggioni, MA (2002) Clustering dynamics and the location of high-tech firm. Physica, Heidelberg.

Maggioni MA, Bramanti A (2001) Le macroregioni europee e le politiche per lo sviluppo 'locale'. In: Quadrio Curzio A (ed.) Profili della Costituzione economica europea. Il Mulino, Bologna, pp 475–528.

Maggioni MA, Nosvelli M (2003) La cultura dei sistemi produttivi territoriali tra formazione e innovazione. In: Osservatorio Impresa e Cultura (ed) Cultura e competitività per un nuovo agire imprenditoriale. Rubettino, Catanzaro, pp 307–347.

Mancini A (2000) Una verifica del Modello di Krugman per l'Italia. In: Del Colle E, Esposito GF (eds) Economia e statistica per il territorio. Introduzione all'analisi operativa delle economie locali. F. Angeli, Milano, pp 81–83.

Martin R, Tyler P (2000) Regional employment evolutions in the European Union: a preliminary analysis. Regional Studies 34:601–616.

Martini M (1993) Metodi statistici per la costruzione di aree funzionali. In: Zani S (ed.) Metodi statistici per le analisi territoriali. F. Angeli, Milano, pp 122–141.

Ministero del Lavoro e delle Politiche Sociali (2001) Libro bianco sul mercato del lavoro in Italia. Proposte per una società attiva e per un lavoro di qualità. Ministero del Lavoro e delle Politiche Sociali, Roma.

Murat M, Paba S (2001) Flussi migratori e modelli di sviluppo industriale. L'esperienza italiana dal dopoguerra agli anni '90. In: Lunghini G, Silva F, Targetti Lenti R (eds) Politiche pubbliche per il lavoro. Il Mulino, Bologna, pp 305–337.

Nosvelli M (1999) I mercati locali del lavoro: un'analisi dei distretti lombardi. Economia e Lavoro 33:63–89.

O'Donoghue D (2000) Some evidence for the convergence of employment structures in the British Urban System from 1978 to 1991. Regional Studies 34:159–167.

OECD (2000) Employment outlook. OECD, Paris.

Overman HG, Puga D (2002) Unemployment clusters across European regions and countries. Economic Policy, 34:117–147.

Owen DW, Gillespie AE, Coombes MG (1984) 'Job shortfalls' in British local labour market areas: a classification of labour supply and demand trends, 1971–1981. Regional Studies 18:469–88.

Owen DW, Green AE (1989) Labour market accounts for travel-to-work areas, 1981–1984. Regional Studies 23:69–72.

Pacinelli A (1998) Sull'autocontenimento del lavoro nei sistemi locali del lavoro dell'Italia peninsulare. Un'analisi esplorativa dei SLL dell'Italia peninsulare. Economia & Lavoro 32:73–90.

Paniccia I (2001) Industrial districts: evolution and competitiveness in Italian firms. Edward Elgar, Aldershot.

Pellegrini G (2001) Polarizzazione dello sviluppo e vincoli di prossimità nell'economia italiana: Un'analisi empirica a un livello territoriale molto disaggregato. In: Mazzola F, Maggioni MA (eds) Crescita regionale ed urbana nel mercato globale. Modelli, politiche, processi di valutazione. F. Angeli, Milano, pp 158–174.

Pellegrini G, Fabiani S (1998) Un'analisi quantitativa delle imprese nei distretti industriali italiani: redditività, produttività e costo del lavoro. L'industria 4:811–831.

Plummer P, Taylor M (2001) Theories of local economic growth (part 1): concepts, models and measurement. Environment and Planning A 33:219–236.

Prasad ES, Utili F (1998) The Italian labour market: stylized facts, institutions, and directions for reform. IMF Working Paper 9842.

Puhani PA (2001) Labour mobility. An adjustment mechanism in Euroland? Empirical evidence for Western Germany, France and Italy. German Economic Review 2:127–140.

Scott A (1988) New industrial spaces. Pion, London.

Sestito P (2001) Le politiche del lavoro in Europa e in Italia: alcune considerazioni critiche. In: Lunghini G, Silva F, Targetti Lenti R (eds) Politiche pubbliche per il lavoro. Il Mulino, Bologna, pp 21–33.

Sforzi F (1987) L'identificazione spaziale. In: Becattini G (ed.) Mercato e forze locali: il distretto industriale. Il Mulino, Bologna, pp 143–168.

Sforzi F (1997) Il cambiamento economico nel sistema urbano italiano. In: Dematteis G, Bonavero P (eds) Il sistema urbano italiano nello spazio unificato europeo. Il Mulino, Bologna, pp 205–241.

Signorini FL (ed.) (2000) Lo sviluppo locale. Un'indagine della Banca d'Italia sui distretti industriali. Meridiana-Donzelli, Roma.

Storper M, Scott A (1990) Work organization and local labour markets in an era of flexible production. International Labour Review 129:513–531.

Storper M, Walker R (1989) The capitalism imperative, Basil Blackwell, Oxford, UK.

Taylor J, Bradley S (1997) Unemployment in Europe: A comparative analysis of regional disparities in Germany, Italy and the UK. Kyklos 50:221–245.

Tobler W (1970) A computer movie simulating urban growth in the Detroit Region. Economic Geography 46 Supplement:234–240.

Volpe M (2001) La mobilità del lavoro e la fedeltà al distretto. In: Tattara G (ed.) Il piccolo che nasce dal grande. F. Angeli, Milano, pp 130–189.

Weber A (1929) Theory of the location of industry, Chicago University Press, Chicago.

5 Labour Market Reform and the Beveridge Curve across Italian Regions

Sergio Destefanis and Raquel Fonseca

University of Salerno, Italy

5.1 Introduction[*]

According to the OECD (1994, 2000), Italy used to be, together with Spain, one of the countries with the highest labour market rigidity indexes in the OECD. The situation has quite recently undergone some change: labour legislation (on part-time work, temporary employment, fixed-term contracts, and similar flexible arrangements) was modified and the share of non-standard over total employment in Italy changed from 5.4 per cent in 1983 to 7.8 per cent in 1997 to 10 per cent in 2000. This chapter investigates to what extent the recent changes in Italian labour legislation, and in particular the so-called Treu Act (a law which considerably eased the regulation of temporary work and fostered its growth in Italy), have affected the unemployment-vacancy relationship across regional and skill labour markets. Although the Treu Act aroused considerable interest in the press and among labour market participants, to date extensive scientific analysis of its effects has not been conducted.

Previous studies on this de-regulation process include Adam and Canziani (1998), who examined labour policy measures in the 1980s. In particular, they analysed fixed-term training contracts and compared the economic impact of their de-regulation in Italy against the Spanish case: fixed-term training contracts have been widely used in Spain whereas their adoption has been more limited in Italy. More recent studies include Nannicini (2004a, 2004b), and they centre on temporary employment in Italy. Nannicini (2004a) analyses the diffusion of this type of 'non-standard' employment (legalised by the Treu Act) at industry level. He concludes that industries using temporary employment have experienced a more marked after-liberalisation decrease in their share of permanent employment. Nannicini (2004b) analyses the tendency of temporary work to become permanent in certain industries. Closer to our concerns here are the studies by Centra et al. (2001) and by Ichino et al. (2005), who analyse temporary work at regional and

---

[*] We are very grateful to drs. Malgarini from ISAE, Mocavini and Paliotta from Isfol, Pirrone and Sestito from Ministero del Lavoro for kindly providing us with data on vacancies, and useful feedback on our research. The usual disclaimer applies. Financial support from MIUR, Italy is also gratefully acknowledged.

skill level, investigating region by region the duration of temporary work and its probability of becoming permanent.

We investigate whether the liberalisation of employment protection laws has improved matching between vacancies and the unemployed at the regional and skill level. The general idea put forward is that with higher flexibility, both hirings and firings may be easier for the firm, with an ambiguous final effect on labour market tightness. As job turnover increases, labour market tightness may increase or diminish depending on different heterogeneities across jobs, regions and workers: shifts in the Beveridge Curve may subsequently be indeterminate.

Our analysis is also of interest because the unemployment–vacancy relationship has been very seldom analysed in the Italian literature, mainly because of the lack of official vacancy data, and estimates of the Beveridge Curve are essentially non-existent since 1990. We adopt a fairly recent empirical approach: the matching function, re-parameterised as a Beveridge Curve, is modelled and estimated as a production frontier.

In empirical labour economics, the efficiency of labour markets has often been analysed by means of matching functions. Furthermore, the interpretation of the matching function as a production function is quite common, and some research has sought to reveal the micro foundations of this 'black box' (see Petrongolo and Pissarides 2001). However, only recently has the matching function been used to analyse matching efficiency with the tools of production frontier analysis (after the seminal study by Warren 1991, see Ibourk et al. 2001, for France; Fahr and Sunde 2002, for Germany; Ilmakunnas and Pesola 2003, for Finland).

We apply this relatively novel technique to Italian data,[1] with the effects of the Treu Act as the main focus of interest. We concentrate on the 1993–2000 period, adopting the ISAE labour scarcity indicator as a measure for vacancies. Our evidence shows that the Treu Act did indeed generate a higher vacancy supply, especially in the North and Centre of Italy, but also a slight outward shift of the Beveridge Curve in the South of Italy. As a consequence, it may be concluded that the Treu Act reduced unemployment in the more developed regions of the country.

The chapter is structured as follows. Section 5.2 provides a fairly brief account of the main features of the Treu Act, as well as its main implications in the light of Pissarides (1990, 2000). Section 5.3 considers the relationships between matching functions and production frontiers, introducing the empirical specification adopted, while the Italian literature on the Beveridge Curve is surveyed in Section 5.4. Data and econometric results are presented and commented on in Section 5.5. Section 5.6 contains some concluding remarks.

---

[1] To the best of our knowledge, the first application of frontier analysis to the Italian labour market is to be found in Destefanis and Fonseca (2004).

5.2 Labour market reform and matching efficiency

In recent years one of the main structural changes to have affected OECD economies has been the advent and success of previously uncommon types of employment contracts (part-time, temporary employment, fixed-term contracts, and similar).[2] In Italy, non-standard employment has grown to significant proportions only very recently. It is widely believed that the Italian labour legislation enacted during the 1960s and 1970s produced a system characterised by high hiring and firing costs.[3] In practice, these regulatory rigidities were bypassed by means of various forms of flexibility, some specific (the lay-off scheme known as *Cassa Integrazione Guadagni*), others *ad hoc* (industrial rescues) or informal (shadow economy). Yet, a slow drift to non-standard employment had already begun by the late 1980s, and a decisive legislative measure in favour of non-standard employment was enacted in the late 1990s: Law 196/1997, the so-called *legge Treu* (Treu Act, which took the name of the then minister of Labour and Welfare, Tiziano Treu). In particular, the Treu Act legalised temporary work agencies (Law 196/1997, articles 1–11). In the typical employment relationship ensuing a temporary work agency hires a worker (usually for a fixed term) with a view to placing him/her in a client firm for a temporary assignment. This kind of relationship was forbidden in certain cases: the substitution of workers on strike; firms that had made collective dismissals in the previous twelve months; firms experiencing a time-of-work reduction; jobs requiring medical supervision. The Treu Act does not impose a limit on the cumulated duration of temporary contracts or legal reasons for using temporary labour, leaving the implementation of such regulations to collective bargaining. Collective agreements usually stipulate that temporary workers cannot exceed 8–15 per cent of the normal workforce (depending on the industry) and state some acceptable reasons for their use: peak activity; one-off work; expertise not available within the firm. According to the collective agreement for agency workers, firms cannot extend an individual contract more than four times and for a cumulated period longer than 24 months.

The Treu Act, whose actual implementation took place in the second half of 1998, brought about decisive growth in the number of temporary workers, who already numbered 250 000 in 1999 and 470 000 in 2000 (Confinterim 2000). Temporary, fixed-term employment rapidly expanded, particularly in manufacturing and in the more developed northern regions of Italy.

The impact of the Treu Act on the diffusion of non-standard employment naturally calls for evaluation of the economic and social effects of this new institution. An obvious question, which has already been analysed by some studies (Centra et al. 2001; Ministero del Lavoro e delle Politiche Sociali 2001, pp. 123–25; Nannicini 2004a, 2004b; Ichino et al. 2005) is whether temporary work leads to some kind of permanent employment relationship. To be asked more generally is whether temporary work enables entry into the formal labour market by workers previously excluded from it. Most of the uncertainty relating to the economic out-

---

[2] See on this Felstead and Jewson (1999).
[3] See OECD (1994), Bertola and Ichino (1995), Sestito (1996).

comes of the Treu Act boils down to the following questions. Does the greater flexibility implied by temporary work increase the chances of the unemployed finding jobs, but also the probability of a subsequent job separation? And which is the stronger of the two effects? A novel and potentially interesting approach to this issue involves the modelling and specification of matching functions.

The matching function is based on the idea that the existence of frictions in the labour market means that firms (jobs) and workers can match each other only with some delay (this account is largely based on the approach developed in Pissarides 1990, 2000). New matches between workers and jobs produce new hirings, a process which can be described by the following function:

$$H_{it}=h(U_{it-1},V_{it-1})e_{it} \tag{5.1}$$

where i are the units defining the labour market (areas, industries, occupations), t is the time period, H are hirings, U the number of job-seekers (here proxied by the unemployed) and V the number of vacancies. Higher levels of e_{it}, usually defined in the literature as the efficiency term, bring about higher H_{it} levels, for given U_{it-1} and V_{it-1} stocks. This term is influenced by the search intensity of firms and workers, by the effectiveness of search channels, by the labour mismatch across micro markets defined over areas, industries or skills. Obviously, it is extremely important to ascertain whether it varies over time and across categories.

There is a growing body of literature which analyses the implications of short-term contracts for unemployment (Saint-Paul 1996 is a very important reference in this field). A key intuition concerns the role of screening devices performed by fixed-term contracts (Jovanovic 1979, 1984), which should enable employers to observe the productivity of the job-worker pair during a maximum probation period and thus improve matching efficiency. For our purposes here, a particularly important study is Wasmer (1999), which uses a matching model à la Pissarides with two kinds of jobs in order to explain the increasing share of non-standard employment across Europe. Wasmer concludes that the rise in the share of non-standard jobs shifts the Beveridge Curve to the right, because a larger number of job vacancies is required to keep employment constant. However, in order to determine the total effect of the diffusion of non-standard work on unemployment, one must also examine its impact on firms' supply of vacancies. Depending on the probability for a worker with temporary contract of obtaining the renewal of a temporary contract, or a permanent contract, the vacancy supply curve moves rightwards or leftwards, and the total effect on unemployment is ambiguous.

Section 5.5 explores the explanatory power of this framework, concentrating on the impact of the de-regulation of employment protection legislation on the Italian Beveridge Curve during the 1990s. The production frontier set-up will allow the focus to be trained on the possible differences arising at the regional level.

5.3 Matching functions and production frontiers

Some interesting studies have conducted empirical analysis of the matching function by exploiting the close conceptual and analytical resemblance between this function and the commonly adopted production function. Consider again Eq. (5.1). If the estimation of this function concentrates on the term e_{it}, its evolution and its determinants, then the analysis can profit from the methodologies developed in the field of stochastic production frontiers (see in particular Kumbhakar and Lovell 2000).

Stochastic production frontiers are based on the assumption that the technical efficiency of a productive unit is measured by the distance between the input and output mixes observed for the unit itself and the input and output mixes on the point of the production frontier relevant to the observed unit. In the case of the matching function, consider Fig. 5.1, where various mixes of U_{it-1} and V_{it-1}, all of them able to produce the output H_{0t}, are considered along an isoquant.

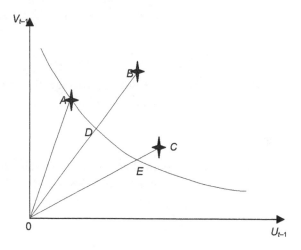

Fig. 5.1. The matching function as an isoquant

Obviously, the U_{it-1} and V_{it-1} combinations on the isoquant are efficient points. For each value of U_{it-1} on the isoquant they single out the minimum V_{it-1} value consistent with obtaining H_{0t}, and vice versa. It will always be possible to obtain H_{0t} for U_{it-1} and V_{it-1} values higher than those on the isoquant, but this will not be technically efficient. Then, both points B and C are inefficient, while A is technically efficient. Adopting the measure of technical efficiency proposed in Farrell (1957), that is, the largest radial input contraction consistent with obtaining a given output (in this case H_{0t}), the technical efficiency of C is $0E/0C$, that of B is $0D/0B$ and that of A is $0A/0A$. The last, being fully efficient, has an efficiency score equal to one. On the other hand, the technical efficiency of C is higher than that of B, which is situated further away from the isoquant.

This framework can be utilised not only to measure the distance of each observation from the isoquant, but also to assess which factors determine the efficiency of these observations. More precisely, consider for simplicity the following specification (it is assumed that panel data are available):

$$h_{it} = \alpha + \mathbf{x}_{it-1}\boldsymbol{\beta} + \varepsilon_{it} - \upsilon_i \tag{5.2}$$

where h_{it} is the natural log of H_{it}; $\mathbf{x}_{it-1}$ is the vector containing the natural logs of U_{it-1} and V_{it-1}; $\boldsymbol{\beta}$ is a parameter vector; ε_{it} is a stochastic variable assumed to be iid. $N\left(0, \sigma_\varepsilon^2\right)$ and independent from $\mathbf{x}_{it-1}$ and υ_i. The last is a stochastic non-negative variable measuring technical inefficiency (the complement to one of the above-defined notion of technical efficiency). By assumption, the inefficiency terms υ_i do not vary through time. Furthermore, without any loss of generality, we consider a Cobb-Douglas functional form. Naturally, α is the constant term of the function. Setting now $\alpha_i = \alpha + \upsilon_i$, we obtain the model proposed in Schmidt and Sickles (1984):

$$h_{it} = \alpha_i + \mathbf{x}_{it-1}\boldsymbol{\beta} + \varepsilon_{it} \tag{5.3}$$

This model can be easily estimated by means of a Within procedure. If we now define $\hat{a} = \max_i\{\hat{\alpha}_i\}$, the technical efficiency of observation i is defined by:

$$ET_i = \exp\{-\hat{\upsilon}_i\} = \exp\{\hat{\alpha} - \hat{\alpha}_i\} \tag{5.4}$$

The above model can be straightforwardly modified in order to allow variations through time of technical efficiency. Take for instance the model proposed in Cornwell et al. (1990):

$$\begin{aligned} h_{it} &= \alpha + \mathbf{x}_{it-1}\boldsymbol{\beta} + \varepsilon_{it} - \upsilon_{it} \\ &= \alpha_{it} + \mathbf{x}_{it-1}\boldsymbol{\beta} + \varepsilon_{it} \end{aligned} \tag{5.5}$$

where $\alpha_{it} = \alpha + \upsilon_{it} = \delta_{i1} + \delta_{i2}t + \delta_{i3}t^2$. If we define $\hat{a}_t = \max_i\{\hat{\alpha}_{it}\}$, from the Within estimates of this model we obtain:

$$ET_{it} = \exp\{-\hat{\upsilon}_{it}\} = \exp\{\hat{\alpha}_t - \hat{\alpha}_{it}\} \tag{5.6}$$

Through the terms $\delta_{i1} + \delta_{i2}t + \delta_{i3}t^2$ this model nests the explanation of inefficiency within the estimation of the production function. Yet, more can be done in this regard by including in (5.5), besides the $\mathbf{x}_{it-1}$ vector, a z_{it} vector of variables potentially determining the technical efficiency of observation i at time t.

The literature on matching functions within the frontier approach is still rather recent. The seminal contribution is Warren (1991). Three more recent studies have been carried out for European countries and are the starting point for the present empirical analysis. All these studies share the assumption of a Cobb–Douglas functional form for the matching function. They fundamentally differ in regard to the data-sets utilised and the variables considered in the explanation of inefficiency.

Ibourk et al. (2001) consider monthly data for the 22 French regions from March 1990 to February 1995. They include in the estimates (besides a linear trend), a rather large number of potential determinants of inefficiency. The list is given in Table 5.1.

Table 5.1. The potential efficiency determinants considered in Ibourk et al. (2001)

Factors	Variables
Search Intensity Discrimination Effects Ranking Effects	share of workers aged under 25 share of workers aged over 50 share of immigrants share of women share of long-term unemployed
Firm Effects Industry Effects	turnover rate share of open-ended contracts[*] net rate of employment growth[**]
Other Factors	share of workers on training programmes density of population

[*] Besides this share (referring to total vacancies), shares refer to the total unemployed.
[**] This variable is taken with a one-month lag in order to avoid spurious correlation.

The results suggest the existence of wide regional differences in efficiency, and that on average a decline in efficiency occurs over the time period considered. The hypothesis of constant returns to scale for the matching function is not rejected. Interestingly, the decline occurring in open-ended contracts over the time period considered has apparently little impact on hirings.

Ilmakunnas and Pesola (2003) consider annual data for the 14 Finnish regions from 1988 to 1997. They too include a linear trend in the estimates and allow for some potential determinants of inefficiency (see Table 5.2). Among the latter of particular interest are the average unemployment and vacancy rates of neighbouring regions. The authors believe that in this way allowance can be made for the spillover effects recently highlighted by Burda and Profit (1996), Burgess and Profit (2001).

Indeed, the average unemployment and vacancy rates of neighbouring regions significantly enter the estimates, and with the expected signs (the average unemployment rate of neighbouring regions has a negative impact on efficiency, while the average vacancy rate has a positive impact). Also the evidence in Ilmakunnas and Pesola (2003) is favourable to the hypothesis of constant returns to scale for the matching function.

Table 5.2 The potential efficiency determinants considered by Ilmakunnas and Pesola (2003)

Factors	Variables
Search Intensity	share of workers aged under 35[*]
Discrimination Effects	share of workers with higher education
Ranking Effects	home ownership index
	share of long-term unemployed
Firm Effects	Level of GDP per capita
Industry Effects	job reallocation rate
	churning rate
Other Factors	average unemployment rate in neighbouring regions
	average vacancy rate in neighbouring regions

[*] Here shares are calculated relative to the labour force.

The analysis by Fahr and Sunde (2002) concerns two different types of annual data, both referring to the German economy. In the former case, 117 local labour markets are considered from 1980 to 1997. In the latter, data are taken from 1980 to 1995 for 82 occupational groups. Hence these authors consider the occupational as well as the territorial dimension of matching.

A feature shared by all the above studies is that no dynamic specification of the matching function is considered. This is somewhat curious, both because of the annual or infra-annual frequency of the data and because of the notorious presence of dynamics in this field (the Beveridge Curve 'loops'). Our empirical analysis will take due account of this consideration.

5.4 The Beveridge curve in Italy. The literature

In Italy there are no official data on vacancies. However, two surveys enable empirical appraisal to be made of the Beveridge Curve, also over a regional dimension. One survey was carried out by CSA (Centro di Studi Aziendali, Florence) and by ISFOL, Rome, on the help-wanted advertisements published in certain leading daily newspapers. Another data source is the quarterly business survey carried out by ISAE (formerly ISCO) in manufacturing where, among other things, firms were asked whether the scarcity of labour prevented them from expanding their activity. Furthermore, until 1999 it was also possible to utilise another (administrative) source: the data from the Ministry of Labour (*Ministero del Lavoro e delle politiche Sociali*) on the vacancy notices posted by firms carrying out certain types of hiring (firms usually only posted these notices when they had already actually decided upon the hiring).

Perhaps because of the absence of official data on vacancies, few studies in Italy have examined the nature and evolution of the Beveridge Curve. Sestito (1988) and Bragato (1990) utilise the ISFOL-CSA data on vacancies and find a significant relationship between unemployment and vacancies only in the presence of a growing linear trend. Bragato (1990) also finds a significant Beveridge Curve for the North and the Centre, but not for the South. A significant difference between the Southern labour market and the rest of the country is also detected by Sestito (1991), where vacancies are measured using the data from the ISAE survey. In this case, however, there is no need to include a linear trend in the estimates to find a significant relationship between unemployment and vacancies. The analysis in Di Monte (1992) is based on a similar econometric specification, but it utilises the Ministry of Labour data on vacancies. The main difference between the results obtained by Di Monte and previous studies is that a significant Beveridge Curve also shows up for the South.

More recent evidence is provided by Mocavini and Paliotta (2000), who examine Beveridge Curve plots based on the ISFOL-CSA data, and by Destefanis and Fonseca (2004), who estimate and compare some Beveridge Curves based on all available indicators (ISFOL-CSA, ISAE and Ministry of Labour). The evidence from these works is largely consistent with previous findings. A Beveridge Curve is also apparent in the 1990s, with some outer shift over this period. Moreover, as in previous studies, the Southern labour market behaves somewhat differently from the rest of the country.

5.5 Labour market reform, vacancies and unemployment. The estimates

The empirical evidence in the Italian literature relates to the Beveridge Curve (and not to the matching function proper). Three different indicators are used for vacancies (ISFOL-CSA: help-wanted advertisements, ISAE: indicator of labour scarcity, Ministry of Labour: data from hiring procedures). Only in Destefanis and Fonseca (2004) is direct comparison made among the three indicators, and it yields, at least as far as the 1990s are concerned, substantially similar results.

A feature shared by all these estimates of the Beveridge Curve is the presence of significant dynamic effects. This obviously increases the perplexity expressed earlier concerning the simple dynamic structure of the matching functions surveyed in Section 5.3. It is well known that, under the hypotheses of constant returns to scale for the matching function and of the existence of a steady state with constant average rate of unemployment, the Beveridge Curve can be obtained as a re-parameterisation of the matching function. It is commonly believed in the literature that the hypotheses of constant returns to scale and of a steady state with constant average rate of unemployment are not particularly restrictive. Hence the empirical exercise performed here consists in the estimation of a Beveridge Curve, with particular attention paid to its dynamic specification. Under the hypothesis of constant returns to scale, Eq. (5.1) becomes:

$$\frac{H_{it}}{U_{it-1}} = h \frac{V_{it-1}}{U_{it-1}} e_{it} \tag{5.7}$$

In its turn, this function can be rewritten as:

$$\frac{H_{it}}{N_{it-1}}\left(\frac{L_{it-1}}{U_{it-1}}-1\right) = h\left(\frac{V_{it-1}}{L_{it-1}} \middle/ \frac{U_{it-1}}{L_{it-1}}\right)e_{it} \tag{5.8}$$

In a steady state with a constant unemployment rate, the hiring rate $\left(H_{it}/N_{it-1}\right)$ is equal to $s + g$, where s is the separation rate and g is the rate of growth of the labour force, L. Hence Eq. (5.8) becomes an inverse relationship among the unemployment and the vacancy rates, the Beveridge Curve, whose position depends on s, g, and e_{it}. The interpretation of the last term does not change vis-à-vis Eq. (5.1); however empirical measures of efficiency will reflect the evolution not only of e_{it}, but also of s and g. This should be kept in mind when interpreting the results.

The main data source used for the analysis was the quarterly ISTAT Labour Force Survey (*Indagine trimestrale sulle forze di lavoro*). This survey is conducted every quarter on about 200,000 persons in 1,400 municipalities throughout the country. In particular, individual data from 1992:4 to 2001:2 were utilised to measure stocks of unemployed and labour force for the three main areas of Italy (North, Centre, South – the level of territorial disaggregation is chosen in order to allow comparison with previous results in the literature). We used data only from 1992:4 onwards because individual data were not available prior to that date. These data are of great importance, not only because of the information that they provide about unemployment, but also for the construction of a series of potential determinants of matching efficiency. Following the studies surveyed in Section 5.3, we considered variables controlling for search intensity, for discrimination or ranking effects, for firm or industry effects, and for other residual factors. All these potential determinants of efficiency are listed in Table 5.3.

Table 5.3. The potential efficiency determinants from the *Indagine trimestrale sulle forze di lavoro*, ISTAT

Factors	Variables
Search Intensity	share of unemployed aged under 25
Discrimination Effects	share of unemployed aged under 35
Ranking Effects	share of unemployed aged over 55
	share of female unemployed
	share of long-term unemployed
Firm Effects	share of labour force in agriculture
Industry Effects	share of labour force in industry
	share of labour force in services
	share of labour force in public administration
Other Factors	share of part-time employment
	share of open-ended contract employment

As an indicator for vacancies we used the ISAE labour scarcity indicator (which arguably gave the best results in Destefanis and Fonseca, 2004). Following the customary practice, a Cobb–Douglas functional form was initially assumed for the Beveridge Curve, implying a log-linear relationship between unemployment and vacancy rates. Actual estimation of the Curve suggested, however, that slightly different functional forms sometimes gave better results (see Table A.1 in the Appendix). We performed a dynamic specification search within an error correction mechanism, where the log differences of the dependent variable depended not only on current and lagged log differences of other variables (as well as of the dependent variable itself), but also on lagged *levels* of the dependent variable and of other variables.

For the sake of clarity, we write below an equation almost identical to the most successful empirical specifications obtained in estimation:

$$\Delta u_{it} = \beta_1 \Delta u_{it-1} + \beta_2 \Delta u_{it-4} + \beta_3 u_{it-1} + \beta_4 f(V)_{it-j} +$$

$$+ \sum_{i=1}^{3} \beta_{4+i} C_i + \sum_{i=1}^{3} \beta_{7+i} T_i + \sum_{i=1}^{3} \beta_{10+i} T^2{}_i + \sum_{m=1}^{p} \beta_{13+m} Z_{mit-1} \qquad (5.9)$$

where $i = 1, 2, 3$, stands for the territorial area, and t for the time period (quarter). In (5.9) the log differences of the rate of unemployment are a linear function of their own one- and four-quarter lagged values, of the one-quarter lagged natural log of the rate of unemployment, of a function of the vacancy rate taken at an unspecified lag,[4] and of a variable vector standing for the potential determinants of matching efficiency. This vector will always include, following the suggestions of Cornwell et al. (1990), a constant term, C, a linear trend term, T, and a quadratic trend term, T^2, for each of the three territorial areas. There is also set of variables denoted by Z, comprising the control variables presented in Table 5.3 (all taken with a one-quarter lag in order to avoid simultaneity problems) and a variable standing for the impact of the Treu Act. The significance of the latter was tested through a binary variable equal to one from 1998:3 onwards, and through a variable (INTERIM) constructed using the information available from Confinterim (the data-set is available on line at http://www.confiterim.com/vilstat)). Because the number of temporary contracts for the whole of Italy was known, it was possible to construct a variable equal to zero until 1998:2 and assuming values of 0.2 for 1998:3 and 1998:4, of 0.4 for the year 1999, and of 1 from 2000:1 onwards (these values are roughly proportional to the actual numbers of temporary work contracts). No allowance was made for regional differences in the numbers of temporary work contracts, since these are more or less stable through time.

Following the specification already adopted for constant terms and trends, the Treu Act indicators could assume different values across the main areas. Moreover, we allowed for the possibility that the Act might affect the slope of the vacancy term. Specifically, we considered three cases: the Act only affected regional intercepts (case 1); it also affected the slope, but uniformly throughout the country

---

[4] The nature of the function and the order of the lag will be specified below.

(case 2); it affected both intercepts and slopes in a different manner across areas (case 3).

With a view to obtaining as much information as possible from the data, Eq. (5.9) was estimated not only on unemployment and vacancy rates relating to the whole labour force, but also on unemployment and vacancy rates calculated on skilled and unskilled labour forces. The criterion used to segment the labour force for this purpose consisted in considering the labour force with university degrees or (non-vocational) high-school diplomas as skilled, and the rest of the labour force as unskilled (see on this Sneessens *et al.*, 1998).

Before we describe the econometric results, it is instructive to consider the evolution of vacancies in Table 5.4.

Table 5.4. The evolution of vacancies in the three areas

	North	Centre	South
1992	2.00	1.25	5.13
1993	1.43	1.25	0.63
1994	7.57	2.75	3.50
1995	11.29	2.50	2.63
1996	6.86	1.50	1.25
1997	8.71	6.50	2.13
1998	15.43	10.25	4.63
1999	15.00	5.50	3.75
2000	32.14	12.75	13.00
2001	23.86	18.00	4.75

From 1998 onwards, vacancies increased markedly in the North and the Centre. This rise in vacancies cannot simply be explained by cyclical factors, because the Italian labour market had already been picking up for some years (see ISTAT 2003, 2004). In the South the evidence on increasing vacancies is less clear.

Turning now to the econometric evidence (in order to save space, reported in the Appendix are only what we regard to be the most significant results), we find evidence which largely bears out the existence of a Beveridge Curve in the 1990s across the main territorial areas. The dynamic specification of the Curve was very similar to that found by Destefanis and Fonseca (2004). Estimates for unskilled and total rates of unemployment were more significant than estimates for the skilled rate of unemployment. In the latter case, significant coefficients for the vacancy rate could only be obtained by dropping the Cobb–Douglas specification in favour of a hyperbolic functional form which more markedly penalised high values of the vacancy indicator. The hypothesis that the slope of the Curve is uniform across regions can be comfortably maintained.[5] However, wide differences emerge between the South and the rest of the country. The Southern labour market turns out to be much less efficient than those of the other two areas.

As far as the significance of the control terms listed in Table 5.3 is concerned, only the share of labour force in industry (negative sign for the skilled, positive sign for the unskilled), the share of labour force in services (positive sign for the skilled, negative sign for the unskilled; less significant than the former variable), the share of female unemployed and the share of unemployed aged under 35 (both with a negative sign for the unskilled) have some degree of significance. When these controls are included in the equation in various combinations the best fit is obtained with the share of labour force in industry plus the share of female unemployed. This suggests that efficiency is positively related to the share of female unemployed and negatively related to the share of the labour force in industry. The fact that other controls are not significant does not mean *per se* that these factors are not relevant. An obvious alternative interpretation of this result is that territorial disparities in these factors are sufficiently well captured by the regional fixed effects and trends.

Focusing now on the impact of the Treu Act, we find that INTERIM is much more significant than a simple binary indicator. The evidence also indicates that INTERIM only acts through different regional intercepts (indeed, the Appendix only reports estimates for case 1, the regional intercept specification of INTERIM). Interestingly, the effect of INTERIM is negative (on unemployment) for the North, insignificant for the Centre, and positive for the South. This obviously means that the Treu Act had a positive impact on efficiency in the North, but a negative impact in the South. Only the latter is consistently significant, especially if the control variables are included in the estimates.

All in all, the evidence suggests that the Treu Act brought about a reduction of unemployment in the more developed regions of the country, but, if anything, it had an unfavourable effect on the efficiency of the Southern labour market. For the South of Italy and for unskilled labour in particular, there is some evidence of a slight outward shift of the Beveridge Curve. This could be explained along the lines suggested by Wasmer (1999): the rise in the share of non-standard jobs shifts the Beveridge Curve to the right, because the probability of job separations increases more than chances for the unemployed to find jobs.

5.6 Concluding remarks

This chapter has used a matching theory approach to assess the impact on the Italian labour market of the so-called 1997 Treu Act (*legge Treu*). Although the Treu Act aroused considerable interest in the press and among labour market partici-

---

[5] We tested for this hypothesis allowing the vacancy coefficients to differ across areas. The test values, available on request, do not reject the null hypothesis of a common coefficient.

pants, to date extensive scientific analysis on its effects has not been conducted. Our study is also of some interest because the relationship between unemployment and vacancies has been very seldom analysed in the Italian literature, mainly because of the lack of official vacancy data. We have adopted a fairly recent empirical approach where the matching function, re-parameterised as a Beveridge Curve, is modelled and estimated as a production frontier.

We have found largely favourable evidence as to the existence of a Beveridge Curve in the 1990s across the main territorial areas examined. Wide efficiency differences have been shown between the South and the rest of the country. Our evidence suggests that the Treu Act fostered an increase in the vacancy supply, especially in the North and in the Centre of Italy. However, for the South of Italy, and for unskilled labour in particular, some evidence has been found of a slight outward shift of the Beveridge Curve. As a consequence, it may be concluded from our evidence that the Treu Act brought about a reduction of unemployment in the more developed regions of the country, but did not greatly affect the efficiency of the Italian labour market. In the future, we intend to obtain more robust evidence on these matters by conducting our analysis at a finer level of territorial disaggregation.

Appendix

Table 5.A.1. Measure of vacancies: ISAE Indicator of Labour Scarcity – No Control Variables among Regressors

	Total Labour Force		Skilled Labour Force		Unskilled Labour Force	
	Coeff.	t–ratio	Coeff.	t–ratio	Coeff.	t–ratio
Δu_{it-1}	0.14	1.11	0.27	2.52	0.01	0.03
Δu_{it-4}	−0.09	−1.15	−0.09	−1.05	−0.20	−2.16
u_{it-1}	−0.89	−6.39	−0.78	−5.63	−0.69	−5.30
$f(\mathbf{V})_{it-2}$	−0.0021	−2.87	0.0006	3.45	−0.0037	−4.34
C_North	−2.31		−2.04		−1.75	
C_Centre	−1.94		−1.71		−1.48	
C_South	−1.39		−1.25		−1.04	
T_North	0.0078	1.36	0.0123	1.39	−0.0004	−0.08
T_Centre	0.0151	3.03	0.0209	3.69	0.0044	0.87
T_South	0.0247	5.14	0.0184	3.20	0.0202	3.74
T^2_North	−0.0005	−2.30	−0.0007	−2.17	−0.0001	−0.57
T^2_Centre	−0.0006	−3.24	−0.0007	−4.10	−0.0002	−1.21
T^2_South	−0.0007	−5.32	−0.0005	−3.13	−0.0005	−3.93
INTERIM_North	−0.08	−1.60	−0.06	−0.79	−0.07	−1.74
INTERIM_Centre	−0.01	−0.16	−0.00	−0.06	−0.01	−0.14
INTERIM_South	0.06	2.76	0.04	1.14	0.06	2.96
Adjusted R^2	0.49		0.33		0.50	

Table 5.A.2. Measure of vacancies: ISAE Indicator of Labour Scarcity – Significant Control Variables among Regressors

	Total Labour Force		Skilled Labour Force		Unskilled Labour Force	
	Coeff.	t–ratio	Coeff.	t–ratio	Coeff.	t–ratio
Δu_{it-1}	0.20	1.32	0.30	2.35	0.08	0.03
Δu_{it-4}	–0.10	–1.22	–0.08	–1.00	–0.19	–2.16
u_{it-1}	–0.91	–6.33	–0.87	–5.69	–0.77	–5.30
$f(V)_{it-2}$	–0.0022	–2.92	0.0005	2.35	–0.0038	–4.34
C_North	–2.25		–1.89		–2.06	
C_Centre	–1.84		–1.66		–1.61	
C_South	–1.29		–1.25		–1.09	
T_North	0.0095	1.55	0.0135	1.58	0.0034	0.62
T_Centre	0.0153	2.84	0.0247	3.86	0.0046	0.91
T_South	0.0251	5.14	0.0206	3.38	0.0225	4.31
T^2_North	–0.0005	–2.35	–0.0007	–2.47	–0.0002	–1.18
T^2_Centre	–0.0006	–3.04	–0.0008	–4.23	–0.0002	–1.27
T^2_South	–0.0007	–5.42	–0.0005	–3.21	–0.0006	–4.36
INTERIM_North	–0.07	–1.32	–0.10	–1.05	–0.05	–1.14
INTERIM_Centre	–0.01	–0.16	0.00	0.11	–0.01	–0.20
INTERIM_South	0.06	2.79	0.03	0.94	0.07	2.84
Industry share$_{it-1}$	0.34	0.62	–1.30	–1.42	1.34	2.64
Female share$_{it-1}$	–0.40	–1.26	–0.02	–0.03	–0.58	–2.18
Adjusted R^2	0.49		0.33		0.54	

Legend of tables and figures

The dependent variable is always Δu_{it}, where $i = 1, 2, 3$, stands for North, Centre and South, and t is a given quarter.

In the case of the skilled labour force, $f(V)$ always stands for the hyperbolic function $1/(V^3)$. Otherwise $f(V)$ is a linear function.

All variables are deseasonalised.

The sample relates to the 1994:1–2001:2 period, for a sum total of $30\times3 = 90$ observations.

T-ratios are obtained from variance-covariance matrices corrected for heteroskedasticity with the White procedure.

Adjusted R^2 is the coefficient of determination corrected for degrees of freedom.

References

Adam P, Canziani P (1998) Partial de-regulation: fixed-term contracts in Italy and Spain. CEP Discussion Paper 386.

Bertola G, Ichino A (1995) Crossing the river. a comparative perspective on Italian employment dynamics. Economic Policy 21:359–420.

Bragato S (1990) La curva di Beveridge e le componenti della disoccupazione in Italia (1980–88). Economia & Lavoro 24:111–122.

Burda M, Profit S (1996) Matching across space: evidence on mobility in the Czech Republic. Labour Economics 3:255–278.

Burgess S, Profit S (2001) Externalities in the matching of workers and firms in Britain. Labour Economics 8:313–333.

Centra M, Linfante G, Mandrone E (2001) Le determinanti territoriali degli esiti del lavoro temporaneo, XVI Convegno Nazionale di Economia del Lavoro, Florence, 4–5 October.

Confinterim (2000), Il lavoro temporaneo. Confinterim, Milan.

Cornwell C, Schmidt P, Sickles RC (1990) Production frontiers with cross-sectional and time-series variation in efficiency levels. Journal of Econometrics 46:185–200.

Destefanis S, Fonseca R (2004) Un nuovo approccio alla misura del mismatch: la funzione di produzione. In: Mocavini A, Paliotta A (eds) La domanda di lavoro qualificato in Italia. F. Angeli, Milano, pp 234–255.

Di Monte P (1992), La disoccupazione in Italia e la natura dei divari territoriali. Economia & Lavoro 26:29–45.

Fahr R, Sunde U (2002) Estimations of occupational and regional matching efficiencies using stochastic production frontier models. IZA Discussion Paper 552.

Farrell MJ (1957) The measurement of productive efficiency. Journal of the Royal Statistical Society, Series A 120:253–281.

Felstead A, Jewson N (eds) (1999) Global trends in flexible labour. Macmillan, London.

Ibourk A, Maillard B, Perelman S, Sneessens HR (2001) The matching efficiency of regional labour markets. A stochastic production frontier estimation, France 1990–1995. Cahiers du CREPP 2001/04.

Ichino A, Mealli F, Nannicini T (1995) Temporary work agencies in Italy: a springboard toward permanent employment?. European University Institute, Florence, mimeo.

Ilmakunnas P, Pesola H (2003) Regional labour market matching functions and efficiency analysis. Labour 17:413–437.

ISTAT (various years), Indagine trimestrale sulle forze di lavoro. ISTAT, Roma.

ISTAT (2003), Rapporto Annuale 2002. ISTAT, Roma.

ISTAT (2004), Rapporto Annuale 2003. ISTAT, Roma.

Jovanovic B (1979) Job matching and the theory of turnover. Journal of Political Economy 87:972–990.

Jovanovic B (1984) Matching, turnover, and unemployment, Journal of Political Economy 92:108–122.

Kumbhakar SC, Lovell CAK (2000) Stochastic frontier analysis. Cambridge University Press, Cambridge.

Ministero del Lavoro e delle Politiche Sociali (2001), Rapporto di monitoraggio sulle politiche occupazionali e del lavoro, Roma.

Mocavini A, Paliotta A (2000) Job vacancies in Italia. Il quadro teorico, le indagini, le evidenze empiriche. ISFOL, Monografie sul Mercato del lavoro e le politiche per l'impiego 6/2000, Roma.

Nannicini T (2004a) The take-off of temporary help employment in the Italian labor market. ECO-EUI Working Paper 09/2004.

Nannicini T (2004b), Temporary workers: how temporary are they?. ECO-EUI Working Paper 23/2004.

OECD (1994) The OECD jobs study, evidence and explanations, Vols. I and II. OECD, Paris.

OECD (2000) Employment outlook. OECD, Paris.

Petrongolo B, Pissarides CA (2001) Looking into the black box: a survey of the matching function. Journal of Economic Literature 39:320–431.

Pissarides C (1990) Equilibrium unemployment theory. First edition Basil Blackwell, London. Second edition (2000), The MIT Press, Cambridge (Mass.).

Saint-Paul G (1996) Dual labor markets: a macroeconomic perspective, The MIT Press, Cambridge (Mass.).

Schmidt P, Sickles RC (1984) Production frontiers and panel data. Journal of Business and Economic Statistics 2:367–374.

Sestito P (1988) Esiste una curva di Beveridge per l'Italia?. Banca d'Italia, Temi di discussione 101.

Sestito P (1991) Disoccupazione e carenza di personale. Politica Economica 1:85–103.

Sestito P (1996) I vincoli ad assunzioni e licenziamenti e la performance dell'occupazione. In: Galli G, Marzotto P (eds) La mobilità della società italiana, SIPI, Roma, vol 1, pp 209–252.

Sneessens HR, Fonseca R, Maillard B (1998) Structural adjustment and unemployment persistence (with an application to France and Spain). EUI Working Paper 98/4.

Warren RS (1991) The estimation of frictional unemployment: a stochastic frontier approach. Review of Economics and Statistics 73:373–377.

Wasmer E (1999) Competition for jobs in a growing economy and the emergence of dualism in employment. Economic Journal 109:349–371.

6 Enterprise Defensive Restructuring: Cross-Country Evidence within Transitional Settings

Polona Domadenik[1] and Maja Vehovec[2]

[1] University of Ljubljana, Slovenia
[2] University of Rijeka, Croatia

6.1 Introduction

For over a decade, Central and Eastern Europe has been undergoing one of the most profound economic and political transformations in history. At the beginning of the 1990s, the region embarked on an ambitious reform programme intended to replace central planning with market-based economies. A decade later, and amid significant difficulties, the region has achieved remarkable successes, with several countries becoming increasingly integrated into the global economy. But, while some countries have attained favourable economic positions, others are lagging behind. It is evident that the faster-reforming countries – those which have pursued a faster and deeper reform path – grew more rapidly during the first phase of transition. As far as future growth prospects are concerned, it is of great importance to identify the factors that induce high economic growth.

Enterprise restructuring has been seen as a key element in the reform process (Earle and Estrin 1997, Svejnar 2002, Estrin 2002). After implementing Type 1 reforms (macroeconomic stabilisation, price and trade liberalisation, privatisation, etc), many transition countries were faced with the challenge of accomplishing Type 2 reforms, which mostly concerned establishment of an efficient institutional environment. Estrin (2002) notes that pro-reform policies have been applied more consistently and effectively in the Visegrad countries (Poland, Hungary, the Czech and Slovak Republics), the Baltic States and Slovenia than elsewhere. Empirical studies show that the restructuring of firms in transition crucially depends on the efficient operation of labour and capital markets (Lizal 1998, Konings et al. 2002, Domadenik et al. 2003). However, to date no empirical study has focused on how different reform paths affect enterprise restructuring, especially in a cross-country perspective. Moreover, given that Slovenia and Croatia were part of the former Yugoslavia and shared a common self-management system, it can be argued that both countries started from similar initial conditions. From this perspective, our study provides potentially interesting evidence on how the pursuit of different reform paths affects enterprise restructuring and the economic performance of a country as a whole.

Following the original study by Roland (1996 and 2000), we divide the restructuring process of the transition firm into two stages: defensive (cost-related) and strategic (revenue-focused). Defensive restructuring has usually been seen as the first response of firms to huge output drops and new market conditions. The introduction of hard budget constraints forced firms to adjust workforce size to demand for their products, considering the new technological requirements and circumstances in the markets. The approach usually adopted when studying defensive restructuring is to apply a labour demand model to obtain evidence on how rapidly firms adjust their workforces to variation in wages and output. The second stage, strategic restructuring, involves investment activity intended to develop firms' main capabilities and comparative advantages. Although Roland (1996 and 2000) perceived the process as sequential, there is some evidence of a complementary process, especially if underdeveloped institutional structures limit labour adjustment (Domadenik et al. 2003, Domadenik. 2003).

This chapter reports the findings of a study on the defensive restructuring of privatised Slovenian and Croatian firms. It uses a panel dataset comprising large and middle-sized firms in the period after privatisation. Although we are aware of the shortcomings due to the fact that data problems prevent us from dealing with strategic restructuring of firms in both countries, we believe that our study contributes to the existing literature in at least two significant ways. First, both countries were part of the former Yugoslavia, which started implementing market reforms in the 1970s. Before transition, they were the most advanced of CEE economies with per capita GDPs well above those of other countries. They shared the same legal and economic system and therefore inherited very similar initial conditions. Both countries successfully implemented macroeconomic reforms, while implementation of Type 2 reforms followed different paths. A decade later, per capita GDP in Slovenia is almost twice as high as in Croatia. Moreover, Croatia has a double-digit unemployment rate while Slovenia records one of the lowest rates among the CEE economies. Hence, the question of interest is whether different reform implementations have affected firms' restructuring and hence key macroeconomic variables. Secondly, both countries have highly protected and underdeveloped labour markets which possibly constrain efficient defensive and strategic restructuring.[1] Moreover, because firms in both countries face severe international competition on domestic and foreign markets, slower labour adjustment may endanger their long-term survival.

The next section describes the institutional and political environment characterising the two countries in the 1990s. The third section outlines the model. The fourth section sets out the data and empirical results, while the last section makes some concluding remarks and draws some policy implications.

---

[1] The present labour market rigidities in both countries have mostly been inherited from the previous self-management system in the former Yugoslavia. In the social ownership system, the labour market existed in very rudimentary? form, being efficient when there was excess labour demand but completely rigid otherwise. At the beginning of transition, employees retained their excessive influence on decision-making processes through unions and legislation which favoured employee participation in firms' decisions (see the Co-Determination Law in Slovenia).

6.2 The institutional framework and policy settings in Slovenia and Croatia

As mentioned in the introduction, Slovenia and Croatia implemented successful macroeconomic stabilisation policies in the early 1990s, and they liberalised prices and foreign trade. However, both countries belatedly introduced a market-oriented legal system and labour market regulations.

Slovenia's economic performance during the 1990s was relatively successful. After a brief period of economic decline in 1990–92, a period of sustained economic growth ensued, with GDP increasing by 2.8 per cent in 1993, 5.3 per cent in 1994, 4.1 per cent in 1995, and 3.5 per cent in 1996. In the 1997–2000 period, Slovenia recorded an average GDP growth of more than 4 per cent. Exports constituted almost 60 per cent of GDP – EU member countries being the main trading partners. Macroeconomic stabilisation policies in the 1990s involved restrictive monetary and fiscal measures which brought inflation down from 22 per cent per month in October 1991 to an annual rate of about 6–7 per cent in the late 1990s. At the micro level, the government rehabilitated the commercial banking sector, writing off losses against capital. The Bank of Slovenia strictly enforced the regulations, compelling the commercial banks to be more careful in screening credit applications by firms. As a result, the financing of firms by domestic banks was limited. Moreover, the role of the newly-established Ljubljana Stock Exchange in supplying and allocating capital was limited as well. With very few issues of securities, the primary capital market was almost non-existent, while the secondary market lacked liquidity. Foreign capital and foreign direct investment played no significant role in Slovenia in the 1990s. Owing to the fact that external financing was constrained, investment activity by firms mostly depended on their ability to generate internal funds (Domadenik et al. 2003). Firms that paid lower wages and had more internal funds exhibited higher levels of investment.

By contrast, the Croatian transition path started with a war that brought huge? destruction of lives and property. More than 10,000 people were killed, almost four times as many were wounded and/or handicapped (Vujcic and Lang 2001). Direct war damage was estimated at USD 29.6 billion, which was equivalent to 157 per cent of 1995 GDP. Although the war delayed many reforms, the Stabilisation Programme was launched in October 1993 and reduced inflation from 1250 per cent in 1993 to minus 3 per cent in 1994. Since stabilisation, Croatian monetary policy may be characterised *ex-post* as a quasi-currency board policy. Although exchange rates were never fixed, they remained very stable. The war also exacted a heavy toll in terms of economic and political isolation (at least until the end of the 1990s). After declaring its independence in 1991, Croatia lost more than 70 per cent of its markets (50 per cent of total exports and 17 per cent of pre war GDP). Yet after substantial economic decline in the years between 1991-and 1993, when GDP declined by 22, 12 and 8 per cent respectively, a period of sustained economic growth began, with GDP increasing by 5.9 per cent in 1994, 6.8 per cent in 1995, 5.9 per cent in 1996, and 6.8 per cent in 1997. But in 1998 GDP growth once again ground to a halt, reaching only 2.5 per cent, and it became negative in the year after. In recent years, Croatia has achieved lower growth than the most successful CEE economies

Firms were gradually privatised in both countries, but with substantial differences in implementation. Slovenia and Croatia lagged behind in large-scale privatisation and enterprise reforms, while they belonged to the first group in the case of small-scale privatisation (EBRD 2000). In Slovenia, former socially-owned enterprises were privatised using a combined voucher and buy-out method.[2] As shown by Gregorič et al. (2000), the present ownership structure in privatised Slovenian firms still reflects the privatisation model chosen, and it is dispersed among privatisation investment funds, state funds, other non-financial enterprises, employees, former employees and retired people. Slovenian corporate governance has been made even more complicated by the 1993 Law on Workers' Co-Determination. Under this Law, in companies with up to 500 employees at least one-third of Supervisory Board members must be workers' representatives, and in companies with over 1,000 employees at least one-half of them must be such.[3] Given the Supervisory Board's important role in supervising a company's affairs and elections of its management, there is relatively little monitoring by outsiders (Prašnikar and Gregorič, 2002).

Privatisation in Croatia is also being carried out gradually, and it is generally considered to be not very successful, for two main reasons (Vujcic and Lang 2001). First, early privatisation took place amid unstable war conditions which engendered? higher costs of transition. Second, there was no general consensus on privatisation procedures. Different privatisation models were adopted on a case-by-case basis and following what were often *ad hoc* decisions. Models included employee and management buyouts, public offerings (including for cash or 'frozen' foreign saving's deposits, and on the? stock exchange), privatisation through restructuring, voucher privatisation to certain groups, and sale to strategic investors (usually foreign). The main motive for privatisation in the early years of transition was ownership change; thereafter, it became the need to finance budget deficits.

During the transition period, the institutional setting of the labour market played an important role in corporate restructuring. The Slovenian and Croatian labour markets underwent dramatic changes similar to those in other transitional countries. The state abandoned its paternalistic role and firms were allowed to lay

---

[2] The 1992 Privatisation Law allocated 20 per cent of a firm's shares to insiders (workers), 20 per cent to the Development Fund, which auctioned the shares to investment funds, 10 per cent to the National Pension Fund, and 10 per cent to the Restitution Fund. In addition, in each enterprise the workers' council or board of directors (if one existed) was empowered to allocate the remaining 40 per cent of company shares for sale to insiders (workers) or outsiders (through a public tender). According to how it was decided to allocate this remaining 40 per cent of shares, firms can be classified as being privatised to insiders (the internal method) or outsiders (the external method).

[3] The Slovenian Companies Act (1993) introduced a two-tier governance structure with the Supervisory Board as the intermediate body between the management and the Shareholders' Assembly.

off redundant workers. Responsibility for finding employment was transferred to individuals. However, the government continued to exert a major influence through the creation of new labour legislation and negotiation and coordination with trade unions and employers' associations.

Most of the reallocation of workers from traditional manufacturing industry, state-owned and large firms, to services, new private SMEs and self-employment took place in the early stage of transition. These changes were concomitant with long-run persistent unemployment and inflow into non-employment with the possibility of early retirement. After a decade of transition, Croatia still has two-digit unemployment rates, the highest among the CEE economies, while Slovenia invariably recorded fairly small, one-digit, unemployment rates. Interestingly, in both countries registered unemployment rates were higher than ILO survey rates, which signalled the existence of generous welfare policies offering incentives to register as unemployed. Registered employment significantly decreased during the transition in all countries. Slovenia had one of the highest employment rates among the EU accession countries, whilst the Croatian employment rate was the lowest among CEE economies, probably owing to a large decrease in the working-age population (caused by war and migration), an unusually large unofficial economy (estimated at around 25 per cent of GDP from 1990–1995:October 1997), and slow labour reallocation.

What is the role of the labour market institutions in all this? Rigid employment legislation that makes employers cautious about hiring new workers is usually believed to be very important in this regard. However, as Svejnar (2002) has recently pointed out, labour market flexibility is an important but not major factor in comparison with market imperfections and rigid regulation in other areas such as the housing market, transportation infrastructure, capital market, corporate governance, legal framework, and the business environment. Indeed, according to the Employment Protection Legislation (EPL) Indexes calculated by Riboud et al. (2002) for EU accession countries and by Biondic et al. (2002) for Croatia, Hungary has the most flexible labour legislation whilst that of Slovenia and Croatia is the most rigid. Yet Slovenia's labour market performance is well on a par with Hungary's.[4]

Further discussion is required of the wage setting process. After the collapse of the socialist system, wage determination became subject to collective bargaining which largely took the form of tripartite negotiations among unions, government and employers' associations. Although this kind of nation-wide wage bargaining may be justified by social consensus, and was used to implement basic reforms at the beginning of transition, it is questionable in later transition stages. When the level of unionisation is quite high, this may imply that wages increase more than productivity.

---

[4] Calculating an EPL index on the Slovenian new labour code (in which came into force at the beginning of 2003) makes the labour market more competitive in terms of regular and temporary employment legislation but not in terms of collective dismissals legislation. Slovenia's collective dismissals regulation was not improved, and together with that of Croatia, it is the most restrictive legislation among EU accession countries.

Slovenia started with general collective agreements in 1990. These agreements were supplemented by industry-specific agreements; and at firm-level, union and management bargained in the context of the firm's annual plan to adjust industry-level wages further. General collective agreements required that officially determined minimum wages for different occupations must not be lowered by firm-level bargaining. This multi-layer bargaining structure resulted in both wage dispersion and rapid wage growth.

Croatia has a large share of unionised workers (50 per cent in the late 1990s). Although declining, unions are still strong social partners in tripartite negotiations with the government and the employers' associations. Time-series analyses of wages and productivity in Croatia (Nestic et al. 2001) confirm that wages grew annually more than productivity – on average by 4.5 per cent points – which worsened Croatia's competitive position *vis-à-vis* Hungary, the Czech Republic and Poland.

To sum up, Croatia and Slovenia had similar pre-transition conditions (as far as GDP per capita and unemployment rate were concerned). Their economies underwent hugely different shocks (the war for Croatia), but their different behaviours in GDP per capita and labour market performance in the 1990s cannot be simply ascribed to those shocks (see for instance how the post-war recovery in Croatia ground to a halt in the late 1990s). The labour market institutions were fairly similar in the 1990s, although union pressure on wages was arguably greater in Croatia. The main hypothesis of this chapter, which will be tested below, is that the diverging evolution of the two economies in the 1990s was due to the more successful strategic response of Slovenian firms to the shocks hitting the two economies. For data reasons, analysis of strategic restructuring in Croatia cannot be conducted directly (the results of Slovenian firm-level analysis are summarised in Domadenik et al. 2003). Yet, following some recent studies (Basu et al. 1997, 2000; Domadenik et al. 2003), we believe that the comparison of short- and long-run elasticities of labour demand can yield useful indirect evidence on the process. The model and the empirical methodology are explained in the next section.

6.3 A general model of dynamic labour demand

Consider the following labour demand model. The firm faces an exogenous output demand (revenue) constraint and quadratic costs d and e in adjusting its labour (L) and capital (K) inputs. The adjustment costs d may reflect explicit financial costs, such as severance payments, or implicit costs such as the perceived difficulty of re-hiring skilled workers that had been laid off. Given the negative output shock, one may realistically assume that the firm determines its employment by minimising input costs C_t:

$$C_t = E_t \sum_{c=0}^{\infty} \left(\frac{1}{1+r} \right)^{\tau} [c_{t+\tau} K_{t+\tau} + W_{t+\tau} L_{t+\tau} + d(\Delta L_{t+\tau})^2 + e(\Delta K_{t+\tau})^2] \qquad \forall t \qquad (6.1)$$

subject to a production constraint

$$Q(L_{t+\tau}, K_{t+\tau}) = Q_{t+\tau}, \quad \forall t, \tag{6.2}$$

where E is the expectation operator, subscript t denotes time, r is the discount rate, c is the user cost of capital, W is the wage, $\Delta L_t = L_t - L_{t-1}$ and $\Delta K_t = K_t - K_{t-1}$ are the one-period (year) adjustments in the labour and capital inputs, respectively, and Q is the firm's output or revenue. Assuming further that the production function is of Cobb–Douglas type, that changes in employment from period to period are not too large, that the exogenous variables follow an autoregressive process of the second degree, and that the institutional features discussed above are important, one obtains a log-linear estimating equation of the form:[5]

$$\ln L_{it} = \alpha_0 + \alpha_1 \ln Q_{it} + \alpha_2 \ln Q_{it-1} + \alpha_3 \ln W_{it} + \alpha_4 \ln W_{it-1} +$$
$$+ \alpha_5 \ln L_{it-1} + \alpha_6'(YEAR_t) + \alpha_7'(IND_i) + \varepsilon_{it} \tag{6.3}$$

In equation (6.3), subscript i denotes firms, Q is the real revenue of the firm, $YEAR$ and IND are annual and industry dummy variables that control for macroeconomic shocks and industry-specific conditions, respectively, while ε_{it} is the error term.

Equation (6.3) permits us to estimate separately the short-term effects that correspond to defensive restructuring, as well as the long-term effects that capture to a greater extent strategic managerial behaviour relating to hiring or/and firing workers. For example, the short-term elasticity of employment with respect to revenue is given by α_1, while the corresponding long-term elasticity is given by the ratio $(\alpha_1 + \alpha_2)/(1 - \alpha_5)$.[6] The short and long-term employment elasticities with respect to wages and the other variables are defined analogously.

In terms of our conceptual discussion, equation (6.3) contains the following interesting hypotheses about the extent and speed of firm restructuring:

> *H1: Firms in transition economies adjust employment significantly in response to changes in the relevant exogenous variables ($\alpha_2 = \alpha_4 = 0$).*

> *H2a: Managements in transition economies adjust employment rapidly in response to exogenous shocks, with the adjustment in employment being completed within one year of a given change in the relevant exogenous variable (complete adjustment model: $\alpha_2 = \alpha_4 = \alpha_5 = 0$).*

> *H2b: Firms in transition economies adjust employment gradually over time in response to exogenous shocks (dynamic model: $\alpha_2 \neq 0$ and/or $\alpha_4 \neq 0$ and/or $\alpha_5 \neq 0$).*

---

[5] See Domadenik (2003) for details on derivation of the empirical model.

[6] The short-term elasticity measures the contemporaneous percentage effect on employment of a one-per cent increase in real revenue in a given year, while the long-term elasticity measures the estimated percentage effect on employment over time of a one per cent increase in the revenue in the given year.

Hypothesis 1 enables us to assess whether the adjustment in employment is significant or whether firms are reluctant to adjust employment and thus resemble the traditional (stodgy) state-owned enterprises (Basu et al. 1997, 2000; Svejnar 2000). Hypothesis 2a states that employment adjustment completely takes the form of short-term, defensive restructuring. In contrast, hypothesis 2b reflects employment adjustment which also takes the form of long-term, strategic restructuring (Domadenik et al. 2003).

Estimating dynamic panel data models such as (6.3) raises issues concerning the inclusion of a lagged dependent variable among the explanatory variables. Since the dependent variable is a function of the error term, the lagged dependent variable is correlated with the error term as well, making the OLS estimator biased and inconsistent even if the error terms less firms' specific component are not serially correlated. A traditional way to remedy this inconsistency is to estimate the model using the Within estimator. However, as Sevestre and Trognon (1996) show, neither the asymptotic covariance between the deviation of lagged dependent variable from its mean nor the deviation of the error term from its mean are zero. Hence, the Within estimator also produces inconsistent results. The degree of inconsistency is negatively related to the panel time horizon and is consequently especially severe in the case of short panels.[7]

Two methods designed to correct for OLS inconsistencies in autoregressive models are instrumental variables (IV) and generalised method of moments (GMM) estimators. However, as GMM is a large-sample estimator and its desirable properties are likely to be achieved only in very large samples[8] we will estimate our dynamic model using the Anderson-Hsiao (1986) IV approach. This implies first differencing the model to get rid of the firm-specific part in the error term. This transformation eliminates the primary cause of inconsistencies but introduces a new problem: a serial correlation of the moving average type in the error term. The choice of valid instruments in this case depends on the order of the moving average process. If disturbances are assumed to be non-correlated, then lagged values of the dependent variables as well as first differences of r.h.s. variables can serve as valid instruments. If disturbances are correlated, then lags of dependent variables have to be chosen and instruments should be higher-power lagged than the corresponding moving average process. Baltagi (2001) points out that this IV estimation method yields consistent but not necessarily efficient estimates of the parameters in the model. Arellano (1989) finds that in this case the estimator using differences rather than levels for instruments has a singular point and very large variances over a significant range of parameter values. In contrast, the estimator that uses instruments in levels has no singularities and much smaller variances, and is therefore recommended. We will consequently use the Anderson-Hsiao approach and instruments in levels lagged by two years.

---

[7] Judson and Owen (1999) report Monte Carlo experiments showing that the bias could be as much as 20 per cent of the true value of the coefficient of interest when the panel data covers 30 years.

[8] Typically, GMM estimators are asymptotically efficient, but they are rarely efficient in finite samples.

6.4 Data and empirical results

Both samples comprised previously socially-owned firms that underwent privatisation in the first years of privatisation. We excluded agriculture, fishery and extraction industries from the full samples. We also excluded firms still state-owned in the period after privatisation, and the financial services' sector. The samples consisted mainly of large and medium-sized firms: around 500 for Croatia and 1000 for Slovenia.[9] In the study we used balance-sheet data obtained from Agencies of Payments in both countries for the period 1995-2000.

In 2000, Slovenian firms in the sample generated 85 per cent of total income and employed 75 per cent of all employees of firms registered with the Slovenian Agency of Payments. In the same year, Croatian firms generated 86 per cent of total income and employed 81 per cent of all employees of all firms registered with the Croatian Agency of Payments.

The representative Slovenian firm in this sample reduced the number of its employees from 258 in 1996 to 244 in 2000 (by 1.076 per cent per year), whilst Croatian firms reduced their employment by more than 22 per cent (4 per cent per year) in the period 1995-2000. However, total sales in Croatia diminished by almost 2 per cent in the six years, whilst in Slovenia total sales increased by almost 7 per cent every year (for exact values see Table 6.1). Moreover, although total sales in Croatia decreased, the average wage rose by more than 18 per cent between 1995 and 2000, and by more than 22 per cent in Slovenia in the same period. Productivity in Slovenia over the five years rose by 77 per cent (11 per cent per year), whilst in Croatia it increased by 30 per cent. Both total sales and wages are measured in 1995 constant prices (using SIT for Slovenia and KN for Croatia).

The parameters were estimated using the Anderson-Hsiao IV estimator and the corresponding elasticities are reported in Tables 6.2 and 6.3. As we expected, the best fit to the data was found for the dynamic labour demand model (the corresponding F-tests were significant). Coefficients have the predicted signs and are statistically significant, except for coefficients on sales in the case of Croatia and coefficients on lagged sales and wages in the case of Slovenia.

Table 6.1. Summary statistics for variables used in estimating labour adjustment and investment equations

Variable	Year	No.	Mean	Description
SLOVENIA				
L	1995	1016	258.08	Number of employees
	1996	1163	243.07	
	1997	1132	236.61	
	1998	1044	240.44	
	1999	1038	234.55	

---

[9] The number of firms in both countries varies from year to year because some firms failed to report their balance-sheet data to Agencies of Payments in some years.

	2000	950	244.08	
$W = y/L$	1995	978	1914.78	Labour costs per employee
	1996	1097	1974.48	
	1997	1060	2094.04	
	1998	974	2169.70	
	1999	974	2304.67	
	2000	827	2347.30	
TS	1995	1018	$2.300*10^6$	Sales
	1996	1176	$2.336*10^6$	
	1997	1146	$2.518*10^6$	
	1998	1059	$2.665*10^6$	
	1999	1057	$2.805*10^6$	
	2000	965	$3.286*10^6$	
TSL	1995	1011	13840.67	Sales per employee
	1996	1160	15396.11	
	1997	1127	17728.79	
	1998	1042	19080.75	
	1999	1034	19979.35	
	2000	949	24188.3	

CROATIA

L	1995	502	252.83	Number of employees
	1996	502	235.03	
	1997	544	209.37	
	1998	531	206.08	
	1999	525	202.92	
	2000	503	199.51	
$W = y/L$	1995	496	43711.74	Labour costs per employee
	1996	500	47520.33	
	1997	540	49987.63	
	1998	530	50315.39	
	1999	519	50463.77	
	2000	494	51639.01	
TS	1995	502	$6.27*10^7$	Sales
	1996	502	$6.43*10^7$	
	1997	544	$6.94*10^7$	
	1998	531	$6.33*10^7$	
	1999	525	$5.87*10^7$	
	2000	503	$6.15*10^7$	
TSL	1995	496	$3.25*10^5$	Sales per employee
	1996	500	$3.40*10^5$	
	1997	540	$4.12*10^5$	
	1998	530	$3.58*10^5$	
	1999	519	$3.58*10^5$	
	2000	494	$4.23*10^5$	

* Variables are measured in constant prices (base is 1995) and 1000 SIT for Slovenia and 1000 KN for Croatia.

Table 6.2. Labour demand estimations for Slovenia and Croatia

	CROATIA	SLOVENIA
Ln *TS*	0.4292 (0.3471)	0.6119[a] (0.2026)
Ln *W*	-0.7825[a] (0.3008)	-1.1899[a] (0.4270)
Ln *L*$_{t-1}$	0.5310[a] (0.1993)	0.5501 (0.4837)
Ln *TS*$_{t-1}$	-0.0675 (0.0971)	-0.2191 (0.3629)
Ln *W*$_{t-1}$	-0.2698[b] (0.1109)	-1.1136 (0.8699)
Constant	-0.0294 (0.0566)	Dropped
Year dummies	Yes	Yes
Industry dummies	Yes	Yes
Adjusted R2	0.2843	0.1838
N	1588	636

Notes
1. a, b and c denote statistically significant values at 1 per cent, 5 per cent and 10 per cent on a two tail test, respectively.
2. Standard errors are reported in parenthesis.
3. In the labour demand estimation for Croatia we used lagged and twice lagged levels of ln *TS*, ln *W* and ln *L* as instruments.
4. In the labour demand estimation for Slovenia we used lagged 3, 4, and 5-year levels of ln *TS*, ln *W* and ln *L* as instruments.

Table 6.3. Short and long run elasticities of labour demand

	$E(L/TS)$	$E(L/W)$
SLOVENIA		
Short run	0.6119[a]	-1.1899[a]
Long run	0.8730	-5.1200
CROATIA		
Short run	0.4292	-0.7825[a]
Long run	0.7712	-2.2437

The key part of our study is the comparison of short and long run elasticity of labour demand in both countries. Surprisingly, there are not large differences in the estimated short-term wage elasticities (–1.19 in Slovenia versus –0.78 in Croatia). With respect to elasticities for other CEE transition countries, the estimated elasticities were similar to those calculated for the Czech Republic and Poland, but they were substantially lower than that for Hungary: for example, the short run elasticity of labour demand with respect to wages for the Czech Republic was estimated at between –0.6 and –1.0, at –0.8 for Poland, between –1 and –2.3 for Hungary, and at –0.3 for the Slovak Republic. (Basu et al. 1997). Similarly, the short-run elasticities of labour demand with respect to sales fall in the same range as for the Czech Republic and Poland. For the Czech Republic it was estimated at between 0.5 and 0.6, at 0.4 for Poland, at 0.3 for Slovak Republic, and at between 0.7 and 0.8 for Hungary.

However, long run wage elasticities for Slovenia and Croatia show substantially higher values for Slovenia, twice as high as the Croatian ones. Long run elasticities of labour demand with respect to sales exhibit similar values to the short run ones. Following the analyses developed in some recent studies (Basu et al. 2000; Domadenik et al. 2003), we interpret the higher long run wage elasticities for Slovenia as evidence in favour of a greater capacity for strategic response by Slovenian firms. Our results support Svejnar's (2002) argument that not only labour market flexibility, but also other factors such as transportation infrastructure and business environment, are the prerequisites for any efficient strategic restructuring.

6.5 Conclusion

Firms' restructuring and market adjustment are core issues in both transition and developed countries. However, they are more important for the former countries because they have to make up for delays in development originating in the previous socio-economic system. In countries with emerging markets, a significant number of firms have to be restructured and adjusted to the new business environment. Discussion of the possible reasons for underachievement in this regard is of interest to policy-makers, firms' decision–makers, and researchers. We believe that our study significantly contributes to the literature comparing the different outcomes of enterprise restructuring (efficient in Slovenia and inefficient in Croatia although both countries started from similar initial conditions).

In the early 1990s Slovenia and Croatia successfully implemented macroeconomic reforms. Then, in the second part of the 1990s, the establishment and enforcement of a market-oriented legal system with its accompanying institutions became the most important economic goal. Although Croatia inherited the same path dependence, and although it was the most developed reforming countries at the beginning of transition, ten years later it substantially lagged behind, with one of the highest unemployment rates among the CEE economies. Our analysis, based on a sample of 1000 Slovenian and 500 Croatian privatised firms, reports that the estimated short run elasticities of labour with respect to wages and sales are very similar in both countries, confirming that firms in both economies have adjusted employment gradually over time in response to exogenous shocks occurring at the beginning of transition (defensive restructuring). Yet, the strategic response has been much more efficient in the case of Slovenian firms, and we may conclude that the main difference between the two economies resides in the extent and efficiency of strategic restructuring. The analysis in Domadenik et al (2003) confirms that Slovenian firms behave similarly to firms in developed economies as regards investment in fixed and soft (training, marketing, R&D) capital. However further research is required to clarify this issue.

References

Arellano M (1989) A note on the Anderson-Hsiao estimator for panel data. Economic Letters 31: 337–341.

Baltagi BH (2001) Econometric analysis of panel data. John Wiley and Sons: New York.

Basu S, Estrin S, Svejnar J (1997) Employment and wage behaviour of enterprises in transition economies: the case of Poland and Czechoslovakia. Economics of Transition 5:271–287.

Basu S, Estrin S, Svejnar J (2000), Employment and wages in enterprises under communism and in transition: evidence from central Europe and Russia. WDI Working Paper 440.

Biondic I, Crnic S, Martinis A, Sosic V (2002) Tranzicija, zastita zaposlenja i trziste rada u Hrvatskoj. Ured za socijalno partnerstvo u Hrvatskoj, Zagreb.

Crnkovic-Pozaic S, Vujcic B. (1998) Country report for Croatia: employment and labour market policies. Mimeo.

Domadenik P, Prašnikar J, Svejnar J (2003) Defensive and strategic restructuring of Firms during the transition to a market economy. WDI Working Paper 541.

Domadenik P (2003) Restructuring of firms in post-privatization period: The case of Slovenia. PhD Thesis. University of Ljubljana.

Earle J, Estrin S (1997) After voucher privatization; the structure of corporate ownership in Russian manufacturing industry. CEPR Discussion paper 1736.

EBRD (2000) EBRD transition report 2000, EBRD, London.

Estrin S (2002) Competition and corporate governance in transition. The Journal of Economic Perspectives 16(1):101–125.

Gregorič A, Prašnikar J, Ribnikar I (2000) Corporate governance in transitional economies: the case of Slovenia. Economic and Business Review 2:183–207.

Hsiao C (1986) Analysis of panel data, Cambridge University Press, Cambridge.

Judson RA and Owen AL (1999) Estimating dynamic panel data models: a guide for macroeconomists. Economic Letters 65: 9–15.

Lizal L (1998) The dynamics of enterprise investment and export influence on investment behavior in the transition period. PhD Thesis, Center for Economic Research and Graduate Education, Prague.

Konings J, Lehmann H (2001) Marshall and labour demand in Russia: going back to basics. WDI Working Paper 392.

Ott K (1997) Gospodarska politika i neslužbeno gospodarstvo. Financijska praksa 21: 29–45.

Prašnikar J, Svejnar J, Domadenik P (2000) Enterprise in post-privatisation period: firm-level evidence for Slovenia. East European Economics 38: 60–92.

Prašnikar J, Gregorič A (2002) The influence of workers' participation on the power of management in transitional countries: the case of Slovenia. Annals of Public and Co-operative Economic 73: 269–297.

Riboud M, Sanchez-Paramo C, Silva-Jauregui C (2002) Does eurosclerosis matter? Institutional reform and labor market performance in central and eastern European countries. In: Funck B, Pizzati L (ed.) Labor, employment, and social policies in the EU enlargement process: changing perspectives and policy options. The World Bank, Washington, pp 315–338.

Roland G (1996) Economic efficiency and political constraints in privatisation and restructuring. Paper presented at the 'Policy Studies to Promote Private Sector Development' workshop, EBRD, London.

Roland G (2000) Transition and economics: politics, firms, markets, MIT Press, Cambridge (Mass.).

Sevestre P, Trognon A (1996) Dynamic linear models. In: Matyas L. and Sevestre P, The econometrics of panel data. Kluwer, Dordrecht, pp 100–118.

Svejnar J (1999) Labor markets in the transitional central and east European economies. Handbook of labor economics, vol 3. Elsevier, Amsterdam, pp 2809–2857.

Svejnar J (2002) Transition economies: performance and challenges. The Journal of Economic Perspectives 16:3–28.

Vujcic B, Lang M (2001) Croatia – GDN project country study. http://www.cerge-ei.cz/pdf/gdn/croatia.pdf.

7 Widening Unemployment Differentials in Italy: the Role of Wage and Labour Productivity

Michele Limosani

University of Messina, Italy

7.1 Introduction[*]

The regional unemployment differential between the southern and the northern Italian regions has steadily increased in the past forty years. Although previous analyses have attempted to determine the causes of these regional variations,[1] they have certain shortcomings. Firstly, the majority of these studies do not specify the theory behind the empirical estimation.[2] Moreover, they tend to focus on the failure of certain adjustment mechanisms in the labour market, and in particular on wage and labour mobility and, more recently, on the interplay between shocks and institutions. They consequently neglect the role of labour productivity. It is likely that institutions shape the effects of some shocks and that wage flexibility may improve the performance of the labour market. Yet widening differentials of unemployment in Italy for such a long period of time, almost forty years, cannot be explained unless consideration is made of the dynamics of labour productivity across regions.

This chapter proposes a simple model with which to analyse the relation between unemployment, productivity and wage differentials in Italy, and it conducts a panel data analysis to explore the direct link among these variables. The first section of the chapter sketches the model, which makes it possible to identify potential channels through which productivity and wage differentials influence regional unemployment. The second section presents some empirical evidence in support of the predictions of the theoretical model. The final section draws some concluding remarks.

---

[*] I wish to thank S Destefanis, FE Caroleo, C Panico, T Thirwall and all participants at the XVII Convegno Nazionale di Economia del Lavoro, Salerno, 26-27 September 2002, for their comments and suggestions. Financial support from the University of Messina is gratefully acknowledged.

[1] On this issue see Attanasio and Padoa Schioppa (1991), Faini et al. (1996) and, more recently, Pench et al. (1999), Boeri et al. (2000), and Brunello et al. (2001a, 2001b, 2001c).

[2] For a survey of theoretical and empirical studies on regional unemployment differentials see Elhorst (2003).

7.2 Theoretical background

The macroeconomic framework used for the theoretical analysis builds on a previous model on regional labour productivity developed by the present author, which has been slightly modified to take account of a differentiated nominal wage at a regional level.[3] In order to simplify the exposition, only given in what follows are the fundamental equations discussed in the previous model, with the main differences being highlighted. The model can be described by the following equations:

$$y_i = n_i + \lambda_i \tag{7.1}$$

$$p_i = w_i - \lambda_i + \eta_i \tag{7.2}$$

$$y_i = I_i - \alpha (p_i - p) \tag{7.3}$$

$$I_i = \gamma Z + v \lambda_i \tag{7.4}$$

where all variables are expressed in logarithms and y is output supply, n the number of employed workers, λ labour productivity, w the nominal wage, I investment spending, p the price level, η the mark-up, and $i = (1, 2, 3 \ldots s)$ refers to the numbers of regions. In this economy, therefore, firms operate under a constant return to scale technology: equation (7.1). Equation (7.2) describes the price setting equation. Unlike in the previous model,[4] where the nominal wage was assumed to be equal across regions, this equation now considers the existence of a regional nominal wage. Although industry-level collective agreements have always played a dominant role in the Italian bargaining system at central level, a potential wage drift across regions may arise because of a second-stage local bargaining process.[5]

Equation (7.3) indicates that regional demand depends on regional investment and on relative price with respect the aggregate price, p, set equal to the international price exogenously given in our analysis. Equation (7.4) describes regional investments as functions of certain macroeconomic factors common to all regions, such as the real interest rate and a measure of national and fiscal and monetary policies, all variables included in the vector Z, and local variables such as the productivity level.

Substituting Eq. (7.4) into Eq. (7.3) and taking Eqs [7.1–7.2] into account, we obtain

$$n_i = \gamma Z - \alpha w_i - \theta \lambda_i - \alpha \eta_i + \alpha p \tag{7.5}$$

where $\theta = (1 - \alpha - v)$ and thus the employment differential between two regions as follows:

---

[3] For a full description of the model see Limosani (2004).
[4] See Limosani (2004).
[5] On this issue see Brunello et al. (2001b) and Brandolini et al. (2001).

$$n_i - n_j = -\theta(\lambda_i - \lambda_j) - \alpha_i(\eta_i - \eta_j) - \alpha_i(w_i - w_j) \tag{7.6}$$

Considering that employment is equal to the labour force, l, minus the number of unemployed people, equation (7.6) becomes:[6]

$$u_i - u_j = \theta(\lambda_i - \lambda_j) + \alpha(\eta_i - \eta_j) + \alpha(w_i - w_j) + (l_i - l_j) \tag{7.7}$$

The dynamics of the unemployment differential are not influenced by the behaviour of aggregate variables; they are instead determined by the evolution of local variables, in particular differentials in nominal wage, productivity, mark-up and the labour force. The empirical analysis in the next section will be organised around a statistical investigation of Eq. (7.7).

7.3 The empirical analysis

The data employed in the analysis are taken from the ISTAT database: u is the unemployment rate, l is the labour force, λ is labour productivity, measured as gross value added per worker, and w is the nominal gross wage.[7] Following previous works on unemployment differentials in Italy,[8] the twenty Italian regions are grouped into four geographical areas, North–West, North–East, Centre, South. When deriving the differentials described in Eq. (7.7) the North–Western region, the most productive area in the 1990s, was chosen as the benchmark and marked with *. The sample covers a period of about forty years between 1960 and 2000.

Figure 7.1 displays the unemployment rate differential between the Southern and the North-Western regions for the entire period considered. The data clearly show that the unemployment differential has widened since 1980. A similar picture, however, emerges if we look at the labour productivity and wage differentials between the two geographical areas as displayed in Figs 7.2 and 7.3.

In the rest of this section we pooled regions and estimate the parameters of interest using the Least Square Dummy Variable (LSDV) estimator. In particular a regression was run which allowed the unemployment differential to depend on labour productivity, the labour force, and the wage differential as suggested by Eq. (7.7):

$$(u - u^*)_{it} = d_i + a(\lambda - \lambda^*)_{it} + b(l - l^*)_{it} + c(w - w^*)_{it} \tag{7.8}$$

---

[6] Recalling that labour force, L, is equal to the number of employed, N, and unemployed people U, $L = N + U$, if we take logarithms and assume that $\log(U/N + 1) \approx \log U/N$, it is possible to write that $\log U/N = \log u \approx \log L - \text{Log } N \rightarrow u \approx l - n$. In the following analysis u is considered to be a good proxy for the rate of unemployment.

[7] Nominal wage is calculated from ISTAT data on 'Occupazione e Redditi da lavoro dipendente' and includes labour tax.

[8] See Brunello e al (2001b) and Limosani (2004).

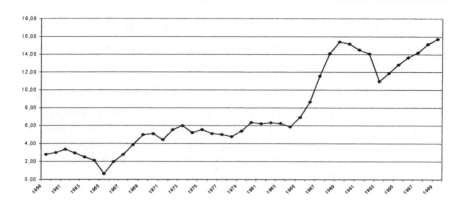

Fig. 7.1. Unemployment differential (South vs. North–West)

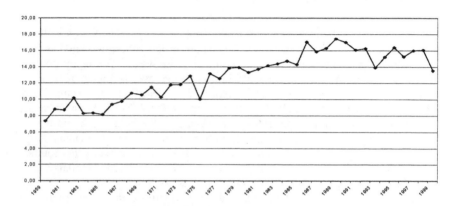

Fig. 7.2. Labour productivity differential (North vs. West–South)

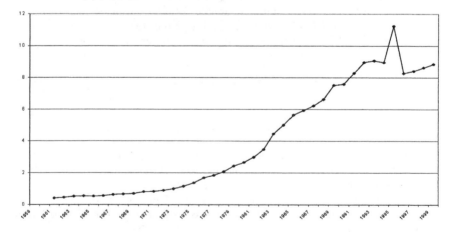

Fig. 7.3. Wage differential (North vs. West–South)

where d_i denotes the regional macro-areas. The estimated coefficients of the regional dummy variables in our specification are also intended to function as a proxy for the behaviour of the mark-up across regions. Table 7.1 reports the results of the estimated model.

Table 7.1. The estimated coefficients of the panel model (sample 1960–2000)

Variables	Coefficients*
$(\lambda - \lambda^*)_t$	-0.35
	(2.85)
$(1 - 1^*)_t$	-0.003
	(2.78)
$(w - w^*)_t$	-0.58
	(5.75)
d_1	$3,52$
	(1.65)
d_2	6.60
	(3.03)
d_3	0.90
	(0.75)
R^2	0.85
Wald test	$\xi\,(3) = 20.12$
Breush-Pagan test	$\xi\,(3) = 21.51$

* t-ratio reported in brackets

The following results point to some interesting conclusions. Firstly, regression performs well in fitting the cross-regions dimension of the panel. The correlation coefficient R^2 suggests that the estimated model explains almost 85 per cent of total variation in the data. Secondly, the results show that unemployment and productivity differentials are negatively correlated across regions: the greater the dispersion of regional productivity, the greater the dispersion of regional unemployment. The coefficient on the productivity differential is significant both economically and statistically. A one per cent increase in the productivity differential leads to a decrease in the unemployment differential of 0.35 per cent.

The coefficient on the wage differential is also statistically significant. According to our estimate, a one percentage point increase in the wage differential will reduce the unemployment differential by about 0.60 points. Moreover, an increase of one per cent in the labour force differential, due to inter-regional migration or exogenous demographic factors, reduces the unemployment rate differential by about 0.003 per cent. This effect is significantly smaller than the productivity or wage impact, but it is still statistically significant. Finally, some regional dummies variables are statistically significant, which suggests that, across geographical areas, there would be a variation in the level of mark-up applied by firms.

It is well known that the existence in the pooled regression model of simultaneous correlations of the disturbances across regions or the presence of group-wise heteroskedasticity, as indicated in Table 7.1 by the Wald and the Breusch-Pagan test statistics respectively, generate incorrect standard errors and biased and inefficient OLS estimates.[9] In order to produce corrected standard error estimates for our panel, we therefore re-estimated our previous model by means of Prais-Winsten regression. While removing the potential autocorrelation within the cross-sectional units, the Praise-Winsten technique computes the standard errors of variance-covariance estimates by allowing the disturbances to be heteroskedastic and simultaneously correlated across panels. The estimation results are reported in Table 7.2.

Table 7.2. The estimated coefficients of the Praise-Winsten regression (sample 1960–2000)

Variables	Coefficients[*]
$(\lambda - \lambda^*)_t$	− 0.26
	(2.87)
$(1 - 1^*)_t$	− 0.001
	(2.08)
$(w - w^*)_t$	− 0.48
	(2.70)
d_1	3.68
	(1.62)
d_2	6.90
	(2.91)
d_3	1.91
	(1.41)
R^2	0.87
AR	(1)

[*] t-ratio reported in brackets

While providing further robust empirical estimation, the new estimated model largely confirms our previous conclusions. Taken together, the results of both estimations indicate that besides wage flexibility, the labour productivity differential is another of the main determinants to consider when seeking to explain the evolution of unemployment differentials in Italy.

7.4 Concluding remarks

Unemployment differentials in Italy have widened steadily since 1960. Although previous research into the causes of these spatial differences has improved our understanding of why they may occur, there is still much work to be done. This chapter has focused on labour productivity and wage differentials as two of the main driving forces of unemployment differentials over time. To this end, it has

---

[9] See Greene (2003).

proposed a simple model in order to highlight the potential channels through which these variables may influence unemployment, and it has provided empirical evidence in support of this relation. The results of the empirical investigation strongly suggest that both wage and productivity differentials are important factors in explaining the dynamics of unemployment disparities in Italy over the past forty years.

References

Attanasio O, Padoa Schioppa F (1991) Regional inequalities, migration and mismatch in Italy, 1960-1986. In: Padoa Schioppa F (ed.) Mismatch and labour mobility. Cambridge University Press, Cambridge, pp 237–320.

Boeri T, Layard R, Nickell S (2000) Welfare to work and the fight against long term unemployment. Report to prime minister Blair and D'Alema. Department of Education and Employment Research Report 206, London.

Brandolini A, Cipollone P, Sestito P (2001) Earnings dispersion, low pay and household poverty in Italy 1977–1998. Banca d'Italia, Temi di Discussione 427.

Brunello G, Lupi C, Ordine P (2001a) Effetti differenziati della politica fiscale nei mercati del lavoro locali. Rivista di Politica Economica 8:257–271.

Brunello G, Lupi C, Ordine P (2001b) Widening differences in Italian regional unemployment. Labour Economics, 8:103–129.

Brunello G, Lupi C, Ordine P, Parisi M (2001c) Beyond national institutions: labour taxes and regional unemployment in Italy. CESifoWorking Paper 414.

Elhorst JP (2003) The mystery of regional unemployment differentials. Theoretical and empirical explanations. Journal of Economic Surveys 17:709–748.

Fabiani S, Locarno A, Oneto G, Sestito P (2001) The sources of unemployment fluctuations: an empirical application to the Italian case. Labour Economics, 8:259–89.

Faini R, Galli G, Rossi F (1996) Mobilità e disoccupazione in Italia: un'analisi dell'offerta di lavoro. Centro Studi Confindustria Working Paper 6.

Greene WH (2003) Econometric analysis, MacMillan, New York.

Layard R, Nickell S, Jackman R (1991) Unemployment. Macroeconomic performance and the labour market. Basil Blackwell, Oxford.

Limosani M (2004) Beyond regional institutions: widening unemployment differentials in Italy. Labour 18:503–514.

Pench LR, Sestito P, Frontini E (1999) Some unpleasant arithmetics of regional unemployment in the EU. Are there any lessons for EMU?. European Commission Economic Paper 134, Brussels.

8 Skill Mismatch and Regional Unemployment in Poland

Andrew Newell

University of Sussex, United Kingdom

8.1 Introduction

This chapter reports estimates of the impact of structural features of local labour markets on the geographical distribution of unemployment in Poland. Here structure is defined primarily in terms of industry and education. The education structure of the potential labour force is taken to reflect the skill mix of labour supply. The industrial and sometimes occupational structures of employment are taken to reflect, as least in part, the skill structure of labour demand.

Why choose education as a key structural feature? There are three outstanding *a priori* reasons. First, most of the formerly centrally planned economies featured a much larger industrial sector, and correspondingly smaller service sector than their Western counterparts. Industry generally employs a much greater share of manual workers with vocational and primary education than services. A shift towards services was one of the most predictable changes to occur through transition. Second, on the supply side, there was a massive rise in completed education levels among Poland's population of working age, through the 1990s. This is documented below. Thirdly, there is a universal and reliable inverse relationship between broad educational rankings and unemployment rates. By and large, lower educated or less-skilled workers have higher unemployment rates. There are several reasons for this inverse relationship, which are briefly discussed in what follows. This inverse relationship holds for Poland and again this is documented below.

These three facts fairly naturally combine to suggest the hypothesis tested in this chapter, which can be restated as follows. If the regions of Poland differ markedly in their skill structures and experienced different sized shifts in these structures, then these changes should account for some of the regional unemployment picture over the 1990s.

The study covers 1994–1998 inclusive. It was a time of rapid economic growth in Poland. Over this period the data source, the Polish Labour Force Survey, categorised industries, occupations and regions in a consistent way. After 1998 the 49 administrative regions of Poland, the *wojewodstwa*, were reduced to 17, with many new boundaries. The regions will be referred to by the anglicised expression *voivodship*. Because of this administrative change, researchers of Poland's regional evolution have concentrated on this period.

Let us briefly summarise some relevant findings from three fairly recent papers. Newell and Pastore (2000) demonstrate that unemployment rates and indices of industrial and occupational change are positively and significantly correlated across voivodships. They also show that inflow rates to unemployment are also correlated with these indices of change. The indices that Newell and Pastore use reflect only the volume of structural change,[1] rather than the skill content. Newell and Pastore also show that for individuals, the probability of inflow to unemployment from employment is strongly inversely related to completed education levels. Lastly, Newell and Pastore document that there is strong persistence in regional unemployment patterns.

Faggio and Konings (2003) demonstrate the wide diversity across voivodships in the nature and timing of industrial restructuring. Deichmann and Henderson (2000) study regional evolutions from the economic geographer's perspective. They find that Poland experienced little internal migration over the period, much less than they would have expected from the study of other countries. They argue plausibly that housing market imperfections are at the heart of this lack of mobility. Deichmann and Henderson also study the regional concentration of industries. They find that manufacturing and agriculture were initially quite highly concentrated, but that after the initial contraction of manufacturing following the 'Big Bang' reforms, manufacturing began to become regionally less concentrated. Also, they find no evidence of more rapid manufacturing growth in regions of high unemployment. Lastly, Deichmann and Henderson find growing concentration in services, in the large urban centres.

There is now quite a long list of facts. Let us summarise. Firstly, there is little migration and a fair amount of persistence in relative unemployment rates. Secondly, there is wide diversity in industrial and skill structure and across voivodships. Also, these structures changed markedly over the period.

The next section reviews the data, documenting the large shift in skills, the regional diversity of skills and industrial structures and the changes in these structures across voivodships. Section 8.3 discusses theoretical issues in order to give foundations to the interpretation of the empirical work. Section 8.4 discusses the econometric results and Section 8.5 concludes. We find, plausibly, that higher skilled populations tend to generate lower unemployment rates and that controlling for population skill levels, lower levels of relative demand for unskilled workers raises a region's unemployment rate. These equilibrium and disequilibrium phenomena can explain about half of the regional variance in Polish unemployment rates.

---

[1] The typical index used by Newell and Pastore (2000) was of the form:

$$I_t = \frac{1}{2} \sum_i \left| \Delta s_{it} \right|$$

Here s_{it} is sector i's share of employment and Δ is the change over a period ending at t.

8.2 Unemployment and structural change across Poland's regions

8.2.1 The inverse relationship and the big shift in skills

Table 8.1 demonstrates the shift in completed education levels. The middle section of the table shows a rise of around 8 percentage points in the share of the working age population with completed secondary or higher education. Clearly, older, less-qualified people were retiring and being replaced by well-qualified young people. The table also shows that Polish unemployed people were less educated than employed workers in Poland during 1993: see the first and seventh lines of the table. To put it another way, less educated workers had higher unemployment rates. As already mentioned, this is a well-documented phenomenon, visible in many countries. It reflects the inverse relationship between job turnover and inflow rates to unemployment on the one hand, and skill (or education) level on the other hand (see Layard et al. 1991, Chap. 6). Layard et al. also show that differences in unemployment durations by skill also exist, but are less pronounced. We illustrate these relationships for Poland in 1997/8 in Tables 8.2 and 8.3a and 8.3b.

Table 8.1. The big shift in skills: changes in the distributions of employment, the working age population[1] and unemployment by level of completed education, 1993–1999

	Tertiary	Secondary	Lower Vocational	Primary or lower
Share in employment in 1993	10.5	26.3	35.6	27.6
Share in employment in 1999	15.6	34.2	35.2	15.0
Change in employment share 93-99	5.1	7.9	–0.4	–12.6
Share in population in 1993	7.8	23.8	31.4	37.0
Share in population in 1999	10.5	29.7	31.0	28.8
Change in population share 93-99	2.7	5.9	–0.4	–8.2
Share in unemployment in 1993	3.8	25.6	43.4	27.2
Share in unemployment in 1999	5.5	30.9	42.0	21.5
Change in unemployment share 93-99	1.7	5.3	–1.4	–5.7

[1] Population aged 15–60
Source: Polish Labour Force Survey

Table 8.2. The inverse relationship, Poland 1998

Completed education level	Unemployment rate (%)	Participation rate (%)	Share of population aged 16-60 (%)
Tertiary	4.1	90.3	10.7
Secondary	9.9	75.0	28.7
Lower Vocational	12.4	79.3	32.0
Primary	16.1	39.0	28.6

Source: Polish Labour Force Survey.

Table 8.3a. Tenure and turnover by broad completed education level, Poland 1997–98

	Average uncompleted job tenure, November 1997, in years	Percentage of the employed in November 1997 who were not in the same job by November 1998
Tertiary	5.8	7.7
Secondary	5.6	11.6
Lower Vocational	5.2	15.9
Primary or lower	4.5	25.4

Note: The sample was non-agricultural workers aged under 40 in November 1997.
Source: Polish Labour Force Survey, November 1997 and November 1998.

Table 8.3b. Average uncompleted unemployment duration by educational attainment, Poland 1998

Completed education level	Average uncompleted unemployment duration (months)
Tertiary	9.2
Secondary	12.8
Lower vocational	12.2
Primary of less	13.5

Source: Polish Labour Force Survey

Table 8.2 shows the inverse relationship very clearly. Primary educated workers experienced an unemployment rate almost four times that of tertiary-educated workers. The first column of Table 8.3a shows that uncompleted job tenures increase with completed education levels. The second column of Table 8.3a shows that turnover rates decrease sharply with education.[2] Table 8.3b shows that unemployed workers with tertiary education experienced shorter spells of unemployment than other workers, but differences between other groups are milder.

In the period 1993 to 1999, this gap in the average levels of completed education between the employed and the unemployed grew significantly. The third and seventh lines of Table 8.1 show a much larger shift towards higher levels of education among the employed than among the unemployed. If we construct a Dun-

---

[2] The sample used for Table 8.2 excludes workers over 40 years old. In Poland in the 1990s, older workers tend to have lower education levels but longer tenures. Selecting workers under 40 crudely eliminates this heterogenity.

can and Duncan (1955) segregation index[3] to quantify the differences in education structure, it increases from 7.8 for 1993 to 13.6 for 1999, a rise of almost 75 per cent.

To reiterate the scale of the change, over this six-year period there was a drop of over 12 percentage points in the share of primary-educated workers in employment, and a corresponding rise of 13 percentage points in the share of workers with at least secondary education.

The shift in employment was both a shift towards the employment of better-educated workers within industries and a shift in industrial structure towards education-intensive sectors. Table 8.4 illustrates this. Comparing the positions in 1993 and 1998, there is a within-industry shift away from the employment of lower vocational and primary-educated workers for all the major industrial groupings. Between industries, there was a dramatic fall in employment in agriculture, an industry that employs mostly workers with lower levels of education. The main gains in employment share came in trade and public services, both of which employ majorities of better-educated workers. The relative importance of between and within industry change can be gauged by a shift-share decomposition. Using 1-digit industry level data, the aggregate change in the proportion of secondary or higher educated employment is roughly half between-industry change and half within-industry change. Of course, as Table 8.4 suggests, this balance is altered if agriculture is omitted. In non-agricultural employment the share of tertiary and secondary-educated workers increases from 47.9 per cent in 1993 to 54.2 per cent in

Table 8.4. The structure of employment by major industrial sector and education, Poland 1993 and 1998

	Tertiary and secondary share in industry (%)	Lower vocational and primary share in industry (%)	Industry share in total employment (%)
Agriculture, 1993	13.1	86.9	38.8
Agriculture, 1998	16.4	83.5	21.3
Manufacturing, 1993	31.5	68.5	18.9
Manufacturing, 1998	37.5	62.5	20.5
Trade and related, 1993	52.5	47.5	9.6
Trade and related, 1998	56.3	43.7	15.1
Public administration, health and education 1993	69.9	30.1	17.6
Public administration, health and education, 1998	75.3	24.7	21.3
Total, 1993	34.4	65.6	100
Total, 1998	46.1	54.9	100

Source: Polish Labour Force Survey

---

[3] If s_{ne} is the share of employment with education level e and s_{ue} is the share of unemployment with education level e, then the Duncan and Duncan (1955) segregation index, D, is

$$D = \frac{1}{2}\sum_{e}\left|s_{ne} - s_{ue}\right| * 100 .$$

1998, an increase of 6.3 percentage points. A shift-share analysis of this increase reveals that 5.8 percentage points of the change, over 80 per cent, were within-industry.

8.2.2 Regional variations in skill and unemployment

Table 8.5 illustrates the variety of unemployment and skill structure that existed across the voivodships in 1994. Perhaps it is easiest to obtain an impression by looking at the maximum and minimum voivodship values for the variables. Unemployment rates ranged from moderate but substantial to extremely high. There are wide variations in educational shares, partly reflecting, no doubt, the geographical distribution of economic activity generated in the communist period. The default category includes all those with primary of lower levels of education. There is similar variety in occupational shares, which are calculated from non-agricultural employment. The industrial shares show the greatest spatial variation.

Table 8.6 reports the regional distribution of percentage point changes for 1994-1998 in the same set of variables as in Table 8.5. For all variables, there are voivodships where significant falls are recorded and others where the variable rose.

Table 8.5. Voivodship variations in unemployment, industry and skill, levels, 1994

	Average	Std. deviation	Maximum	Minimum
Unemployment rate	14.7	4.1	28.0	8.0
Completed education shares				
Tertiary	8.1	2.9	20.0	4.0
Secondary	23.0	3.6	36.0	16.0
Lower voc.	25.3	4.4	35.0	14.0
Industry[1] shares				
Agriculture	36.0	9.4	68.0	21.0
Industry	34.5	9.1	56.0	12.0
Services	29.5	15.3	66.0	3.0
Non-agricultural occupational[2] shares				
Non-manual 1	33.2	4.6	47.0	18.0
Non-manual 2	19.8	2.9	27.0	15.0
Manual	47.0	5.0	61.0	32.0

[1] Industry includes mining, manufacturing, utilities, construction and transport. Services include public administration, education, health, other services, financial and business services, and trade.
[2] Non-manual 1 includes professional, managerial and technical workers. Non-manual 2 includes clerical and sales workers.

Source: Polish Labour Force Survey

Table 8.6. Voivodship variations in changes in unemployment, industry and skill, percentage point changes 1994–1998

	Average	Std. Deviation	Maximum	Minimum
Unemployment rate	−3.6	3.1	2.0	−13.0
Completed education shares				
Tertiary	0.8	1.7	5.0	−3.0
Secondary	1.5	2.6	8.0	5.0
Lower voc.	1.2	2.8	8.0	−5.0
Industry shares				
Agriculture	−4.9	5.3	7.0	−18.0
Industry	1.0	4.8	12.0	−9.0
Services	4.0	4.2	14.0	−4.0
Non–agricultural occupational shares				
Non-manual 1	−0.3	5.9	14.0	−13.0
Non-manual 2	1.8	4.1	11.0	−7.0
Manual	−1.4	5.4	13.0	−20.0

[1] Industry includes mining, manufacturing, utilities, construction and transport. Services include public administration, education, health, other services, financial and business services, and trade.
[2] Non-manual 1 includes professional, managerial and technical workers. Non-manual 2 includes clerical and sales workers.

Source: Polish Labour Force Survey

8.3 Theoretical issues

First, what gives rise to the inverse relationship between skill and unemployment rates? All the most obvious theories rely on lower rates of job turnover for skilled workers converting into lower inflows to unemployment. The textbook answer involves non-wage labour costs. For highly-skilled workers, hiring, training and firing costs are usually greater (see e.g. Filer at al. 1996). This gives rise to lower lay-off probability. In addition, in the face of these fixed costs, there is a greater incentive for firms to pay efficiency wages to reduce turnover due to quits. How could this generate skill-related unemployment differentials? There follows a labour market model in which skill mix affects equilibrium unemployment.

8.3.1 Labour demand

The demand side of this model is entirely conventional. Regional production takes place within a representative firm with constant-returns-to-scale technology production:

$$Y_i = f(K_i, S_i, N_i) \text{, for regions } I = 1, ..., R.$$

where K is capital, S is skilled labour and N is unskilled labour. Taking logs of the profit-maximising first order conditions and total differentiation will yield Marshallian demands. If we assume a CES production function, then the resulting system is, letting lower case represent logs and dropping subscripts:

$$s = c_s - \frac{1-\rho}{1-\beta-\gamma}\left(w_s - \gamma\left[w_s - w_n\right]\right) \tag{8.1}$$

$$n = c_n - \frac{1-\rho}{1-\beta-\gamma}\left(w_n + \beta\left[w_s - w_n\right]\right) \tag{8.2}$$

The parameters β and γ are positive and less than unity and can be thought of as the income shares of skilled and unskilled workers. The parameter ρ is related to the elasticity of substitution,[4] assumed to be less than unity. For Cobb–Douglas $\rho = 0$. We shall assume that, without loss of generality, w_s and w_n are the (log real product) wages of skilled and unskilled workers respectively.

The constants c_s and c_n are functions of the parameters of the underlying technology and of the capital stock. If (8.1) and (8.2) are derived as approximations to the first order conditions obtained using a CES production function, and we separately allow for skill-augmenting and unskilled labour-augmenting technical progress, then c_s will rise with skill-augmenting technical progress and fall with unskilled-labour augmenting technical progress. The opposite is true for c_n.

Approximate the unemployment rate, u, of a group of workers as the difference between the log labour force and log employment, i.e. $u = l - n$, then:

$$u_s = l_s - c_s + \frac{1}{1-\beta-\gamma}\left(w_s - \gamma\left[w_s - w_n\right]\right) \tag{8.3}$$

$$u_n = l_n - c_n + \frac{1}{1-\beta-\gamma}\left(w_n + \beta\left[w_s - w_n\right]\right) \tag{8.4}$$

Now before developing models of wages, write the aggregate unemployment rate, the (log) aggregate labour force, l, and the log aggregate wage, w, as weighted sums of skill-specific measures, so that, for instance $u = (1 - \alpha)u_s + \alpha u_n$, where α is the share of skilled workers in the labour force. Then aggregate unemployment is:

$$u = (l-c) + \frac{1}{1-\beta-\gamma}\left(w + \left[(1-\alpha)\beta - \alpha\gamma\right]\left[w_s - w_n\right]\right) \tag{8.5}$$

This equation yields some insights. First, if wages are set at the national level, then regions with low levels of capital will experience higher unemployment. Next, imagine a fully specified model that yields equilibrium regional unemployment rates and wages by skill. In that case, this equation gives us the impact effects of disequilibrium wages on unemployment. For instance, if the average real

---

[4] The elasticity of substitution is $\sigma = \frac{-1}{1-\rho}$.

wage is 1 percentage point higher than its steady-state level, then the unemployment rate will be $1/(1-\beta-\gamma)$ percentage points higher than its equilibrium value. Similarly, if the skilled-unskilled wage gap is 1 percentage point above its equilibrium level, the unemployment rate is $\left[(1-\alpha)\beta-\alpha\gamma\right]/(1-\beta-\gamma)$ percentage points above steady state. This effect is naturally ambiguous and its sign follows the sign of $(\beta/\gamma)-\left[\alpha/(1-\alpha)\right]$. In words, if the relative share of skilled workers in output exceeds the relative share of skilled workers in the labour force, then a high relative wage for skilled workers raises aggregate unemployment. However, by adding some realism to the interpretation of the parameters, we can make further progress in pinning this down. First, note the more-or-less universal facts that skilled wages are higher than unskilled wages and skilled workers also experience lower unemployment rates than unskilled workers. If technology is Cobb–Douglas, then by taking the first-order conditions underpinning (8.1) and (8.2) it is straightforward to deduce that $(\beta/\gamma)-\left[\alpha/(1-\alpha)\right]$ is positive.[5]

To summarise, if firms are on their labour demand curves, then medium-term unemployment derives from too high an aggregate real wage or from out-of-equilibrium relative wages, in particular, too high a wage mark-up for skilled workers.

8.3.2 Wages

The model of wage formation is also fairly conventional, with one minor twist. We imagine that real product wages are set either by bargaining between firms and workers, or by the firms alone, perhaps motivated by efficiency wage considerations. Following a host of researchers, a recent example being Nickell and Quintini (2003), we suppose that wages respond to local labour market conditions, summarised by unemployment rates. One issue is whether wages by skill respond only to unemployment among own skill group, or more generally to all unemployment. We plan to investigate this empirically, but to allow that either may be true we suggest the following wage equations:

$$w_s = C - \lambda(\delta u_s + (1-\delta)u_n) \qquad (8.6)$$

$$w_n = D - \lambda\left(\frac{\alpha}{1-\alpha}(1-\delta)u_s + \left\{\frac{1-2\alpha}{1-\alpha} + \frac{\alpha\delta}{1-\alpha}\right\}u_n\right) \qquad (8.7)$$

---

[5] The ratio of first-order conditions is

$$\frac{\beta N_n}{\gamma N_s} = \frac{W_s}{W_n} \text{ or } \frac{\beta(1-u_n)(1-\alpha)}{\gamma(1-u_s)\alpha} = \frac{W_s}{W_n},$$

from which the deduction follows.

Here, C and D are wage shift factors. Think of them as the inner products of vectors of wage shift variables on the one hand and vectors of impact coefficients on the other hand. They will contain some, if not all, common effects. Among the variables likely to be included are those that directly impinge on the bargain, such as taxes and the wedge between consumer and producer prices, as well as variables reflecting the external environment: unemployment rates and replacement rates, for example.

The parameter $\lambda \, (> 0)$ measures the responsiveness of wages to unemployment. For simplicity this is assumed common to both groups of workers. The parameter δ is assumed to take values between α and unity. Therefore δ measures the extent to which the skill groups care about their own unemployment ($\delta = 1$) or about aggregate unemployment ($\delta = \alpha$).

The next step is to consolidate the constants in the labour demand functions (8.3) and (8.4). Letting A and B represent skill-specific labour demand shift factors as follows:

$$u_s = \frac{1}{1-\beta-\gamma}\left(w_s - \gamma[w_s - w_n]\right) + A \tag{8.3a}$$

$$u_n = \frac{1}{1-\beta-\gamma}\left(w_n + \beta[w_s - w_n]\right) + B \tag{8.4a}$$

Equations (8.3a), (8.4a), (8.6) and (8.7) are the system, which solves for wages and employment by skill. To gain further insights, let us begin the analysis by studying the two-equation system derived from subtracting (8.4a) from (8.3a) and (8.7) from (8.6). Subtracting (8.4a) from (8.3a) yields:

$$u_s - u_n = A - B + w_s - w_n \tag{8.8}$$

Subtracting (8.7) from (8.6) yields:

$$w_s - w_u = C - D - \lambda\left(\frac{\delta-\alpha}{1-\alpha}(u_s - u_n)\right) \tag{8.9}$$

Solving (8.8) and (8.9) yields:

$$u_s - u_n = \frac{(1-\alpha)(A-B+C-D)}{1-\alpha+\lambda(\delta-\alpha)} \tag{8.10}$$

$$w_s - w_u = \frac{(1-\alpha)(C-D) - \lambda(\delta-\alpha)(A-B)}{(1-\alpha)+\lambda(\delta-\alpha)} \tag{8.11}$$

Before we can gain insight from these equations we need to insert some more realism, or at least meaning, into the shift factors A, B, C, and D. First note that since unemployment rates are always lower among skilled workers than among unskilled workers, and skilled wages are always higher that wages for unskilled work, then from (8.8) and (8.10) we should have:

$$A - B \leq u_s - u_n \leq A - B + C - D \leq 0,$$

which implies that $C - D \geq 0$.

Under these circumstances, changes λ and δ have similar effects upon relative wages and relative unemployment rates, unless $\delta = \alpha$.[6] An increase in either λ or δ will reduce the unemployment rate gap between skilled and unskilled workers and increase the wage gap between skilled and unskilled workers. An increase in α, the population skill proportion reduces the skilled wage premium and increases the gap between skilled and unskilled unemployment rates.

From previous discussions, a rise in skill-augmenting technology is modelled through a fall in A-B. From (8.10) and (8.11) this would raise the skilled wage premium and lower the relative unemployment rate of skilled workers. By contrast, a rise in the relative bargaining power of skilled workers is modelled through a rise C-D. From (8.10) and (8.11) this raises the skilled wage, but raises the relative unemployment rate of skilled workers.

Solving the system for u_s, u_n and $u = \alpha u_s + (1 - \alpha) u_n$ yields

$$u_s^* = \frac{1}{1 + \lambda - \beta - \gamma}\left\{C - \gamma B + (1 - \beta)A + \frac{(1-\alpha)\lambda(1-\delta)-\gamma}{1-\alpha+\lambda(\delta-\alpha)}(A-B+C-D)\right\}$$

$$u_n^* = \frac{1}{1 + \lambda - \beta - \gamma}\left\{D + (1 - \gamma)B - \beta A + \frac{(1-\alpha)\beta-\lambda\alpha(1-\delta)}{1-\alpha+\lambda(\delta-\alpha)}(A-B+C-D)\right\}$$

$$u^* = \frac{1}{1 + \lambda - \beta - \gamma}\left\{(1-\alpha)D + \alpha C + (1-\beta-\gamma)[(1-\alpha)B + \alpha A] + \right.$$
$$\left. + [(1-\alpha)\beta - \alpha\gamma](w_s^* - w_n^*)\right\}$$

This somewhat ugly expression is actually quite simple and symmetric. Note the expression multiplying the equilibrium skilled wage premium. Exactly as in (8.5), the impact on unemployment of greater equilibrium skilled wage differences, see equation (8.10), depends upon the sign of the expression $(1-\alpha)\beta - \alpha\gamma$, which we take as positive.

We can show that a rise in the population proportion of skilled workers will lower the total unemployment rate u^*.[7]

---

[6] If $\delta = \alpha$, then none of the parameters, α, δ or λ affect equilibrium relative wages and unemployment rates.

[7] $\frac{\partial U^*}{\partial \alpha} = \left[\frac{A-B+C-D}{1+\lambda-\beta-\gamma}\right]\left[\frac{(1-\alpha)^2(1-\beta-\gamma)+\lambda(\delta-\alpha)(1-\alpha)(2-\beta-\gamma)+\lambda^2(\delta-\alpha)^2+(1-\delta)\lambda[(1-\alpha)\beta-\gamma\alpha]}{[1-\alpha+\lambda(\delta-\alpha)]^2}\right] \leq 0$

8.3.3 Possible extensions

A natural way to develop this model into a model of regional unemployment is to suggest that labour immigration, and therefore the labour force, responds positively to a region's relative wage, and negatively to a region's unemployment rate. This would mean adding two more equations to our model, for l_s and l_n. If the parameters of these labour supply functions were identical by skill, these would add little to our analysis, other than add wages and unemployment rates for other regions as shift variables.[8]

One attractive alternative is to imagine that skilled labour tends to migrate to areas with concentrations of skilled workers, following the tastes model of Fernandez and Rogerson (2001), but we do not pursue the matter here.

This is our theory. Regions with higher skilled workforces will exhibit lower unemployment rates; but controlling for that, low levels, or negative changes in demand for manual/low-skill workers will also generate higher medium term mismatch unemployment.

8.4 Econometric results

Data on the 49 old voivodships 1994–98 were combined to make a panel of 245 observations. Also data from 16 new voivodships, combining 6 half-yearly PLFS rounds from Autumn 1999 to Spring 2002 were used to create a 96 observation data set. The skills of a region's workforce were measured by the shares of workers with different levels of completed education. The share of workers aged over 25 years was also included as a rough inverse proxy of the level of adaptability of the workforce. The characteristics of the unemployed, such as their previous work experience, were also added in initial experiments. Few were significant, perhaps surprisingly. The structure of employment is captured by occupational shares.

Table 8.7 gives results of static unemployment estimates using two sets of data. The first set is our panel of 49 old voivodships over five years, 1994–98. The second data set is our panel of 16 new voivodships of 6 half-annual observations from Autumn 1999 to Spring 2002. The skill mix of the population of working age is measured using the shares of people with different levels of completed education. The skill mix of labour demand, D, is measured by the shares of broad occupational groups in regional employment; on the other hand, employment shares by occupation. Initial estimation was by OLS. Both models were also estimated by fixed and random effects panel methods, yielding very similar results.[9] As expected, regional unemployment rates vary inversely with the education level of the

---

[8] In a simplified setting, let $u = l - k + \beta w$ and $l = p - k + \eta w - \lambda u$, then substitute to create a new reduced form unemployment equation.

[9] The fixed effects panel estimator offered very similar, though less precise estimates. The between and within estimates were broadly similar, suggesting no great difference in variation between the cross-section and time-series dimensions.

population. Also the skill intensity of labour demand has the predicted positive effect on regional unemployment, for the sample 1994–98, at least. The explanatory variables account for just over a half of the voivodship unemployment rate variation in the earlier sample, and much more in the later sample.

Table 8.7. Static estimates of the influence of structural supply and demand features on voivodship unemployment rates, (A) Annual panel 49 voivodships 1994–1998. (B) Half-annual panel 16 new voivodships Autumn 1999–Spring 2002

Dependent variable: log(unemployment rate)

Method of estimation	OLS	OLS
Sample	49 voivodships over 5 years, 1994–1998	16 voivodships, Autumn 1999–Spring 2002
Population shares by education level (base group = primary or lower) and age		
Tertiary	–0.83(6.3)	–1.46(6.6)
Secondary	–0.42(4.8)	–0.31(2.6)
Lower vocational	–0.40(6.6)	–0.63(9.4)
Aged 25+	0.45(4.6)	
Occupational structure of employment (default = agricultural worker)		
Managerial, professional and technical share	0.26(3.1)	0.02(0.2)
Clerical and sales share	0.30(2.9)	0.21(2.0)
Share of agriculture in employment	–0.05(1.1)	–0.73(16.1)
R^2, Adj R^2	0.55, 0.53	0.87, 0.86
N	245	96
BP het. Test	0.37	0.31
Normality	3.36	3.46

Note: Heteroskedastic-consistent absolute values of t-ratios in brackets. See footnotes to Table 8.5 for industrial definitions. The estimation allows for time fixed effects. See text for discussion.

In the first column of Table 8.8, we reduce the sample to two years, in order to estimate a dynamic unemployment equation, using industrial shares as the measure of employment structure. This specification is a simplification from an equation that included the levels and changes of all the forcing variables plus some other variables. The restrictions imposed to reach the reported equation yield a Chow (12, 74) test statistic of 0.6 and cannot be rejected. Note that none of the change variables survive. Indeed, this equation adds little to the information gained from the results in Table 8.7, except that regional unemployment adjusts reasonably quickly to changes in labour market structure.

The second column in Table 8.8 is perhaps a harder test of the importance of structural features of labour markets in the short run. Here the dependent variable is the change in the (log) unemployment rate 1994–98. Most of the structural variables are also subject to the same transformation. Perhaps surprisingly, about 40 per cent of regional variations in unemployment changes are explained by this regression, suggesting that evolution of the skill structure of a regional labour market has significant and quite fast-acting effects on a region's unemployment.

Table 8.8. Estimates of the influence of structural supply and demand features on voivodship unemployment rates, allowing for dynamic effects, 1996 and 1998

Method of estimation	Instrumental variable	OLS
Dependent variable	Log (unemployment rate)	Change in the log unemployment rate 1994–1998
Population shares by education level (default = primary or lower) and age		
Tertiary	−5.11 (2.7)	
Secondary	−0.33 (0.3)	
Lower vocational	−2.41 (3.0)	
Δtertiary, 1994–98		−3.66 (1.8)
Δsecondary, 1994–98		−2.70 (2.2)
Δlower voc., 1994–98		−0.52 (0.4)
Lower vocational, 1994		−3.21 (3.1)
Characteristics of the unemployed		
Share of new entrants$_{t-1}$	1.05 (2.8)	
Industrial structure of employment (default = agriculture)		
Industry share	1.06 (2.8)	
Services share	1.24 (1.6)	
Occupational structure of employment (default = agricultural worker)		
Δmanagerial, professional and technical share 94–98		3.96 (4.0)
Δclerical and sales share 94–98		2.25 (2.9)
Δnon-agricultural manual share 94-98		1.86 (2.9)
Non-agricultural manual share, 1994		1.86 (4.0)
Log unemployment rate$_{t-1}$	0.59 (2.7)	
Log vacancy rate 1995	−0.51(1.9)	−0.13 (2.6)
R^2, Adj R^2	0.56, 0.50	0.53, 0.41
N	98 (49 voivodships, 2 years)	49
BP het. Test		1.32
Normality		0.42

Note: Heteroskedastic-consistent t-ratios in brackets. For other conventions, see notes to tables 8.6 and 8.7.

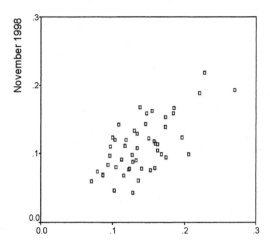

Fig. 8.1. Polish regional unemployment rates

8.5 Conclusions

This chapter reports the estimation of the extent to which the pattern of regional unemployment in Poland 1994–1998 can be explained by regional variations in skill levels. We find, plausibly, that higher skilled populations tend to generate lower unemployment rates and that controlling for population skill levels, lower levels of relative demand for unskilled workers raises a region's unemployment rate. These equilibrium and mismatch structural phenomena can explain about half of the regional variance in Polish unemployment rates, and a significant amount of the variance of changes in those rates.

References

Deichmann U, Henderson V (2000) Urban and regional dynamics in Poland. World Bank Research Working Paper 2457.

Duncan OD, Duncan B (1955) A methodological analysis of segregation indices. American Sociological Review 20:210–217.

Faggio G, Konings J (2003) Job creation, job destruction and employment growth in transition countries in the 90s. Economic Systems 27:129–154.

Fernandez R, Rogerson R (2001) Sorting and long-run inequality. Quarterly Journal of Economics, 126:1305–1342.

Filer R, Hamermesh D, Rees A (1996) The economics of work and pay. Sixth edition, Harper Collins, New York.

Fujita M, Krugman P, Venables A (1999) The spatial economy. Cities regions and international trade. MIT Press, Cambridge (Mass.).

Layard R, Nickell S, Jackman R (1991) Unemployment. Macroeconomic performance and the labour market, Oxford University Press, Oxford.

Newell A, Pastore F (2000) Regional unemployment and industrial unemployment in Poland. IZA Discussion Paper 194.

Newell A, Symons J (1991) Endogenous separations in a matching model. CEP Discussion Paper 35.

Nickell SJ, Quintini G (2003) Nominal wage rigidity and the rate of inflation. Economic Journal 113:762–781.

Overman H, Puga D (2002) Regional unemployment clusters. Economic Policy 34:116–147.

Tinbergen J (1975) Income distribution, analysis and policies. North-Holland, Amsterdam.

9 The Wage Curve and Agglomeration

Jens Südekum

University of Konstanz, Germany

9.1 Introduction

It has been recognised for quite some time that in most OECD countries, particularly in Europe, production and income are very unevenly spread across regions. The same can be said about unemployment rates. East versus West Germany, or South versus North Italy, are popular examples of how dramatically different unemployment rates can exist *within* a nation.[1] Moreover, if one looks at the European economic landscape from a bird's-eye perspective, one finds that regional unemployment rates exhibit a quite distinct spatial pattern. Unemployment tends to be organised in transnational clusters that closely resemble the core/periphery structure of regional GDP per capita. Regional unemployment rates are low in the rich core regions of the European Union where population, production and income are agglomerated. By contrast, high unemployment rates are found in the small and economically peripheral regions (Südekum 2003).

Traditionally, economists have addressed the issue of regional labour market disparities with the neoclassical theory pioneered by Harris and Todaro (1970) and Hall (1970, 1972). Since regions are much more closely linked than nations by the possibility of labour migration, an uneven regional distribution of unemployment rates can only exist for a non-transitory period if individuals in the high-unemployment areas are compensated by other economic factors, for instance by high regional wages. This compensating differentials argument implies that real wages and unemployment rates are positively correlated in equilibrium (Roback 1987; Marston 1985). The 'wage curve' literature pioneered by David Blanchflower and Andrew Oswald (hereafter B/O), however, has forcefully challenged this neoclassical view. After having performed large scale empirical research with micro-data, the authors claim to have found an "empirical law of economics", according to which a doubling of the regional unemployment rate will drive down regional wages down by roughly 10 per cent. This implies that regional wages and regional unemployment rates are in fact *negatively* correlated in equilibrium.

Although the wage curve is today widely accepted *empirically* (see e.g. Card 1995; Buettner 1999; Blien 2001; Bell et al. 2002), the theoretical account of the wage curve still has a number of loose ends. In partial equilibrium, there is by now convincing theoretical evidence for the wage curve. A negative relationship between regional wages and regional unemployment rates can arise in efficiency

---

[1] See OECD (2000) for an extensive descriptive overview of the facts.

wage and collective bargaining models, as well as in contract theoretic or search theoretic frameworks.[2] But its integration into a general equilibrium model has still not been convincingly accomplished.

Much of this paper will be devoted to discussion of why the existing wage curve models are on their own insufficient to account for the spatial structure of unemployment in reality, for instance in the EU. The existing literature is useful for determining regional unemployment rates if the corresponding wage levels are exogenously given. But wage curve theory is ill-equipped to explain endogenously *why* there are such pronounced disparities in the real world. Moreover, the wage curve has an inherent tendency to erosion due to the mobility of labour in the B/O model. It turns out that the assumption of perfect competition and constant returns in production are crucially responsible for these problems. In such a world, prices, wages, trade patterns etc. are essentially determined exogenously by factor endowments and preferences. Hence, regional disparities must essentially be assumed, and are not explained endogenously. Secondly, in such a world, labour migration will almost inevitably lead to a convergence of factor prices and unemployment rates. In sum, it is difficult to argue convincingly that a wage curve will prevail in the long run.

These criticisms will be used to outline an alternative product market specification, and to marry this with a conventional partial equilibrium foundation for the wage curve. The alternative production structure is built around the central idea of agglomeration economies. If production is characterised by localised increasing returns to scale, there is an endogenous force that pushes for regional disparities. *A priori* identical regions may develop in entirely different manner over time, and labour migration will not ameliorate regional inequalities but may even reinforce them. In such a world, which shares some characteristics with the models of Krugman (1980, 1991), Ethier (1982) and Matusz (1996), the wage curve quite naturally arises as a long-run equilibrium relation.

The rest of this chapter is organized as follows. Section 9.2 introduces the essential ideas of the wage curve model of B/O. Section 9.3 points up some problems of this model and argues that on its own it is ill-suited to furnishing understanding of the regional disparities in the EU. Section 9.4 outlines an alternative model structure with an increasing returns technology. Section 9.5 concludes.

9.2 The theory of the wage curve

On an aggregate view, the wage curve implies that regional real wage levels and regional unemployment rates within a country are negatively correlated. At any point in time, there exist regions with both high wages and low unemployment rates, and regions with low wages and high unemployment rates. This relationship

---

[2] Originally, B/O only used the first three microfoundations. Sato (2000) subsequently showed that a wage curve also develops in a search theoretic framework in combination with a monocentric city structure.

has frequently been represented graphically. Qualitatively, the wage curve is a non-linear downward sloping curve in the real wage/unemployment rate space, as depicted by Fig. 9.1.

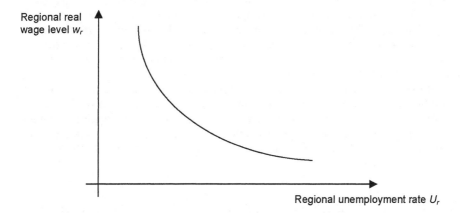

Fig. 9.1. The wage curve

In the theoretical part of their work, B/O present three partial equilibrium frameworks where a higher regional unemployment rate depresses the regional wage level: the first is based on implicit contracts; the second on collective bargaining and the third on efficiency wages. The approach based on implicit contracts is probably the most complicated but the least convincing of the three (see Card 1995, p. 796; Blien 2001, p. 84). The logic of the collective bargaining approach and the efficiency wage approach is relatively straightforward. Put briefly: a higher regional unemployment rate reduces the bargaining power of regional trade unions and hence regional wages: or alternatively, it acts as a disciplining device for workers, who do not shirk and provide work effort because regional unemployment is high. The necessity to pay efficiency wages is therefore reduced. Which of the two accounts is most appropriate for analysis of regional labour market disparities in the European Union? It is often maintained that union models fairly well reflect the institutional situation in continental Europe, whereas the efficiency wage models apply more to the 'flexible' labour markets of the UK and the USA. One might thus expect a collective bargaining approach to be more appropriate for analysis of European unemployment. However, recall that from now on we are concerned with the *regional* dimension of an economy. It is true that continental European labour markets are highly unionised; but they are also characterised by a very low degree of regional differentiation of union wages (Faini 1999). Collective bargaining in, for example, (West) Germany takes place at the sectoral level but with virtually nil regional differentiation of contracted wages. If at all, regional differentiation in Germany arises from differences in *effective earnings* that come about when employers in different areas consciously pay above the union minimum wage (Südekum 2004; Schnabel 1995).

Hence, an approach that bases a wage curve on regional differences in the bargaining strength of inherently regional unions is not appropriate, given the institutional structure of most continental European countries. On the contrary, one can argue that it is *precisely because* of the low degree of regional differentiation of union wages that intra-national unemployment disparities are so evident (Faini 1999; Südekum 2004). Efficiency wages thus seem to be the more appropriate micro-foundation of the wage curve, since the regional differentiation of effective wages in European countries (the wage drift) is presumably due to efficiency wage considerations (Blien 2001, p. 86).

B/O use a modified version of the shirking approach developed by Shapiro and Stiglitz (1984). This chapter will use an even more simplified version in order to keep the formal analysis as straightforward as possible. It considers an economy consisting of two regions $r = \{1,2\}$ populated with risk-neutral workers who gain utility from wage income w_r, but disutility from work-effort e_r. Utility V_r is assumed to be linear.

$$V_r = w_r - e_r. \tag{9.1}$$

Effort at work is a technologically fixed number $e_r > 0$. Individuals can choose to 'shirk' at work and spend zero effort $e_r = 0$. Shirking individuals run the risk of being detected and then fired. The detection and firing probability $(1 - \gamma) < 1$ is less than perfect. Once fired, an individual enters the pool of the unemployed. Yet, following Shapiro and Stiglitz (1984), there is also an exogenous destruction rate of firms $R_r > 0$ that likewise gives rise to an inflow from employment to unemployment. For simplicity, we assume that unemployed persons have no source of income.[3]

Unemployed individuals have a chance α_r of re-entering work. This endogenous variable depicts the flow from unemployment back into the pool of the employed. In the steady state equilibrium, the two labour market flows must be equal. Given that nobody will shirk in equilibrium, we can write this condition as $R_r N_r = \alpha_r (L_r - E_r)$, where L_r is the labour force and E_r is employment. The definition of the unemployment rate is $U_r = 1 - E_r/L_r$. This determines the function α_r to be $\alpha_r = (R_r/U_r) - R_r$. Thus, the outflow probability from unemployment is decreasing in the regional unemployment rate U_r. The only decision to be made by an individual is whether or not to shirk. The utility of an unemployed individual (V_{ur}) is given by

$$V_{ur} = \alpha_r (w_r - e_r). \tag{9.2}$$

Non-shirking employed workers and shirkers have utility levels V_{enr} and V_{esr} respectively

---

[3] In most parts of their efficiency wage framework, B/O assume that regions may differ with respect to the level of unemployment benefits. This case is not considered here, because it is irrelevant for most continental European countries. Unemployment benefits are generally not differentiated across regions. We therefore assume that unemployment benefits b_r are equalized on the level $b_r = 0$. This normalization, however, is only for analytical simplification.

$$V_{enr} = w_r - e_r \tag{9.3}$$

$$V_{esr} = \gamma\, w_r + (1 - \gamma)[\alpha_r(w_r - e_r)]. \tag{9.4}$$

Because it is in the interest of the firm to prevent shirking, it will pay efficiency wages that are just sufficient to ensure equal utility for shirkers and non-shirkers, i.e. $V_{esr} = V_{enr}$. Equating (9.3) and (9.4) yields after some manipulations

$$w_r = e_r + \frac{\gamma_r e_r}{(1 - \gamma_r)\left[1 - \alpha_r(U_r)\right]} \tag{9.5}$$

Equation (9.5) is the regional wage curve and can be interpreted as the aggregate non-shirking condition in region r. If we abstract from structural differences between the two single regions and assume that e_r and γ are the same in both regions, it is warranted that both regions face the same wage curve locus.

The wage curve (9.5) represents 'one half' of the full equilibrium in the B/O-model. More precisely, it describes the labour market in both locations of this two-region economy. In order to move from partial to general equilibrium, one has to introduce the product market structure, i.e. the labour demand side.

The way in which B/O (1994, p. 77 ff.) deal with this issue is in fact very simple. They assume that each of the two regions produces a distinct tradable commodity under constant returns to scale and perfect competition. The production function for the regional tradable good Y_r is given by $Y_r = f(N_r, K_r)$. K_r is assumed to be an essential input of production whose price i is determined on world markets. Labour N_r and capital K_r have to be used in fixed proportions. Under constant returns to scale, total minimum costs are simply the product of minimum unit cost (c_r) and the quantity of output Y_r.

$$C_r(Y_r, w_r, i) = \min_{N_r, K_r} \left\{ w_r N_r / Y_r + i K_r / Y_r \right\} = Y_r\, c_r(w_r, i) \tag{9.6}$$

Perfect competition and zero profits imply that $c_r(w_r, i)$ must equal the product price p_r, which is exogenous to any single firm. Without loss of generality, B/O normalize the given product price for the good from region 1 to unity. The price of the product from region 2 is denoted by p. In either region, product and labour market must be jointly in equilibrium. Since both regions face the same wage curve locus, the graphical representation of the general equilibrium can be illustrated in just one diagram, Fig. 9.2.

If $p < 1$, nominal wages are higher and unemployment is lower in region 1. With freely tradable goods, workers from both regions face the same consumer price index and nominal wage differences are equal to real wage differences. In this constellation, individuals from region 2 have an incentive to migrate to region 1. But for a full interregional equilibrium to come about, all migration incentives must also have vanished. In the situation depicted in the diagram, this is not yet the case.

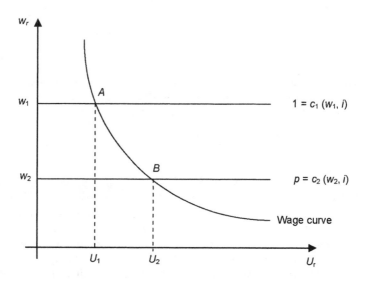

Fig. 9.2. Full equilibrium in both regions in the Blanchflower/Oswald model

What are the effects of this internal migration? B/O (1994, p. 81) are not very explicit about the technological effects on labour productivity and wages if migration occurs. This will of course crucially depend on the properties of the underlying production function. If firms can adjust the essential capital input proportionally to the additional stock of workers, the marginal product of labour, and ultimately the zero profit curves in Fig. 9.2 will remain unchanged. The incentive for migration will remain constant, as the regional wage gap is independent of the number of migrants and only depends on the exogenous product prices. Matters are different if the capital stock cannot be adjusted. In this case, every additional worker has a marginal productivity of zero. But the total amount of labour (measured e.g. in working hours) that is technologically efficient for the given capital stock can simply be shared among a higher number of workers. The total wage income in both regions will thus remain constant, but the wage per worker in region 1 and 2 will converge through labour migration.

Migration will thus lead to convergence of per capita remunerations and ultimately to an erosion of the wage curve relation. However, B/O (1994, pp. 81–82) avoid discussion of these matters by assuming that there are intrinsic regional amenities that compensate for the 'economic' variables w_r and U_r. They introduce a utility supplement ξ_r and assume that it is negatively proportional to the population density of region r. In other words, as workers move to region 1, the latter gradually becomes crowded and therefore unattractive. With this element of congestion, it is possible to produce a configuration where the two regions are located along the wage curve locus, but with no further migration incentives. Regions on the 'bad side' of the wage curve will compensate individuals with inherent regional amenities – in this case with the fact that there is little congestion. In terms of the observable economic variables w_r and U_r, however, a wage curve is visible in the data. Regional wages and regional unemployment are negatively correlated in equilibrium, and these regional disparities persist and show no tendency to vanish. Hence, the wage curve is interpreted to be stable over time.

9.3 A critical review of the Blanchflower/Oswald model

Several criticisms can be made of this wage curve model, and they all have to do with the product market specification. Most importantly, the substantial origin of the regional differences remains unexplained. Regions are assumed to produce different final goods and sell them at exogenous prices under perfect competition. The fact that one region is assigned to produce a 'better' good gives rise to disparate regional development.

There is an apparent identification of regions with sectors or specific products. This is problematic for several reasons. Firstly, regions in Europe are far from being specialized in one or only a few products. Similarly, specific industries are not highly concentrated in only one region. The regional concentration of industries may be increasing as a result of the European integration process. At the moment, however, it is certainly not of a magnitude to set regions equal with industries. Moreover, it seems to be a well-established empirical fact that differences in regional unemployment rates can be only weakly attributed to the sectoral specialisation patterns of regions.[4] Rather, there seems to be a truly spatial dimension to the problem of regional unemployment disparities which cannot be explained by sectoral components.

Furthermore, the B/O model does not specify why regions specialise in certain products and why they do not change their specialisation patterns if other commodities yield a better regional economic performance. This *complete* exogeneity might not even be that critical. One can think of model extensions where regions are characterised by different factor endowments that shape the sectoral specialization patterns through comparative advantages. However, such an approach would probably still be insufficient. There are good reasons to believe that the regional economic landscape in Europe is not driven by comparative advantage alone (Ottaviano and Puga 1998). Economic activity in the EU-15 is characterised by an evident core/periphery structure. The rich core regions clearly do not have their status *only* because of underlying endowments. Instead, the current spatial economic configuration is also the result of endogenous cumulative processes and circular causation mechanisms. A product market specification like B/O's cannot take account of such processes.

---

[4] See e.g. OECD (2000), Martin (1997), Taylor and Bradley (1983), or Elhorst (20003) (and the references therein), who concludes that "most empirical applications have indicated that spatial differences in industry mix account for little, if any, of the variation in unemployment rates between regions. The same industry seems to experience different unemployment rates in different regions."

Another criticism concerns the issue of labour mobility. In Fig. 9.2, individuals from region 2 would want to move to region 1. But B/O assume, in an 'ad-hoc' way, that the dislike of regional congestion operates as an obstructive factor. It must be noted, however, that the construction chosen is a very special case. Furthermore, the assumption that regions with high unemployment and low wages are otherwise particularly attractive because of low population density is rather implausible. Research in urban economics does not support the idea that people dislike density in general.

Blien (2001) points out another critical aspect: within the general equilibrium model the original causality of the wage curve, running from unemployment to wages, suddenly changes without explicit notice. Wage curve theory is meant to provide a rationale for the wage effects of unemployment. But in the B/O model, exogenous product prices determine a wage rate via the zero profit condition for firms. Unemployment is determined only in a second step, but in an unusual manner such that high wages are associated with low unemployment. Blien's criticism seems valid, even though one can think of the regional values of wage and unemployment rate as being simultaneously determined. It is still one more representation of the fact that in B/O's model everything is essentially driven by the exogenous product prices.

Blien (2001) presents his own approach to integrating the wage curve into a general equilibrium context. He presents a multi-region setup and assumes that every region is specialised in a single product or industry (just as B/O implicitly do). But Blien analyses the product market in a more dynamic manner by using the idea of product cycles. New products tend to face largely unsatisfied demand, and the price elasticity is high. But products age over time, demand becomes largely satisfied and the price elasticity decreases. Appelbaum and Schettkat (1995) have shown that an exogenous productivity improvement (= falling prices) leads to an increase in employment if the price elasticity of demand is greater than one. Similarly, unemployment will increase in response to productivity improvements if product demand reacts inelastically. Consider the regional consequences of product cycles if the single regions are completely specialized. Blien (2001) assumes that improvements in labour productivity are exogenous and identical for all regions. This has different effects on the single regions, depending on the state of the specific products within the cycle. Those which specialise in old products will be harmed, because higher productivity effectively leads to more unemployment. The opposite is true of regions with young products at the beginning of the cycle. There is a high elasticity of demand for the specific commodity, and productivity improvements (= falling prices) translate into higher employment. Turning to the long run, Blien (2001) acknowledges that workers will move to those areas where wages are high and unemployment is low. But he rightly points out that migration is not an instantaneous reaction to small differences in economic variables. It is a costly and slow process. He argues that migration will take place gradually in response to regional inequalities. As a consequence, the regional disparities will slowly fade away, other things being equal. The wage curve is thus not a long-run equilibrium relation in his model, but rather one of temporary short-run equilibria. The wage curve relationship is visible in regional data because the equilibrating forces are weak, and frequent impulses from product markets keep the labour market permanently in motion.

Although Blien's (2001) model has incorporated an appealing dynamic element into the product market, most of the B/O model's problems persist in his approach, because regions are identified with sectors and the specialisation patterns are assumed rather than explained. Both models essentially lack a truly endogenous reason for regional disparities, or indeed any *spatial dimension* at all. Recent years have seen a marked revival of theories that analyse why economic activity in market economies tends to be organised unevenly across space; why there is a tendency for agglomeration; and why regional disparities may endogenously unravel and persist. These theories have departed from traditional assumptions typical of neoclassical models and also used by B/O and Blien. This most importantly concerns the assumptions of constant returns to scale and perfect competition. The new trade and location approaches instead work with localised increasing returns to scale and monopolistic competition. Under this set of assumptions it is possible to explain the endogenous emergence and persistence of core/periphery structures. The remainder of this chapter will show how this alternative product market specification is a natural complement to the wage curve as a labour market equilibrium relation.[5]

9.4 Endogenous agglomeration economies

To outline this alternative product market specification, we consider a two-region economy $r = \{1,2\}$ that produces (without using labour) a final consumption good Y_r using a large variety of N_r single, non-tradable intermediate inputs $X_{i,r}$. The production function of the final product Y_r is given by the symmetrical CES function

$$Y_r = \left(\sum_{i=1}^{N_r} X_{r,i}^{\theta} \right)^{1/\theta} \tag{9.7}$$

with $0 < \theta < 1$. The parameter θ is a measure of the differentiability of single intermediate inputs. If θ is close to one, inputs are nearly perfect substitutes. The elasticity of substitution between the single intermediates is given by $\sigma = 1/(1-\theta)$.

The minimum cost function of Y_r, given the variety of domestic intermediate inputs, can be obtained by minimizing total consumption expenditure subject to (9.7). This yields

$$C_r(p_{r,1}, ..., p_{r,N_r}, Y_r) = \left(\sum_{i=1}^{N_r} p_{r,i}^{\theta/(\theta-1)} \right)^{\frac{\theta-1}{\theta}} \cdot Y_r \tag{9.8}$$

---

[5] The full details of the model as well as several generalisations can be found in Südekum (2005).

The term

$$G_r \equiv \left(\sum_{i=1}^{N_r} p_{r,i}^{\theta/(\theta-1)} \right)^{\frac{\theta-1}{\theta}}$$ (9.9)

can be understood as a minimum unit cost function for the final good Y_r in region r. The conditional factor demand curve for every single intermediate is given by

$$X_{r,i} = (p_r)^{1/(\theta-1)} \cdot (G_r)^{\theta/(1-\theta)} \cdot Y_r$$ (9.10)

Assuming that all intermediate inputs enter symmetrically into the production function and have the same price within region r, the function G_r simplifies to

$$G_r = \left(N_r (p_r)^{\theta/(\theta-1)} \right)^{(\theta-1)/\theta}$$ (9.11)

where p_r is the price of one symmetrical intermediate produced in region r. As can be seen, the minimum unit costs decrease with N_r. According to Ethier (1982) and Matusz (1996), this is intended to capture Adam Smith's famous 'pin factory' idea: it is an advantage for an economy to have a deeper division of labour, that is, more narrowly defined sub-steps into which a specific production task (Y_r) is partitioned. The factor demand curve facing a single firm, equation (9.10), shifts inwards, however, when N_r increases.

An important assumption by Matusz (1996), and which will also be used here is perfect competition in the Y_r sector which ensures that profits must always be equal to zero. It is furthermore assumed that the final product Y_r, unlike the intermediate inputs, can be freely traded across space. There is thus price equalization across regions. We use the price of the final good p^Y as the numeraire and normalize it to one. Zero profits in the Y-sector thus entail that minimum unit costs G_r must equal the product price $p^Y = 1$.

Each of the N_r single intermediates $X_{r,i}$ is produced by one firm under increasing returns to scale and within a monopolistically competitive market. Labour is the only production factor. The labour requirement necessary to produce the quantity X is given by

$$\ell = \alpha + \beta X \qquad \text{with } \alpha > 0, \beta > 0 \qquad (9.12)$$

A firm maximizes profits subject to (9.10) and (9.12), taking G_r as given. It optimally sets a price p_r that is as a constant mark-up over marginal costs βW_r.

$$p_r = \frac{\beta}{\theta} \cdot W_r$$ (9.13)

Profits for every X-firm are driven down to zero by the entry of potential competitors. Using (9.13), this implies that all X-firms operate at a unique scale of output where fixed costs are just covered by operating profits,

$$X = \left(\frac{\alpha}{\beta} \right) \left(\frac{\theta}{1-\theta} \right)$$

and every firm employs

$$\ell = \frac{\alpha}{1-\theta}$$

manufacturing workers. Therefore, the number of locally produced intermediates is restricted by regional employment, $(1 - U_r)L_r$, where L_r is the exogenous regional labour supply.

$$N_r = (1 - U_r) \frac{L_r}{\ell} \tag{9.14}$$

9.4.1 Short-run equilibrium

It is now easy to compute the product market equilibrium wage. Without loss of generality, we set $\beta = \theta$ for notational convenience, we apply the equilibrium condition $G_r = 1$ and then use (9.11) and (9.14) to derive

$$W_r = \left((1 - U_r) \frac{L_r}{\ell} \right)^{\frac{1-\theta}{\theta}} \tag{9.15}$$

With wages given by (9.15) there is profit maximization and zero profits in both sectors and regions. As can be seen, the nominal (= real) regional wage W_r is increasing in regional employment. If, for example, employment in region 1 is higher than in region 2, then the product market equilibrium condition (9.15) entails that the wage rate W_1 must be higher than W_2. The intuition for this scale effect is straightforward. We have seen that production costs for the final product decrease in the number of available regional intermediate inputs. But the price p^Y is the numeraire and always equal to one. Suppose L_1 and hence N_1 increases. On instance there will be positive profits in the Y sector, because costs have decreased at constant sales prices. With perfect competition, new entrepreneurs will enter the market for Y and reduce profits to zero. This must be done by paying more for intermediate products. On the assumption of zero profits in the X-sector, these price increases will be absorbed by higher wages. In other words if more intermediates can be produced, the increasing returns to scale can be better exploited. This will lead to higher wages in region r.

Let us now graphically illustrate the short-run equilibrium with immobile agents. The locus VV in Fig. 9.3 represents the familiar wage curve locus, which is the same for both regions. This is the graphical illustration of all combinations of wages and unemployment rates where shirking is just prevented for workers in the intermediate goods sector. For all points to the right of VV, unemployment is too high for any given wage. Consequently firms can hire new workers and be confident that they will not shirk. Hence, equilibrium unemployment must fall. This determines the phase arrows in the horizontal direction.

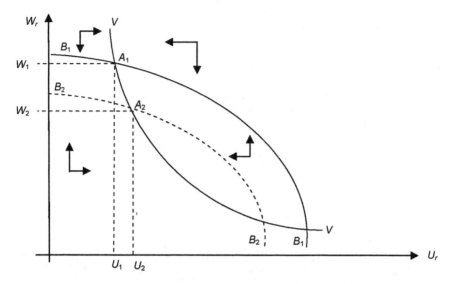

Fig. 9.3. Equilibrium in the two-region economy with immobile agents

The product market equilibrium curves are given by the curves B_1B_1 and B_2B_2, where it has been assumed that $L_1 > L_2$. These equilibrium curves are no longer horizontal lines as in the B/O model but are now downward sloping curves. The greater the difference between L_1 and L_2, the further apart are B_1B_1 and B_2B_2. For all points below the *BB*-schedule, wages are too low for a given unemployment rate. This determines the vertical phase arrows.

The stable equilibrium points are at points A_1 and A_2 respectively. As can be seen, region 1 has both the higher equilibrium wage and the lower unemployment rate.[6] The reason is the better exploitation of the increasing returns in production. For any given wage rate, this region has a higher labour demand, which drives down unemployment in the first instance and simultaneously increases the need to pay efficiency wages in order to prevent individuals from shirking. In equilibrium, the larger region ('the core') has an advantage over the smaller one along two dimensions: higher wages and a lower unemployment rate. The fact that larger regions pay a wage premium in the presence of increasing returns has already been

---

[6] Note that the equilibrium unemployment is strictly involuntary. Workers would in principle be willing to work at going wages w. But employers know that further recruiting would induce the incumbent workers to shirk at going wages. Therefore they do not hire additional workers. Put differently, the combination with full employment ($U = 0$) and wages equal to $\overline{w}$ might be desirable, but it is not feasible, since rational individuals would respond to this constellation with shirking behaviour.

noted by Krugman (1980). Yet, the existence of unemployment exacerbates this: it is not solely due to technological factors and better exploitation of scale economies. With efficiency-wage based unemployment, we can see that the larger region must pay an additional wage premium to deter shirking in view of the low unemployment rate.

9.4.2 Labour mobility and long-run equilibrium

We have not yet accounted for the effects of labour mobility in this economy. But spatial differences as indicated in Fig. 9.3 would of course spur migration from region 2 to region 1. It is important to note that labour migration is *not an equilibrating force* in our model. Rather it perpetuates regional disparities. In fact, if workers were *perfectly* mobile across regions, there would always be full concentration of all economic activity in one region, regardless of the level of transportation costs.

This can be shown very easily. For notational convenience, let us normalize the size of the total national labour force to $\bar{L} = L_1 + L_2$. A fraction λ lives and works in region 1, $L_1 = \lambda\bar{L}$. The remaining fraction $(1-\lambda)\bar{L}$ is located in region 2. From (9.15), the relative regional wage $\hat{w} = W_1/W_2$ is given by

$$\hat{w} = \frac{W_1}{W_2} = \left(\frac{(1-U_1)\lambda}{(1-U_2)(1-\lambda)} \right)^{\frac{1-\theta}{\theta}} \tag{9.16}$$

The relative wage $\hat{w}$ is increasing in λ and greater than one if $\lambda > \frac{1}{2}$. This is so for two reasons. Firstly, the better exploitation of increasing returns implies a higher production wage. Secondly, unemployment is lower in region 1, and higher efficiency wages must consequently be paid. All workers would thus migrate up to the point with $\lambda = 1$ under perfect mobility. This equilibrium also prevails if we assume that the labour force is initially distributed equally across the two regions, i.e. with no regional disparities ex-ante.

Put differently, with perfect mobility the increasing returns technology implies extreme regional divergence in the long-run. This is quite the opposite of the B/O's results, where perfect mobility (without regional amenities) would lead to regional convergence. Consequently, introducing imperfect labour mobility – for instance, in an *ad hoc* way by postulating different intrinsic regional preferences or by assuming congestion as a dispersion force – would not prevent convergence as in the B/O model; instead, it would impose an upper bound on the degree of regional agglomeration.

Let us briefly illustrate this. Suppose that the symmetrical situation with $\lambda = \frac{1}{2}$ exists initially. Now we add an individual-specific discount factor $\kappa_i > 0$ that captures the relative attractiveness of region 1 perceived by individual i. Let the value κ_i be equal to one if an individual has no intrinsic preference for either region. Values $\kappa_i > 1$ indicate a preference for region 1, whereas $\kappa_i < 1$ indicates a discount for living in that location. We assume that half of the total labour force located in region 1 also has an intrinsic preference for this area (i.e. $\kappa_i > 1$). The other half of $\bar{L}$, which is located in region 2, instead dislikes region 1.

Consider all $\bar{L}$ workers in the nation arranged in a line from $i = 0$ to $i = \bar{L}$. We assume that the distribution of the individual preference parameter κ_i over the entire working population will be described by the following function

$$\kappa_i = \left(\frac{\bar{L}-i}{i}\right)^{1/d} \qquad \text{with } d \geq 0. \qquad (9.17)$$

All workers in the range from $\lambda = 0$ to $\lambda = \frac{1}{2}$, i.e. those originally located in region 1, have values of $\kappa_i > 1$. By contrast, workers indexed in the range $i \in \left[\bar{L}/2 ; \bar{L}\right]$ discount to live in region 1. The individuals at the extremes, $i = 0$ and $i = \bar{L}$, have values $\kappa_i = \infty$ and $\kappa_i = 0$ respectively, and are thus inevitably tied to one specific region. The parameter d is a measure of the overall home bias in the population. The lower is d, the more pronounced are the preferences for one specific region. In the extreme case with $d = 0$, all individuals are completely tied to their region of birth. For $d \to \infty$, all individuals are intrinsically indifferent between locations.[7]

The workers living in region 2 face the following trade-off: given the technology alone, they would all want to move to region 1. However, they are intrinsically attached to their home location 2. Thus, these workers must receive a premium in order to move. They will move if and only if the relative wage of region 1 is greater than their individual dislike of that location, i.e. if

$$\hat{w} > \frac{1}{\kappa_i}.$$

To get a better intuitive feel for this trade-off, consider Fig. 9.4. The thick solid line represents the relative regional wage $\hat{w}$ from (9.16). The dotted lines represent three different examples of the inverted regional preferences $1/\kappa_i$ from (9.17). The steeper is the $1/\kappa_i$–curve, the more biased are individuals towards their home region, i.e. the lower is the parameter d.

People move only if the curve $\hat{w}$ runs above curve $1/\kappa_i$. For the case with strong regional preferences (the steepest curve), the final equilibrium will be the symmetrical initial situation, because the higher relative wage (the technological advantages from concentration) can never compensate for the individual dislike of

---

[7] Note that the preferences κ_i only capture intrinsic preferences for region 1 independently of the actual degree of spatial concentration in that location. The term κ_i does not represent a dislike of congestion etc.. However, given that the construction of regional preferences is 'ad-hoc' anyway, one could easily extend the preference formation and introduce a term $\kappa(\lambda)$ that depends on the overall degree of spatial concentration. Total individual preferences might e.g. look like $\kappa(i, \lambda) = \kappa_i + \kappa(\lambda)$, where the former term captures purely individual factors and the latter the preference for or against congestion.

region 1. The opposite happens with a low home bias, the flattest dotted line. In this case, there will be complete agglomeration. With intermediate regional preferences, the equilibrium distribution of the workforce λ^* is given by the intersection point of the two curves.

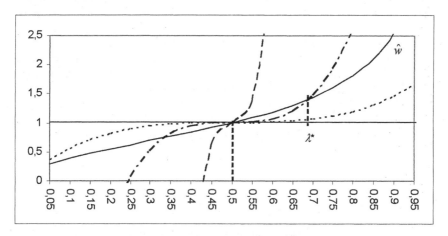

Fig. 9.4. Distribution of the labour force with intrinsic regional preferences

The regional preferences do not change the fundamental result that the larger region is better off than the periphery with respect to both W_r and U_r. The existence of κ introduces parameter constellations in which migration does not occur due to a very pronounced attachment to home. Importantly, the construction with regional preferences allows for less-than-full agglomeration. There are interior equilibria $\frac{1}{2} < \lambda^* < 1$, where regional preferences just compensate for the worse 'economic' situation in region 2. This enables us to draw implications from the *degree of agglomeration* (λ) for the magnitude of regional disparities. The more agglomeration-fuelling migration occurs, the stronger regional divergence becomes. Intrinsic preferences in this model are not responsible for a slow convergence speed as in B/O. On the contrary, they prevent further disparities. This result implies that the wage curve is a stable interregional relation with no tendency of erosion.

9.5 Discussion and conclusion

We have pointed out some fundamental criticisms with respect to B/O's wage curve model. In short, we have criticised the model in that (a) regional disparities cannot develop endogenously but must be exogenously assumed, (b) regions are essentially identified with sectors, and (c) labour mobility erodes the wage curve, so that long-run stability crucially hinges on restrictive *ad hoc* assumptions.

Our alternative approach gives rise to different conclusions with respect to all three of these points. Since we have incorporated a scale effect into the production function, we have envisaged an *endogenous* mechanism for the emergence of regional disparities, namely the presence of localised increasing returns to scale. Sectoral specialisation patterns play no crucial role in our model. Both locations are engaged in production activities within the same sectors. Differences in the production structure exist only in so far as the larger region can produce more industrial intermediates. But all regional differentiation, and all interregional trade, is of an intra-industry type. Lastly, the wage curve is not put under strain by labour mobility as in the B/O-model but is instead strengthened by it.

Hence, if one works with an increasing returns technology, the theoretical case for the existence of a wage curve is even stronger than argued by B/O themselves. No 'ad-hoc' construction of compensating regional amenities is needed for the long-run stability of the wage curve. Our model leaves the possibility of compensating regional amenities, but nevertheless the wage curve does not erode through labour migration. Hence, increasing returns in production seem to be a natural complement to the wage curve.

References

Appelbaum E, Schettkat R (1995) Employment and productivity in industrialized economies. International Labor Review 134: 605–623.

Bell B, Nickell S, Quintini G (2002) Wage equations, wage curves and all that. Labour Economics 9: 341–360.

Bispink R (1999) Tarifpolitik und Lohnbildung in Deutschland am Beispiel ausgewählter Wirtschaftszweige. WSI Discussion Paper 80.

Blanchard O, Katz L (1997) What we know and do not know about the natural rate of unemployment. Journal of Economic Perspectives 11: 51–72.

Blanchflower D, Oswald A (1994) The wage curve. MIT Press, Cambrige (Mass.).

Blien U (2001) Arbeitslosigkeit und Entlohnung auf regionalen Arbeitsmärkten. Physica, Heidelberg.

Buettner T (1999) Agglomeration, growth, and adjustment. Physica, Heidelberg.

Card D (1995) The wage curve: a review. Journal of Economic Literature 33: 785–799.

Carlin W, Soskice D (1990) Macroeconomics and the wage bargain. a modern approach to employment, inflation and the exchange rate. Oxford University Press, Oxford.

CER (1998) Il lavoro negli anni dell'Euro. Rapporto CER 3. CER, Milano.

Dixit A, Stiglitz J (1977) Monopolistic competition and optimum product diversity. American Economic Review 67: 297–308.

Elhorst JP (2003) The mystery of regional unemployment differentials. Theoretical and empirical explanations. Journal of Economic Surveys 17:709–748.

Ethier W (1982) National and international returns to scale in the modern theory of international trade. American Economic Review 72: 389-405.

Faini R (1999) Trade unions and regional development. European Economic Review 43: 457–474.

Hall R (1970) Why is the unemployment rate so high at full employment?. Brookings Papers on Economic Activity 3: 369–402.

Hall R (1972) Turnover in the labour force. Brookings Papers on Economic Activity 3: 709–756.

Harris J, Todaro M (1970) Migration, unemployment and development: a two-sector analysis. American Economic Review 60: 126–142.

Hughes G, McCormick B (1985) Migration intentions in the U.K. – Which households want to migrate and which succeed?. Economic Journal 95 Supplement:113–123.

Krugman P (1980) Scale economics, product differentiation, and the pattern of trade. American Economic Review 70: 950–959.

Krugman P (1991) Increasing returns and economic geography. Journal of Political Economy 99: 483–499.

Layard R, Nickell S, Jackman R (1991), Unemployment. Macroeconomic performance and the labour market. Oxford University Press, Oxford.

Marston S (1985) Two views of the geographic distribution of unemployment. Quarterly Journal of Economics 100: 57–79.

Martin R (1997) Regional unemployment disparities and their dynamics. Regional Studies 31: 237–252.

Matusz S (1996) International trade, the division of labour, and unemployment. International Economic Review 37: 71–84.

OECD (2000) Disparities in regional labour markets. Employment Outlook. OECD, Paris.

Ottaviano G, Puga D (1998) Agglomeration in the global economy: a survey of the "new economic geography". World Economy 21: 707–731.

Roback J (1987) Determinants of the local unemployment rate. Southern Economic Journal 53: 735–750.

Sato Y (2000) Search theory and the wage curve. Economics Letters 66: 93–98.

Schnabel C (1995) Übertarifliche Entlohnung: einige Erkenntnisse auf Basis betrieblicher Effektivlohnstatistiken. In: Gerlach K, Schettkat R (eds) Determinanten der Lohnbildung. Ed. Sigma, Berlin, pp 28–49.

Shapiro C. Stiglitz J (1984) Equilibrium unemployment as a worker discipline device. American Economic Review 73: 433–444.

Südekum J (2003) Agglomeration and regional unemployment disparities. PhD Thesis, Peter-Lang, Frankfurt.

Südekum J (2004) Selective migration, union wage setting, and unemployment disparities in West Germany. International Economic Journal 18: 33–48.

Südekum J (2005) Increasing returns and spatial unemployment disparities. Papers in Regional Science. Forthcoming.

Taylor J, Bradley S (1983) Spatial variations in the unemployment rate: a case study of North-West England. Regional Studies 17: 113–124.

10 A Panel of Regional Indicators of Labour Market Flexibility: the UK, 1979–1998

Vassilis Monastiriotis

London School of Economics, United Kingdom

10.1 Introduction[*]

It is a widely held view that labour market flexibility has advanced over the last two decades in many OECD and other economies. Indeed, the 1980s experienced a global shift of economic policy towards the relaxation of the rigidities imposed in the labour and product markets during the period of Keynesian regulation and Fordist development. This underlined the belief that market forces, when left free to operate, can lead to optimal economic (but also social) outcomes and that policy intervention can only distort the market clearing equilibria, thus generating unemployment and lowering the rates of economic growth. Under such considerations, a number of measures were introduced (or relaxed) in many countries to facilitate increased flexibility of their labour markets. Despite this, and the voluminous research into its economic impact, little effort has been put into producing consistent measures of flexibility.[1] Rather, flexibility is assumed to increase each and every time deregulation occurs, despite wide recognition that the former is conditioned on a range of factors outside regulation and, thus, should not be equated with deregulation (see Pollert 1991, or Solow 1998, for a theoretical discussion and Addi-

---

[*] I have benefited from comments by P Cheshire, S Destefanis, R Jackman, R Martin, D Perrons, A Rodriguez-Pose, V Sena and participants at the RSA and AIEL conferences and the DTI/EMAR seminar on Labour Market Flexibility (November 2003). Financial support by the SSF (IKY) and the ESRC (Ref.: T026271203) is acknowledged. All errors and omissions remain with the author. The LFS, FES, GHS and WIRS surveys are Crown Copyright and have been used under permission. The aggregate indexes presented here are available from the author upon request.

[1] Among the few relevant attempts (always at the national scale), the ILO and the OECD indexes (for example, ILO 1999; OECD 1997) are the most detailed and consistent over time, although they lack reference to theory. Some researchers have used single-year small-scale survey data to quantify flexible employment relations, but the measures produced are not comparable across studies or over time (see for example Burchell et al. 1999, based on the Job Insecurity and Work Intensification Survey). Finally, since 1998 the ONS has produced a relatively consistent indicator of flexible forms of employment based on QLFS data. This indicator is closely related to the more detailed indexes presented in this chapter.

son and Hirsch 1997, for relevant empirical evidence).[2] As a result, little is known empirically about the levels (let alone the specific forms, spatial variation or temporal evolution) of flexible labour relations that actually obtain in the labour market.

The UK in particular experienced a significant shift away from the government protectionism regime of the 1970s (for political as well as economic reasons) and is in many respects one of the most characteristic examples of labour market deregulation. During the 1980s Thatcherism provided the political and ideological platforms for the deregulation of labour relations and the flexibilisation of the UK labour markets.[3] The trend towards labour market deregulation continued (and in some cases, intensified) in the following Conservative and, more importantly, the new Labour governments (Work and Parents Taskforce 2001; OPSR 2002). From the beginning of the 1980s, the 1980 Employment Act imposed restrictions on the rights to strike and to organise into a trade union and removed some of the benefits related to unfair dismissal and maternity rights. At the end of the decade, the 1989 Employment Act further restricted such rights and imposed clauses that reduced job and employment security (dismissal protection and redundancy payments). Although the 1993 Trade Union Reform and Employment Rights Act redefined or re-introduced some of the employment rights related to maternity leave and dismissal protection, the same act completely abolished the Wage Councils responsible for the determination of minimum levels of pay (although only for overtime and hourly wage rates and for only a few occupations, since the 1986 Wage Act). More recent Employment Acts (e.g., 1996, 1999) have re-introduced some of the previously removed employment rights (e.g., re-introduction of a national minimum wage and restrictions introduced on the length of the working day and week). Nevertheless, labour market flexibility remains central for policy.

The policies employed to enhance labour market flexibility never obtained a clear regional dimension. Even in 1999, with the introduction of the new minimum wage, labour market policy did not assume a regional dimension, despite the recognition by at least some academics that this might be necessary (Sunley and Martin 2000) and the known differences in incomes and average wages among some UK regions (especially the South East and the rest of the country) (Gregg and Machin 1994). Of course, this probably reflects the belief that nation-wide labour market policies can have regionally uneven effects rather than a neglect of the regional economic problems of the country.[4] Such effects can mainly arise

---

[2] Following this consideration, a distinction is employed throughout between deregulation (the implementation of policies aiming at enhancing flexibility) and flexibility (the actual conditions created as a response to deregulation). In another part of the work on which this chapter is based (Monastiriotis 2002), I derive a labour market model which makes flexibility endogenous to the fundamentals of the labour market, as well as to levels of regulation.

[3] Although the term 'flexibilisation' is a neologism that is not particularly appealing aesthetically, we use it extensively to describe 'increases in labour market flexibility'.

[4] From this viewpoint, it has been argued that labour market deregulation constituted an indirect regional economic policy (Armstrong and Blackaby 1998), at least in the 1980s.

from cross-regional differences in the implementation of deregulation policies. In turn, these differences will depend on a number of region-specific factors that will determine the way in which each region will respond to any uniform (i.e., national) deregulation policy.

Acknowledging the possibility of regional differences in labour market flexibility, the purpose of this chapter is twofold. First, to construct a series of measures that would reflect the extent of flexible arrangements in the UK labour market, over two decades of significant regulatory and economic changes. Second, to derive such measures at the sub-national (regional) level and examine spatial patterns of differentiation and clustering. The next section makes some theoretical considerations that help identify the elements that comprise labour market flexibility. Section 10.3 discusses the empirical issues relating to the quantification of these elements into cardinal indexes. Section 10.4 examines the evolution over time and across space of the constructed indexes. The last section concludes with some considerations for policy.

10.2 Labour market flexibility and its elements

Defining labour market flexibility as the extent to which labour market forces determine labour market outcomes, it follows that a totally flexible labour market is one where no financial, institutional, linguistic, political and cultural impediments (or indeed any impediments) are present. In this respect, any factor entering the labour market other than the forces of demand and supply – themselves determined by the profit and utility maximising economic agents and their preferences – potentially impose rigidities in the labour market and lead to labour market inflexibilities.

10.2.1 Defining labour market flexibility

Although under this definition, there are many factors that can be related to labour market rigidities, by far the most prominent is labour market regulation, not only for ideological reasons but also practically, as government regulations are particularly binding and, more importantly, insensitive to labour market and general economic conditions. Because of this – and under the specific conditions that were created after the slowdown of economic growth in the 1970s – labour market deregulation became an issue with many advocates and few opponents. The policies that were developed thereafter related to the flexibilisation of the housing and financial markets and the reduction of barriers to geographical mobility, but more importantly, to the relaxation of policies that keep minimum wages, hiring and firing costs, costs related to overtime and non-wage compensations (maternity leave, paid holidays, sick leave, etc) and unemployment benefits at high levels.[5]

---

[5] It has to be noted, though, that labour market deregulation effectively constitutes a re-regulation of labour markets under more flexible and (mainly) cost-effective rules

Nevertheless, following from the above definition, labour market flexibility cannot be simply reduced to the absence of government-imposed regulations in the labour market. One has to keep in mind that often such regulations are not simply introduced to protect workers, but mainly to organise the operation of labour markets in a systematic way, to achieve continuity, and to establish commonly accepted 'rules of the game' which should benefit both employees and employers.[6] Moreover, they often serve the goal of neutralising the impact of other sources of labour market rigidity, e.g., the existence of market power on the side of firms or individual employees. It is well known that firms' monopsony power produces inflexibilities and sub-optimal outcomes in terms of employment, output, prices and wages. The same may be true for some types of labour monopoly power, as has been shown for example in the insider-outsider literature (Lindbeck and Snower 1988). Because of the presence of such 'inflexibilities', it follows that one cannot simply equate labour market deregulation with what could be called 'labour market flexibilisation'. Indeed, deregulation is neither a sufficient nor a necessary condition for flexibilisation to occur, as flexibility can increase without a change in regulation (for example if other labour market rigidities are removed), while on the other hand deregulation can occur without subsequent changes in observed levels of flexibility (Brosnan and Walsh 1996; Ozaki 1999).[7]

Reflecting these considerations, we prefer to think of flexibility more as an outcome, rather than a potential. Such a perspective suggests that labour market flexibility is endogenous to labour market conditions, so that it is not the potential for flexible employment arrangements that is important, but rather the extent to which such flexible arrangements are identifiable in a labour market. The latter will depend on the degree of regulation and the specific economic conditions prevailing in the labour market and will affect the extent to which regulations are used. This is the perspective we employ in what follows, both in terms of the construction of the measures of flexibility and of the analyses of these measures.

(Streeck 1989; Peck 1992). It is thus conceptually different from labour market flexibility and not at all symmetrically opposite to labour market regulation.

[6] For example, regulations on working times reflect the socially acceptable standards with respect to work intensity, working time and health and safety. Minimum wages reflect the minimum 'acceptable' compensations (minimum value that the society gives to an hour's work). Unemployment benefits provide incomes for those temporarily out of employment and probably help sustain product demand or at least stabilise it over the business cycle.

[7] Imagine for example that, certain rules regulating fringe benefits were withdrawn (deregulation). Firms would have the option to reduce their fringe benefits in order to reduce their (labour) costs. If, however, such a reduction led to lower labour supply or to reduced workers' effort (probably in an efficiency wages rationale), it is possible that this could reduce production efficiency and output. A profit-maximising firm would possibly find it more profitable to keep its fringe benefits at their pre-deregulation levels, rather than reduce them. Addison and Hirsch (1997) discuss such an empirical case with respect to mandatory advance dismissal notices.

10.2.2   Types of flexibility

It follows from the above discussion that labour market flexibility is neither uniform nor homogeneous. Instead, it is a composite aggregate, with elements that can often move in opposing directions. The literature introduces a number of typologies that help identify particular elements of flexibility (Atkinson 1984, Pollert 1991, Dawes 1993, Osaki 1999, Burchell et al. 1999, Weiss 2001). Such typologies consider different characteristics of the constituent elements of flexibility, for example, their function, their aims, their areas of influence, or the particular forms that they take in the labour market.

Starting from a rather abstract viewpoint, a first decomposition of flexibility can be made along two axes: one measuring numerical versus functional flexibility (or, 'tactical' versus 'operational'; Weiss 2001) and a second measuring internal versus external flexibility.[8] This two-way decomposition produces four distinct functional types. The first type, internal numerical flexibility, refers to the adjustability of labour inputs already employed by the firm. It includes the adjustability of working hours (short shifts, overtime) working time (weekly hours, variable shifts), and leave and holidays. In contrast, external numerical flexibility represents the adjustability of the labour intake from the external labour market. It is thus related to temporary and part-time employment, the relaxation of hire-and-fire regulations and increased wage flexibility. The third type, internal functional flexibility, can be defined as "the ability of companies to improve their operating efficiency by reorganising the methods of production and labour content (multi-skilling, decreases in job demarcations, increased employee involvement) in order to keep pace with changing [demand conditions or] technological needs" (Koshiro 1992, p. 14). Finally, external functional flexibility captures the ability of firms to externalise or diversify parts of their production (vertical disintegration), mainly through sub-contracting.

A more empirical perspective would consider labour market flexibility as the extent to which market forces are allowed to operate freely in three broad domains: 'production function flexibility', 'labour costs flexibility' and 'supply-side flexibility',[9] with each of these consisting of smaller sub-domains. Thus, production-function flexibility includes 'flexibility in the labour input' (adjustability of labour input to changing economic conditions) and 'flexibility in the work content'. Correspondingly, labour-costs flexibility includes 'flexibility in non-wage costs' and 'pay flexibility'. Two distinct elements can be further identified within the latter: 'flexibility in the determination of reservation wages' and '(average)

---

[8] This classification resembles that produced by the Institute of Manpower Studies (Atkinson 1984; Meager 1985; Atkinson and Meager 1986). There, however, functional flexibility was mostly identified as internal, while numerical flexibility was considered external. A third type of financial flexibility, which here we consider external to the labour market and do not discuss, was also identified.

[9] Alternatively, these domains have been labelled 'institutional flexibility', 'wage flexibility' and 'individual flexibility' (Dawes 1993).

wage flexibility'. Finally, supply-side flexibility can be split into 'labour mobility' and 'flexibility in skills acquisition'.

As illustrated in Fig. 10.1, this typology comprises seven distinct areas of flexibility. Such a typology is broadly related to two other dimensions, those of the aims and of the sources of flexibility. In terms of sources, flexibility can come from the side of the government, trade unions, employers, or the individual workers (Ozaki 1999). Specifically, it can be the outcome of changes in the organisation of production and the micro-economic behaviour of firms (e.g., demand for temping or sub-contracting). It can be related to changes in labour market institutions and the governance and macro-operation of labour markets, for example, changes in unemployment benefits, or the responsiveness of wages to changes in unemployment. Finally, it can be the outcome of changes in behavioural patterns on the side of employees (e.g., voluntary shift-working) and the provision of employment policies (e.g., government training programmes). Similarly, flexibility can be purely aimed at reducing labour (and production) costs (cost-reducing role), or targeting efficiency increases and a higher responsiveness to a more volatile product demand (efficiency-enhancing role), or finally aimed at increasing labour and total factor productivity in the workplace (productivity-increasing role).

It is clear from the above considerations that there is no direct correspondence between the areas presented in Fig. 10.1 and the various sources and targets of flexibility, or indeed the functional types identified earlier. Rather, each of the

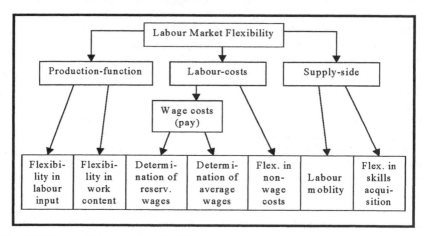

Fig. 10.1. Types of labour market flexibility

seven areas can be to varying degrees influenced by the behaviour of firms, unions, the government, or individuals, as well as serving different objectives (e.g., cost-reduction and productivity increases). Similarly, each of these areas includes elements of functional, numerical, internal, and external flexibility. As an example, labour can move within (internal) or between firms (external) and across occupations (functional) or labour markets (numerical). Thus, depending on the level of detail that one seeks, it is possible to identify a probably very large number of types of labour market flexibility. Instead of pursuing such a detailed analysis, the next sub-section considers directly the various elements of labour arrangements that are empirically observable in the labour market and can be associated with labour market flexibility.

10.2.3 Observable components of flexibility

There is a plethora of practical examples of flexible labour arrangements in the labour market, many of which existed well before the issue of flexibility obtained its contemporary prominence. In this respect, it is the extent and, more importantly, the ways such arrangements are used that places them at the heart of the debate about labour market flexibility. To review the most widely recognised of them, it is useful to organise them into a number of aggregate groups.

The first group consists of non-standard employment arrangements that allow firms to hire workers while avoiding a permanent commitment to them (and the related non-wage costs). Elements included in this category of 'flexible employment' are part-time work (especially when related to a fixed task), temporary placements (either fixed-term contracts or contracts for a fixed task), seasonal work, and casual employment (irregular or occasional work and home-working).[10] These non-standard employment arrangements also connect to elements related to the 'casualisation of employment', with the deregulation of dismissal protection (job security). Such elements make the permanency of a job less secure and dismissals less costly. Consequently, labour becomes cheaper (lower non-wage costs) and therefore more responsive to demand and general economic conditions.

The second group, described by the ILO as 'working-time flexibility' (Ozaki 1999), reflects the ability of firms to adjust their internal labour input relatively costlessly. It is thus related to labour-input and internal numerical flexibility and includes, among others, flexible working hours, shift-work and use of overtime work. Hence, the relaxation of regulations covering (paid and unpaid) overtimes, working maxima (regarding hours per week, hours per day, or days per week), the continuity of the working day (shift-work) and of the working week (weekend-working) allows firms to adjust internally their labour inputs and distribute them more evenly, so as to achieve continuity of production and respond immediately to demand changes. An example of such an arrangement would be the annualisation of working time, whereby overtime is no longer calculated on a weekly basis and weekly hours can vary substantially, sometimes including a week's holiday per month in return for weekend work or longer workdays.

---

[10] It is to be noted that, especially in the UK, part-timing often has characteristics more closely related to the internal numerical element. However, we decided to classify part-timing as an external numerical flexibility element, in a sense to avoid double-counting, since the 'internal' aspects of part-timing can be largely captured by elements like overtimes and irregular working hours. Instead, we assigned higher significance to 'external' elements such as dismissal costs and employee representation rights.

A third group of flexible labour arrangements relates to the 'content of work', which includes arrangements on multi-tasking, team-working, broadened job definitions, and within-job occupational mobility. Next, is a broad category of 'flexibility in labour standards', which includes elements that largely represent extra production costs, but also aspects related to the adjustability of the labour input. Elements that fall into this broad group are arrangements on employee representation rights, working conditions, health and safety regulations, the right to organise in a union, as well as arrangements on holidays, (sickness or maternity) leave, work-breaks, and working hours.

Two other groups of flexible labour arrangements represent what was earlier framed as supply-side flexibility. These are 'flexibility in worker training', including active labour market policies and arrangements about formal education and job-related training, and 'flexibility in labour mobility', which captures the propensity of workers to move across occupations, sectors, regions, or simply jobs (and, thus, also includes the average length of job tenure). Finally, the last group identified relates to 'pay flexibility'. This includes wage flexibility (the elasticity of wages with respect to unemployment), arrangements that determine the levels and coverage of minimum wages and unemployment benefits, the structure of wage bargaining and union power (including the structure and coverage of the union movement, as well as levels of co-ordination between and among unions and employers and the degree of centralisation or individualisation in the wage bargaining process), but also payroll taxes, which affect the distance between production and consumption wages (the 'wedge').

Note that the groups considered here and the arrangements each group includes are not exclusive. Rather, significant overlapping exists among groups, in the same way as the latter do not correspond directly and exclusively to specific flexibility types, as discussed earlier. However, the consideration of the above list of flexible labour arrangements, and of their types and groupings, is essential in that it facilitates the organisation of the analysis that follows. Hence, following the discussion in the present section, it is possible to move next to the empirical focus of the chapter and consider the construction of a series of measures of labour market flexibility for the UK and its regions.

10.3   Construction of the indexes of flexibility

Clearly, there is a substantial qualitative element in the arrangements under consideration. However, quantification is not the main problem; in the construction of the measures of flexibility severe limitations are imposed by data availability. The UK has a significant number of data sources, available for sufficiently long time-periods, and is thus one of the least problematic cases in this respect. We discuss the data sources and technical details about the index construction process later in this section. However, in order to keep reference with the preceding theoretical considerations, we start by presenting the various indicators that it was possible to construct. These indicators reflect – in the best possible way – the types and groupings of flexible labour arrangements that were presented earlier. As can be seen, these indicators were developed in a multi-layer process. Thus, first, we produced measures of the various observable elements of labour arrangements that are generally associated with flexibility. Then, we aggregated them into groups, and then further into functional types. These grouped indexes are presented next (see also Table 1, which presents the full list of indexes and their data sources). The last layer is the aggregate index of overall labour market flexibility, which reflects the average level of flexibility in the UK labour market(s).

10.3.1 The constructed indexes

The first index measures **internal numerical** or **working-time flexibility** and includes four components: *work-time* (the share of employees who are happy with their weekly hours of work and would not prefer to work much more or much less than their actual hours for the going wage rate); *irregular hours* (average of (i) the share of employees working variable hours, (ii) the share of average weekly overtime to average weekly standard hours, and (iii) the share of unpaid to total overtime); *shift-work* (the percentage of employees doing shifts); and *weekends* (the percentage of employees working during weekends). The second index refers to **flexible employment** or **external numerical flexibility** and includes *part-time* (average of (i) the share of part-time to total employment and (ii) the share of involuntary to total part-timing), *temping* (average of (i) the share of temps to total employment and (ii) the share of involuntary temps to total temporary employment), *dismissal* and *employment protection, home-working* and *alternative workers* (occasional and seasonal work). Owing to data limitations, the last three components were impossible to quantify in a meaningful way and are thus not represented in the index.[11]

Similar data-related problems were encountered in the construction of the index for **work-content** or **internal functional flexibility** and in particular in the case of *employee representation rights* (the extent of workers' involvement in decision-making), *labour standards* (general working conditions) and *multi-tasking*. Thus, the only component included in this index is *within-job mobility*, measured as the number of employees who changed occupation over the last year while remaining with the same employer, as a share of all the employees who changed occupation in the same period.[12]

As with internal functional flexibility, many of the elements related to labour-cost flexibility were impossible to obtain for a reasonably large number of observations. This was the case for *minimum wages*, average *duration of unemployment benefits*, and the *structure of wage bargaining* (labour market co-ordination, union

---

[11] This implicitly introduced the assumption that elements/groups within a functional type follow largely the same temporal and spatial patterns. Clearly, such an assumption is restrictive, as it is possible that within the same functional type various elements will be used with variation over time and across labour markets.

[12] This variable has been adjusted for the business cycle using the regional unemployment rate.

coverage and union power). However, three indexes were possible to calculate. Thus, **unemployment flexibility** was calculated on the basis of information on *replacement ratios* (the share of the representative[13] unemployment benefit to average wage). **Wage flexibility** was based on the estimated *wage elasticity* of unemployment (see Appendix 10.A.1 for details), while **unionism** (or **wage bargaining flexibility**) was proxied by the inverse of *union density* (the share of employed union-members to total employment).[14]

Data on **labour mobility,** the seventh index, were in general much easier to obtain. *Regional mobility* is the share of gross migration flows to regional population, adjusted for the five-year average unemployment rate (to control for business cycle effects). *Sectoral (occupational) mobility* is the number of employees who changed industry (occupation) over the last year as a share of the total number of employees who changed job during the same period. *Job mobility* is an indicator measuring the average employment length in the region (in 8 intervals), adjusted for regional unemployment. *Housing flexibility,* finally, is the share of employees who changed address for a job-related reason to total employment, again adjusted for regional unemployment. Following the theoretical discussion, a last index would measure flexibility in the **skills input,** based on the three elements of supply-side flexibility (*training, educational attainment* and *active labour market policies*). However, none of these were possible to quantify for a sufficiently large part of the sample and thus this element of flexibility is not included in the analysis.

Following the classification of Fig. 10.1, a further set of three composite indexes was constructed on the basis of the indexes described above. These indexes are: (i) **production function flexibility,** which includes labour-input flexibility and flexibility in the work content and is proxied by the indicators reflecting internal, external, numerical and functional flexibility; (ii) **labour cost flexibility,** which includes wage flexibility, unemployment flexibility, and union flexibility, thus capturing practically only the wage element of the broad labour costs category of Fig. 10.1; and (iii) **supply-side flexibility,** which includes all the elements of labour mobility. These three indexes were finally integrated into one composite index of **labour market flexibility,** capturing the overall picture of flexibility in the labour market. The technical details of the index construction and the aggregations made are discussed next.

---

[13] We use the word 'representative' here to show that the average unemployment benefit (derived from OECD data on national unemployment benefit replacement ratios) was adjusted for the household composition of the 'average' unemployed person (based on information derived from the Family Expenditure Survey series).

[14] Regional union density data are not available prior to 1989. For this reason an extrapolated series of union density was constructed for the period 1979-1998, using data on union recognition from WIRS80 and WIRS84, data on union membership from WIRS84, WIRS90, LFS89-91 and QLFS92-98 and national union density data.

10.3.2 Technical details

In order to collect the necessary information for the construction of these indexes, a large number of available data-sources were used. The primary data source was the Labour Force Survey series (LFS and QLFS). This is a national quarterly (bi-annual for 1973–1983, annual for 1984–1991) household survey under the responsibility of the Office for National Statistics (ONS). Additional sources were the Family Expenditure Survey (FES) and the General Household Survey (GHS) series, as well as the various Workplace Industrial Relations Surveys (WIRS 1980, 1984, 1990; New Workplace Industrial Relations Survey 1990; Workplace Employee Relations Survey 1998). Finally, some published data were also used, mainly derived from the ONS Regional Trends database, the OECD Database on Social Expenditures and the OECD Employment Outlook series. With this information we achieved the construction of a large panel of 240 observations (12 regions for 20 years), for seven operational aggregate labour market flexibility indicators, measured in percentage points from their maximum value.

The nature of the data sources (surveys), with their frequent changes in the content of the questions asked, made it particularly difficult to obtain consistent time-series for all the indicators. For this reason, in certain cases some data had to be estimated by interpolation. When this was necessary, the typical procedure was to estimate group averages for the data from years where the relevant information was available, and then calculate the values for the year of interest, assuming that the distribution of characteristics across the groups had remained (relatively) constant.

For example, data on household relocation for job-related reasons at a regional level were not available for the years 1980–1983 and 1985. To estimate the missing values, we calculated average relocation rates by region, sector and occupation for the years for which all information was available (e.g., 1979, 1984) and interpolated the household relocation shares for the missing years using national information on relocation rates and on regional, sectoral and occupational employment. This implied the assumption that the share of people moving house for job-related reasons in a region relative to the national share, given differences in the sectoral and occupational composition of employment, remained constant between two years (say, 1979 and 1980). Such an assumption, although restrictive, is not implausible.

Out-of-sample projections were also used when a change in definitions (for the survey data) made the derived indicators non-comparable through time. For example, the figures for sectoral mobility derived from the Quarterly Labour Force surveys were not directly comparable to those derived from the annual Labour Force surveys, because the definition of job mobility (the control variable) changed between the two survey series. In adjusting the two series we made the assumption that job mobility followed the same trend before and after 1992, relative to the unemployment rate. When inter- and extrapolation were not possible (or did not seem reliable), we had to accept a reduction in the sample size for the specific indicator. This was the case with a few indicators for values before 1982 (for example, information on irregular hours, weekend work and shift-work) and for household relocation for job-related reasons for values after 1991.

Table 10.1. Indexes of labour market flexibility

Flexibility Indicators			Data Sources			
Basic indexes	Intermediate indexes	Aggregate indexes	LFS	WIRS	FES/ GHS	ONS/ OECD
Work time	Internal numerical	Production function	•	•		
Irregular hours	Internal numerical	Production function	•			
Shift work	Internal numerical	Production function	•			
Weekend work	Internal numerical	Production function	•			
Home-working	External numerical	Production function	*	*		
Alternative workers	External numerical	Production function		*		
Part-time workers	External numerical	Production function	•			
Temporary employment	External numerical	Production function	•			
Dismissal protection	External numerical	Production function	*	*		
Employment protection	External numerical	Production function		*		
Within-job occ. mobility	Internal functional	Production function	•			
Empl. representation rights	Internal functional	Production function		*		
Labour standards	Internal functional	Production function		*		
Multi-tasking	Internal functional	Production function		*		
Replacement rate	Unemploy- ment flexibility	Labour costs			•	•
Minimum wages	Unemploy- ment flexibility	Labour costs	*			*
Duration of benefits	Unemploy- ment flexibility	Labour costs				*
Structure of wage bargaining	Wage flexibility	Labour costs		*		
Co-ordination (unions-firms)	Wage flexibility	Labour costs		*		
Wage elasticity	Wage flexibility	Labour costs			•	
Union density	Union Flexibility	Labour costs	•	*		
Union coverage	Union Flexibility	Labour costs		*		
Union power	Union Flexibility	Labour costs		*		
Regional mobility	Labour mobility	Supply side	•		•	•
Sectoral mobility	Labour mobility	Supply side	•			
Occupational mobility	Labour mobility	Supply side	•			
Job mobility / Tenure	Labour mobility	Supply side	•			
Housing flexibility	Labour mobility	Supply side			•	
Training	Skills-input flexibility	Supply side				*
ALMPs	Skills-input flexibility	Supply side				*
Educational attainment	Skills-input flexibility	Supply side				*

Note: Dots (•) show a valid data source used in the construction of the corresponding indicator. Stars (*) correspond to potential data sources that, for various reasons (sample size, accuracy, change in definitions over time, regional detail, etc), we were unable to use.

In constructing the indexes, an important decision that had to be made was whether they should be weighted (and how). Admittedly, many of the indicators used exhibit cross-industries and cross-occupational variation. But should such variation be considered endogenous (and, thus, controlled for) to labour market regulation? In other words, are flexible labour markets such because of the firms that operate in them (i.e., is flexibility exogenous to the labour market), or are flexibility-type firms locating in flexible labour markets (endogenous)? For example, is temporary employment more common in London because of its large share of service sector employment (which also attracts a lot of temping), or is it that service sector firms tend to be attracted by London because of its flexible labour market? The decision that was approved was to control most of the indicators for industrial composition, but not for occupational composition, as the latter is much less exogenous to labour market flexibility than is the former. We also made some adjustments based on the regional unemployment rates (deviations from the regional means) for those indicators for which the literature suggested that they depend on the business cycle (for example, household relocation and within-jobs occupational mobility; see Evans 1999).

A second important issue related to the aggregation of the detailed components and the construction of the broad indexes. Since no prior knowledge could be assumed regarding the significance of each element for the broader category to which it belonged, we did not weight the indicators when aggregating them. This should not be much of a problem. A potential source of serious bias, however, was in cases where some data were not available for all years (for example, temping in the case of external numerical flexibility). To calculate an unbiased measure of external numerical flexibility, given the missing values for temping and the fact that the constituent elements (temping and part-timing) were not necessarily correlated with one another, we applied a weighted extrapolation procedure, as described in Appendix 10.A.2.

10.4   Labour market flexibility in the UK, 1979–1998

10.4.1 Evolution over time – the national picture

The set of labour market flexibility indicators that was produced based on the above procedures and considerations, despite their probably inherent limitations, for a first time allows detailed examination to be made of the evolution of labour market flexibility in the UK. As stated earlier, this is particularly important since the UK is probably the country where one of the most intensive labour market deregulation programmes was applied, especially in the 1980s.

Figure 10.2 plots the temporal evolution of the seven functional indexes of flexibility for the period 1979–1998. A very interesting observation can be made straightaway: the evolution of the different elements of labour market flexibility exhibits significant variability. Indeed, correlation between the indexes varies from –0.36 (internal functional against external numerical) to 0.97 (internal numerical against union flexibility). Internal numerical and union flexibility exhibit an almost linear increase throughout the period, increasing by 36 per cent and 47 per cent in the twenty years between 1979 and 1998, respectively. Unemployment flexibility has also followed a linear-like increase (especially in the 1980s, as it seems to have stabilised in the 1990s), but at a rather slow pace, at 12 per cent in the twenty-year period. External numerical flexibility followed a rather similar trend, but with a significant structural break in the late 1980s, which seems to be related more to the business cycle than to changes in the regulatory framework affecting part-timing and temping.

Probably also related to the business cycle is the evolution of the labour mobility element, which was slowly increasing in the 1980s but subsided in the early 1990s, before catching up again after 1994. In the twenty years since 1979 this element of flexibility increased by 10 per cent, or just over 0.5 per cent per annum.

The evolution of the last two elements of flexibility is significantly different. Wage flexibility was stable, if not declining, in the 1980s, fell sharply in the early 1990s, probably as a result of the recession that hit the country in that period, but has since 1994 returned to its 1980s levels. But the most interesting temporal evolution is exhibited by the element measuring internal functional flexibility. Its increasing trend in the 1980s was brought to an end during the recession years. Between 1988 and 1992 internal functional flexibility (i.e., within-jobs occupational mobility) followed a (pro-)cyclical path – which seems directly related to the turmoil in the labour market at the same period. By 1993 it had returned to its early-1980s levels and continued to fall throughout the 1990s.

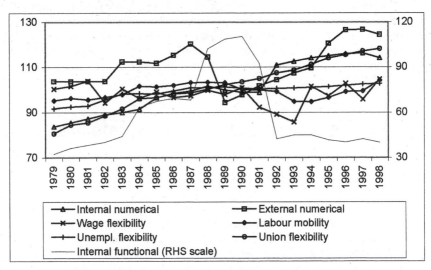

Fig. 10.2. Functional elements of labour market flexibility, UK

Due to these evolutions, the relative importance of the different elements of flexibility also changed. Thus, as one would probably expect, internal numerical and union flexibility became much more significant in the late 1990s. In contrast, increases in other elements of flexibility were much more modest, so that in relative terms such elements became less important. This obviously reflects qualitative characteristics of the type of deregulation supported by the UK governments throughout the period, as well as particular needs that the changing labour market regulations came to serve. It can be argued that the labour market arrangements that became more prominent in the twenty-year period under examination were related to the need to enhance flexibility inside the workplace, by increasing the adjustability of the labour intake within the firm and reducing the collective voice of workers, mainly through union de-recognition, which was reflected in the declining rates of union membership. Other elements seem much less significant, in that they have increased much more slowly, if at all. It is not possible to know whether this reflects inefficiencies of the deregulation programme that was followed, or structural factors that are reflected in the behaviour of the firms. Nevertheless, it is probably reasonable to assume the latter, especially given the fact that the deregulation of the UK labour market was to a large extent an across-the-board phenomenon – at least in the 1980s. Although these developments are in line with intuition, the information presented in Fig. 10.2 is very important in that it provides a quantitative measurement of such developments and verifies the conventional expectations. Furthermore, it shows that changes in labour market arrangements have been overall rather smooth with no clearly identifiable structural breaks. In other words, increases in flexibility do not seem to follow immediately after a change in labour market regulations; rather, they tend to follow a gradual adjustment procedure.

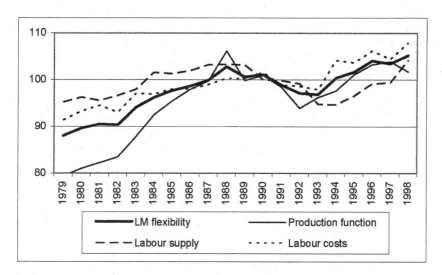

Fig. 10.3. Aggregate indexes of labour market flexibility, UK

Thus, it seems that the main factor leading to increases in labour market flexibility was related to what we earlier labelled as production-function flexibility. Indeed, this element increased by 28 per cent in the period 1979–98, exhibiting very fast growth rates especially in the 1980s. As is depicted in Fig. 10.3, the recession of the early 1990s led to a sharp decline in production function flexibility, which took the best part of the 1990s to offset, although the trend growth of this element of flexibility since the mid-1990s is very similar to that prior to the recession. The evolution of labour costs flexibility is rather similar, although the increase is much smoother but also much slower (at 18 per cent or 0.9 per cent annually). Labour costs flexibility was in relative terms much more important in the 1980s than it is today, although in 1998 it was the most prominent element of labour market flexibility. In contrast, labour supply flexibility has lost in relative importance in the 1990s. Whereas this element was increasing in the 1980s, the cyclical behaviour observed for labour mobility in the 1990s resulted in an overall growth for the twenty-year period of 9.5 per cent.

Together, these evolutions are responsible for the picture of overall labour market flexibility that is presented in Figure 10.3. Labour market flexibility was increasing rather fast (at 1.75 per cent per annum) in the 1980s, that is, during the period of labour market reform under the Thatcher governments. It declined rather sharply (by almost 1 per cent per annum) in the period 1989–93, which corresponds to a recession period, and has returned to its earlier rates of growth (at 1.7 per cent per annum) in the economic recovery since 1993. This cyclical behaviour can of course be quite puzzling at first glance; one could reasonably expect that, with increasing labour market flexibility, when the economy was hit by a recession the prevailing pattern would relate to even faster growth of flexible labour arrangements. This is clearly consistent with the view of such arrangements as mechanisms that serve to offset the impact of exogenous shocks to the economy. However, on closer inspection such reservations are less justified. As Fig. 10.2 shows, the impact of the recession was largely absorbed by evolutions across specific elements of flexibility. While functional and wage flexibility were declining, external numerical flexibility, which was pro-cyclical, was increasing rather fast, clearly even faster than the steadily increasing elements of internal numerical and union flexibility. Thus, while the recession affected access to some flexible labour market arrangements (e.g., adjustability of wages, since with above-average unemployment rates wages became less responsive to changes in unemployment) the labour market responded by putting increasing strain in other elements of flexibility which, as discussed earlier, were mainly related to numerical and union flexibility.[15]

Two other observations are important here. First, the cyclical behaviour observed is consistent with our definition of flexibility as an observable outcome rather than an only partially realised potential. The above considerations support our decision to follow this definition. By looking at outcomes rather than potentials, it was possible to examine real changes in the quality and extent of flexible arrangements prevailing in the labour market and thus gain important insights into the behaviour of the UK labour market during the period under examination and

---

[15] This behaviour is very interesting and offers significant insights in the behaviour of the labour market. Without entering into a detailed discussion, it is worth noting that there seems to be some element of substitutability among types of flexible labour arrangements, in the sense that when economic conditions adversely affect elements of flexibility that are exogenous to the firm (e.g., wage flexibility or labour mobility), when the institutional framework allows it, firms will respond by enhancing flexibility in other domains, mainly related to numerical flexibility. Clearly, the opposite reaction is also possible; this is at least not rejected by the negative correlation between wage flexibility and internal numerical flexibility observed in our data.

the role of labour market flexibility for the operation and performance of the labour market across the business cycle. Further, it must be noted that the recession of the early 1990s was quite peculiar in that it was rather sector- and region-specific (Martin 1993). Specifically, while during the recession employment was declining in the south of England, the northern parts of the country were still growing, especially in the service sector, which was the sector most heavily affected in the south. This observation stresses the importance of regional evolutions, and it is to these evolutions that we turn our attention next.

10.4.2 Regional evolutions – flexibility in the UK regions

We saw earlier that different types of flexibility increase faster in different parts of the economic cycle. The same should be also true for changes in different labour markets within the country, for any or all of the following reasons: (a) differences in the regional economic cycles, (b) differences in the regional economic structures and conditions, and (c) differences in responsiveness to changes in the regulatory framework. The last reason is directly related to specific policy and theoretical considerations. Following the predictions of economic orthodoxy, the UK governments in the 1980s expected that, with deregulation, flexibility would increase faster in the more rigid labour markets. To the extent that rigidities were associated with poorer economic performance, convergence in labour market flexibility would further translate in regional economic convergence (DTI 1983). Thus, on viewing flexibility as a response to economic and institutional changes, it follows that deregulation should create an environment of spatially uneven changes in labour market flexibility. Without entering into a detailed examination of the causes and policy consequences of these changes, we review the evolution of labour market flexibility in the UK regions as illustrated by the indexes that we constructed.

The three panels of Fig. 10.4 summarise the regional performance in terms of the seven flexibility elements across three time periods (1979–81, 1988–90 and 1996–98). As can be seen, regional variations in levels of flexibility seem to be quite small relative to the existing differences across types of elements as reviewed earlier. In the early 1980s flexibility was higher in the south of the country (South East, Greater London, East Anglia, but also South West), with the areas outside England lagging rather significantly behind. Interestingly, in the same period, flexibility types associated with production function flexibility were typically smaller in the south, even in absolute terms.[16] Thus, the flexibility advantage of the south of England in the early 1980s was mostly attributable to structural macro-factors, especially factors related to the elements of union, unemployment, and wage flexibility.

---

[16] Quite surprisinlgy, the region with the highest level of overall labour market flexibility (East Anglia) was the one with the lowest level of internal numerical flexibility.

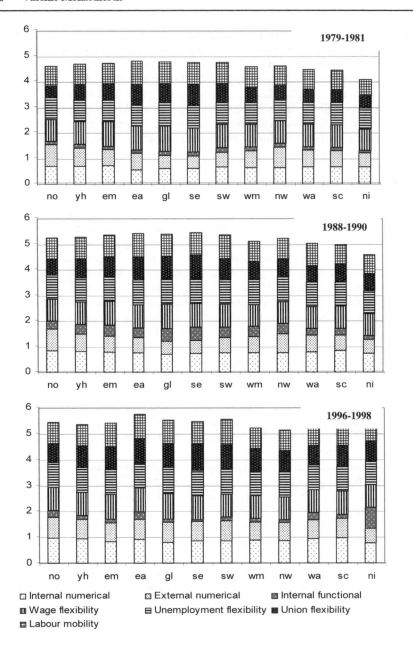

Fig. 10.4. Labour market flexibility in the UK, by region and functional type

There are few significant changes that can be observed in the late 1980s (second panel). Labour market flexibility increased in all regions, with the more significant increase being related everywhere to internal functional flexibility, probably for reasons discussed earlier. In the late 1980s the South East was the region with the most flexible labour market, enjoying a significant decline in union membership for its workforce. The most rigid labour markets were still outside England, mainly due to factors related to unionism, labour mobility and functional flexibility.

By the late 1990s the picture had changed significantly, with the regions exhibiting signs of convergence but also diversity across different types of flexibility. Flexibility increased very fast outside England, mainly the production function element. The south of England remained the area of highest labour market flexibility, with very high values for union flexibility and labour mobility, although production function flexibility in that region was still very low (especially internal numerical, despite the fact that it increased by around a half in the twenty-year period; the external numerical element increased even faster and caught up with the rest of Britain). In Northern Ireland a substantial increase in internal functional flexibility was combined with persistence (and, hence, divergence) in terms of the other elements of production function flexibility. Consistent with what we saw earlier for the UK as a whole, internal functional flexibility subsided from its late 1980s level in all regions.

Figure 10.5 offers a visual illustration of these regional variations. Each of the maps depicts a picture of regional differentiation in levels of flexibility for the mid-to-late 1990s period (1994–1998). Production function flexibility has been consistently higher outside the South East and the North West. Starting from a clear North-South divide in the early 1980s, however, the picture has transformed into a more mixed core-periphery relationship. For labour costs flexibility, the North-South divide pattern is clearer throughout the period and persists to the late 1990s, but is inversed. This domain (as well as labour supply flexibility, which is not shown if Fig. 10.5) has higher values in the south and is mainly concentrated in the greater London region. As a result, levels of overall labour market flexibility are also higher in the south, although an East-West dichotomy also emerges at this level. In the second part of the 1990s East Anglia was the region with the highest levels of labour market flexibility in the UK.

In summary, the information depicted in Figs 10.4 and 10.5 confirms the expectation that the south of England has a more flexible labour market now and throughout the period. Inequalities related to elements of production-function flexibility remained rather stable, if not increased, despite the fact that the external numerical element showed signs of convergence. Regional disparities in supply-side flexibility were rather stable in the 1980s but increased fast in the 1990s. On the other hand, disparities in labour-cost flexibility declined throughout the period. Thus, regional levels of overall labour market flexibility have followed a convergent path especially since the mid-1980s. The general pattern that can be identified through these evolutions shows the south of England specialising in supply-side and labour-costs flexibility, with many areas in the rest of the UK exhibiting a relative specialisation in production-function flexibility. If anything, this pattern does not seem to lend support to the view of flexibility as a spatially and qualitatively uniform phenomenon. In accordance with at least one interpretation of the expectations of regional policy, deregulation facilitated regional differentiation in levels of flexibility. Furthermore, the strong patterns of regional specialisations in functional types of flexibility suggest that structural factors play a significant role in influencing the quality, extent and type of flexible labour arrangements that prevail in each regional economy. Such factors could be related to regional economic specialisations (e.g., industrial composition), socio-economic structures (e.g., skill levels), or even external forces, like transport infrastructure, openness to trade, and globalisation, but the examination of such potential influences would be beyond the scope of the present study.

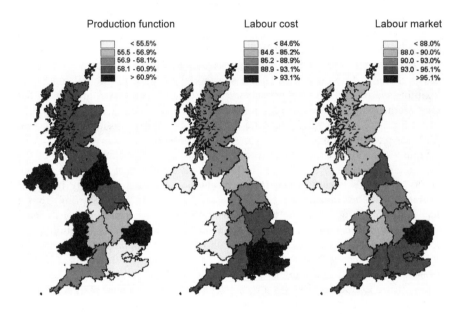

Fig. 10.5. UK labour market flexibility in the late 1990s by domain and region

10.5   Concluding remarks

Measuring, over a twenty-year period, a number of elements that together comprise what is commonly understood as labour market flexibility, the present analysis has allowed for detailed examination of the evolution of flexible arrangements in the UK national and regional labour markets. Our analysis at the national level has revealed some interesting facts that largely seem in accordance with expectations. Labour market flexibility increased more or less throughout the period. This increase was cyclical but otherwise rather smooth, with no significant structural breaks that could be related to episodes of deregulation, thus suggesting a relative hysteresis in the response of flexibility to policy changes. Despite the upward trend, not all elements of flexibility moved in the same direction at all times. Rather, some evidence of substitutability was also found.

Turning our attention to the regional evolutions, it is noticeable that despite the differences labour market flexibility increased in all regions and, possibly with the exception of Northern Ireland, which has a much more rigid labour market, differences between the south and the rest of Britain have, if anything, declined. Convergence, although slow, has been identified in the cases of labour-costs flexibility, supply-side flexibility, and some elements of production-function flexibility.

On the other hand, the most interesting observation has been that, despite the common temporal evolutions, there exist persistent regional differences in the levels and types of labour market flexibility. The south of England shows higher levels of wage flexibility and labour mobility. Conversely, production-function flexibility is higher in the rest of Britain. Thus, rather than the south being more flexible compared to the rest of the country, it seems likely that different regions within the country utilise – or are driven to exploit – different types of labour market flexibility.

Significant implications for policy stem from this observation. If, as is perfectly plausible, regional differences in labour market flexibility are structural, in that regions with different economic (and social) structures differ in their intensity of use of the various forms of flexible labour relations, then it follows that labour market deregulation is not regionally neutral in terms of the levels and types of flexibility and thus the type of employment relations that it produces. Such a rationale would suggest that the design of labour market deregulation (and re-regulation) policies must obtain a regional focus, at least to the extent that regional cohesion and harmonisation are among the targets of national economic policy.

It is important that further research is undertaken to explore this issue in more detail. By attributing specific developments of labour market flexibility to specific labour market (economic) and wider social conditions, research can inform policy not only about the necessity of a regionally focused labour market regulation programme, but also of the specific regional variations that such a programme can take so as to optimise its economy-wide effects. Future research could focus – together with extending and probably improving the indexes presented here – on the social, economic, and technological determinants of labour market flexibility, examining the factors that influence on the quality and quantity of flexible arrangements that prevail in the labour market. Additionally, of course, future research should examine in detail the extent and ways in which the spatio-temporal evolutions examined here have impacted on labour market and overall economic performance both at the national and the regional level.

Appendix

10.A.1 Construction of the wage flexibility indicator

Measures of wage flexibility are typically estimated as the wage elasticity of unemployment, using a standard Phillips-curve equation (Layard et al. 1991, Blanchflower and Oswald 1994). Wage growth is regressed on unemployment and expected inflation (usually inflation lagged one period) and the coefficient of unemployment is interpreted as a measure of wage flexibility. This standard procedure, however, can only produce a time-series of coefficients (when derived from cross-sectional regressions for each year) or a simple cross-section of coefficients (when derived from time-series regressions for each region). For the purposes of our research, it was necessary to obtain a panel of such coefficients, corresponding to each observation in our sample. To do so, one possibility would have been to estimate the cross-sectional and time-series Philips curves (12 time-series, one for each region in our sample, and 20 cross-sections, one for each sample year), thus deriving one wage flexibility measure for each year and one for each region, and then to calculate the average of the two wage flexibility measures corresponding to each observation. The problem with this procedure is that estimates for the wage elasticity of unemployment often vary significantly between cross-sectional and time-series regressions. Averaging may therefore produce values that are artificially constructed and do not correspond to the specific conditions characterising the specific region at the specific year.

Instead, we used an alternative procedure based on the inverse of individual contributions. We first estimated a Phillips-curve equation for the whole panel of our data (240 observations). We then re-estimated the same regression 240 times, each time dropping one single observation (corresponding to a specific region for a specific year). For each of the 240 obtained coefficients, we calculated the ratio of this coefficient to the one obtained from the full sample. We then subtracted these ratios from unity and obtained a new panel of coefficients. These coefficients measure the percentage change in overall (average) wage flexibility when a specific observation was excluded. Hence, this measure is rather relative (to the universally mean value) than absolute.

To illustrate this procedure better, an example can be used. The universal estimate of wage flexibility was –0.2 (which is slightly over, but in line with, wage flexibility estimates obtained elsewhere; see for example, Blanchflower and Oswald 1992, Abraham, 1996, Baddeley et al. 1999). Assume that excluding the value for London in 1990 resulted in a new estimate of –0.21. This would mean that, when not taking into account the specific situation of London 1990, the estimated wage flexibility increases. We can roughly interpret this as evidence that London in 1990 had less flexible wages than all the regions throughout the period under investigation, on aggregate. It is further possible to quantify this difference. By calculating

$$WFLEX_{L90} = (WFLEX_{TOTAL} - WFLEX_{excl.\{L90\}})/WFLEX_{TOTAL}$$

we obtain $1 - (0.21/0.20) = 1 - 1.05 = -0.05$. Therefore, wage flexibility in London in 1990 was by an estimated value of 5 per cent lower than the average value for our full sample. We attached the value of 0.95 (= $1 + WFLEX_{L90}$) to the corresponding observation. This procedure is intellectually appealing and produces quite plausible results (flexibility varies among the 12 regions over the 20 years period from 95 per cent to 113 per cent).

10.A.2 Construction of aggregate indexes with missing values

For the calculation of the aggregate (intermediate) indexes in the cases where there were missing values for some of their components, the following procedure was employed, which we illustrate using the case of external numerical flexibility (temping and part-timing). First, we projected the missing (in our example, temping) data backwards, assuming the same time-trend (that flexibility was growing during the missing years at the same pace as it was growing in the sample years) and the same trend of regional convergence/divergence in terms of levels of flexibility (temping in this case). We then calculated a temporary index of external numerical flexibility as the un-weighted sum of all the detailed indicators. Further, we calculated correlation coefficients between this temporary index and the full series (part-timing), one for the period for which all data were available and a second for the period for which we undertook the extrapolation. We then created the ratio (k) of the two correlation coefficients (smaller over greater, in absolute terms) and used this ratio as a weight, multiplying the extrapolated series of the aggregate index with k and the original part-timing series (for the same period) with $1- k$ and adding the two products. This resulted in a series (for the 'extrapolated' period) which was closer to the behaviour of the original part-timing data, the more our extrapolation produced a correlation that was further away from the one in the 'actual' sample.

References

Abraham F (1996) Regional adjustments and wage flexibility in the EU. Regional Science and Urban Economics 26:51–75.

Addison J, Hirsch B (1997) The economic effects of employment regulation: what are the limits?. In: Kaufman B (ed.) Government regulation of the employment relationship. Industrial Relations Research Association, Cornell University Press, Ithaca, pp 125–178.

Armstrong D, Blackaby D (1998) Regional labour markets and institutions in the United Kingdom. In: van der Laan L, Ruesga S (eds) Institutions and regional labour markets in Europe. Elgar, Ashgate, pp 81–103.

Atkinson J (1984) Flexibility, uncertainty and manpower management. IMS Report 8.

Atkinson J, Meager M (1986) Changing working patterns: how companies achieve flexibility to meet new needs. Institute of Manpower Studies, National Economic Development Office, London.

Baddeley M, Martin R , Tyler P (2000) Regional wage rigidity: the EU and US compared. Journal of Regional Science 40:115–141.

Blanchflower D, Oswald A (1992) International wage curves. NBER Working Paper 4200.

Blanchflower D, Oswald A (1994) The wage curve. MIT Press, Cambridge (Mass.).

Brosnan P, Walsh P (1996) Plus ça change...: the Employment Contracts Act and non-standard employment in New Zealand, 1991–1995. Victoria University, Wellington, Industrial Relations Centre Working Paper 4/96.

Burchell B, Day D, Hudson M, Ladipo D, Mankelow R, Nolan J, Reed H, Wichert I, Wilkinson F (1999) Job insecurity and work intensification: flexibility and the changing boundaries of work. Joseph Rowntree Foundation, YPS, UK.

Dawes L (1993) Long-term unemployment and labour market flexibility, Centre for Labour Market Studies, University of Leicester, mimeo.

DTI (1983) Regional industrial development, HMSO.

Evans P (1999) Occupational downgrading and upgrading in Britain. Economica 66:79–96.

Gregg P, S Machin (1994) Is the UK rise in inequality different?. In: Barrell R (ed) The UK labour market: comparative aspects and institutional developments. Cambridge University Press, Cambridge, pp 13–125.

ILO (1999) Key indicators of the labour market, International Labour Organisation, Geneva.

Koshiro K (ed.) (1992) Employment security and labour market flexibility: an international perspective. Local Economics and Policy Series, Wayne State University Press, Detroit.

Layard R, Nickell S, Jackman R (1991) Unemployment. Macroeconomic performance and the labour market, Oxford University Press, Oxford.

Lindbeck A, Snower D (1988) The insider-outsider theory of employment and unemployment, MIT Press, Cambridge (Mass.).

Martin R (1993) Remapping British regional policy: the end of the North-South divide". Regional Studies 27:797–805.

Meager N (1985) Temporary work in Britain: its growth and changing rationales. IMS Report 106.

Monastiriotis V (2002) Labour market flexibility and regional economic performance in the UK, 1979–1998. PhD Thesis, Department of Geography and Environment, LSE.

OECD (1997), Employment outlook. OECD, Paris.

OPSR (2002), Reforming our public services. The Prime Minister's Office for Public Services Reform (available on-line from http://www.pm.gov.uk/opsr).

Ozaki M (ed.) (1999) Negotiating flexibility: The role of the social partners and the state, International Labour Office, Geneva.

Peck J (1992) Labour and agglomeration: control and flexibility in local labour markets. Economic Geography 68:325–347.

Pollert A (ed.) (1991) Farewell to flexibility?. Blackwell, Oxford.

Solow R (1998) What is labour-market flexibility? What is it good for?. Keynes Lecture in Economics, Proceedings of the British Academy 97:189–211.

Streeck W (1989) Skills and the limits of neo-liberalism: the enterprise of the future as a place of learning. Work, Employment and Society 3:89–104.

Sunley P, Martin R (2000) The geographies of the national minimum wage. Environment and Planning A 32:1735–1758.

Weiss C (2001) On flexibility. Journal of Economic Behavior and Organization 46:347–356.

Work and Parents Taskforce (2001), About time: flexible working, Report to the Government, London (available on-line from http://www.workandparentstaskforce.gov.uk/news.htm).

11 Regional Wage Flexibility: the Wage Curve in Five EU Countries

Víctor Montuenga[1], Inmaculada García[2] and Melchor Fernández[3]

[1] Department of Economics and Business Studies, University of La Rioja, Spain
[2] Department of Economic Analysis, University of Zaragoza, Spain
[3] Department of Economics, University of Santiago de Compostela, Spain

11.1 Introduction[*]

At the beginning of the 1970s, unemployment levels in Western Europe were essentially the same as in the United States (US). However, since that time the two unemployment rates have diverged, principally because of the significant increase in the European levels. Thus, by the 1990s the difference between the European Union (EU) and the US average unemployment rates was some seven points, and has remained more or less unaltered over the past ten years (see Fig. 11.1). The current situation is that the 'equilibrium' unemployment rate in the US stands at around 5 per cent, this being just half of the average EU values. Furthermore, within the EU, the member-state distribution of unemployment rates varies considerably. Figure 11.1 shows that, in some countries (for example, the UK and Portugal), these rates are around 7 per cent, whereas in others they reach levels of more than 11 per cent (e.g. Spain, Italy, France).

Differences among labour market institutions (Nickell, 1997; Nickell and Layard, 1999), in their response to shocks (Blanchard and Katz, 1992; Decressin and Fatàs, 1995; Jimeno and Bentolila, 1998), and in the interaction of both elements (Blanchard and Wolfers, 2000), have been considered as fundamental reasons for dissimilar evolution of unemployment rates across countries. A common finding is that countries with the highest rates of unemployment usually also have quite rigid labour institutions. This rigidity prevents the labour market from responding rapidly to external shocks, so that the adjustment process takes some time.

[*] We thank the comments and suggestions made by participants at the seminars at CELPE, University of Salerno, and at the Department of Economics, University of Girona. The financial support provided by the Spanish Ministry of Education, Culture and Sports under project BEC2000-0163 to Fernández and Montuenga; and by the Spanish Ministry of Science and Technology, under project SEC2002-01350, to García and Montuenga is gratefully acknowledged. Finally, Fernández and Montuenga are also indebted to the Xunta de Galicia for support provided under project-code PGIDT01PXI20102A.

In Chap. 10, Monastiriotis provides a wide-ranging discussion on the topic of labour market flexibility within which the notion of pay flexibility is one of the most closely debated themes. This flexibility is commonly represented by the elasticity of wages with respect to unemployment, and the estimation of such elasticity is the central concern of this chapter. Over the last twenty years or so, two broad strands of research have sought to compute this wage response against changes in the unemployment rate. Historically, the first approach, applied during the 1980s and the early years of the 1990s, consisted of studying wage flexibility on a

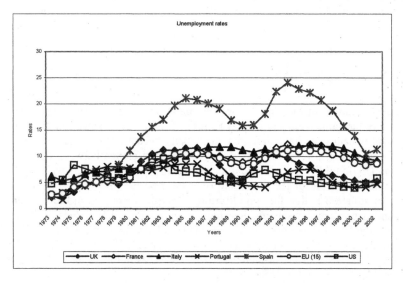

Fig. 11.1. Unemployment rates in the US, the EU, and the five EU sample countries

Source: Eurostat

country-by-country basis, using aggregated time series of wages and unemployment rates (Grubb et al. 1986; Bean et al. 1986; Andrés et al. 1990; Layard et al. 1991). The usual result was that wage flexibility varies considerably across countries, this being explained by arguments such as differences in the institutional structure, in the labour force composition, in workers' mobility, or in the skill composition of the labour force. This general result coincided with the forecasts made by modern non-competitive theories of the labour market, so that it became a widely-accepted starting point for analysis.

However, more recent evidence seems to support the idea of uniformity in wage flexibility across countries. This result, obtained when micro data are used, represents a sharp break with the previous line of thought. Since the initial work for 12 OECD countries by Blanchflower and Oswald (1994), there has been a growing body of evidence on a very broad set of countries throughout the world.[1] A common result emerges from all this work: irrespective of the country analysed, the period under consideration and the data used, an 'empirical law of economics' has been identified which states that a doubling of the unemployment rate implies a one-tenth decrease in wages. This result is comprised in a more general framework, that is to say, the existence of a negative relationship between wages and unemployment rates when both are measured locally. This relationship is commonly called the wage curve.

Estimating wage curves has two clear advantages when calculating wage flexibility. First, the use of individual data enables identification of the personal and labour characteristics of workers in such a way that the composition and aggregation biases are avoided. Secondly, provided that the unemployment rates are measured regionally, each worker is associated with his/her relevant labour market (the local labour market). Therefore, the regional dimension emerges as an obvious condition for determination of the actual impact of unemployment on wages.

Against this background, this chapter estimates wage curves for five European Union (EU) member states, considering the wage elasticity to unemployment to be a proper indicator of wage flexibility. In this regard, the use of a homogenous database, the European Community Household Panel (ECHP), has a clear advantage in that the survey methodology is common to all the countries analysed, with the result that it is possible to draw reliable comparisons.

The rest of the chapter is organised as follows. Section 11.2 discusses the issues of wage curve and wage flexibility in some detail. Section 11.3 describes the data sources, the underlying theoretical model and the estimation procedure, whilst Section 11.4 presents the results of the estimation with emphasis on the differing patterns of behaviour across countries and hence on a heterogeneous pattern of wage flexibility. Section 11.5 closes the chapter with a review of the main conclusions.

11.2   The wage curve and the measurement of wage flexibility

Let us first consider the concept of the wage curve as a measure of wage flexibility. In their seminal study, Blanchflower and Oswald (1994) found that, when measured locally, wages and unemployment are negatively related. More precisely, an individual living in a low unemployment region, other things being equal, earns more that the same individual living in another region where the unemployment rate is higher. The evidence for this has been widely studied and con-

---

[1] Among the various examples, we cite those of Bratsberg and Turunen (1996) and Turunen (1998) for the US, Winter-Ebmer (1996) for Austria, Jansenss and Konings (1998) for Belgium, Baltagi and Blien (1998) for Germany and Kennedy and Borland (2000) for Australia. For a summary, see Montuenga and Ramos (2005).

firmed for many countries; and a common result has emerged, namely that unemployment elasticity is around –0.1.

The reason for this negative link between wages and unemployment has been examined from different points of view. Blanchflower and Oswald (1994 and 1995) have themselves promoted the bargaining and efficiency wage models. According to the bargaining framework, in a low unemployment region the trade unions are able to claim higher wages because of the bargaining power that they enjoy. As regards the efficiency wage hypothesis, when the unemployment rate is considered as a discipline effort device (Shapiro and Stiglitz 1984), regions with high unemployment rates may reduce the incentives to workers to 'shirk', so that it is not necessary to pay them 'extra' wages.

It was once widely held that, in the case of the European countries, the explanation for a wage curve based on the bargaining between workers and employers was more appropriate, since unions are more closely involved in negotiations than in the US, where, by contrast, the efficiency wage hypothesis appeared more cogent. However, recent empirical evidence seems to show the limited relevance of the bargaining premise. Thus, in highly centralised and strongly unionised countries, such as the Nordic states, the non-existence of a wage curve is the usual finding (see Albaek et al. 2000, Barth et al. 2002), which questions the validity of this bargaining hypothesis. Additionally, when unionised and non-unionised workers are distinguished, the wage curve is found to exist only for the latter.

The most recent justifications for a wage curve relationship rely on the alternative hypotheses of efficiency wage models. Campbell and Orszag (1998) argue that unemployment discourages voluntary exits from jobs: when unemployment is high, workers are less interested in looking for high-wage alternative jobs, and, as a consequence, employers are not obliged to pay higher wages to prevent workers from leaving. What to the best of our knowledge is the latest evidence (Kennedy and Borland 2000, and Morrison et al. 2000), tends to support this wage curve approach. Other concepts of the existence of a wage curve explicitly take account of regional mobility and the agglomeration problem. Buettner (1999) stresses the need to consider the spatial contiguity between regions, since labour mobility and economic integration expand the labour market dimension. Sato (2000) obtains a wage curve from a search model where workers live in a city with a monocentric structure and where congestion costs prevent total concentration. Puga (2002) notes that differences in unemployment rates across the European regions have tended to increase over the past decades, in spite of the general process of convergence among national rates. Overman and Puga (2002) conclude that unemployment rates in Europe have polarised between clusters of regions with high unemployment and others with low unemployment. Finally, in Chap. 11, Südekum sets the wage curve concept in relation to the regional dimension of unemployment on the basis of the New Economic Geography. Garcia and Montuenga (2003) have estimated the wage curve for Spain and shown that limited wage flexibility may help explain the increase in regional unemployment differentials.

Wage elasticity to unemployment, estimated with micro data, has been widely viewed as a suitable indicator of wage flexibility (Blanchflower and Oswald 1995, Nickell 1997, and Nickell and Layard 1999). This elasticity is a measure of the responsiveness of workers' remuneration to the amount of excess supply in a local labour market. The local unemployment rate is usually expressed contemporaneously, relating the current unemployment rate to current wages, according to the functioning of a spot labour market. In this context, wages are equally flexible against either increases or falls in unemployment rates. However, several labour market theories predict that past conditions of that market also affect current wages. Thus, implicit contract models, bargaining models and wage efficiency considerations offer support for the argument that current wages are related to past values of the unemployment rate. Consequently, the typical measure of wage flexibility, based on wage elasticity to current unemployment, may be misleading because the spot market models do not offer a good representation of reality (see Beaudry and Di Nardo 1991).

If this is the case, a more interesting indicator of wage flexibility is based on the hypothesis that wages are downwardly rigid over time (see Canziani 1997). The underlying idea is that of the existence of a dual form of behaviour: when the economic situation is favourable, wages are likely to increase, whereas when the economy is in recession, wages do not fall, thereby causing a rise in unemployment rates (see Demertzis and Hugues Hallet 1996). Specifically, when workers are mobile between employers, wages are negotiated at the beginning of the contract, but when economic conditions improve, they must be revised upwards to prevent workers from being 'poached' by other firms. Therefore, individual wages are considered to be flexible if they increase, or remain stable, whenever the unemployment rate falls or rises, respectively. According to this definition, flexible wages are correlated to the minimum of unemployment since the date of hiring.

Alternatively, when job mobility is limited, wages are correlated to the unemployment rate at the moment of hiring, so that this measure depicts the economic situation when the labour contract was stipulated. In Western European countries, where labour markets have been characterised by average real wages that have slightly increased or remained stable over time, together with significant increases in unemployment, it is probable that these additional measures provide more information about wage flexibility. In the case of the US, Beaudry and Di Nardo (1991) find that wages are very flexible, given that current wages are negatively correlated to the minimum unemployment rate since the moment of hiring and not at all correlated to the contemporaneous unemployment rate. Canziani (1997) has studied the cases of Italy and Spain, finding that whilst wage flexibility is limited in Italy, it is high in Spain. Canziani notes that wages in Spain are only related to the current unemployment rate, which indicates wage flexibility in terms of the spot market model: wages continuously adjust to changes in the unemployment rate.[2] By contrast, for Italy she finds that only the unemployment rate at the moment of hiring is significant, which reflects the low responsiveness of wages to labour market conditions.

In what follows, we consider wage flexibility in five EU member states, namely France, Italy, Portugal, Spain and the UK, by measuring the wage response against unemployment rates, with the latter being expressed in three different forms: the

---

[2] The possible explanation for this result is 'the high ratio of fixed-term contracts with short duration among employed people' (Canziani 1997, p. 24).

contemporaneous (current) unemployment rate; the unemployment rate at the moment of hiring; and the minimum unemployment rate since the moment of hiring. By adopting this approach, we hope to obtain a more robust evaluation of wage flexibility in this geographical area.

11.3   The data and the model

As mentioned earlier, the data used in this study is drawn from the ECHP database. This was compiled from a common survey which was originally carried out in twelve EU member states at the beginning of 1994 and then progressively included an extra country for each year until 1996. The database provides abundant information on both the personal and labour characteristics of individuals. This information is homogenous across the sample countries, given that the questionnaire was the same and the elaboration process was coordinated by Eurostat. Regional unemployment rates are provided by the REGIO European Statistic Database, which also ensures homogeneity in the data collection.[3] For more detailed information on the data sources, see the Appendix.

We study the wage curve of the five countries in question for the period 1994–96. Unfortunately, it has not been possible to include other EU countries, given that the data corresponding to them is not region or industry-identified, an aspect that is necessary in order to compute the wage curve. Consequently, although the five countries belong to the EU, which implies certain common features, they nevertheless exhibit quite heterogeneous patterns of behaviour as regards their labour markets (see Nickell and Layard 1999; Blanchard and Wolfers 2000). In the UK, for example, labour regulation is less rigid and bargaining coverage less extensive than in the other sample countries; by contrast, unemployment benefit coverage is less generous in Spain and Portugal than in the rest of the countries. Table 11.1 sets out some basic statistics on unemployment benefit systems and collective bargaining institutions in the five countries, the former being described in terms of generosity (replacement rates) and coverage, and the latter in terms of the degree of unionisation, centralisation and coordination. The Table also shows the wage and unemployment rate averages for the five countries over the period in question.

Turning to the model, we chose to apply the one proposed by Blanchflower and Oswald (1994). Thus, wage flexibility was computed by estimating the following wage equation:

$$\ln(w_{irt}) = a + bX_{irt} + \beta \ln(u_{rt}) + \varepsilon_{irt} \tag{11.1}$$

for each individual i in region r and at a given point in time, t, where w is the wage, u the unemployment rate and X a set of individual and labour characteristics

---

[3] REGIO is Eurostat's harmonised regional statistical database. It covers the main aspects of economic and social life in the European Union, classified to the first three levels of the Nomenclature of Statistical Territorial Units (NUTS).

Table 11.1. Labour Market Features

	France	Italy	Portugal	Spain	UK
Benefits System[a]					
B. Generosity	37.5	NA	35.2	31.7	18.1
B. Coverage	77	NA	43	40	97
Bargaining Institutions[a]					
Coverage	95	82	71	78	47
Unionisation	9	50	58	25	91
Centralisation	2	1	2.2	2	2
Co-ordination	2	1	2.5	2	2
Average values					
Wage[*]	7.3	7.0	3.7	6.7	6.3
Unemployment Rate[b]	11.83	11.73	7.13	23.33	8.90

Notes: NA = not available; [*] 1994–96 average hourly wage expressed in ECUs

Sources: [a] Employment outlook, OECD, 1999; [b] REGIO database, several years

(such as gender, education, experience, occupation, etc.). Because both wages and unemployment are expressed in logs, the interpretation of β is the elasticity of wages with respect to unemployment. One advantage of this logarithmic form is that it facilitates comparisons between countries, given that the results are invariant to currency differences. Blanchflower and Oswald (1994) have shown that this is the preferred specification.

Time-period and region fixed effects are then added to this basic equation. The former controls for all those variables that vary over time but are common to all the regions (i.e., business cycle variables), whereas the latter allows for controlling variables that are time-invariant but particular to each region. In this way, any permanent component of the relationship between wages and unemployment is captured by these regional fixed effects, and the unemployment coefficient β only reflects the temporary component of that relationship (see Card 1995). Consequently, the equation to be estimated takes the form:

$$\ln(w_{irt}) = a + f_r + d_t + bX_{irt} + \beta \ln(u_{rt}) + \varepsilon_{irt} \tag{11.2}$$

where f_r is a regional fixed effect and d_t a time fixed effect.

However, direct estimation of this equation is affected by various biases, as Blanchflower and Oswald (1995) and Card (1995) have shown. To solve these biases, we have taken the following precautionary steps. First, wages are expressed in hourly terms in order to eliminate the bias generated by the negative correlation between the response in worked hours to changes in aggregate demand and the local unemployment rate.

Secondly, the real number of degrees of freedom is not the number of observations, but rather the number of different regional unemployment rates. In our study, the region category comes determined by the ECHP survey, where the degree of disaggregation is limited because it classifies individuals from the NUTS 1 geographical areas (see the Appendix). As a result, the total number of degrees of freedom is itself rather limited. One way to increase variability in unemployment rates across labour markets is to use additional measures of such rates disaggregated by certain worker characteristics (gender, age, etc.), an approach used by Canziani (1997) and Kennedy and Borland (2000). In this chapter we accordingly present estimates for the regional unemployment rate and the region by gender and by age group unemployment rates.[4] Consequently, although dispersion at the level of the purely regional unemployment rates is limited (the number of the NUTS 1 regions in each country times three periods), it grows more informative as we disaggregate by gender and by age group. According to Blanchflower and Oswald (1994), as the unemployment variable is measured more accurately, so the estimates obtained become more reliable, thereby allowing for more robust estimation of the wage curves.

Thirdly, and this is related to the previous point, the unemployment rate variable is measured at a more aggregated level than that of the other independent variables, and particularly at a more aggregated level than that of the dependent variable. This may generate a correlation across individuals belonging to the same region, giving rise to an upwards bias in the estimate of the t-statistics (see Moulton 1986). A first way to overcome this problem is to estimate a 'cell-mean' wage regression (Blanchflower and Oswald 1994 and Baltagi and Blien 1998) where the dependent variable and all explanatory variables are defined by the region and by yearly averages. Unfortunately, since the number of explanatory variables is larger than the number of region-by-year cells, it is not possible to use this estimation method with our data.

Alternatively, other authors (Canziani 1997 and Blanchard and Katz 1997: among others) have used a two-step approach, as suggested in Card (1995).[5] This method uses micro-level data to estimate the coefficients of the individual-level variables. The second step then fully accounts for the presence of correlation across individuals in the same market. In our study, this approach suffers from the problem that, as the number of regional dummies increases (when considering measures of the unemployment rate computed by region, by gender and by age group), so there are subgroups in the second stage with no individuals represented in the survey.

These two procedures have been widely used, especially when the data derive from repeated cross-sections. A number of authors (for example, Bratsberg and Turunen 1996 and Turunen 1998) have proposed that, when a panel structure of

---

[4] Two additional measures of unemployment have also been used, namely the region by gender and the region by age group unemployment rates, respectively. However, for the sake of brevity we only include the results by region and by the joint measure of region, age and gender, given that the other results do not differ substantially from these. The choice of the joint measure derives from the fact that it is the most refined, as well as being the most appropriate one with which to capture the relevant rates of unemployment for different groups of people (i.e. young, women, etc).

[5] It works as follows. In the first stage, equation (2) is estimated excluding the unemployment variable and the time-period dummies. Then, in the second stage the estimated region dummies are regressed on year dummies and the regional unemployment rate.

the data is available, Eq. (11.2) is estimated, but with individual effects permitted. Panel estimation is important to control for unobservable characteristics, thus reducing the probability of specification bias (Card 1995). In addition, controlling for individual heterogeneity makes it possible to alleviate both aggregation and composition biases.[6] Thus, the estimated equation becomes:

$$\ln(w_{irt}) = a_i + f_r + d_t + bX_{irt} + \beta \ln(u_{rt}) + \varepsilon_{irt} \tag{11.3}$$

where a_i is the individual effect. Throughout the study, all the coefficients presented have been estimated taking these three aspects into account.

11.4 Empirical results

Table 11.2 shows the panel estimation results for the three alternative concepts of the unemployment rate and for all the countries analysed. By using disaggregated measures of the unemployment rate it is possible to have more than 250 'degrees of freedom' for Italy, almost 200 for France and nearly 170 for Spain and Portugal. Unfortunately, disaggregated measures of the unemployment rate are not available for the UK, which means that in this case we can only give estimates for the regional unemployment rate. For the sake of brevity, we simply present the coefficients that correspond to the unemployment rate, i.e., β.

When estimating the wage curve we carried out several preliminary tests which are thoroughly discussed in the Appendix.[7] Table 11.2 summarises the principal results of our investigation, which will be described in more detail below. However, we must first draw attention to two features. First, it is generally accepted that estimates using the disaggregated unemployment rates are more appropriate. In particular, all the results shown here correspond to the unemployment rate expressed by region, by gender, and by age group. Two main reasons can be adduced in support of this choice: the considerable increase in the degrees of freedom (from about 30 to around an average of 200, depending on the countries), and the subsequent gain in both precision and efficiency in the estimates. Additionally, the cases of young people and of women are especially controlled for when this expression of unemployment rate is used. These two cases are of particular interest, given the extremely high values that these rates assume in some of the countries studied.

Secondly, we only show the results for the case of individual effects. The pooled estimation was discarded according to the usual LM test (see Appendix).

---

[6] Studies using repeated cross-sections do not control for changes in the unmeasured characteristics of the individuals over the cycle. This may be a source of bias in the elasticity of real wages with respect to unemployment (Solon et al. 1994).

[7] The full set of estimates for the parameter β is presented in Tables 11.A.1 and 11.A.2 in the Appendix. The former shows the results when the regional unemployment rate is used, whilst the latter gives the estimates when the unemployment rate is expressed by region, by gender and by age group.

Table 11.2. Fixed effects estimation of the wage curve in the five sample EU countries. The unemployment rate is expressed by region, by gender, and by age group[1]

	Individual			Pairs						Triples		
	u_t	u_h	u_{min}	u_h	u_{min}	u_h	u_t	u_{min}	u_t	u_t	u_h	u_{min}
France	-0.106 (-3.65)	-0.106 (-3.65)	-0.098 (-3.31)	1,484 (4.03)	-1.558 (-4.31)	-0.197 (-2.29)	0.099 (1.12)	-0.115 (-1.30)	0.018 (0.20)	0.037 (0.41)	-1.565 (-4.32)	1,457 (3.89)
Italy	-0.039 (-3.27)	-0.088 (-4.64)	-0.105 (-5.41)	0.392 (4.60)	-0.678 (-5.38)	-0.075 (-3.50)	-0.016 (-1.20)	-0.097 (-4.38)	-0.011 (-0.79)	-0.013 (-1.00)	0.395 (4.64)	-0.674 (-5.33)
Portugal	0.007 (0.37)	0.026 (1.27)	0.039 (1.93)	-0.070 (-1.33)	0.072 (1.97)	0.035 (1.34)	-0.013 (-0.57)	0.056 (2.16)	-0.024 (-1.04)	-0.018 (-0.77)	-0.061 (-1.13)	0.075 (2.03)
Spain	-0.154 (-5.06)	-0.159 (-4.08)	-0.222 (-4.75)	-0.006 (-0.09)	-0.216 (-2.43)	-0.198 (-1.96)	-0.094 (-1.94)	-0.168 (-3.01)	-0.080 (-1.76)	-0.090 (-1.86)	0.048 (0.60)	-0.210 (-2.36)
UK²	-0.238 (-2.78)	-0.191 (-1.09)	-0.313 (-1.36)	-0.132 (-0.71)	-0.262 (-1.09)	-0.211 (-1.20)	-0.445 (-2.82)	-0.376 (-1.63)	-0.462 (-2.92)	-0.464 (-2.93)	-0.139 (-0.75)	-0.323 (-1.33)

Notes:

[1] t-statistics between parentheses.

[2] The unemployment rate is expressed only at regional level.

u_t denotes the contemporaneous unemployment rate; u_h the unemployment rate at the time of hiring; and u_{min} the minimum unemployment rate. Under the heading 'individual', each concept of unemployment rate is introduced alone in the estimate equation; under the heading 'pairs' those concepts are introduced in pairs (three possibilities); finally, under the heading 'triples' the three concepts are simultaneously introduced.

The panel structure of the data then allowed us to control for unobservable individual heterogeneity and to alleviate the aggregation and the group effects biases. Additionally, the Hausman test showed that the fixed effects estimation was appropriate, given the correlation between some of the regressors and the unobservable individual effects. Consequently, all the results presented in Table 11.2 were obtained when the unemployment rate was expressed regionally by gender and by age group and the fixed effects estimation was applied.

The estimated coefficients of parameter β appear in the respective columns corresponding to each of the alternative estimation procedures being considered. More specifically, the first columns show the results when the contemporaneous unemployment rate was used, this being the typical wage curve as estimated in Blanchflower and Oswald (1994). The estimated values confirm the existence of a wage curve relation for these countries (except for Portugal, see Montuenga et al., 2003). However, wage elasticity to unemployment varies considerably across countries, ranging from the lowest (absolute) value of Italy (−0.039) to the highest for the UK (−0.238).[8] This is preliminary evidence of a diverse degree of wage flexibility across the EU countries.

The results set out in column 2 were obtained when the current unemployment rate was substituted by the unemployment rate at the time of hiring. Our intuition here is that the level of unemployment at the moment of hiring is significant in explaining current wages only in those circumstances where labour mobility is limited. The estimated coefficients are also negative (again, except for Portugal), indicating a reverse relationship between unemployment rates and wages. The estimated values in column 3 were obtained when the unemployment rate corresponded to the minimum unemployment rate since the moment of hiring. In principle, if mobility costs are low, then changes in unemployment will have a dual effect on individual wages: (i) increases in the unemployment rate will not engender a fall in wages; and (ii) when labour market conditions improve, workers will adjust their wages upwards, since they can credibly threaten to quit their current employment to start new jobs at higher wages. The estimates obtained also support this hypothesis. In the case of Portugal, the estimated coefficient is positive and slightly significant. The fact that the unemployment rate measured at the moment of hiring is non-significant, but significant when the minimum unemployment rate is used, allows us to interpret this finding as an indication of a certain degree of wage flexibility in the Portuguese labour market. However, the mechanism may work in the reverse direction: wages are downwards-flexible in bad times and remain controlled when the economy is recovering.[9]

---

[8] All the estimates corresponding to the UK were obtained when the unemployment rate was measured regionally only. In Chap. 10, Monastiriotis obtains a fairly similar estimate for the wage flexibility in the UK of −0.2.

[9] The case of Portugal is especially interesting given its distinctive behaviour (characterised by low wages and low unemployment rates) which has given rise to a significant group of studies (see Blanchard and Jimeno 1995; Bover et al. 1997 and Blanchard and Portugal 2001).

Inspection of this first set of results shows that the three coefficients are negative and significant (again except for Portugal), confirming a negative relationship between wages and any concept of the unemployment rate. To appraise the magnitude of each of these concepts, we adopted a procedure similar to that employed in Beaudry and DiNardo (1991). First, the alternative concepts of unemployment rate were introduced in pairs in order to study their joint significance, with the estimates being shown in the following three pairs of columns. The three alternative measures were then jointly estimated: the results are presented in the last three columns.

The simultaneous inclusion of the unemployment rate measured at the time of hiring and by the minimum since that date yields noticeably extreme values for France and Italy. This may be due to the exceptionally high correlation between both measures for these two countries (0.99), which may produce a misleading inference. For the case of Portugal, the minimum unemployment rate is positively significant, albeit only slightly so, whereas for Spain it is negatively significant.

When the contemporaneous unemployment rate is introduced jointly with the unemployment rate at the time of hiring, or with the minimum unemployment rate, or with both simultaneously, the following patterns can be observed. In France and Italy, the contemporaneous unemployment rate is no longer significant, whilst the other concepts remain significant. However, we cannot determine which of the measures is at work because of the earlier-mentioned high positive correlation. In the case of Spain, the three concepts are still negatively significant. Nevertheless, when they are introduced at the same time, only the minimum and contemporaneous unemployment rates are significant. For the UK, the results must be treated with caution, given the data limitation due to the availability of exclusively regional unemployment rates. That said, the estimates seem to indicate that only the contemporaneous unemployment rates are related to wages. For the case of Portugal, we can see that only the minimum unemployment rate is significant, but with a positive sign. As mentioned above, this result may be interpreted in terms of a certain degree of downwards wage flexibility, together with limited growth of real wages in boom phases. Furthermore, unemployment benefits and the requirements for entitlement to them are rather strict in Portugal (see Castillo et al. 1998). All this corroborates the high wage flexibility reported in the study by Marimon and Zilibotti (1998) which allowed for shocks to be absorbed without increasing unemployment.

In the light of the foregoing discussion, we may draw the following conclusions. First, wages are negatively related in all three unemployment rate concepts considered in this chapter (except in the case of Portugal). Moreover, unemployment elasticity differs among the five countries analysed. In particular, when computing wage flexibility in terms of the contemporaneous unemployment rate (as is usually done in other studies), a ranking of wage flexibility can be constructed from the less flexible – Portugal and Italy – to the most – the UK – with France and Spain located somewhere in the middle of the scale.

Secondly, when the contemporaneous unemployment rate is introduced together with other alternative measures, it does not affect wages in France, Italy and Portugal, refuting the existence of a spot labour market as described by Beaudry and Di Nardo (1991). In the case of France, the unemployment rate at the time of hiring seems to be the most relevant measure in determining wages, with an estimated coefficient of –0.1, indicating low mobility in the labour market. For Italy, both alternative measures are negatively significant when introduced separately with the contemporaneous unemployment rate. However, a non-conclusive result is obtained when the both concepts are considered simultaneously.

Thirdly, the estimates for Portugal show a markedly different pattern of behaviour with respect to the other countries, in that only the minimum unemployment rate seems to be correlated with current wages, although with a positive sign. This result can be interpreted as one of dual behaviour in the wage response, but running in the opposite direction.

Fourthly, in Spain the minimum unemployment rate is most prominent, even though the contemporaneous unemployment rate also plays an important role. This can be viewed as indicative of a more flexible process of wage determination, which may be explained by sharp segmentation of the labour market (permanent versus temporary workers), as noted in previous articles (Canziani 1997 and Ferreiro and Serrano 2002). Thus, whilst wages respond to the current situation in the labour market (through temporary workers), it is also possible for them to respond favourably in a boom environment (through permanent, insider workers).

Finally, the case of the UK is the one most similar to that of the spot functioning of the labour market where only the contemporaneous unemployment rate affects wages. This result tends to coincide with the process of labour-market liberalisation under way in the UK since 1990 (see Demertzis and Hugues Hallet 1996).

11.5 Conclusions

The high rates of unemployment found in most EU countries have led many governments to set themselves the objective of achieving less rigid labour markets. With this aim in mind, both economists and legislators have stressed the importance of measuring the wage response to unemployment as an indicator of the speed at which the labour market absorbs accruing negative shocks. Consequently, the issue of wage flexibility is today regarded as being of especial importance in practically all countries.

This chapter has attempted to appraise the magnitude of wage flexibility in five EU countries by examining their respective wages curves. A wage curve captures the negative relationship between wages and unemployment rates at the local level: in this respect, the regional dimension is clearly important, because it enables identification of the relevant labour market where the decisions of both employers and employees are made.

However, the typical estimation of a wage curve concentrates solely on the relationship between current wages and current unemployment rates, which prevents consideration of alternative descriptions of wage flexibility. Beaudry and Di Nardo (1991) and Canziani (1997) noted that lagged values of unemployment rates influence current wage levels. Thus, if workers have only limited mobility across jobs, the unemployment rate at the time of hiring must be especially relevant to the current level of wages. Alternatively, when workers are highly mobile, wages are sticky downwards in bad times but easily increase as the economy recovers. Therefore, the minimum unemployment rate since the moment of hiring emerges as the appropriate measure of labour market tightness. On these grounds, we applied the methodology proposed by Beaudry and Di Nardo (1991) using an homogenous database for the cases of France, Italy, Portugal, Spain and the UK. Our main results can be summarised as follows.

First, the degree of 'typical' wage flexibility varies across the five sample countries, indicating different patterns of behaviour by their respective labour markets. This finding offers support for the predictions of modern non-competitive labour market theories as confirmed by time series-aggregated studies (e.g. Layard et al., 1991), and questions the belief in an 'empirical law of economics' – namely a –0.1 wage elasticity to unemployment – as argued by Blanchflower and Oswald (1994).

Secondly, the functioning of a spot labour market, where wages are only related to current values of the unemployment rates, is discarded for France, Italy and Portugal. In the case of France, our estimates seeming support the idea of low mobility in the labour market, whereas for Italy the results are non-conclusive. Canziani (1997) finds that Italy displays a similar pattern of behaviour to France's. The case of Portugal is of particular interest, given the positive relationship between the minimum unemployment rate and the current wages. Our intuition is that the dual behaviour envisaged by Beaudry and Di Nardo (1991) is at work here, but it operates in the reverse direction. We can only attribute a spot labour market to the case of the UK. In Spain, the contemporaneous unemployment rate exhibits a significant negative influence of about –0.09, even though its significance is overshadowed by the minimum unemployment rate. This situation, which highlights the importance of the current unemployment rate, can be explained by the high proportion of fixed-term contracts in the Spanish economy (around one-third of total labour contracts), which are strongly affected by the business cycle (Canziani, 1997). Furthermore, the collective bargaining system in Spain, and its ample coverage of the workforce, may make it easier to achieve wage improvements during boom phases of the economy.

Appendix

The regional classification used in this study (which is defined by the ECHP) is the 'Nomenclature of Territorial Units for Statistics', commonly known by its French acronym, NUTS. The regions examined by this are NUTS 1 regions, of which there are 77 in the EU. Specifically, in the case of the sample countries, there are 11 regions for Italy, 11 for the UK, 8 for France, 7 for Portugal and 7 for Spain (see Table 11.A.1 for an overall description). In each country, we selected from the complete survey those individuals who are wage earners working in the industrial and services sectors and who furnished all the relevant information for the estimation through the first three waves of the survey, 1994, 1995 and 1996. Therefore, the final data sizes used in the estimation for each year are: 3,740 individuals for France, 3,589 for Italy, 2,777 for Portugal, 2,641 for Spain and 2,113 for the UK.

The survey provides information on earnings, as well as job and personal characteristics. In particular, we used the following variables:

- *Log real wage per hour.* Nominal wages deflated by the corresponding weighted regional CPI, taken from the National Statistic Institutes.
- *Log unemployment rate.* Four alternative measures were used: the regional unemployment rate; the region-by-gender unemployment rate; the region-by-age group unemployment rate (the corresponding age groups being between 16 and 19, between 20 and 24, between 25 and 54 and over 55); and the region-by-gender and by-age-group unemployment rate. Only the estimates for the first and the last measures are presented. The data were drawn from the National Labour Force Surveys.
- *Age.* This was used to proxy working experience. We also introduced it to the second power (divided by 100) in order to shape the decreasing returns on experience.
- *Gender.* Male = 1, female = 0.
- *Marital status.* Married = 1, otherwise = 0.
- *Part-time work*: Working fewer than 30 hours per week = 1, working more than 30 hours = 0.
- *Education level of the employee*: This divided into three categories: no formal and primary education, secondary education, and university and technical education.
- *Occupation group.* This variable describes the type of employee specialisation, divided into eight categories: managers, professional technicians, supporting professional technicians, administrative staff, simple service workers, skilled craftsmen and technicians, assemblers, and unskilled workers.
- *Seniority.* The number of years that a worker had been employed in his/her current position. This divided into three categories: less than 2 years, between 2 and 10 years, and more than 10 years.
- *Type of activity.* In principle, this classification comprises agricultural, industrial and service activities. However, once we eliminated agricultural workers, it became a dummy variable. Industry worker = 1, services worker = 0.

The NUTS 1 areas used for the investigation were those in Table 11.A.1.

The full set of estimates of the wage elasticity is presented in Tables 11.A.2 and 11.A.3 The first table shows the results when the unemployment rate is measured only at regional level. As discussed in the main text, more disaggregate expressions of the unemployment rate were preferred, given that they provide a larger number degrees of freedom, with the resulting gain in precision and efficiency. Therefore, Table 11.A.3 presents the estimates when the unemployment rate is expressed by region, by gender, and by age group. The column scheme is the same as that used in Table 11.2 in the main text. As regards the row scheme, the first row contains the results when the pooled estimation was used; the second and third rows collect the estimates when individual heterogeneity was considered, through fixed coefficients in the second row and through random effects in the third. The LM tests, shown in the fourth row, reject the pooled specification in favour of the panel one; finally, the Hausman tests, shown in the fifth row, tend to favour the within estimation over the random effects.

Table 11.A.1. Regional (NUTS 1 and NUTS 2) disaggregation in the five EU sample countries

FRANCE	NUTS 1 ZEAT	NUTS 2 Régions
Region 1	Île de France	Île de France
Region 2	Bassin Parisien	Champagne-Ardenne, Bourgogne, Picardie, Haute-Normandie, Centre, Basse-Normandie
Region 3	Nord – Pas-de-Calais	Nord – Pas-de-Calais
Region 4	Est	Lorraine, Alsace, Franche-Comté
Region 5	Ouest	Pays de la Loire, Bretagne, Poitou-Charentes
Region 6	Sud-Ouest	Aquitaine, Midi-Pyrénées, Limousin
Region 7	Centre-Est	Rhône-Alpes, Auvergne
Region 8	Méditerranée	Languedoc-Roussillon, Corse Provence-Alpes-Côte d'Azur
ITALY	NUTS 1 Gruppi di regioni	NUTS 2 Regioni
Region 1	Nord Ovest	Piemonte, Valle d'Aosta, Liguria
Region 2	Lombardia	Lombardia
Region 3	Nord Est	Trentino-Alto Adige, Veneto Friuli-Venezia, Giulia
Region 4	Emilia-Romagna	Emilia-Romagna
Region 5	Centro	Toscana, Umbría, Marche
Region 6	Lazio	Lazio
Region 7	Abruzzo-Molise	Abruzzo, Molise
Region 8	Campania	Campania
Region 9	Sud	Puglia, Basilicata, Calabria
Region 10	Sicilia	Sicilia
Region 11	Sardegna	Sardegna
PORTUGAL	NUTS 1 Continente	NUTS 2 Regiones Autónomas
Region 1	Continente	Norte
Region 1a		Centro
Region 1b		Lisboa e Vale do Tejo
Region 1c		Alentejo
Region 1d		Algarve
Region 2	Açores	Açores
Region 3	Madeira	Madeira
SPAIN	NUTS 1 Agrupación de Comunidades Autónomas	NUTS 2 Comunidades Autónomas
Region 1	Noroeste	Galicia, Asturias, Cantabria
Region 2	Noreste	País Vasco, Navarra, La Rioja, Aragón
Region 3	Comunidad de Madrid	Comunidad de Madrid
Region 4	Centro	Castilla-León, Castilla-La Mancha, Extremadura
Region 5	Este	Cataluña, Comunidad Valenciana, Baleares
Region 6	Sur	Andalucía, Murcia, Ceuta, Melilla
Region 7	Canarias	Canarias

UNITED KINGDOM	NUTS 1 Government Office Regions	NUTS 2 Counties
Region 1	North East	Tees Valley and Durham; Northumerland; Tyne and Wear
Region 2	Yorkshire and Humberside	East Riding and North Lincolnshire; North Yorkshire; South Yorkshire; West Yorkshire
Region 3	East Midlands	Derbyshire and Nottinghamshire; Leicestershire, Rutland and Northants; Lincolnshire
Region 4	Eastern	East Anglia; Essex; Bedfordshire; Hertfordshire; London
Region 5	South East	Berkshire, Bucks and Oxfordshire; Surrey; East and West Sussex; Hampshire and Isle of Wight Kent
Region 6	South West	Gloucestershire, Wiltshire and North Somerset; Dorset and Somerset; Cornwall and Isles of Scilly Devon
Region 7	West Midlands	Herefordshire, Worcestershire and Warks; Shropshire and Staffordshire; West Midlands
Region 8	North West	Cumbria; Cheshire; Greater Manchester; Lancashire; Merseyside
Region 9	Wales	West Wales and The Valleys; East Wales
Region 10	Scotland	North Eastern Scotland; Eastern Scotland; South and Western Scotland; Highlands and Islands
Region 11	Northern Ireland	Northern Ireland

Table 11.A.2. Estimation of the wage curve in the five sample EU countries: regional unemployment rate

Country	Estimation	Individual u_i	Individual u_h	Individual u_{min}	Pairs u_i	Pairs u_h	Pairs u_{min}	Pairs u_i	Pairs u_h	Pairs u_{min}	Triples u_i	Triples u_h	Triples u_{min}
France	Pool	-0.134 (-3.69)	-0.859 (-29.19)	-1.014 (-30.26)	-0.230 (-2.79)	-0.859 (-29.19)	-0.769 (-8.19)	-0.273 (-1.18)	-1.014 (-30.26)	-0.275 (-1.19)	-0.274 (-1.19)	-0.230 (-2.79)	-0.769 (-8.19)
	Fixed effects	-0.810 (-4.49)	-0.810 (-4.49)	-0.256 (-1.32)	-3.706 (-8.24)	-0.804 (-4.46)	3.383 (-7.02)	-0.272 (-1.73)	-0.251 (-1.30)	-0.282 (-1.80)	-0.261 (-1.67)	-3.694 (-8.21)	3.375 (-7.01)
	Random effects	-0.158 (-4.62)	-0.861 (-21.27)	-0.966 (-21.31)	-0.454 (-3.94)	-0.860 (-21.26)	-0.487 (-3.76)	-0.274 (-1.74)	-0.966 (-21.31)	-0.277 (-1.76)	-0.275 (-1.75)	-0.454 (-3.93)	-0.488 (-3.76)
	LM	2944	3202	3142	3146	3203	3144				3148		
	Hausman	287	512	556	614	394	322				488		
Italy	Pool	-0.081 (-7.21)	-0.291 (-11.52)	-0.662 (-23.72)	-0.138 (-1.36)	-0.291 (-11.50)	-0.643 (-20.66)	-0.103 (-1.30)	-0.662 (-23.74)	-0.128 (-1.64)	-0.126 (-1.62)	-0.037 (-1.33)	-0.644 (-20.68)
	Fixed effects	-0.109 (-1.87)	-0.371 (-3.09)	-0.508 (-5.08)	-0.045 (-0.31)	-0.353 (-2.92)	-0.487 (-4.05)	-0.092 (-1.58)	-0.503 (-5.04)	-0.101 (-1.74)	-0.100 (-1.71)	-0.020 (-0.14)	-0.494 (-4.10)
	Random effects	-0.076 (-7.32)	-0.309 (-8.99)	-0.623 (-17.65)	-0.045 (-1.19)	-0.308 (-8.95)	-0.601 (-15.11)	-0.086 (-1.49)	-0.624 (-17.67)	-0.113 (-1.96)	-0.111 (-1.92)	-0.042 (-1.12)	-0.603 (-15.16)
	LM	2206	2572	2373	2373	2573	2375				2374		
	Hausman	152	115	120	122	127	127				126		
Portugal	Pool	0.076 (-3.2)	0.165 (-6.25)	-0.493 (-19.78)	0.164 (-6.38)	0.165 (-6.25)	-0.493 (-19.82)	-0.006 (-0.07)	0.124 (-1.79)	0.005	-0.002 (-0.03)	0.164 (-6.37)	-0.493 (-19.82)
	Fixed effects	0.007	0.043 (-0.58)	0.124 (-1.79)	-0.021 (-0.25)	0.042 (-0.57)	0.132 (-1.71)	0.005	0.004	-0.09	0.005	-0.021 (-0.25)	0.132 (-1.71)
	Random effects	-0.008 (-0.14)	0.136 (-3.81)	-0.387 (-12.77)	0.188 (-5.38)	0.136 (-3.82)	-0.406 (-13.33)	-0.005 (-0.10)	-0.388 (-12.77)	-0.07	-0.003 (-0.01)	0.188 (-5.38)	-0.406 (-13.33)
	LM	2886	3013	2841	2833	3013	2841				2833		
	Hausman	318	358	500	482	323	414				400		
Spain	Pool	-0.143 (-3.58)	-0.615 (-16.12)	-1.057 (-24.34)	0.024 (-0.47)	-0.614 (-16.11)	-1.076 (-17.95)	-0.053 (-0.30)	-1.057 (-24.33)	-0.029 (-0.17)	-0.030 (-0.17)	0.024 (-0.47)	-1.076 (-17.95)
	Fixed effects	-0.120 (-0.96)	-0.603 (-3.75)	-0.155 (-1.08)	-0.946 (-4.21)	-0.593 (-3.67)	0.44 (-2.18)	-0.172 (-0.57)	-0.146 (-1.01)	-0.111 (-0.88)	-0.072 (-0.57)	-0.936 (-4.15)	0.44 (-2.18)
	Random effects	-0.235 (-1.85)	-0.617 (-11.89)	-0.926 (-16.60)	-0.064 (-0.91)	-0.616 (-11.87)	-0.876 (-11.28)	-0.048 (-0.38)	-0.925 (-16.58)	-0.040 (-0.32)	-0.038 (-0.30)	-0.063 (-0.90)	-0.876 (-11.28)
	LM	1793	2135	1941	1940	2136					1940		
	Hausman	149	114	147	165	114					165		
UK	Pool	-0.298 (-6.60)	0.283 (-6.78)	-0.442 (-8.01)	0.347 (-8.25)	0.283 (-6.76)	-0.516 (-9.29)	-0.419 (-1.90)	-0.443 (-8.04)	-0.458 (-2.08)	-0.442 (-2.02)	-0.517 (-9.31)	-0.516 (-9.29)
	Fixed effects	-0.238 (-2.78)	-0.191 (-1.09)	-0.313 (-1.36)	-0.132 (-0.71)	-0.211 (-1.20)	-0.262 (-1.09)	-0.445 (-2.82)	-0.376 (-1.63)	-0.462 (-2.92)	-0.464 (-2.93)	-0.323 (-1.33)	-0.262 (-1.09)
	Random effects	-0.244 (-2.76)	0.238 (-4.26)	-0.436 (-5.88)	0.296 (-5.28)	0.235 (-4.21)	-0.495 (-6.66)	-0.422 (-2.67)	-0.441 (-5.96)	-0.459 (-2.90)	-0.446 (-2.82)	-0.500 (-6.72)	-0.495 (-6.66)
	LM	1534	1453	1452	1411	1457					1414		
	Hausman	67	238	225	257	78					79		

Table 11.A.3. Regional (NUT 1 and NUT 2) disaggregation in the five EU sample countries

		Individual			Pairs						Triples		
		u_t	u_h	u_{min}	u_h	u_{min}	u_t	u_{min}	u_t	u_h	u_t	u_h	u_{min}
France	Pool	-0.188 (-6.01)	-0.388 (-27.23)	-0.401 (-26.96)	-0.342 (-3.77)	-0.048 (-0.51)	0.401 (11.83)	-0.583 (-26.81)	0.468 (13.19)	-0.647 (-27.20)	0.458 (12.75)	-0.160 (-1.76)	-0.477 (-4.76)
	Fixed effects	-0.106 (-3.65)	-0.106 (-3.65)	-0.098 (-3.31)	-1.558 (-4.31)	1.484 (4.03)	0.099 (1.12)	-0.197 (-2.29)	0.018 (0.2)	-0.115 (-1.30)	0.037 (0.41)	-1.565 (-4.32)	1.457 (3.89)
	Random effects	-0.182 (-9.79)	-0.320 (-18.46)	-0.324 (-18.07)	-0.502 (-4.02)	0.191 (1.47)	0.398 (10.35)	-0.557 (-19.48)	0.433 (10.82)	-0.599 (-19.39)	0.42 (10.24)	-0.343 (-2.75)	-0.238 (-1.77)
	LM	2964	3185	3182	3184		3167		3142			3145	
	Hausman	430	483	492	500		542		582			596	
Italy	Pool	-0.082 (-7.21)	-0.137 (-13.08)	-0.178 (-16.03)	-0.337 (-10.66)	-0.151 (-11.34)	0.025 (1.74)	-0.232 (-15.50)	0.036 (2.37)	-0.257 (-16.50)	0.081 (5.49)	0.163 (5.58)	-0.396 (-11.87)
	Fixed effects	-0.039 (-3.27)	-0.088 (-4.64)	-0.105 (-5.41)	-0.678 (-5.38)	-0.075 (-3.50)	-0.016 (-1.20)	-0.097 (-4.38)	0.035 (1.34)	0.105 (1.97)	-0.013 (-1.00)	0.569 (4.64)	-0.674 (-5.33)
	Random effects	-0.074 (-6.54)	-0.130 (-10.66)	-0.163 (-12.78)	-0.358 (-8.53)	-0.132 (-9.18)	0.004 (0.34)	-0.181 (-11.78)	0.025 (1.46)	-0.231 (-11.06)	0.026 (2.07)	0.193 (4.86)	-0.375 (-8.79)
	LM	2186	2566	2529	2524		2560		2486			2477	
	Hausman	132	109	106	117		113		149			166	
Portugal	Pool	-0.069 (-4.14)	0.003 (0.24)	-0.105 (-10.36)	-0.067 (-3.07)	-0.294 (-16.15)	0.207 (12.76)	-0.181 (-12.69)			0.066 (2.84)	0.187 (10.64)	-0.273 (-16.46)
	Fixed effects	0.007 (0.37)	0.026 (1.27)	0.039 (1.93)	-0.013 (-0.57)	-0.198 (-1.96)	-0.070 (-1.33)	0.056 (2.16)			-0.018 (-0.77)	-0.061 (-1.13)	0.109 (2.03)
	Random effects	-0.088 (-6.64)	0.009 (0.73)	-0.072 (-5.82)	-0.028 (-1.38)	-0.265 (-11.28)	0.204 (9.36)	-0.112 (-7.06)			0.019 (0.95)	0.197 (8.51)	-0.236 (-11.02)
	LM	2790	3036	2972	2914		3025		2924			2904	
	Hausman	386	356	394	407		462		383			430	
Spain	Pool	-0.101 (-2.76)	-0.281 (-17.35)	-0.349 (-21.11)		-0.390 (-11.88)	0.042 (1.61)	-0.374 (-20.28)	0.077 (3.01)		0.072 (2.8)	0.03 (0.94)	-0.399 (-12.10)
	Fixed effects	-0.154 (-4.07)	-0.159 (-4.08)	-0.222 (-4.75)		-0.216 (-2.43)	-0.094 (-1.94)	-0.168 (-3.01)	-0.080 (-1.76)		-0.090 (-1.86)	0.048 (0.6)	-0.210 (-2.36)
	Random effects	-0.126 (-5.06)	-0.259 (-12.65)	-0.333 (-15.60)		-0.378 (-9.01)	0.016 (0.55)	-0.346 (-14.54)	0.035 (1.22)		0.028 (0.94)	0.04 (0.97)	-0.380 (-9.05)
	LM	1796	2113	2057	2057		2111		2048			2048	
	Hausman	121	119	109	108		536		665			664	

Note: As explained in the text, problems of data availability do not allow estimation for the UK

References

Albaek K, Asplund R, Blomskog S, Barth E, Gudmundsson B, Karlsson V, Madsen E (2000) Dimensions of the wage-unemployment relationship in the Nordic Countries: wage flexibility without wage curves. Research in Labor Economics 19:345–382.

Andrés J, Dolado JJ, Molinas C, Sebastián M, Zabalza A (1990) The influence of demand and capital constraints in Spanish unemployment. In: Dreze J, Bean C (eds) Europe's unemployment problem. MIT Press, Cambridge (Mass.), pp 366–408.

Baltagi B, Blien U (1998) The German wage curve: evidence from the IAB employment sample. Economics Letters 61:135–142.

Barth E, Bratsberg B, Naylor R, Raaum O (2002) Explaining variations in wage curves: theory and evidence. University of Oslo, Memorandum 03/2002,

Bean C, Layard R, Nickell S (1986) The rise in unemployment: a multi-country study. Economica 53 Supplement:1–22.

Beaudry P, Di Nardo J (1991) The effects of implicit contracts on the movement of wages over the business cycle: evidence over micro data. Journal of Political Economy 99:663–668.

Blanchard O, Jimeno J (1995) Structural unemployment. Spain versus Portugal. American Economic Review 85:212–218.

Blanchard O, Katz L (1992) Regional evolutions. Brookings Papers on Economic Activity 1:1–75.

Blanchard O, Katz L (1997) What do we know and we do not know about the natural rate of unemployment. Journal of Economic Perspectives 11:51–73.

Blanchard O, Portugal P (2001) What hides behind an unemployment rate. Comparing Portuguese and U.S. unemployment. American Economic Review 91:187–207.

Blanchard O, Wolfers J (2000) The role of shocks and institutions in the rise of European unemployment: the aggregate evidence. Economic Journal 110:1–33.

Blanchflower D, Oswald A (1994) The wage curve. MIT Press, Cambridge (Mass.).

Blanchflower D , Oswald A (1995) An introduction to the wage curve. Journal of Economic Perspectives 9:153–167.

Bover O, García-Perea P, Portugal P (1997) A comparative study of the Portuguese and Spanish labour markets. Bank of Spain DT 9807.

Bratsberg B, Turunen J (1996) Wage curve evidence from panel data. Economics Letters 51:345–353.

Buettner T (1999) The effect of unemployment, aggregate wages, and spatial contiguity on local wages: an investigation with German district level data. Papers in Regional Science 78:47–67.

Campbell C, Orszag J (1998) A model of the wage curve. Economics Letters 51:345–353.

Canziani P (1997) The wage curve in Italy and Spain: are European wages flexible?. CEP Discussion Paper 375.

Card D (1995) The wage curve: a review. Journal of Economic Literature 33:785–799.

Castillo S, Dolado J, Jimeno J (1998) A tale of two neighbour economies: does wage flexibility make the difference between Portuguese and Spanish unemployment?. FEDEA DT 98–02.

Decressin J , Fatàs A (1995) Regional labour markets in Europe. European Economic Review 39:627–55.

Demertzis M., Hughes Hallett A (1996) Regional inequalities and the business cycle: an explanation of the rise in European unemployment. Regional Studies 30:15–29.

Ferreiro J, Serrano F (2001) The Spanish labour market: reforms and consequences. International Review of Applied Economics 15:31–53.

Garcia I, Montuenga V (2003) The Spanish wage curve: 1994–1996. Regional Studies 37:929–945.

Grubb D, Jackman R, Layard R (1986) Wage rigidity and unemployment in OECD countries. European Economic Review 21:11–39.

Janssens S, Konings J (1998) One more wage curve: the case of Belgium. Economics Letters 60:223–227.

Jimeno J, Bentolila S (1998) Regional unemployment persistence (Spain, 1976–1994). Labour Economics 5:25–51.

Kennedy S, Borland J (2000) A wage curve for Australia?. Oxford Economic Papers 52:774–803.

Layard R, Nickell S, Jackman R (1991) Unemployment. Macroeconomic performance and the labour market, Oxford University Press, Oxford.

Marimon R, Zilibotti F (1998) Actual vs. virtual employment in Europe. European Economic Review 42:123–53.

Montuenga V, García, Fernández M (2003) Wage flexibility: evidence from five EU countries based on the wage curve. Economics Letters 78:169–174.

Montuenga V, Ramos JM (2005) Reconciling wage curve and Phillips curve. Journal of Economic Surveys. Forthcoming.

Morrison P, Papps K, Poot J (2000) Local labour markets, migration and wage determination: theory and evidence for the wage curve in New Zealand. Victoria University of Wellington, GSBGM 1/00,

Moulton B (1986) Random group effects and the precision of regression estimates. Journal of Econometrics 32:385–397.

Nickell S (1997) Unemployment and labor market rigidities: Europe versus North America. Journal of Economic Perspectives 11:55–74.

Nickell S, Layard R (1999) Labor market institutions and economic performance. In: Ashenfelter O, Card D (eds) Handbook of labor economics, Vol 3, Elsevier, Amsterdam, pp 3029–3085.

Overman H, Puga D (2002) Unemployment clusters across European countries and regions. Economic Policy 34:117–14.

Puga D (2002) European regional policy in light of recent location theories. Journal of Economic Geography 2:372–406.

Sato Y (2000) Search theory and the wage curve. Economics Letters 66:93–98.

Shapiro C. Stiglitz J (1984) Equilibrium unemployment as a worker discipline device. American Economic Review 73: 433–444.

Solon G, Barsky R, Parker J (1994) Measuring the cyclicality of real wages: how important is composition bias?. Quarterly Journal of Economics 109:1–26.

Turunen J (1998) Disaggregated wage curves in the United States: evidence from panel data of young workers. Applied Economics 30:1665–1677.

Winter-Ebmer R (1996) Wage curve, unemployment durations and compensating differentials. Labour Economics 3:425–434.

12 Large-Scale Labour Market Restructuring and Labour Mobility: the Experiences of East Germany and Poland

Vania Sena

Aston Business School, United Kingdom

12.1 Introduction

During the past two decades large-scale restructuring in the labour market has occurred in many countries. The causes of these adjustments, which have required a substantial reallocation of labour across sectors and caused high unemployment during the often pro-longed adjustment period, are of various kinds, and in some cases they are disputed. Established market economies in Western Europe and North America have experienced a sharp decline of employment in traditional manufacturing sectors and an expansion of the service sector, with a loss of unskilled jobs in particular. This development has been variously attributed to the decline in resource-based industries (such as mining in United Kingdom), skill-biased technological progress, and increased competition from low labour cost countries. The transition economies in Central and Eastern Europe and in the Commonwealth of Independent States have experienced – as part of their transition from centrally planned economies to market ones – large-scale adjustments in the labour market as privatised firms, as well as those that continue to be state-owned, have had to restructure and lay off a substantial number of workers.

The distinction between labour market adjustments in response to structural changes within the context of an established market economy and adjustments that occur as part of transition from a centrally planned economy to a market economy is obviously important. It is principally so because, in the latter case, a regulatory framework for insurance coverage in the event of job losses and other income support programmes has had to be established largely simultaneously with the privatisation of state-owned enterprises and the liberalisation of prices (Boeri 1997). Despite these differences, however, one can outline a common theoretical framework within which to consider large-scale labour market restructuring and the various policy options available to eliminate the worst social costs and promote the efficient use of human resources. Indeed, at any point in time, there are three pools of individuals in the labour market: (1) the employed; (2) the unemployed; and (3) the non-employed. Structural changes in the labour market increase the outflow from employment, typically by destroying jobs in the shrinking sector. The speed at which workers move into the expanding sector depends on the speed at which jobs are destroyed in the shrinking sector and created in the expanding sector; but it also depends on the incentives for seeking employment rather than leaving the labour force or accepting extended spells of unemployment. The speed at which jobs are destroyed in the shrinking sector depends on numerous factors, including government policy on such issues as subsidies and strict employment-protection legislation (e.g. non-negligible severance pay). Successful restructuring requires a fairly dynamic labour market with high job turnover and mobility. In this respect, the paramount role of territorial mobility as far as transition economies are concerned was given early emphasis by Burda (1993).[1] Government policies include passive labour market policies (such as unemployment benefits and social assistance) and active labour market policies (such as training, job search services, and public employment programmes).

The purpose of this chapter is first to present a very simple theoretical framework which enables assessment of the government's role in the labour reallocation across sectors and regions. The gist of the model is that, at the beginning of transition, wage rigidities in the labour market may slow down the speed at which workers move from the shrinking sector to the expanding one. They thus contribute to the creation of an unemployment pool (consisting mostly of unskilled workers priced out by the market) that may become stagnant unless the government actively intervenes. Two case studies are then considered: East Germany and Poland, which have undergone this reallocation process with mixed outcomes in terms of resulting unemployment and the long-term working of the labour market. The structure of the chapter is as follows. Section 12.2 describes the model, while Sections 12.3 and 12.4 present the cases of East Germany and Poland respectively. Finally, Section 12.5 makes some concluding remarks.

12.2   Permanent shocks and labour market adjustment: an analytical framework

This section presents a two-sector model in which labour moves from a shrinking manufacturing sector to an expanding service sector, and in which there are labour market frictions based on a simple efficiency wage mechanism. Unlike the model of Aghion and Blanchard (1994), which is a model of optimal reallocation speed between sectors, the emphasis here is on comparative static solutions, and explicit consideration is made of the influence that price adjustment of tradable and non-tradable goods may exert on sectoral reallocation. The latter element reflects the sometimes overlooked fact that the shrinking sector in most transition countries is the manufacturing (whose output was typically traded within the COMECON area), while the expanding sector is generally services catering to the domestic market (Economist Intelligence Unit 2003).

Consider an open economy consisting of a representative consumer supplying one unit of labour and two firms. The latter produce two different types of consumption good: a tradable good Y_t^S and a non-tradable good Y_t^{NS}. Each firm is

---

[1] The central role of geographical mobility for macroeconomic adjustment has since been emphasised in Oswald (1997).

endowed with a stock of private capital (assumed to be equal between the two firms), but for simplicity its choice is not modelled (i.e. the model has a short-run set-up). The exogenous interest rate is assumed to be equal to one throughout the model. In the first part of the model we analyse the agents and their objective functions, and derive the labour demands, while in the second part we assess the effects of an adverse shock to productivity on unemployment.

The tradable good, Y_t^S is produced by firm S with the following constant returns to scale technology:

$$Y_t^S = a_t K_t^{S,\theta} L_t^{S,1-\theta} \tag{12.1}$$

where K_t^S is the amount of physical capital employed by firm S at time t, L_t^S is the labour employed at time t and a_t is total factor productivity at time t, assumed to be exogenous for simplicity[2] and therefore dictating the evolution of the economy over time. Equation (12.1) can be expressed in intensive form as:

$$y_t^S = a_t k_t^{S,\theta} \tag{12.2}$$

The non-tradable good, Y_t^{NS}, is produced by firm NS, using the following linear homogenous production function:

$$Y_t^{NS} = K_t^{NS,\beta} L_t^{NS,(1-\beta)} \tag{12.3}$$

where L_t^{NS} is the labour employed at time t. In intensive form (12.3) is equal to:

$$y_t^{NS} = k_t^{NS,\beta} \tag{12.4}$$

Firms maximise profits subject to their technology. For firm S, profits π_t^S are:

$$\pi_t^S = y_t^S - w_t L_t^S \tag{12.5}$$

where y_t^S is the tradable output produced at time t and $w_t L_t^S$ is the wage bill. The price of the tradable goods is determined outside the local economy and can be normalised to unity. For firm NS, profits π_t^S are equal to:

$$\pi_t^{NS} = p_t y_t^{NS} - w_t L_t^{NS} \tag{12.6}$$

---

[2] Indeed, we can conceive total factor productivity as a function of a variety of factors like the availability of infrastructures, social capital and so on. However, at this stage, modelling these factors is beyond the scope of the model.

where y_t^{NS} is the non-tradable output produced at time t, p_t is the price of non-tradable goods at time t and $w_t L_t^{NS}$ is the wage bill for firm NS. The price of the non-tradable goods (relative to the tradable goods), p_t, is determined by the market clearing conditions in the domestic market.

Profit maximisation yields the following first-order conditions:

$$a_t(1-\theta)k_t^{S,\theta} = w_t \tag{12.7}$$

$$p_t(1-\beta)k_t^{NS,\beta} = w_t \tag{12.8}$$

where (12.7) and (12.8) are the first-order conditions with respect to labour for both firms. Labour demand by firm S can be computed from (12.7) as:

$$L^S = K^S a_t^{\frac{1}{\theta}} (1-\theta)^{\frac{1}{\theta}} w_t^{-\frac{1}{\theta}} \tag{12.9}$$

Labour demand increases in total factor productivity and decreases in wage as:

$$\frac{\partial L^S}{\partial a_t} = \frac{1}{\theta} K^S a_t^{\frac{1-\theta}{\theta}} (1-\theta)^{\frac{1}{\theta}} w_t^{-\frac{1}{\theta}} > 0$$

$$\frac{\partial L^T}{\partial w_t} = -\frac{1}{\theta} K^T a_t^{\frac{1}{\theta}} (1-\theta)^{\frac{1}{\theta}} w_t^{\frac{\theta-1}{\theta}} < 0$$

From (12.8) labour demand by firm NS is equal to:

$$L^{NS} = K^{NS} p_t^{\frac{1}{\beta}} (1-\beta)^{\frac{1}{\beta}} w_t^{-\frac{1}{\beta}} \tag{12.10}$$

An increase in the price of the non-tradable good increases labour demand, whereas an increase in the wage decreases it:

$$\frac{\partial L^{NS}}{\partial p_t} = \frac{1}{\beta} K^{NS} p_t^{\frac{1-\beta}{\beta}} (1-\beta)^{\frac{1}{\beta}} w_t^{-\frac{1}{\beta}} > 0$$

The consumer provides one unit of labour to the economy, so that equilibrium in the labour market is defined by the following equality:

$$L^S + L^{NS} + U = 1 \tag{12.11}$$

The government levies a unit tax, t, on both firms' wages in order to finance the benefit programme providing financial assistance to the unemployed. The government faces a simple budget constraint:

$$B_t = T_t \tag{12.12}$$

because total expenditure on the benefit programme is equal to total tax revenues, which are in turn equal to $t(L^S + L^{NT})$. Equation (12.11) can be used to rewrite (12.12) as:

$$bU_t = (1 - U_t)t \tag{12.13}$$

where U_t is the unemployment at time t, b is the unemployment benefit per capita.

Assume that wages are set according to an efficiency wages set-up. Wages must be such that the value for the consumer of being unemployed is equal to the value of being employed plus a premium:

$$V_E = V_U + c \tag{12.14}$$

where V_E is the value of being employed, V_U is the value of being unemployed, and c is a premium assumed here to be constant for simplicity. For the consumer, the value of being unemployed is equal to the benefit plus the increase in value associated with moving from the unemployed state to the employed state, weighted by the probability of being employed, π:

$$\rho V_U = b + \pi(V_U - V_E) \tag{12.15}$$

where ρ is the discount rate, which can be assumed to be equal to the interest rate and therefore equal to one. The value of being employed is defined equal to the wage net of the fixed cost of moving to a new sector, m. This cost can be interpreted as the cost associated with learning new skills and adapting to the new working environment; for simplicity it is assumed to be constant. Hence:

$$\rho V_E = w_t - m \tag{12.16}$$

On substituting (12.15) and (12.16) into (12.14), the equilibrium wage is:

$$w_t = (b + m) + c\pi \tag{12.17}$$

The wage must be equal to the benefit plus the adjustment cost with a premium that is in itself a function of the probability of finding a new job. From (12.13), the benefit per capita is a function of the tax levied by the government and the level of unemployment; Eq. (12.17) becomes:

$$w_t = ((1 - U_t)U_t^{-1}t + m) + c\pi \quad \text{with} \quad \frac{\partial w_t}{\partial U_t} = -\frac{t}{U_t^2} < 0; \tag{12.18}$$

that is, as unemployment increases, wages are pushed downwards for a given wage premium and cost of adjustment, m. However, this adjustment is influenced negatively by t: a high tax rate prevents the firms from reducing their wage costs below the level that could help absorb the existing unemployment.

Let us now move to analysis of the equilibrium in this economy. Total factor productivity in equilibrium is equal to a^*. The price of the non-tradable good can be derived by combining (12.7) and (12.8) and recalling that the capital intensities are uniform across firms:

$$p^* = a^* \left(\frac{1-\theta}{1-\beta} \right) \tag{12.19}$$

where:

$$\frac{\partial p^*}{\partial a^*} = \left(\frac{1-\theta}{1-\beta} \right) > 0$$

Thus, in equilibrium a decrease in the total factor productivity of the tradable sector reduces the price of non-tradable goods as long as $0 < \beta < 1$ and $0 < \theta < 1$.

Now consider equilibrium unemployment. Take the labour market equilibrium condition (12.11) and substitute the labour demands of the two firms:

$$K^S a_t^{*\frac{1}{\theta}} (1-\theta)^{\frac{1}{\theta}} (w)^{-\frac{1}{\theta}} + K^{NS} p_t^{\frac{1}{\beta}} (1-\beta)^{\frac{1}{\beta}} (w)^{-\frac{1}{\beta}} + U_t = 1 \tag{12.20}$$

where the wage is given by (12.18). The unemployment rate can thus be computed from (12.20) as a function of the characteristics of the technology for the two firms (as embodied by β and θ), of the tax, t, of the wage premium, c, of the probability of being re-employed, π and of the cost of moving to the other firm, m:

$$U^* = U(\theta, \beta, T, c, \pi, m) \tag{12.21}$$

Let us now consider the impact of a negative permanent shock to total factor productivity on equilibrium unemployment.[3] The analysis can be divided into two stages. In the first, it can be easily shown that the negative shock exerts a direct impact on unemployment through the labour demand of the two firms for a given wage. The shock will first reduce the demand for labour by firm S. Unemployment builds up and the price of non-tradable goods decreases owing to lower total factor productivity. This increases the demand for non-tradable goods and the corresponding labour demand. The net effect on unemployment can be evaluated by considering:

$$\frac{\partial U^*}{\partial a^*} = -\frac{1}{\theta} K^S (a^*)^{\frac{1}{\theta}-1} (1-\theta)^{\frac{1}{\theta}} (w)^{-\frac{1}{\theta}} - \frac{1}{\beta} \frac{\partial p^*}{\partial a^*} K^{NS} p^{\frac{1}{\beta}-1} (1-\beta)^{\frac{1}{\beta}} (w)^{-\frac{1}{\beta}} < 0 \tag{12.22}$$

The adverse shock on productivity has the effect of increasing unemployment in spite of the fact that the effect on the price of the non-tradable good works in the opposite direction. This can be explained by recalling that the price rise fol-

---

[3] Following Blanchard and Kremer (1997), the dislocation of trade links within the COMECON during the early 1990s can be interpreted along these lines.

lowing the negative shock to productivity is a fraction of the size of the initial shock to productivity, so that the positive impact on the labour demand by firm *NS* will always be smaller than the negative impact on the labour demand by firm *S*. However, as unemployment builds up, wages start to move downwards, amplifying the effect of the increase in the price of non-tradable goods on employment in firm *NS*. But the extent of this adjustment depends on the tax rate (and indirectly on the size and coverage of the benefit programme): a higher tax rate (necessary to finance an extensive benefit programme) reduces the extent of wage adjustment and therefore contributes to creation of a long-term unemployment pool.

This simple theoretical framework can be used to illustrate a number of important points. First, the role of wage flexibility. In the model, downward real wage rigidity is modelled through the tax rate. In reality, other variables (trade union pressure, EPL, and so on) may play a similar role by pricing less productive workers, typically non-skilled ones, out of employment. Yet, as suggested by the experience of the transitional countries, this occurs mainly at the beginning of transition. Once the pool of the long-term unemployed people has built up, reducing real wage rigidities does not greatly help; the government must devise policies to assist the non-skilled unemployed in upgrading their skills and becoming employable in the expanding sector.

The second point is the impact of the size and coverage of the benefit system on the build-up of a long-term unemployment pool. Benefit entitlement enters the consumer's work decision and affects the equilibrium wage on the labour market. It is important to ensure that policy measures and institutions developed to deal with transitional adjustment problems do not have adverse effects on active job searching. One way to make sure that this does not happen is to reduce the retention rate and the benefit duration, possibly *pari passu* with the business cycle. At the same time, the unemployed must be supported by local job centres in their job searches. Unemployment traps must be prevented from arising as well: benefits, including housing allowances, should be related to the market wage for unskilled workers. This can be done in two ways. The first is to accept a differential between the lowest (market) wage and the unemployment benefit, but introducing an employment subsidy for low-earners. The second is to eliminate minimum wages, reducing the duration of unemployment benefits and introducing individual transfers to all adult workers independently of their employment status. This would, however, reduce the insurance element of the benefit system.

In addition to these policies, which specifically target those at risk of unemployment, housing policy may have important implications for the cost of large-scale labour adjustment, in that restructuring requires workers to relocate geographically and there are large regional differences in the availability and cost of housing.

12.3 East Germany

12.3.1 The labour market performance

Soon after the fall of the Berlin Wall in 1989, East Germany became part of the Federal Republic of Germany and adopted West Germany's legal, administrative and economic infrastructure. In addition, the West German currency (DM) became legal tender at the very favourable 1:1 exchange rate, and firms located in the new states had immediate access to the common market in the European Union. Monetary union with West Germany meant that nominal assets were converted at a very favourable exchange rate. This, together with the fact that the federal government was able to finance expensive labour market (and other restructuring) programmes, helped to sustain or even raise the standard of living in East Germany, despite the transition recession and high levels of unemployment. Second, West German labour market institutions and rules were imported, with the result that wages between the two parts of Germany converged fairly rapidly. This also helped to keep standards of living high. Thus, labour market adjustment in East Germany was associated with less material hardship than in other transition countries. The down-side to the 'human' approach to labour market adjustment – besides its financial cost – was that it created a number of adverse incentive effects that contributed to keeping unemployment high long after the effect of the initial transition shock had disappeared.

East Germany started the transition process without any open or recorded unemployment. Open unemployment started to increase in the second half of 1990, and by 1992 it had reached an average of 14.8 per cent (see Table 12.1) With minor cyclical fluctuations, unemployment stayed around this level for the rest of the decade. The rise in unemployment was accompanied by an increase in non-employment (see again Table 12.1). A common perception among economists is that the unemployed pool in East Germany is stagnant. However, this is true only for the early 1990s where the monthly average outflow rate from unemployment was about 10 per cent compared to 15 per cent in West Germany. By the mid-1990s, the East German outflow rate had reached a level comparable to that of West Germany (Wolff 2003). Another significant consequence of transition, documented in Table 12.2, has been a reduction in the participation rates of some worker categories (particularly married females and elderly workers). However, participation by unmarried females has risen, making the overall drop in the participation rate fairly small: female participation rates are still much higher than in the East. Aggregate participation by men has not changed significantly and is comparable with that of West Germany.

Table 12.1. Unemployment and non-employment rates in East and West Germany, 1991–2001

	Unemployment (per cent)		Non-Employment (per cent)	
	East	West	East	West
1991	10.3	6.3	26.8	27.1
1992	14.8	6.6	34.0	27.1
1993	15.8	8.2	35.1	27.9
1994	16.0	9.2	34.1	28.5
1995	14.9	9.3	33.4	28.7
1996	16.7	10.1	34.2	29.0
1997	19.5	11	35.0	28.5
1998	19.5	10.5	35.2	27.9
1999	19.0	9.9	34.8	26.9
2000	18.8	8.7	34.2	26
2001	18.9	8.3	33.9	25.1

Note: Non-employment rate is defined as 100 minus the employed share of the working population.

Source: Bundesanstalt für Arbeit (2003).

Table 12.2. Labour market participation rates in East and West Germany, by gender, 1991 and 1998

	East 1991	East 1998	West 1998
All male	59.9	58.2	57.0
All female	50.0	48.6	39.7
Female, unmarried	27.6	34.4	33.5
Female, married	73.0	67.1	49.4
Female, widowed	30.7	9.3	25.6

Note: Participation rate: self-employed, employed and unemployed persons as percentages of total working-age population (in that group).

Source: Bundesanstalt für Arbeit (2003)

12.3.2 Collective bargaining, unemployment insurance and territorial mobility

With political unification in 1990, West German labour law and collective bargaining arrangements were introduced in the East. Although some labour market policies were introduced specifically to deal with the adjustment of the labour market in the East, the key to understanding what happened to the East German labour market is the lack of appropriateness of West German institutions and rules to the transition situation.

In 1991, following the adoption of the West German system of industrial relations based on industry-wide collective bargaining, employers and unions agreed to increase East German wages to Western levels. The first round of negotiations following unification resulted in an average wage increase of 60 per cent for East German workers. The wage settlements were driven by a desire to equalise pay conditions in the two parts of the country with little regard to the substantial productivity differences between them. Jobs were lost as firms substituted capital for (expensive) labour in the restructuring process or simply laid off expensive labour (Aidt and Tzannatos 2002).

Hunt (2001) has investigated how this wage hike affected the relative earnings of different types of workers. Her analysis suggests that, at least at the beginning of the transition, the biggest gains in relative terms were made by those at the bottom of the wage distribution, who were to a large extent unskilled workers. Union wage policy not only increased average wages, it also compressed the wage distribution. Not surprisingly, data from the German Socio-Economic Panel analysed by Hunt (1999) show that the unemployment pool of the 1990s consisted primarily of low-skilled manufacturing workers, who lost their jobs as a consequence of the restructuring of the state-owned enterprises, as well as of female and of older workers. Together with age and (female) gender, (low) skills seem to be the most important factors in explaining prolonged unemployment spells.

Another important factor in the surge of unemployment, and in particular of long-term unemployment, was the extension of the West German unemployment insurance system to the East. Although this system achieved the goal of maintaining the standard of living of those hit by unemployment and providing insurance against loss of income, it produced a number of unfortunate disincentive effects. Firstly, the high replacement ratios without doubt contributed to increasing the reservation wage of low-skilled workers, many of whom preferred to live on benefits or aid rather than take on low-paid jobs. Secondly, the open-ended nature of the unemployment aid programme reduced the incentive to search for a new job and the willingness to move geographically to gain employment.

Early retirement and provisional retirement schemes were a third kind of labour market policy designed to ease adjustment in the labour market. The programme allowed those aged over 55 to retire and receive generous benefits at Western levels. Not surprisingly, almost all workers eligible for the programme took advantage of it before it ended in December 1992. This caused a large-scale exodus of low-skilled elderly workers from the labour force, documented in Table 12.2 by the falling participation rates of widowed (mostly elderly) women. Note, however, that the main reason for the fall in the participation rate of married females was the decrease in the supply of subsidised childcare facilities. Under Communism, childcare had been cheap and readily available because it was usually provided by the enterprise where the mother worked.

Given the high level of unemployment in East Germany, one would expect migration from East Germany to West Germany to take place, facilitated by a common language and similar education systems. Between 1989 and 1990, about 2.5 per cent of the East German population moved to West Germany. However, once unification was agreed, emigration virtually stopped. Several factors may explain why. First, the geography of Germany, in particular the position of the West Berlin enclave, meant that daily (or weekly) commuting from East to West was a feasible alternative to migration, and it was preferred by many who did not want to incur the fixed costs of moving. Second, the unemployment insurance and welfare systems created strong disincentives against moving, as many unemployed workers simply preferred to stay in the Eastern part of the country and live off the generous unemployment benefits. Third, wage convergence between East and West eliminated much of the expected benefit of moving westwards.

A number of studies have examined the determinants of East-West migration using individual-level data. Burda (1993) finds that high household income and a high subjective (self-reported) probability of job loss, as well as specific (family) links with the West, positively affect the probability of migrating. Hunt (2000) finds that the probability of migrating is high for high-skilled and young workers and for individuals experiencing a non-employment spell. These results can be explained by the fact that the wage distribution in East Germany is compressed at the top of the scale (because unions have acted mainly to improve the wages conditions of low-skilled workers), so that a skilled or highly educated worker may be able to find a better-paid job by migrating to West Germany.

12.3.3 Active labour market policies

The federal government has intervened in the East German labour market by implementing various active labour market policies. At the beginning of the transition (until 1992), the federal government financed mainly 'short-term work' programmes, which were the quickest way to respond to the surge of unemployment caused by the initial transition shock. These programmes basically subsidised employment for a short period of time by paying the wage cost of the relevant workers in the participating public or private organisations and/or firms. In 1991, as much as 20 per cent of the East German labour force was involved in such programmes. While the short-term work programmes were clearly temporary measures, a number of additional ones, such as retraining programmes and job creation schemes, were introduced in the early-to-mid 1990s. The purpose of these programmes was to address the mismatch problem by facilitating training or subsidising job creation. The most important measures were the Public Employment Programme, the Public Sponsored Training Programme, and the On-the job Training Programme.

The Public Employment Programme aimed at creating additional jobs by providing a wage subsidy (in some cases up to 100 per cent) to participating employers (in the public or private sector). The programme was targeted at workers who were already unemployed, and it was expected to provide on-the-job training and work experience that would help participating workers return to the regular labour market when they completed the programme (after 1–2 years). The On-the-Job Training programme aimed at upgrading workers' skills. There were no specific requirements on the type of training to be provided by participating firms; the only condition being that the trainee had to be employed by a firm that agreed to bear part of the costs of training. The Public Sponsored Training Programme subsidised training via the labour offices, which assumed the full costs of training as well as any living expenses of the participating workers. These programmes created what is now known as a 'secondary labour market' in Germany. Indeed, the net income of households benefiting from active labour market policies in East Germany amounts to three-quarters of the representative employment income.

The effectiveness of active labour market measures in East Germany in facilitating re-employment has been extensively studied. A simple analysis of participants' employment status shortly after completion of one of these programmes suggests that active labour market policies have been rather successful. Roughly one-third of the participants in qualification programmes and one-quarter of the participants in job creation programmes have re-entered the regular labour market after the programme (Bonin and Zimmermann 2001). However, these results have been criticised on the ground that the performance of the unemployed not taking part in the labour market programmes has been neglected. Consequently, several micro-econometric studies have been conducted by constructing a control-group of non-participants (Lechner 1998; Eichler and Lechner 2000, 2002). In general, training programmes seem to have promoted re-employment more successfully than job creation programmes. Fitzenberger and Prey (1997) show that vocational training schemes had a positive employment effect in the first period after reunification. On-the-job training seems to have very limited employment effects, which suggests that the employment success of programme participants has been offset by the displacement of other workers. Moreover, Bonin and Zimmermann (2001) report that the beneficial effects have been limited to male workers. Evidence of detrimental effects has been found by Lechner (1998), according to whom training and the chance of re-entering the labour market are inversely related. Public job creation has not been successful in bringing workers back into stable employment. Empirical evaluation of these measures by Kraus et al. (2000) uniformly indicates insignificant or even negative effects on the re-employment prospects of participants in this programme. One explanation offered for the poor performance of these schemes is that they do not match current demands in the labour market and therefore give the potential employer wrong signals as to the skills of the prospective worker. A notable exception in this literature is the study by Eichler and Lechner (2002), who found a positive re-employment effect of public job creation using a sample from Saxony–Anhalt. This result is possibly linked to the relatively high development of that region's economy.

12.4   Poland

12.4.1   Labour market performance

Poland started its transition to a market economy without open unemployment; by 2002, its unemployment rate stood at 18.1 per cent and a stagnant unemployment pool had been created. During the 1990s, the Polish labour market underwent a dramatic transformation. The transition to a capitalistic system of production required privatisation of state-owned enterprises and restructuring of those enterprises to fit the new economic environment. On average, the private sector share of total employment rose from 33 per cent to 72 per cent over the period, with sectors such as trade and construction moving almost completely into private ownership. Even though privatisation of the large enterprises in the manufacturing sector proceeded relatively slowly, 72 per cent of total employment in industry was in the private sector by 1999. Table 12.3 shows the evolution of unemployment in Poland over the 1990-2002 period.

Table 12.3. Total unemployed, unemployment and eligibility rate, Poland 1990–2002

Year	Number of regis- tered unemployed	Unemployment rate	Eligibility rate
	Millions	%	%
1990	1.1	6.5	79.2
1991	2.2	12.2	79.0
1992	2.5	14.3	52.3
1993	2.9	16.4	48.3
1994	2.8	16.0	50.1
1995	2.6	14.9	58.9
1996	2.4	13.2	51.9
1997	1.8	10.3	24.7
1998	1.8	9.6	23.0
1999	2.3	12.0	23.6
2000	2.7	14.0	20.3
2001	3.1	16.1	20.0
2002	3.2	18.1	19.5

Notes:
Eligibility Rate is the number of people registered as unemployed who are entitled to benefits as a percentage of all those registered as unemployed.
The unemployment rate is the number of registered as unemployed as a percentage of the total work force.

Source: EIU Country Data (2003)

Unemployment grew rapidly in 1990–1993. Poland's unemployment figures were the highest in Europe at the time, and in 1991 and 1992 about 1 million people, or 6 per cent of the working-age population, were made redundant each year. Massive redundancies affected employees of state-owned enterprises, while newly established private enterprises were unable to provide sufficient employment opportunities. Since the criteria for obtaining unemployment benefits were relatively lenient, the latent unemployment inherited from the socialist system manifested itself in open, recorded unemployment. The years 1994–1997 were marked by an improvement in the economic situation. Employment increased in this period by around 1.1 million, as investment and consumer demand picked up after the initial recession. The number of registered unemployed declined steadily during this period, not only because of the macroeconomic turnaround in the labour market situation. The tightening of the eligibility criterion for claiming unemployment benefits introduced in 1991 made it less attractive for individuals to register as unemployed. Also, and more importantly, many workers preferred to withdraw from the labour force altogether and rely on disability pensions as their main source of income. The participation rates dropped for both genders, but most significantly for women. The years 1998–2002 once again witnessed economic stagnation and a growth in the unemployment rate, as well as in the number of registered unemployed. Rising unemployment among middle-aged, male, urban workers signalled that intense restructuring was in progress. Most layoffs occurred in the private sector, mostly manufacturing, and were mainly the result of rationalisation and restructuring measures prompted by increasing competition from Western firms and by the Russian crisis in 1998. Furthermore, reform of the pensions and health insurance system in 1999 contributed to the increase in the number of registered unemployed, also because it encouraged individuals to register as officially unemployed in order to obtain health insurance coverage. These facts suggest that most of the buffers used to absorb unemployment in the earlier stages of transitions have become exhausted in recent years. Moreover, it seems that agriculture can no longer provide alternative employment for displaced industrial workers, given that there is now widespread unemployment in rural areas as well.

12.4.2 The emergence of a stagnant unemployment pool and territorial mobility

Poor labour market performance during transition has many causes, but it is clear that the particular income support institutions put in place at the beginning of the transition have contributed to the build-up of unemployment and to the reduced labour market participation of certain groups (low-skilled workers in particular). The fact that the privatisation process (with the unavoidable layoffs) gained pace at much the same time as income support and insurance programmes were introduced meant that the system was designed under the pressure of an increasing number of unemployed, many of them without any real job prospects. As a result, Poland was the only transition country in which the initial increase in the number of registered unemployed was *bigger* than the aggregate employment losses.

The Polish unemployment pool is stagnant. In particular, workers who lose their jobs find it difficult to re-enter employment in the official sector (Boeri and Flinn 1997). According to the Polish Statistical Office (GUS), 40.4 per cent of the unemployed at the end of 1998 had been out of work for more than 12 months, while 23.4 per cent had been out of work for more than 24 months. By the end of 2001, these figures had risen to 48.4 per cent and 27.7 per cent. In addition, there is a relatively large underground economy in which approximately 800,000 persons are unofficially employed, according to the GUS estimates. These 'unofficial' employees typically come from rural areas and work in cities as construction workers. The vast majority of workers who find it difficult to exit the unemployment pool are low-skilled workers, with basic vocational education. In the second half of the 1990s, this group of workers made up over 70 per cent of the unemployment pool (World Bank 2001). In addition, young workers joining the labour force with basic vocational educations accounted for about two-thirds of those entering the unemployment pool during the same period. This problem is particularly acute in rural areas, where educational attainment is typically lower than in urban areas.

The high unemployment rate among low-skilled workers can be attributed to a number of factors. The new private sector hired mainly skilled workers. This created a *skill mismatch* that the educational system has not yet been able to remedy and left a large number of workers with insufficient skills in the unemployment pool. Importantly, the excess supply of less-skilled workers did not translate into a substantial widening of earnings differentials. The earnings of those in the bottom 10 per cent of the wage distribution still accounted for around 56 per cent of the median income in 1998, after standing at around 60 per cent at the beginning of the decade. This rigidity in relative wages contributed to the persistence of the unemployment problem among low-skilled workers and induced firms to substitute capital or skilled workers for low-skilled workers. The two main factors slowing the adjustment in earnings at the lower end of the skill distribution were the existence of a minimum wage (around 40 per cent of the average wage during the 1990s) and the fact that the social security benefit system effectively acted as a minimum wage. Both factors established a floor for wages that workers in the lower tail of the wage (and skill) distribution were willing to accept.

The 1989 economic reform programme enacted a complex set of measures to alleviate the social cost of unemployment. One of these measures was a very generous unemployment benefit system. The level of the benefit was linked to the person's last wage, and it was gradually reduced over the period of unemployment, starting at 70 per cent of the last wage during the first three months of unemployment, and then falling to 50 per cent during the subsequent six months, and to 40 per cent thereafter. The 1989 Act made the benefits payments open-ended. People who had not worked could register as unemployed and obtain a benefit equal to the level of the minimum wage. In 1991, the Act on Employment and Unemployment dramatically changed the benefit system in Poland. First, a limit was set on the duration of unemployment benefits, and a maximum period of 12 months was introduced. In addition, the government passed a number of measures to make the period of benefit payment more flexible: if the unemployment rate was particularly low, the benefit period was reduced to three months; if the unemployment rate was high, it was prolonged. In 1996 this mechanism was replaced by a lump-sum payment that effectively decoupled the unemployment benefit from wage growth. In addition, the reform of the system in 1996 effectively transformed an earnings-related system, which was neutral with respect to the dispersion of earnings, into a *de facto* flat-rate system. The flat-rate benefits system increased the opportunity cost of employment disproportionately across workers with different skills, increasing the wage aspirations of the least productive workers more than the wage claims of the more productive ones. As a consequence, the distribution of the reservation wages of the individuals did not increase uniformly, but rose mainly at its lower end. This contributed both to the persistent compression of the wage distribution and to the persistently high unemployment among unskilled workers.

Whilst cushioning the worst social consequences of the initial shock to the economy, it is clear that the very generous benefit system initially put in place in 1989 gave rise to adverse incentive effects. The subsequent changes in the system can be seen as attempts to strike a more appropriate balance between adverse incentive effects and the need to provide insurance and income support to those workers laid off in the process. Nonetheless, the unemployed often preferred to live on social security transfers (unemployment benefits, social security assistance, and so on) and to take casual jobs in the informal sector (like self-employment, part-time work, and so on), rather than search for a job in the (official) private sector. This phenomenon was reinforced in the countryside because family ties are stronger there than in urban areas. These ties often formed a support network that encouraged unemployed workers to stay out of the labour market and to use casual jobs to supplement their unemployment benefits. Góra and Schmidt (1998), for example, find that, during the period 1990-1995, unemployment benefits only accounted for around 20 per cent of the income of the long-term unemployed. They also report that social assistance accounted for around 7 per cent of the income of the long-term unemployed, which suggests that this group of workers was able to supplement their income to a significant extent from other sources *without* entering the official labour market.

A striking feature of the Polish labour market is the huge unemployment differences among regions. Almost half of all unemployed workers live in rural areas. More specifically, residents of rural areas accounted for 45.6 per cent of registered unemployment in December 1998, 43.7 per cent in December 2000, 42.7 per cent in December 2001, and 42.1 per cent at the end of March 2002. This pool of unemployed workers is made up of two separate groups. The first consists of workers laid-off by collective, state-owned farms, and it is a legacy from the previous system and the first stage of transformation. In the second half of the 1980s, a total of 800,000 people were employed in state-owned farms, a large number of which went bankrupt after the political system changed because of a rapid increase in interest rates on outstanding credits, the abolition of the state monopoly on the importing of foodstuffs, and the reduction of customs duties. The former employees of these farms proved to be the most passive and helpless social group in Poland: most of them remained in the countryside and lived off welfare or unemployment benefits. The second group consisted of laid-off industrial workers who have migrated to the countryside, after they had cashed in the severance pay or a disability pension, and given up searching for a job in the new private sector. They preferred to move to the countryside because of the presence there of relatives owning plots of land, and they lived largely on benefits.

More generally, since the beginning of the transition, there has been a decline in the regions (voivodships) in which there was limited output diversification. The highest unemployment rates have been in the regions where the (bankrupt) state-owned firms used to operate in the past (the northern and western parts of Poland). According to data published in March 2002, the unemployment rate was highest in the voivodships of Warminsko-Mazurskie (29.2 per cent), Lubuskie (25.2 per cent) and Zachodniopomorskie (25 per cent), which are largely rural areas or areas with a single dominant industry prior to 1989. Moreover, employment growth has been slow in regions where the service sector was underdeveloped (Newell also finds this in Chap. 8). At the other end of the spectrum, with low unemployment, we find the voivodeships of Mazowieckie (13.6 per cent) and Matopolskie (14.3 per cent). In addition, unemployment is relatively low in the large cities which are capitals of voivodships: 5.8 per cent in Warsaw, 6.3 per cent in Poznan, 7.7 per cent in Katowice, 9.3 per cent in Gdynia, and 9.8 per cent in Rzeszów. The regional disparities in unemployment that emerged in the early 1990s have proved to be remarkably persistent. Regions where unemployment was high in 1993 still had high unemployment in 2000 despite several years of economic growth. This persistence of regional differences in unemployment reflects very low inter-regional migration flows. This, in turn, is due partly to a poorly functioning housing market and partly to the fact that the migrants (usually with basic vocational educations) have little chance of finding a new job by moving from one region to another.

The differences in unemployment levels among regions mainly reflect differences in job creation (Newell and Pastore 2000; see also Chap. 8 in this book). Among the most important determinants of job creation are the following:

1. Sectoral composition: the hiring rate is higher in regions with a developed service sector.
2. Education levels: the hiring rate is higher in regions where a large proportion of the population has a secondary or higher education.
3. Wage dispersion: the hiring rate is higher in regions where productivity is high relative to wages and there is some wage dispersion at the lower end of the earnings distribution.

Not surprisingly, job creation is faster in regions with better educated populations, higher wage flexibility, and dynamic service sectors. It should be noted, however, that in the aftermath of recent economic decline some large cities, particularly Warsaw, have been affected by high and growing unemployment. Jobs became more difficult to come by in Warsaw in the early spring of 2002 – partly as a result of mergers in the banking and insurance sectors and the closing down of some brokerage houses. While it seems that the peak of the wave of massive job losses is now past, employment is still declining in small enterprises in the Polish capital.

12.4.3 Active labour market policies

In 2000, Poland spent more than one per cent of its GDP on active labour market policies designed to alleviate the unemployment problem. These were (a) retraining programmes aimed at equipping unemployed people with skills sought by employers in the expanding sectors; (b) public works programmes for short-term, direct job creation, with employment (lasting up to 12 months) on projects organised by government agencies, including municipal governments; (c) graduate programmes similar to the public works programmes but targeted on school leavers, their purpose being to create opportunities for graduates to gain experience and on-the-job training that improve their labour market prospects; (d) programmes providing loans to employers who create jobs for the unemployed for at least two years, and for unemployed individuals who set up their own businesses; (e) programmes specifically targeted on high-risk groups in the labour market: these include the long-term unemployed, women, young people aged under 24, workers laid off by enterprises undergoing restructuring, and the unemployed in rural areas.

Evaluations of active labour market policies for Poland generally conclude that they have a significant positive short-run impact on the probability of leaving unemployment for both men and women (Fretwell et al. 1999). However, there are medium and long-term effects only for men (Kluve et al. 1999; Kluve et al. 2002). Puhani (1999) finds that training has positive effects for both men and women, but the effect is significant only for men. Evaluation of programmes providing wage subsidies find that they are particularly unfavourable to males and have no effect on unemployed women (Kluve et al. 1999; Kluve et al. 2002; Puhani 1999). As for public work programmes, Kluve et al. (1999) and Puhani (1999) show that they have significant negative effects on existing unemployment and on future employment, this negative impact being stronger for men. The authors conclude that this may be because these programmes seem to stigmatise low-productivity workers. All this strongly suggests that the programmes that are effective gateways to lasting employment are those that explicitly up-grade the skills of participants.

12.5 Conclusions

Large-scale restructuring of the labour market has been widespread in the past two decades. It has coincided with the onset of the decline of resource-intensive sectors and the growth of the service sector in both Europe and North America, and with transition to the market economy in both the Central and Eastern Europe and the Commonwealth of Independent States. Whatever the cause of restructuring, management of the adjustment process is a major challenge for the governments involved. When designing policies to deal with large-scale labour market adjustments, governments are faced by a trade-off between on the one hand creating incentives for workers to leave shrinking sectors and move into the expanding ones as fast and effectively as possible, and on the other, providing social assistance to reduce the hardship associated, in the short run, with the structural change. While well-designed government policies may enable the labour market to adjust more smoothly to structural shocks, badly-designed policies that create perverse incentives may have the opposite effect and encourage prime-aged workers to leave the labour force or to enter a pool of long-term unemployment with significant private and social welfare costs as a consequence. Successful restructuring requires a fairly dynamic labour market with high job turnover and mobility: the paramount role of territorial mobility in this respect was given early emphasis in Burda (1993).

This chapter has tackled these issues from two different perspectives. On the one hand, it has presented a very simple theoretical framework to show how the design of both active and passive labour market policies can affect the ability of the expanding sector to absorb the surplus workers released by the shrinking sector. On the other hand, it has analysed the experiences of East Germany and Poland in managing transition. Even though they started from diametrically different initial positions (East Germany joined one of the economic powerhouses of the developed world while Poland had to cope with the shambles that followed collapse of the Soviet Union), both areas have converged to a common labour market outcome. They both suffer from the existence of a pool of long-term unemploy-

ment consisting mostly of low-skilled workers priced out of the market by compression of the wage distribution. The unemployment benefit system (in both
cases characterised by a generous replacement ratio and long duration) has also
contributed to the increase in unemployment by increasing reservation wages and
thus reducing job-search efforts by the unemployed. Furthermore, it seems that
only some of the active labour market policies aimed at skill upgrading have accelerated the outflow from unemployment.

References

Aghion P, Blanchard OJ (1994) On the speed of transition in central Europe. In: Fischer S,
    Rotemberg JJ (eds) NBER Macroeconomics Annual, MIT Press, Cambridge (Mass.),
    pp 283–320.
Aidt TS, Tzannatos Z (2002) Unions and collective bargaining. World Bank, Washington.
Betcherman G, Olivas K, Dar A (2003) Impacts of active labour market programs: new
    evidence from evaluation with particular attention to developing and transition coun-
    tries, Social Protection Unit, World Bank, Washington.
Blanchard OJ, Kremer A (1997) Disorganisation. Quarterly Journal of Economics
    112:1091–1126.
Boeri T (1997) Market-market reforms in transition economies. Oxford Review of Eco-
    nomic Policy 13:126–140.
Boeri T, Flinn CJ (1999) Returns to mobility in the transition to a market economy. Journal
    of Comparative Economics 27:4–32.
Boltho A, Carlin W, Scaramozzino P (1997) Will East Germany become a new Mezzog-
    iorno?. Journal of Comparative Economics 24:241–264.
Bonin H, Zimmermann KF (2000) The post-unification German labour market. In: Riphahn
    R, Snower DJ, Zimmermann KF (eds) Employment policy in transition. Springer, Ber-
    lin, pp 8–30.
Bundesanstalt für Arbeit (2002) Official bulletin of the federal employment institute, Ber-
    lin.
Burda M (1993) The determinants of East-West German migration: some first results.
    European Economic Review 37: 452–462.
Economist Intelligence Unit (2003) Country Data. The Economist, London.
Eichler M, Lechner M (2000) Some econometric evidence on the effectiveness of active la-
    bour. WDI Working Paper 318.
Eichler M, Lechner M (2002) An evaluation of public employment programmes on the East
    German state of Sachsen-Anhalt. Labor Economics 9:143–186.
Fitzenberger D, Prey H (1997) Assessing the impact of training on employment: the case of
    East Germany. Zeitschrift für Empirische Wirtschaftsforschung 43:71–116.
Fretwell DH, Benus J, O Leary CJ (1999) Evaluating the impact of active labour programs:
    results of cross country studies in Europe and Central Asia. World Bank, Social Pro-
    tection Discussion Paper 9915.
Góra M, Schmidt CM (1997) Long-term unemployment, unemployment benefits and social
    assistance: the polish experience. WDI Working Paper 110.
Hunt J (1999) Determinants of non-employment and unemployment durations in East Ger-
    many. CEPR Discussion Paper 2182.

Hunt J (2000) Why do people still live in East Germany. CEPR Discussion Paper 2431.

Hunt J (2001) Post-unification wage growth in East Germany. The Review of Economics and Statistics 83:190–195.

Kluve J, Lehmann H, Schmidt CM (1999) Active labour market policies in Poland: human capital enhancement, stigmatization, or benefit churning?. Journal of Comparative Economics 27:61–89.

Kluve J, Lehmann H, Schmidt CM (2002) Disentangling treatment effects of Polish active labour market policies: evidence from matched samples. CEPR Discussion Paper 3298.

Kraus F, Puhani P, Steiner V (2000) Do public works programs work? Some unpleasant results from the East German experience. Research in Labor Economics 19:275–313.

Lechner M (1998) Training the East German labour force, Physica, Heidelberg.

Newell A, Pastore F (2000) Regional unemployment and industrial unemployment in Poland. IZA Discussion Paper 194.

Oswald A (1997) The missing piece of the unemployment puzzle. Inaugural Lecture, University of Warwick.

Puhani PA (1999) Evaluating active labour market policies: empirical evidence for Poland during transition. Physica, Heidelberg.

Sinn HW, Westermann F (2001) Two Mezzogiornos. NBER Working Paper 8125.

Wolff J (2003) Unemployment benefits and the duration of unemployment in East Germany. SFB386 Discussion Paper 344

World Bank (2001) Poland's labour market: the challenge of job creation. World Bank Country Study 23033, Washington.

13 Macroeconometric Evaluation of Active Labour Market Policies in Germany. A Dynamic Panel Approach Using Regional Data

Reinhard Hujer[1], Uwe Blien[2], Marco Caliendo[3] and Christopher Zeiss[4]

[1] Goethe-University, Frankfurt, Germany
[2] Institute for Employment Research, Nuremberg, Germany
[3] German Institute for Economic Research (DIW), Berlin, Germany
[4] Goethe-University, Frankfurt, Germany

13.1 Introduction[*]

In view of the immense spending on active labour market policies (ALMP) in Germany (about 43 bn DM in 2001) and the debatable success of the latter, the evaluation literature has been growing rapidly in recent years.[1] Most studies focus on the microeconometric approach using individual data. The importance of this approach is straightforward and the framework for such an analysis is well developed.[2] However, because the microeconometric approach usually ignores impacts on non-participants, it should be seen as a first step towards complete evaluation which must necessarily be followed by macroeconometric analysis. Instead of looking at the effect on individual performance, we shall seek to determine whether ALMP represent a net gain for the whole economy. This is likely to be the case only if the total number of jobs is positively affected by ALMP.

Most macroeconometric evaluations of ALMP are based on panel data models, since a single time series for one country or region does not usually provide enough observations. Two main strands can be distinguished in these studies. First, authors like Forslund and Krueger (1997) or Calmfors and Skedinger (1995) use variation in programme scale across regional units (jurisdictions) combined with

[*] The authors thank SO Becker, B Christensen, O Hübler and A Vassiliev for their valuable comments. We are indebted to S Bond and F Windmeijer for fruitful discussion and their help with implementation of the dynamic panel data estimators. The chapter has also benefited from several comments during our presentations at the IZA Summer School in Labour Economics (2002), and the annual conferences of the European Association of Labour Economists (2002), Verein für Socialpolitik (2002) and the European Regional Science Association (2002). Our especial thanks go to S Kaimer and E Hummel for their valuable help with the data-handling. All remaining errors are our own.

[1] See Hagen and Steiner (2000) or Hujer and Caliendo (2001) for extensive overviews of micro- and macroeconometric evaluations of ALMP in Germany.

[2] See e.g. Heckman et al. (1999) or Smith (2000).

data at the regional level to estimate the effects. Second, authors like Jackman et al. (1990), Layard et al. (1991) or OECD (1993) use variation in programme scale across different countries, even though such analysis may suffer from the heterogeneity of policy measures among countries. Given that we intend to evaluate the effects of ALMP in Germany over recent years, our analysis will use a regional data set that enables estimation of the net effect of ALMP for Germany. Owing to the structural differences between West and East Germany we analyse the regions separately.

In 1998 the legal basis for labour market policy in Germany became the new Social Code SGB III. Changes were made not only to the objectives, like a more intense focus on problem groups in the labour market, but also to the institutional organisation of labour market policy, giving rise to decentralisation and more flexibility in the regional allocation of resources among measures. On the one hand, this decentralisation allows adjustment to the situation in the local labour markets, on the other, it requires that any evaluation must make closer consideration of regional aspects than was previously the case. To be stressed is the importance of suitable data allowing regional heterogeneity to be taken into account. This is especially problematic in East Germany, owing to frequent adjustments made to the regional boundaries of the labour office districts ('Arbeitsamtsbezirke'). In contrast to other evaluation studies, this is not problematic for us because no such changes occurred during the time span considered.

The aim of the study is to add a new perspective to the evaluation of ALMP in Germany. This is done by using regional data to obtain the macroeconomic or net effects of these measures. The chapter is organised as follows. The next section discusses the micro- and macroeconometric evaluation approaches. It highlights the advantages and shortcomings of each approach and shows that complete evaluation necessarily requires them as additional ingredients. Section 13.3 gives an overview of ALMP in Germany and Section 13.4 presents the data used. The chapter then briefly discusses the possible effects of ALMP in a macroeconomic framework, before describing the empirical analysis and presenting the results. The last section concludes and gives indications for further research.

13.2   Micro- and macroeconometric evaluation

The ideal evaluation process consists of three steps. First, the impact of the programme on the participating individual should be estimated. Second, whether or not the impacts are large enough to yield net social gains should be examined. Finally, it should be determined whether this is the best outcome that could have been achieved for the money spent (Fay 1996). We will discuss the first two steps, namely the micro- and the macroeconometric evaluation.

The main question addressed by microeconometric evaluations is whether the outcome variable for an individual is affected by participation in an ALMP programme. That being done, the direct gain can be compared with the associated costs, and the success of the programme can be judged. However, almost all microeconometric approaches estimate the effect of treatment on the treated. An important concept in this regard is the stable unit treatment value assumption (SUTVA, Rubin 1980), one of whose implications is that the effect of the intervention on each individual is not affected by the participation decision of any other individual: that is, the treatment effect for each person is independent of the treatment of other individuals. This assumption guarantees that average treatment effects can be estimated independently of the size and composition of the treatment population. Among other things, SUTVA excludes cross effects or general equilibrium effects. Even though its validity facilitates creation of a manageable formal setup, whether it holds in practical applications it is frequently questionable. In view of the immense amounts spent on ALMP in Germany (for details see Section 13.3) and the large scale of the programmes, spillover effects on non-participants are very likely.[3] Therefore, the microeconometric approach is partial-analytic, and it should be regarded as only one step towards complete evaluation. Or as Heckman (1999) puts it, microdata are no panacea and must be used in conjunction with aggregate time-series data to estimate the full general-equilibrium consequences of policies.

The main problem is that a positive effect at the individual level may not necessarily be positive at the aggregate one. ALMP, especially, are often suspected of having a positive effect at the individual level but a zero or even a negative effect for the economy as a whole. In this context, deadweight losses and substitution effects have received substantial attention in the literature (see e.g. Layard et al. 1991 or OECD 1993). If the outcome of the programme is no different from what would have happened in its absence, one talks of a deadweight loss. A commonly cited example is a hiring from the target group that would have occurred even without the programme. If a worker is taken on by a firm for a subsidised job instead of an unsubsidised worker who would otherwise have been hired, one talks of a substitution effect. The net short-term employment effect in this case is zero. Such effects are likely in the case of subsidies for private-sector work. There is always a risk that employers will hold back on ordinary job creation so that they can take advantage of the subsidies available. In order to minimise this risk, a principle of additionality may be imposed. Another potential problem is that ALMP may crowd out regular employment. This can be seen as a generalisation of the so-called 'displacement effect', which typically concerns displacement in the product market: for example, firms with subsidised workers may increase output but displace (reduce) output among firms which do not have subsidised workers. Calmfors (1994) also stresses the importance of tax effects, in the sense that programmes must be financed by taxes which distort the choices of both participants and non-participants.

---

[3] On the other hand, in the case of the typically small-scale U.S. programmes, the occurrence of such effects is less likely.

13.3   Institutional setup and instruments of ALMP

Labour market policies in Germany are organised by the Federal Employment Office ('Bundesanstalt für Arbeit'). Until 1998, the legal basis for labour market policy in Germany was the Work Support Act ('Arbeitsförderungsgesetz', AFG) of 1969, which was replaced by the new Social Code SGB III ('Sozialgesetzbuch'). The latter made changes not only to objectives, like a more intense focus on problem groups in the labour market, but also to the institutional organisation of labour market policy, giving rise to decentralisation and more flexibility in the regional allocation of resources among measures.[4]   Whereas the AFG had been implemented under full employment conditions, the SGB III was created in a more turbulent economic situation where labour market policy was affected by narrower budget constraints. Some of the AFG's objectives, like securing a high employment ratio and avoiding low-quality employment, were dropped and the focus shifted to the (re-)integration of problem groups in the regular labour market (§ 7.3 SGB III) whilst using resources efficiently ('Grundsatz der Wirtschaftlichkeit und Sparsamkeit'). Furthermore, the self-responsibility of the individual was emphasised, and the 'reasonableness clause' ('Zumutbarkeitsklausel'), which makes it harder for unemployed to turn down job offers, was tightened.[5]

Table 13.1 summarises the spending on, and the participants in the most important measures, these being vocational training ('Förderung der beruflichen Weiterbildung', VT) on the one hand, and subsidised employment consisting of traditional job creation schemes ('Arbeitsbeschaffungsmaßnahmen', JCS) and structural adjustment schemes ('Strukturanpassungsmaßnahmen', SAS) on the other.

In principle, public vocational training under the AFG comprised three types of training measures, namely further training ('Fortbildung'), retraining ('Umschulung') and training to familiarise workers with a new occupation ('Einarbeitung'). The first two types have been summarised in one item (§§ 77–96, 153–159, 517 SGB III), whereas the last is now part of employment subsidies and will not be discussed here.[6] The Federal Employment Office pays the costs of the training measures and a subsistence allowance ('Unterhaltsgeld') to participants which

---

[4] For a good overview of the main reforms see Fitzenberger and Speckesser (2002). Sell (1998) conducts extensive discussion of the new SGB III, with especial regard to the self-responsibility of employees for their own labour market success. Fertig and Schmidt (2000) explain and classify the various measures of employment promotion and explicitly distinguish between non-discretionary and discretionary measures. Brinkmann (1999) discusses aspects of decentralisation and regionalisation, as well as the now mandatory output evaluations.

[5] Other interesting new features of the SGB III, like the special programme to combat youth unemployment ('JUMP'), individualised support through 'free promotion' as well as the reform law regarding the ALMP instruments ('JOB-AQTIV'), cannot be discussed here. For a comprehensive survey see Fitzenberger and Hujer (2002).

[6] See Hujer et al. (2004) for an overview of employment subsidies.

Table 13.1. Labour market policies and unemployment in Germany, 1999-2001

	West-Germany						East-Germany					
	1999		2000		2001		1999		2000		2001	
Spending (in bn DM % of total)												
Total Spending	83.25	–	78.14	–	80.29	–	52.04	–	47.83	–	48.35	–
Passive Labour Market Policies	53.31	64.03	47.11	60.29	48.72	60.68	27.88	53.58	26.82	56.08	27.1	56.05
Active Labour Market Policies	22.98	27.6	23.92	30.62	24.3	30.26	22.32	42.89	19.12	39.97	19.35	40.01
Vocational training (VT)	7.78	9.34	7.94	10.16	8.19	10.2	5.43	10.43	5.37	11.24	5.47	11.3
Job Creation Schemes (JCS)	2.14	2.58	2	2.56	1.69	2.1	5.66	10.88	5.2	10.87	4.13	8.55
Structural Adjustment Schemes (SAS)	0.25	0.3	0.25	0.32	0.25	0.31	1.23	2.36	1.15	2.4	1.45	3.01
SAS-East for Private Firms (SAS-East)	0.14	0.16	0.03	0.04	0.01	0.01	3.43	6.59	1.24	2.6	0.4	0.81
Participants (Entries)												
Vocational Training	264,811		285,921		338,516		166,745		190,751		226,616	
Job Creation Schemes	85,003		78,684		61,890		210,496		181,395		130,147	
Structural Adjustment Schemes	11,183		10,657		11,466		45,836		43,555		42,581	
SAM-East for Private Firms	5,581		940		333		145,420		45,482		26,939	
Unemployed (in millions)	2.76		2.53		2.48		1.34		1.36		1.37	
Unemployment Rate (in %)	9.9		8.7		8.3		19.0		18.8		18.9	

Source: Bundesanstalt für Arbeit (2002)

amounts to 60 per cent (67 for participants with one or more children) of the previous net income (equal to unemployment benefit). The main goals are to reintegrate the unemployed by improving their skills and to counter the risk of unemployment for employees at risk.

Subsidised employment programmes consist of traditional job creation schemes and structural adjustment schemes. JCS (§§ 260–271 SGB III) should support activities of value to society and additional in nature, which means that without the subsidy they could not be executed. They include limited employment so that the long-term unemployed can improve their labour market prospects. The FEO usually pays between 30 per cent and 75 per cent of the costs for 12 months and the rest is paid by the implementing institution, which is usually a non-profit organisation (public or private legal entities, mainly municipalities). Priority is given to projects which improve the chances of finding permanent employment, which support structural improvement in social or environmental services, or which aim at the integration of extremely hard-to-place individuals. Structural adjustment schemes (§§ 272-279 SGB III) play a prominent role especially in East Germany. Like the JCS, their goal is integration into regular employment, but less severe eligibility criteria apply to participants, so that not only unemployed workers but also individuals at risk of unemployment may participate. The SAS consist of a wage subsidy equal to the average amount of unemployment benefit or assistance (including contributions to the social security system) paid on the Federal territory, typically for a maximum period of 36 months. In East Germany, the SAS may be implemented by public institutions and private companies ('SAM Ost für Wirtschaftsunternehmen', SAS-East), whereas in West Germany only the first solution is possible.[7]

Besides the above-mentioned change of objectives, there have been organisational changes as well, which have increased the flexibility of ALMP at a regional and local level. The local employment offices are now given relative freedom in the allocation of their budgets among measures. The decision on the mix of instruments to adopt is left to the particular regional branch of the FEO (Brinkmann, 1999), so that adjustment can be made to conditions in local labour markets. Typically, in situations with marked labour–market imbalances, JCS are preferred to training measures, whereas in areas with low unemployment rates hardly any JCS are undertaken.

Consequently, the measure predominantly used in the West (unemployment rate in 2001: 8.3 per cent) is VT, on which expenditures amounted to DM 8.19 bn in 2001, corresponding to a 10.2 per cent share of total spending. The next most important measures are JCS, with a share of 2.1 per cent, and SAS with 0.31 per cent. In East Germany (unemployment rate in 2001: 18.9 per cent), the situation is much more balanced. VT is again the most important programme (DM 5.47 bn, 11.3 per cent), but JCS (DM 4.13 bn, 8.55 per cent) follow closely behind. This is also clear if we inspect the number of participants entering the two types of programmes. Whereas in West Germany in 2001 over 338,000 individuals entered VT, only around 72,000 participated in subsidised employment programmes. In

---

[7] Since January 1998 SAS-East can also be requested in West Berlin.

East Germany, by contrast, around 226,000 individuals participated in VT and nearly 200,000 in subsidised employment programmes. Besides the spending on the various measures and their participants, also of interest is the average duration of measures. This should give us important hints on the lag structure for our subsequent analysis. The average duration of the measures under consideration in 1999 ranged between 8 and 10 months. JCS had the shortest duration with 8.3 months, followed by VT (8.4 months), and then SAS with 9.8 months (Bundesanstalt für Arbeit 2000).

13.4   The dataset

The data used in this study refer to the labour market regions defined by the administrative areas of the regional offices of the FEO. These are adequate units of the analysis, since, as we have seen, the regional offices take important decisions concerning the mix of active labour market policy measures. Moreover, funds are allocated according to indicators calculated for these areas. These indicators are the following: the local job seeker rate (this is the unemployment rate augmented by the number of people participating in active labour market policy measures); the growth rate of employment; the long-term unemployment rate; and the number of people who leave unemployment to enter regular jobs (Blien 2002). The data are taken from internal administrative sources of the FEO (Pallas-reg system of the Institute for Employment Research), and given that they are used for the allocation of funds and for administrative purposes associated with legal claims, they are especially reliable.[8] A particular difficulty faced by regional labour market analyses is that the regional units used (i.e. the administrative areas of the local offices) are not constant in time. Especially in East Germany their boundaries have been frequently changed. It is therefore not always clear whether, for example, a change in the number of unemployed registered at a particular office is due to a change in the conditions on the local labour market, or whether it is due to a change in the size of the area covered by that office. However, for the time span in question, 1999–2001, no such changes occurred, so that difficult recalculation procedures were not necessary.

Table 13.2 summarises the data used. We exploited a pooled time-series cross-section data set for the German labour office districts. The time span extended from the first quarter of 1999 to the fourth quarter of 2001, which gave us 12 observations for each labour office district. The immense differences between the East and the West German labour markets made it necessary to analyse both areas separately, so that we had 141 cross sections in West Germany and 34 in East Germany.[9] The regional variation in the data is interesting: there are huge differ-

---

[8] Recently, administrative checks have shown that some data from the same origin are biased. One particular variable, which gives the figure of job placements made by the local offices of the BA, is affected by this bias. This variable is not used in our study. There is no evidence of similar problems with other variables.

[9] Due to data limitations, Berlin is excluded from the analysis.

ences not only between West and East Germany but also within each region. If we look at the regional job-seeker rate, we find an average of 9.79 per cent in the time span under consideration in West Germany, whereas the average is around 25.32 per cent in East Germany. The extreme values for the job-seeker rate are 2.95 per cent in Freising (South Germany, north of Munich) and 34.9 per cent in Sangershausen (East Germany). Very different labour market situations are discernible under the institutional structure of one country. Even if only Western Germany is considered, there are marked differences, with 18.1 per cent in Wilhelmshaven as the maximum value. These regional disparities give rise to very different ALMP strategies, with the consequence that any evaluation of the efficiency of these measures must give closer consideration than before to regional aspects.

Table 13.2. Descriptive statistics

	West-Germany			East-Germany		
	Mean	Min	Max	Mean	Min	Max
Quarterly regional information on:						
Participants in JCS	356	3	2181	3882	1048	12547
Participants in SAS	62	0	1241	3105	514	9091
Participants in VT	1227	255	8500	3813	1139	8197
Unemployed	17092	3331	88317	36462	10671	74296
Dependent Labour Force	201539	59864	991637	194258	54113	368984
Unemployment Rate (in %)	8.85	2.68	18.07	19.12	12.85	26.89
Job Seeker Rate (in %)	9.79	2.94	19.37	25.32	16.57	34.86
Number of labour office districts			141			34
Number of observations			1692			408
Time range	1999:Q1-2001:Q4			1999:Q1-2001:Q4		

13.5   Macroeconomic analysis of ALMP

The estimation of macroeconomic effects is not straightforward, and compared to the number of micro analyses, the existing literature is relatively small. The major obstacle, however, is that a macroeconometric analysis of ALMP should be based on a theoretical framework that explains the relevant labour market variables (e.g. regular employment or unemployment). Thus the main problem is not the availability of an appropriate theory but the availability of suitable data with which to implement the theory in an econometric model.

On considering the available theories, the question arises as to which theoretical framework is appropriate for the analysis of ALMP. Leaving aside the traditional way to 'cheat the Phillips curve', i.e. improve the unemployment/inflation trade-off and thereby reduce the nonaccelerating inflation rate of unemployment (Baily and Tobin 1977), a model is needed that generates a positive equilibrium unemployment rate and is also able to incorporate ALMP. The two models most frequently used for the theoretical analysis of ALMP are the Layard and Nickell (1986) framework and the search model framework (see e.g. Pissarides 2000). These models differ in their primary explanation of equilibrium unemployment. In the Layard and Nickell framework, unemployment is generated through a wage setting process that pushes the wage rate above the equilibrium rate generated by labour demand and labour supply. One possible explanation for these wage distortions is the power of unions in the wage bargaining process or efficiency wages. The Layard and Nickell framework is particularly suited to analysis of the effects of ALMP on labour markets where wage distortions are a serious problem.

Search models on the other hand consider the cause of unemployment to be a time and cost consuming matching process. The matching process serves as a proxy for the differences in geographic and skill characteristics between job vacancies and job seekers. The matching process can thus be used to summarise mismatch problems and structural imbalances on the labour market. Given that the traditional purpose of ALMP is to overcome these problems, the matching process should be an important element in analysis of ALMP. Theoretical considerations based on the impacts of ALMP in these two frameworks have been put forward by, for example, Johnson and Layard (1986), Holmlund and Linden (1993) or Calmfors and Lang (1995). A combination of both frameworks as presented by Calmfors and Lang (1995) is obviously useful for analysis of ALMP, since mismatch and wage distortions are labour-market problems in Germany especially. Calmfors (1994) and Calmfors et al. (2002) have identified various effects of ALMP within such a theoretical framework. In what follows we shall outline the most important of them.

Effects on the Matching Process: ALMP are able to improve the matching process through several channels. First, they can improve the active search behaviour of participants. Second, they can speed up the matching process by adjusting the structure of the labour supply to demand. Here the reference is principally to retraining programmes that adapt the skills of the unemployed to the requirements of vacant jobs. Third, participation in an ALMP programme may serve as a substitute for work experience that reduces the employer's uncertainty about the employability of the job applicant. If ALMP are able to improve the matching process, the question is what their effects are on regular employment or on wages. Firstly, an improved matching process means that for a given stock of vacancies there is a greater inflow into employment.[10] Moreover, the improved matching process reduces the average time that a vacancy remains unfilled. Since this reduces the costs of maintaining a vacancy, firms provide more vacancies, which is equivalent to an increase in labour demand. The same effect also improves the firm's position in wage bargaining, since the firm can expect to fill a vacancy much rapidly if a worker has been laid off. Therefore, the improved matching process also reduces the wage rate. ALMP programmes are also expected to have negative effects on the matching process. These are so-called 'locking-in effects'. If participation in an ALMP programme is associated with full-time employment, there may be insufficient time to actively search for a regular job. In this case, the search effectiveness of participants is lower than the search effectiveness of the openly unemployed (Holmlund and Linden 1993). Since this locking-in effect vanishes at the

---

[10] This is equivalent to an inward shift of the Beveridge Curve.

moment when the programme expires, the question is whether the positive effects on search effectiveness persist after the participation has ended.

Effects on the Welfare of the Unemployed: If an ALMP programme raises re-employment probability, or if the compensation level is higher than unemployment benefit, the ALMP programme increases the expected welfare of the unemployed. This is due to the fact that an unemployed person has a positive probability of being placed in a programme and thus faces a rise in expected income. In the context of a wage bargaining process, this is the same as an increase in the fallback income: that is, the income obtained if the bargaining fails and the worker becomes unemployed (Layard et al. 1991). The increase in the fallback income gives rise to a higher outcome for the wage rate, since the position of the workers in the bargaining process is improved. This effect of ALMP on the wage pressure is unavoidable, in fact, since every improvement in the situation of the unemployed is connected with a reduction in welfare losses.

Effects on Competition in the Labour Market: ALMP (especially training programmes) are expected to improve the skills of participants: that is, they make participants more competitive. Consequently, there not only improved competition between the unemployed but also an improvement in the competition between the employed and the unemployed, or between insiders and outsiders. Additionally, ALMP may affect the competition if they stimulate participants to search more actively (i.e. if they counteract the discouraged worker effect) or help increase labour force participation. In both cases there is a rise in the effective labour supply that leads to a reduction in the wage rate.

Effects on Productivity: ALMP programmes that improve the skills of participants or serve as a substitute for work experience can be expected to improve or to maintain the productivity of the participants. Considering a conventional labour demand condition, a rise in productivity would lead to an increase in employment for a given wage rate. Calmfors (1994) notes that the rise in productivity is not self-evident because on the other hand it is possible to produce the same output with fewer but more efficient workers. Additionally, Calmfors et al. (2002) note that the increased productivity of participants may also have a wage raising effect which works through a rise in the participants' reservation wage.

When setting up the econometric model for the evaluation, the preceding discussion can be used to find the relevant relationships. In particular, the theory suggests that there are effects on the matching process, on employment and on the wage rate. Therefore, a straightforward empirical implementation would be estimation of a matching function (see e.g. Boeri and Burda 1996) or a wage equation (see Calmfors and Forslund 1991). Unfortunately, data limitations prevent us from estimating these structural relationships. For this reason we adopt the strategy of Calmfors and Skedinger (1995) and base our empirical analysis on a reduced form relationship explaining the total unemployment rate in the economy. Here we define total unemployment as the stock of job-seekers, i.e. the sum of openly unemployed and programme participants. This is necessary to avoid estimating the effect whereby a programme expansion leads automatically to a reduction in the stock of the openly unemployed.

13.6 Econometric methods

The above-described reduced form approach enables us to estimate the total net effect of ALMP, i.e. the effect through all channels discussed (Calmfors et al. 2002). The basic equation that we want to estimate is

$$c(L)s_{it} = a_0 + \sum_{j=1}^{3} a_j(L)\psi_{it}^j + \sum_{k=1}^{K} b_k(L)x_{it}^k + u_{it} \tag{13.1}$$

where s_{it} is the regional rate of total job-seekers relative to the labour force, ψ_{it}^j (for $j = 1, 2, 3$) is a measure for the ALMP programmes and x_{it}^k (for $k = (1,..., K)$) is a set of K other explanatory variables. As usual in the panel context, all variables are indexed by $t = (1,..., T)$ as a time index and $i = (1,..., N)$ is an index for the regions. $c(L) = 1 - c_1 L - c_2 L^2 - \cdots - c_p L^p$, $a_j(L) = a_{j0} + a_{j1}L + a_{j1}L^2 + \cdots + a_{jq}L^q$ and $b_k(L) = b_{k0} + b_{k1}L + b_{k2}L^2 + \cdots + b_{kq}L^q$ are associated polynomials in the lag operator with p and q as the maximum lag, where q need not be the same for all explanatory variables. The rate of total job-seekers is given by the sum of unemployed and participants in ALMP programmes relative to the labour force. The ALMP programmes we analyse are divided into job creation schemes P_{it}^1, structural adjustment schemes P_{it}^2 and training programmes P_{it}^3. Since the job-seeker rate contains the ALMP participants, direct use of the participation rates (i.e. programme participants relative to the labour force) would bias our results. To avoid this, we follow Calmfors and Skedinger (1995) and utilise so-called accommodation ratios to express the regional ALMP activity. The accommodation ratios are defined as the stock of participants in a specific type of programme relative to the total rate of job-seekers, i.e. $\psi_{it}^j = P_{it}^j / (U_{it} + \sum_{k=1}^{3} P_{it}^k)$ for $j = (1, 2, 3)$. For the further analysis, the ALMP accommodation ratios will be summarised as $\psi_{it} = [\psi_{it}^1, \psi_{it}^2, \psi_{it}^3]$. Finally $X_{it} = [x_{it}^1,..., x_{it}^K]$ includes national variables like the national unemployment and vacancy rate, and seasonal dummies to control for seasonal factors.

The imposed dynamic specification of Eq. (13.1) not only enables us to control for the high persistence of quarterly labour market data but also to analyse the time lag between a change of ALMP activity and the associated impact on the regional job-seeker rate. This is particularly advisable if we bear possible locking-in effects of ALMP programmes in mind. Our description of the German situation in Section 13.3 showed that the average duration of the programmes is between 8 to 10 months. Therefore a lag of 4 quarters for the accommodation ratios is advisable. In particular, we will impose four lags for the job-seeker rate and for the ALMP measures.

Equation (13.1) can be seen as a reduced form relationship that explains the job-seeker rate as a function of the ALMP measures and other variables.[11] For the residual, we assume a one way error-component structure

$$u_{it} = \mu_i + v_{it} \qquad (13.2)$$

where μ_i is a regional specific effect and v_{it} is a residual varying over regions and time.

In order to estimate the parameters of Eq. (13.1) it is reasonable to assume that our explanatory variables are correlated with the regional specific effect. This problem is especially obvious for the lagged dependent variable. To overcome this problem we apply the first-differenced GMM estimator suggested by Arellano and Bond (1991) and the system GMM estimator suggested by Blundell and Bond (1998). Both estimators utilise linear moment conditions that rely on the equations in first differences. For the lagged job-seeker rate we set up the following linear moment conditions,

$$E(s_{it-g}\Delta u_{it}) = 0 , \text{ for } t = 6,\dots,T \text{ and } 2 \le g \le t-1, \qquad (13.3)$$

where the start at $t = 6$ is due to the inclusion of four lags.

A major problem of the macroeconometric evaluation of ALMP is the interdependence between ALMP and the unemployment rate. Given that the purpose of ALMP is to counteract unemployment, it is most natural to think of the decision on how much money is spent on ALMP being determined by the unemployment rate. Generally, the level of ALMP activity is assumed to be determined by a policy reaction function where the unemployment rate is only one argument besides others (Calmfors and Skedinger 1995). As our discussion in Section 13.3 showed, this is also true for Germany, as the allocation of funds to the local labour offices is done according to several indicators, including the job-seeker rate and long-term unemployed.

As Calmfors and Skedinger (1995) note, one can hope that the use of accommodation ratios in order to measure ALMP activity reduces the problem of interdependence, because it is not clear *a priori* whether an increase in the unemployment rate gives rise to a more or less proportional increase in programme participation. Since the unemployment rate is a major part of the job-seeker rate, it is reasonable to assume that the job-seeker rate and the accommodation ratios are determined simultaneously. Following this discussion, we assume that the ALMP

---

[11] Using the job-seeker rate as dependent variable allows us to draw conclusions for the regular rate of employment, which is defined as $n = 1 - s$. The use of the job-seeker rate would be problematic if ALMP programmes attracted people from outside the labour force into the labour force. In this case there would be a movement in the job-seeker rate that should not be interpreted as a programme effect. But since nearly all programme participants are drawn from the stock of the unemployed this problem is negligible.

accommodation ratios are endogenous, i.e. $E(\psi_{ig}v_{it}) \neq 0$ for $g \geq t$. These considerations enable us to build the following linear moment conditions analogously to the lagged dependent variable:

$$E(\psi_{it-g}\Delta u_{it}) = 0 \text{, for } t = 6,\ldots,T \text{ and } 2 \leq g \leq t-1. \tag{13.4}$$

We assume that the explanatory variables in X_{it} are strictly exogenous, and therefore simply use the ΔX_{it} to instrument themselves: that is, we impose the following K moment conditions:

$$E(\Delta X_{it}\Delta u_{it}) = 0. \tag{13.5}$$

The first-differenced GMM estimator is then calculated from the moment conditions (13.3), (13.4) and (13.5).

As shown in Ahn and Schmidt (1995), the linear first-differenced GMM estimator does not utilise all available moment conditions. Furthermore, Monte Carlo results obtained by Blundell and Bond (1998) and Blundell et al. (2000) have shown that in certain cases the first-differenced GMM estimator tends to be biased. As shown by Blundell and Bond (1998) and Blundell et al. (2000), poor performance of the first-differenced GMM estimator may result from a highly persistent pattern in the dependent variable, or if the variance of the regional effect μ_i exceeds the variance of the residual v_{it}. Unfortunately, both cases seem to be an issue for our analysis.

To overcome these drawbacks of the first-differenced GMM estimator, we additionally implement the system GMM estimator suggested by Blundell and Bond (1998). The system GMM estimator uses additional moment conditions for the equations in levels that result from restrictions on the initial conditions. These conditions relate to the assumption that the first differences of the dependent variable are uncorrelated with the regional effect. Applied to our case this implies that we can build the following moment conditions for the job-seeker rate

$$E(u_{it}\Delta s_{it-g}) = 0 \text{; for } t = 6,\ldots,T \text{ and } g = 1,\ldots,4, \tag{13.6}$$

where we account for the inclusion of four lags in Eq. (13.1).[12] Note that if $E(u_{it}\Delta \psi_{it-g}) \neq 0$, obviously Δs_{it} would be correlated with μ_i. Therefore we also need to assume that the ψ_{it} process is uncorrelated with the regional effect in first differences. In this case the following moment conditions are valid:

$$E(u_{it}\Delta \psi_{it-g}) = 0 \text{; for } t = 6,\ldots,T \text{ and } g = 1,\ldots,4, \tag{13.7}$$

---

[12] Note that due to the presence of the moment condition (13.3) the moment conditions for $g > 4$ would be redundant. Additionally the following moment conditions are valid in our situation: $E(u_{i5}\Delta s_{i5-g}) = 0$ for $g = 1, 2, 3$.

where g starts at 1 because we assume that ψ_{it} is an endogenous regressor. For the remaining variables which are not determined by a regional specific component, we merely impose the following k moment conditions: that is, these variables are used to instrument themselves:

$$E(u_{it}X_{it}) = 0 \qquad (13.8)$$

For the calculation of the system estimator we use the full set of moment conditions (13.3), (13.4), (13.5), (13.6), (13.7) and (13.8).

In contrast to the first-differenced GMM estimator, there is no one-step estimator that is asymptotically equivalent to the two-step estimator. The consistency of both GMM estimators relies heavily upon the fact that there is no serial correlation in the residuals. Arellano and Bond (1991) provide an asymptotic normal test statistic for first- and second-order serial correlation that is reported in our results. A serious problem found in various Monte Carlo studies are the downward biased asymptotic standard errors of the two-step estimates.[13] This is because the standard expression for the asymptotic variance ignores the presence of the estimated parameters in the weight matrix (Bond and Windmeijer 2002). In order to overcome this problem, we apply the finite sample correction proposed by Windmeijer (2000). Monte Carlo results have shown that the corrected variance of the two-step estimator often provides more reliable inference with size proportions similar to those of the one-step variance (Bond and Windmeijer 2002).

13.7 Empirical results

The estimation of the effects of ALMP on the job seeker rate (JSR) in both regions was performed with the same model, with the exception that for West Germany the structural adjustment schemes were not included because of their minor importance. The other ALMP measures, namely job creation schemes and vocational training were included for both regions.

For West Germany we restricted the number of moment conditions for both GMM estimators. This was because the time dimension $T = 12$ was relatively large compared to the number of cross sections $N = 141$. Since the moment conditions (13.3) and (13.4) use the whole history (e.g. $s_{it-2},...,s_{i1}$) as instruments, the number of overidentifying restrictions becomes rather large. As discussed in Bond (2002) and Arellano and Bond (1998) the inclusion of too many instruments may result in overfitting biases. To avoid this problem we did not use the whole history as instruments in the moment conditions (13.3) and (13.4). For the first-differenced GMM estimator we truncated the history after $t - 8$, and for the system GMM estimator we truncated it after $t - 6$.[14] Note that even if we had used the re-

---

[13] See for example Arellano and Bond (1991).

[14] The presence of the additional moment conditions for the level equations makes it advisable to truncate the history at an earlier point in time compared to the first-differenced GMM estimator.

duced set of instruments for the system GMM estimator, the number of moment conditions would have exceeded the number of cross sections. The specification of the moment conditions (e.g. see Blundell et al. 2000) for the GMM estimators implies that the two-step weight matrix is estimated only from N observations. In our case, the weight matrix for the system GMM estimator was estimated with fewer observations than instruments anyway.[15] Although the system estimator suffered from this problem, there is no evidence of an overfitting bias, so that the results for the system GMM estimator seem most reliable. This problem was more severe for East Germany because we had only 34 cross sections to hand. Owing to the reduced number of cross sections and the unchanged time dimension, the GMM estimators were not applicable for East Germany. Consequently, we will only present the results from a least squares dummy variable (LSDV) estimator.

Table 13.3 reports the estimation results from the first-difference GMM (DIF GMM), the system GMM (SYS GMM) for West Germany and the LSDV estimator for East Germany. The results from the GMM estimators are the two-step estimates with corrected standard errors as proposed by Windmeijer (2000).

Results for West Germany: On considering the results from the DIF GMM and the SYS GMM estimators for West Germany, we did not find evidence of second order serial correlation for any estimator.[16] In contrast, the test for first order serial correlation rejected the null hypothesis for both estimators. The Sargan test of overidentifying restrictions did not reject the set of instruments for both estimators. The difference between both Sargan tests was 8.2 with 66 degrees of freedom, so that the additional set of instruments could not be rejected. Turning to the coefficients for the lagged dependent variable, the results from the SYS GMM were associated with a more persistent pattern in the job-seeker rate compared to the DIF GMM estimates. The coefficients for the job-seeker rate summed to 0.02 for the first-differenced GMM and to 0.95 for the system GMM estimator. The substantial difference between the first-differenced and the system GMM estimator indicates that inclusion of the additional moment conditions for the level equations was essential for identification of the parameters of interest. In order to analyse the effects of the ALMP measures we relied on the cumulated lag coefficients and the long run multiplier. The cumulated lag coefficients describe the total impact of an ALMP extension in t on the job seeker rate in $t + g$.

The long run multiplier is the impact after $t + \infty$: that is, it refers to the total effect of an ALMP extension. The cumulated lag coefficients for West Germany are plotted in Fig. 13.1 up to $t + 6$ quarters and the long run multiplier is given in Table 13.3. For job creation schemes we found an initially significant negative effect which vanished after the first quarter. Only the results from the system estimator evidenced a significant negative effect until t+6. With regard to the long-run

---

[15] In this case the weight matrix is calculated with a generalised inverse (see \cn{AB98} for details).

[16] Since the calculation of the second-order test statistics failed for the corrected standard errors we use the test statistic obtained from the conventional standard errors.

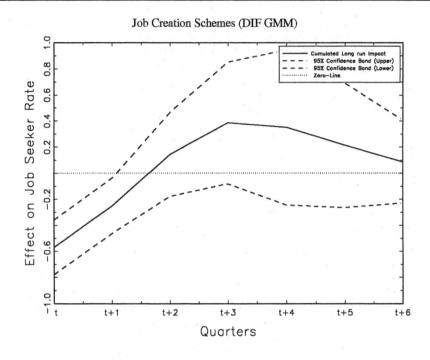

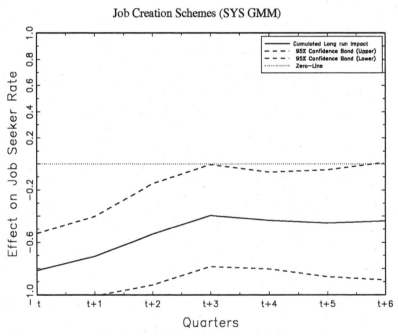

Fig. 13.1. Cumulated lag coefficients West Germany

Vocational Training (DIF GMM)

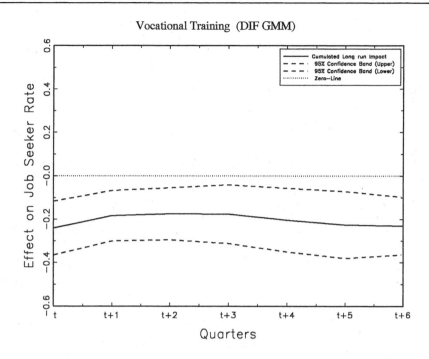

Vocational Training (SYS GMM)

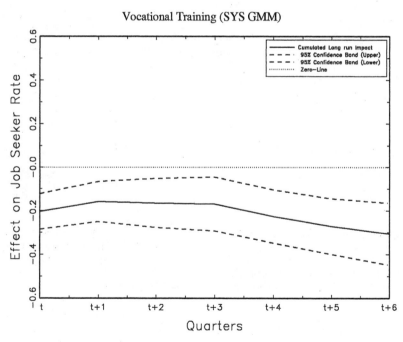

Fig. 13.1. (continued)

Table 13.3. Estimation results[*]

Variable		West–Germany				East–Germany	
		DIF GMM Estimator		SYS GMM Estimator		LSDV Estimator	
		Param.	t–value[**]	Param.	t–value	Param.	t–value
	CONST.	–	–	0.324	5.55	0.2725	3.82
Job Seeker Rate	JSRt–1	0.4618	5.307	0.8678	17.33	0.6563	8.982
	JSRt–2	–0.2517	–4.217	–0.1059	–1.391	–0.2031	–2.042
	JSRt–3	–0.0159	–0.541	0.1023	2.996	0.1112	1.331
	JSRt–4	–0.1702	–0.613	0.0931	0.796	0.4431	5.339
Participants in Job	JCSt	–0.5682	–5.301	–0.8159	–5.68	–0.0117	–0.348
Creation Schemes	JCSt–1	0.5786	4.984	0.8163	5.042	0.0161	0.394
	JCSt–2	0.1082	0.936	–0.012	–0.131	0.001	0.032
	JCSt–3	0.1277	1.545	0.0926	1.418	0.0156	0.593
	JCSt–4	–0.1374	–1.276	–0.08	–1.217	–0.0175	–1.06
Participants in Struct.	SASt	–	–	–	–	–0.1063	–2.703
Adjustment Schemes	SASt–1	–	–	–	–	0.0918	1.771
	SASt–2	–	–	–	–	0.0037	0.082
	SASt–3	–	–	–	–	–0.0227	–0.637
	SASt–4	–	–	–	–	–0.0184	–0.531
Participants in	VTt	–0.2408	–3.801	–0.2035	–4.874	–0.0625	–1.458
Vocational Training	VTt–1	0.1683	5.377	0.2226	6.084	0.0494	1.015
	VTt–2	–0.0782	–3.198	–0.0681	–3.105	–0.0737	–1.608
	VTt–3	0.0049	0.26	0.0265	1.232	–0.0522	–1.21
	VTt–4	–0.0647	–2.144	–0.0394	–1.814	0.0313	0.845
National Unemployed	NURt–1	–0.0475	–0.055	–2.1393	–4.937	–3.0282	–3.253
Rate	NURt–2	0.7782	1.319	–0.2681	–1.027	0.2606	0.32
National Vacancies	NVRt–1	3.0178	0.863	–1.7298	–1.295	0.9597	0.463
Rate	NVRt–2	–3.4925	–3.094	–5.7844	–3.741	–2.5526	–1.236
Seasonal Dummy 1	SD1	0.0045	0.648	–0.0099	–5.14	0.0083	2.269
Seasonal Dummy 2	SD2	–0.0087	–1.042	0.0005	0.065	0.0163	1.292
Seasonal Dummy 3	SD3	–0.0142	–1.397	–0.0017	–0.546	0.0035	0.721
Long Run Multiplier JCS		0.1114	0.748	0.0237	0.023	0.0693	0.506
Long Run Multiplier SAS		–	–	–	–	–0.4407	–1.601
Long Run Multiplier VT		–0.2156	–3.534	–1.4452	–2.592	0.2144	0.788
Wald test of joint significance		(21)	3617.29	(21)	39629.64	(26)	177368.99
Sargan test		(115)	124.06	(181)	132.25	–	–
First–order serial correlation		(141)	–2.23	(141)	–2.12	(34)	3.77
Second–order serial correlation		(141)	–0.74	(141)	0.06	(34)	2.39
No. of observations (N,T)			141,12		141,12		34,12

[*] Degrees of freedom for the test statistics are in parentheses. Asymptotic standard errors and test statistics are asymptotically robust to heteroscedasticity. DIF GMM are the two-step estimates from the first-differenced GMM estimator. SYS GMM are the two-step estimates from the system GMM estimator.

[**] Corrected standard errors as suggested by Windmeijer (2000).

Effects, we did not find any significant effect for JCS. Therefore, although there is a negative impact at the beginning, JCS are not able to reduce the job-seeker rate in the long run. The picture is more promising in the case of vocational training programmes. For both estimators we invariably found a significant negative effect. Furthermore the long-run effects were significantly negative. We consequently conclude that vocational training programmes in West Germany have a permanent negative effect on the job-seeker rate.

Results for East Germany: Turning to the results for East Germany, to be noted is that the LSDV estimator is not consistent in the case of a dynamic panel data model. The consistency depends on T being large relative to N due to the incidental parameter problem. Therefore the results for East Germany should be treated with caution, although the incidental parameter problem should not be too severe in the case of $N = 34$ and $T = 12$. In order to assess the effects of the ALMP measures, we again inspected the cumulated lag coefficients and the long run multiplier. Figure 13.2 shows the cumulated lag coefficients for job creation schemes, structural adjustment schemes and vocational training programmes for East Germany. In the case of JCS, we did not find any significant effect on the job-seeker rate. The cumulated lag coefficients and the long run multiplier were positive but insignificant. On considering structural adjustment schemes, we found an insignificant effect that became significant after 4 quarters; however, the long run multiplier was only just significant at a 10 per cent-level. Finally we found for VT an insignificant positive effect that remained insignificant in the long-run as well. Which means that vocational training is unable to affect the job-seeker rate in East Germany either.

13.8 Conclusions

The chapter has estimated the net effects of ALMP in Germany. Because microeconometric evaluations usually ignore impacts on the non-participants, we have used a macroeconometric approach to analyse the effects of job creation schemes, structural adjustment schemes and vocational training on the employment situation in Germany for the time span from 1999 to 2001.

As the starting-point for our analysis we discussed various channels through which ALMP might influence the whole economy in a theoretical framework. We then stressed the importance of suitable data for evaluation purposes which enable regional heterogeneity to be taken into account. This was especially important for the time period considered because the introduction of the New Social Code SGB III in 1998 decentralised the institutional organisation of labour market policy in Germany, allowing more flexibility in the regional allocation of resources among measures. As a consequence, evaluation must give closer consideration to regional aspects than was previously the case. To this end, we used a regional dataset for 175 labour office districts in West and East Germany. The availability of quarterly data allowed us to take dynamics and persistence in the labour market into

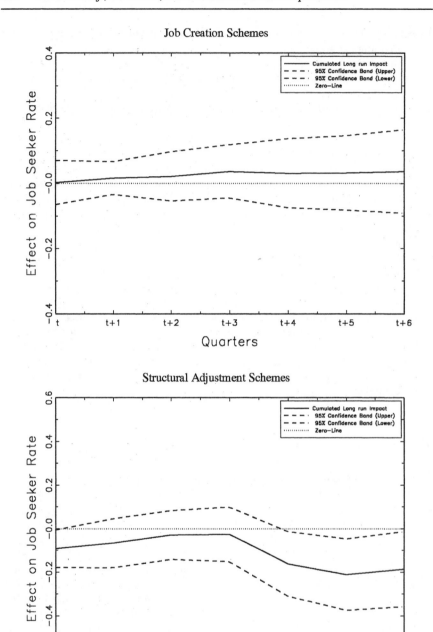

Fig. 13.2. Cumulated lag coefficients East Germany

Vocational Training

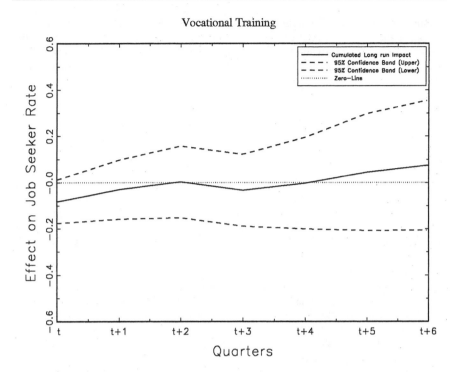

Fig. 13.2. (continued)

account. The fact that there are major differences between the East and the West German labour markets obliged us to make a separate estimation for each area. We based our empirical specification on a reduced form relationship to evaluate the impact of ALMP on the total rate of job-seekers, i.e. the openly unemployed plus programme participants. To control for the problems arising from a dynamic panel data model, we applied the GMM estimation procedures suggested by Arellano and Bond (1991) and Blundell and Bond (1998). Furthermore, we used the two-step standard error correction proposed by Windmeijer (2000) to make reliable inferences about the two-step estimates. By using these methods for dynamic panel data we also accounted for the inherent simultaneity problem of ALMP.

Our results indicate that, for West Germany, vocational training has a significantly negative effect – that is, vocational training is able to reduce the job-seeker rate – whilst job creation schemes do not seem to have any significant effect. Owing to the small number of cross sections in East Germany, the application of the GMM estimators was not feasible. Therefore the results should be treated with caution. For job creation schemes and vocational training we did not find any significant effects, whereas in the case of structural adjustment schemes there was weak evidence for a positive impact on the labour market situation.

A major task for future work is to analyse the various effects of ALMP with a structural model. Since a reduced form approach can only measure the net effect of ALMP, the different channels through which ALMP may affect the economy cannot be detected. The main problem is the lack of data making it possible to consider the effects of ALMP on matching efficiency or on wages. Basically, the ideal macroeconomic evaluation requires three things: first, a well-developed macroeconomic theory which, second, is applicable in an econometric framework and, third, does not fail because of data limitations.

References

Ahn S, Schmidt P (1995) Efficient estimation of models for dynamic panel data. Journal of Econometrics 68:5–27.

Arellano M, Bond S (1991) Some tests of specification for panel data: Monte Carlo evidence and an application to employment equations, Review of Economic Studies 58:277–297.

Arellano M, Bond S (1998) Dynamic panel data estimation using DPD98 for Gauss. http://www.ifs.org.uk/staff/steveb.html.

Baily M, Tobin J (1977) Macroeconomic effects of selective public employment and wage subsidies. Brooking Papers on Economic Activity 2:511–541.

Blien U (2002) Ein Arbeitsmarktgesamtindikator zur Mittelverteilung für die aktive Arbeitsmarktpolitik. Beiträge zur Arbeitsmarkt- und Berufsforschung 250:335–344.

Blundell R, Bond S (1998) Initial conditions and moment restrictions in dynamic panel data models. Journal of Econometrics 87:115–143.

Blundell R, Bond S, Windmeijer F (2000) Estimation in dynamic panel data models: improving on the performance of the standard GMM estimators. In: Baltagi BH (ed) Nostationary panels, panel cointegration and dynamic panels. Elsevier, Amsterdam, pp 53–91.

Boeri R, Burda M (1996) Active labor market policies, job matching and the Czech miracle. European Economic Review 40:805–817.

Bond S (2002) Dynamic panel data models: a guide to micro data methods and practice. Cemmap Working Paper 09/02.

Bond S, Windmeijer F (2002) Finite sample inference for GMM estimators in linear panel data models. Cemmap Working Paper 04/02.

Brinkmann C (1999) Controlling and evaluation of employment promotion and the employment services in Germany. IAB Labour Market Research Topics 36.

Bundesanstalt für Arbeit (2000) Daten zu den Eingliederungsbilanzen 1999. Nürnberg.

Bundesanstalt für Arbeit (2002) Arbeitsmarkt 2001. Nürnberg

Calmfors L (1994) Active labour market policy and unemployment – A framework for the analysis of crucial design features. OECD Economic Studies 22:7–47.

Calmfors L, Forslund A (1991) Real-wage determination and labour market policies: the Swedish experience. Economic Journal 101:1130–1148.

Calmfors L, Lang H (1995) Macroeconomic effects of active labor market programmes in a union-wage-setting model. Economic Journal 105:601–619.

Calmfors L and Skedinger P (1995) Does active labour market policy increase employment? Theoretical considerations and some empirical evidence from Sweden. Oxford Review of Economic Policy 11:91–109.

Calmfors L, Forslund A, Hemström M (2002) Does active labour market policy work? Lessons from the Swedish experience. CESifo Working Paper 675.

Fay R (1996) Enhancing the effectiveness of active market policies: evidence from programme evaluations in OECD countries. OECD Labour Market and Social Policy Occasional Paper 18. OECD, Paris.

Fertig M, Schmidt C (2000) Discretionary measures of active labour market policy – The German employment promotion reform in perspective. Schmollers Jahrbuch 4:537–565.

Fitzenberger B, Hujer R (2002) Stand und Perspektiven der Evaluation der aktiven Arbeitsmarktpolitik in Deutschland. Perspektiven der Wirtschaftspolitik 3:139–158.

Fitzenberger B, Speckesser S (2002) Zur wissenschaftlichen Evaluation der aktiven Arbeitsmarktpolitik in Deutschland. Mitteilungen aus der Arbeitsmarkt- und Berufsforschung, 33:357–371.

Forslund A, Krueger A (1997) An evaluation of the Swedish active labor market policy: new and received wisdom. In: Freeman R, Topel RH, Swedenborj B (eds) the welfare state in transition. Chicago University Press, Chicago, pp 267–298.

Hagen T, Steiner V (2000) Von der Finanzierung der Arbeitslosigkeit zur Förderung von Arbeit – Analysen und Empfehlungen zur Arbeitsmarktpolitik in Deutschland, Nomos, Baden-Baden.

Heckman J (1999) Accounting for heterogeneity, diversity and general equilibrium in evaluating social programs. NBER Working Paper 7230.

Heckman J, LaLonde R, Smith J (1999) The economic and econometrics of active labor market programs. In: Ashenfelter O, Card D (eds) Handbook of labor economics, Vol 3. Elsevier, Amsterdam, pp 1895–2097.

Holmlund B, Linden J (1993) Job matching, temporary public employment and equilibrium, Journal of Public Economics 51:329–343.

Hujer R, Caliendo M (2001) Evaluation of active labour market policy – Methodological concepts and empirical estimates. In: Becker I, Ott N, Rolf G (eds) Soziale Sicherung in einer dynamischen Gesellschaft. Campus, Frankfurt, pp 583–617.

Hujer R, Caliendo M, Radic D (2004) Estimating the effects of wage subsidies on the labour demand in West Germany using the IAB establishment panel. In: Merz J, Zwrett M (eds) MIKAS, vol 1. Statistisches Bundesamt, Wiesbaden, pp 249–283.

Jackman R, Pissarides C, Savouri S (1990) Labour market policies and unemployment in the OECD. Economic Policy 5:450–490.

Johnson G, Layard R (1986) The natural rate of unemployment: explanation and policy. In: Handbook of labor economics. North-Holland, Amsterdam, pp 921–999.

Layard R, Nickell S (1986) Unemployment in Britain. Economica 53:121–170.

Layard R, Nickell S, Jackman R (1991) Unemployment. Macroeconomic performance and the labour market. Oxford University Press, Oxford.

OECD (1993) Employment outlook. Paris.

Pissarides C (2000) Equilibrium unemployment theory. MIT Press, Cambridge (Mass.).

Rubin D (1980) Comment on Basu D. – Randomization analysis of experimental data: the Fisher randomization test. Journal of the American Association 75:591–593.

Sell S (1998) Entwicklung und Reform des Arbeitsförderungsgesetzes als Anpassung des Sozialrechts an flexible Erwerbsformen. Mitteilungen aus der Arbeitsmarkt- und Berufsforschung 29:532–549.

Smith J (2000) A critical survey of empirical methods for evaluating active labor market policies. Zeitschrift für Volkswirtschaft und Statistik 136:1–22.

Windmeijer F (2000) A finite sample correction for the variance of linear efficient GMM two-step estimators. Journal of Econometrics 126:25–61.

14 Evaluating Asymmetries in Active Labour Market Policies: the Case of Italy

Carlo Altavilla[1] and Floro Ernesto Caroleo[2]

[1] University of Naples "Parthenope", Italy
[2] University of Salerno, Italy

14.1 Introduction

Since the beginning of the 1990s, the *OECD Jobs Study* has emphasised the role of active labour market policies (ALMPs) in reducing structural unemployment. Moreover, the *European Employment Strategy*, launched at the Luxembourg Job Summit and restated in the Lisbon strategy, gives ALMPs the task of increasing investments in human capital and of attracting more people into the labour market.

Why a government should adopt ALMPs in reducing unemployment can be demonstrated by a variety of theoretical models in which implementation of ALMP has a positive effect on the matching process as well as on job competition. Other advantages are an increase in productivity, the better allocation of labour among sectors, and greater geographic mobility.

However, in spite of theoretical and political preferences for ALMP spending, real data reveal a quite different picture. In the period from 1985 to 2000, the OECD countries did not significantly increase expenditure on active programmes as a percentage of GDP – less than 1 per cent on average. Moreover, there was no tendency to switch resources from passive to active programmes.

ALMP may in fact have ambiguous effects on the regular labour demand. An active labour policy may engender a crowding-out process through the well-known deadweight effect, the substitution effect, or an accommodation effect on wage setting. For these reasons, the net employment effect of ALMP is an empirical issue, with the consequence that monitoring and evaluating them is important.

There is a large quantity of empirical literature which focuses on whether ALMP have positive effects on unemployment. Most of these studies use microeconometric techniques to evaluate the effects of ALMP on individual performance. Other studies use macroeconometric models to analyse the net effect of ALMP on the economy as a whole.

This chapter takes a macroeconomic perspective. Its empirical analysis is based on a variety of econometric techniques thought to capture the possible effects of ALMP on employment and unemployment dynamics. The aim in particular is to assess whether ALMP may have asymmetric effects in different regions in which they are implemented.

The paper proceeds as follows. Section 14.2 analyses the OECD's view of ALMP effectiveness in reducing structural unemployment. Section 14.3 focuses on the theoretical effects of ALMP. Section 14.4 highlights some peculiarities of the Italian labour market. Section 14.5 moves to the empirical models of labour market policies and presents the results obtained from GMM and P-VAR models. The section also sets out the main results of impulse response analysis and of forecast error variance decomposition. Section 14.6 concludes.

14.2   ALMP and the OECD perspective

The well-known *OECD Jobs Study* (OECD 1994; OECD 1996) emphasised ALMP as a means to combat structural unemployment (Layard et al. 1991). The general conclusion was that the focus of labour market policies should shift from the passive provision of income support to more active measures to assist re-employment, the reason being that subsidies raise the reservation wage and consequently have strong negative effects on the duration of unemployment and on job search intensity. Active labour measures, on the other hand, can improve the match between the labour demand and supply and reduce the long-term unemployment of disadvantaged workers.[1]

The European Employment Strategy (EES), launched at the Luxembourg Job Summit (November 1997) on the basis of the new provisions in the Employment Title of the Treaty, and reiterated in the Lisbon Strategy (Lisbon European Council, March 2000), has given new impulse to ALMPs, stressing their importance not only as alternatives to subsidies but also *per se*. The EES, in fact, gives ALMPs the task of increasing the adaptability of workers and enterprises, attracting more people into the labour market, and of making investment in human capital more effective by adopting a preventive and more active approach to the unemployed (European Commission 2003).

Country surveys, however, have revealed that ALMP have achieved rather limited success in that they suffer from ineffective delivery, monitoring and evaluating mechanisms, as well as poor targeting and other design problems. Consequently, despite theoretical and political preferences for ALMP spending, the data reveal a quite different picture. Average spending on active programmes in the OECD countries increased very little between 1985 and 2000 as a percentage of GDP (from 0.7 to 0.8) (Martin and Grubb 2001). The same trend was apparent in the European countries (from 0.9 to 1.0). There is no tendency to switch resources from passive to active programmes, while both moving in accordance with unemployment. Figures 14.1 and 14.2 show the evolution of expenditure in active and

---

[1] The OECD divides public spending on labour programmes between "active and passive" measures. The former aim at improving the employability of the unemployed by raising their job-related skills and enhancing the functioning of the labour market. It is possible to distinguish among five groups of measures: (1) public employment services, (2) labour market training, (3) youth measures, (4) subsidized employment, (5) measures for the disabled. The latter are income transfers to the unemployed, namely (1) unemployment benefits, and (2) early retirement pensions paid for labour market reasons (Martin and Grubb 2001).

passive policies across various EU and non-EU countries during the 1980s and the 1990s.

In terms of the level of expenditure, measured as a share of the GDP, three groups of countries can be distinguished. The first includes countries such as Denmark, the Netherlands and Belgium, which had high levels of expenditure on both active and passive policy measures during the 1980s. An intermediate group comprises countries with higher-than average expenditure on active, but not passive, income support, such as Sweden and Italy, and countries with higher-than-average expenditure on passive, but not active, measures, such as Spain. The last and largest group includes countries such as Japan, the USA, Austria, Portugal, Greece and Switzerland, with very low levels of expenditure on both active and passive measures. Policies in the three groups of countries have not changed since the 1980s and 1990s. There has been a general reduction in outlays on passive measures, while a group of European countries – Spain, France, Germany and Finland – have substantially increased their spending on active measures. Sweden, by contrast, has reduced its percentage of ALMP expenditure.

Figure 14.3 shows that the hypothesis of a direct negative relation between ALMP expenditures and the unemployment rate does not hold. Indeed, countries with low percentages of ALMP/GDP, but also countries that allocate a higher proportion of GDP to ALMP, have lower unemployment rates. The highest unemployment rate occurs in the countries occupying intermediate positions.

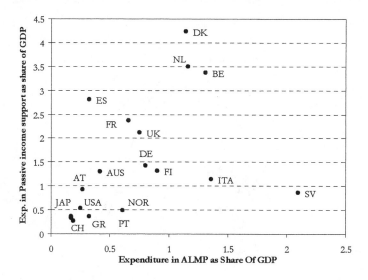

Fig. 14.1. Ratio of active to passive expenditure for employment over GDP (1985)

Source: OECD, Employment Outlook, various issues

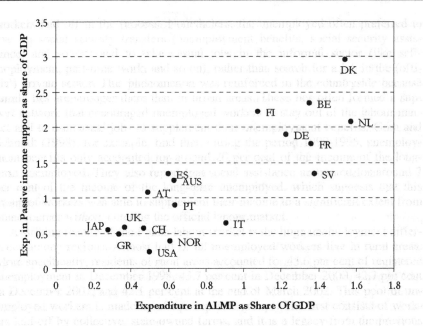

Fig. 14.2. Ratio of active to passive expenditure for employment over GDP (2000)

Source: OECD, Employment Outlook, various issues

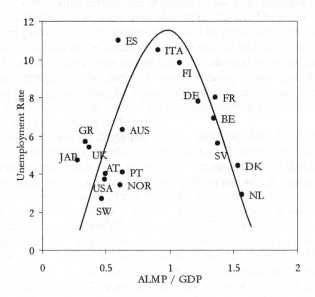

Fig. 14.3. Relation between ALMP expenditures and unemployment rate

Source: OECD, Employment Outlook, various issues

14.3   The theoretical effects of ALMP

From a theoretical point of view, the effects of ALMP can be studied using two models which reach very similar conclusions: the well-known Jackman, Layard and Nickell labour market framework, (Layard et al. 1991; Calmfors 1994; Calmfors and Lang 1995), and the Beveridge curve framework derived from a matching function combined with job search theory.[2] The impact of ALMP on the labour market can be better analysed by means of the latter type of model.

The Beveridge curve (or *uv* curve) represents the non-linear negative relationship between the unemployment rate $u = U/(U + E)$ and the vacancy rate $v = V/(V + E)$, where E is employment:

$$uv = f(u) \qquad f' < 0 \, e \, f'' > 0 \qquad (14.1)$$

It can be shown that the slope and shifts of the curve are due to the behaviour of workers in seeking employment, the behaviour of employers in screening applicants for vacancies, and the 'matching technology' in the labour market by which searching workers and searching firms are brought together.

In a stock-flow model, the change of unemployed stock (ΔU) can be viewed as resulting from the inflow (I) of workers into the unemployment pool from the non-labour force (p) or from employment (e), and the outflow (O) of workers from unemployment to the two statuses, in a period of time (t):

$$\Delta U = (I_t^p + I_t^e) - (O_t^p + O_t^e) \qquad (14.2)$$

The same dynamics can be adopted for change in the stock of vacancies.

$$\Delta V = Q_t - O_t^e \qquad (14.3)$$

Q represents the number of new vacancies registered at time t, and O_t^e is the number of filled vacancies that corresponds to the outflow of unemployed workers to employment, assuming that there are no vacancies which are not either filled by workers from the non-labour force pool or cancelled.

The usual hypothesis is that the inflow from employment into unemployment is a percentage (s) of the employment stock (E):

$$I_t^e = s_t E_t \qquad (14.4)$$

where s is the separation rate.

The outflow from unemployment to employment can be formalized as a percentage (v) of unemployment:

---

[2]   There are two main theoretical foundations for the Beveridge curve: the first is based on a model developed by Hansen and derives the matching function from an aggregation over distinct markets in the presence of frictions and limited labour mobility. The second is a matching model in a stock-flow framework. For a recent survey see Petrongolo and Pissarides (2001).

$$O_t^e = v_t U_t \tag{14.5}$$

where v can be viewed as the average probability that an unemployed worker at the beginning of period t will find a job during period t.

On the other hand, the outflow from vacancies can be written as a percentage (p) of V:

$$O_t^e = p_t V_t \tag{14.6}$$

where p can be described as the probability of *matching*, i.e. the probability that a given vacancy will be filled by an unemployed worker during period t.

Consequently, the change of unemployment stock in period t can be rewritten as:

$$\Delta U = s_t E_t - p_t V_t + I_t^p - O_t^p \tag{14.7}$$

We can refer to the matching model (Hall 1977; Pissarides 1990) to identify the factors determining the matching probability p. As stated before, the matching probability derives (i) from the ways in which the match between unemployed workers and unfilled jobs takes place, (ii) from the behaviour of workers in searching for jobs, and (iii) from the behaviour of employers in screening applicants for vacancies. The probability therefore depends on the probability that an employer with a vacancy will be contacted by at least one job-seeker (contact probability c) and the probability that the job contact took place (acceptance probability r):

$$p_t = c_t r_t \tag{14.8}$$

Under very simple initial assumptions on job-seekers and vacancy supply characteristics (Hall 1977), we can hypothesise that contact probability derives from the relation between unemployment (U) and vacancies (V). In other words, the greater the number of vacancies relative to the number of unemployed, the higher the contact probability, and consequently the higher the probability that an unemployed worker will find a job.

The probability of a job-seeeker contacting an employer is $1/V$. Therefore, the probability that unemployed workers do not contact employers with vacancies can be written, assuming a sufficiently large number of vacancies, as (Hall 1977):

$$\left(1 - \frac{1}{V}\right)^U = \left[\left(1 - \frac{1}{V}\right)^{-V}\right]^{-U/V} \cong e^{-U/V}$$

Probability c depends on two other variables as well: the fraction of active job seekers over total unemployed workers (α), which means that in a labour market where there are many active job-seekers in the unemployment pool, even a small increase in vacancies gives rise to a relatively strong reduction in unemployment; moreover, the probability of contact is due to a mismatch by region, by occupation and by qualification (γ). The contact probability can therefore be written as:

$$c_t = 1 - e^{-\alpha \gamma U_t / V_t} \qquad (14.9)$$

A simple job search model (McCall 1970; Mortensen 1970; Pissarides 1990) furnishes the determinants of acceptance probability r. The decision of a job-seeker to accept a job is based on an optimization problem according to which s/he finds "the optimal duration of a job search by comparing the discounted earnings from the best wage offer found during his search with the discounted search costs" (Frisch 1984, p. 62). The reservation wage (w^r) therefore represents the expected return from pursuing the best stopping rule. This is also influenced by direct and indirect search costs and unemployment benefits. In the same way, the employer's acceptance decision arises from an assessment of the applicant's productive capacity, which is not easy to establish *a priori* and is determined by a screening process affected by variables such as employment subsidies, individual characteristics of the worker, his/her skill level, and his/her reservation productivity level (z^1) for a given job.

The acceptance probability can therefore be written as:

$$r = r(w^r, z^r) \qquad (14.10)$$

with $\dfrac{\partial r}{\partial w^r} < 0; \dfrac{\partial r}{\partial z^r} < 0$

On inserting (14.9) and (14.10) in (14.6), the matching function becomes:

$$O_t^e = r_t(w^r, z^r)(1 - e^{-\alpha \gamma U_t / V_t}) V_t \qquad (14.11)$$

In other words, the matching function can be interpreted as a constant return production function of job matches where the inputs are the unemployed and vacancies.

The essential characteristics of the Beveridge curve can be derived by applying the steady state conditions to the flow model of unemployment. The steady state conditions are $\Delta U = 0$ and $\Delta E = 0$, and the flow equation (14.7), after the substitutions becomes:

$$I_t^p - O_t^p + s_t E_t = r_t(w^r, z^r)(1 - e^{-\alpha \gamma U_t / V_t}) V_t \qquad (14.12)$$

which is a negative convex function of U and V, as the following equations show:

$$\frac{dU}{dV} = -\alpha \gamma \frac{e^{-\alpha \gamma (U/V)}}{\left(e^{-\alpha \gamma (U/V)} - 1 \right) v + \alpha \gamma U e^{-\alpha \gamma (U/V)}} v < O$$

$$\frac{d^2 U}{dV^2} > O \qquad (14.13)$$

Finally, after dividing all variables of (14.12) by labour force L_s, the condition $U = V$ (or $u = v$ where $u = U/L_s$ and $v = V/L_s$) determines the natural rate of unemployment (NRU): that is, the structural and frictional unemployment corresponding to equilibrium in the labour market:

$$NRU = \frac{iq^P - oq^P + sn}{r(w^r, z^r)(1 - e^{-\alpha\gamma})} \tag{14.14}$$

where:

$$iq^P = \frac{I^P}{L_s}; oq^P = \frac{O^P}{L_s}; \frac{E}{L_s} = n$$

The slope of the Beveridge curve consequently depends on the search intensity of job-seekers and on labour market mismatches, while the NRU depends also on the reservation wage and reservation productivity.

As stressed by Jackman et al. (1990), A significantly affect the position and slope of the Beveridge curve (Jackman et al. 1990, p. 480). Indeed, ALMP are supposed to shift the curve towards the origin because they reduce labour market mismatches and search frictions. Moreover, ALMP may make a given job creation programme more effective with regard to employment, flattening the curve. Finally, the matching process is accelerated as obstacles are removed.

Calmfors (1994) analyses various effects of ALMPs, distinguishing between: (i) effects on the matching process; (ii) effects on the competition for jobs; (iii) productivity effects; (iv) effects on the allocation of labour among sectors and geographic mobility; (v) direct crowding-out effects on regular labour demand; and (vi) accommodation effects on wage setting.

ALMP, particularly job-broking and counselling activities, give greater efficiency to the matching process because they promote more active searches by job-seekers. In our model, the coefficient affected by this type of treatment effect is α, i.e. the fraction of active job-seekers in total unemployed workers. The job-seeker pool (S), in fact, consists of unemployed workers (U) and ALMP participants (P). We may write:

$$S = U + a'P$$

where a' is an index of search intensity. If the search intensity of the ALMP participant is greater ($a' > 1$), it is evident that an increase in ALMP participation increases α' and, consequently, improves the matching process.

On the other hand, there may also be an opposite *locking in* effect if a' is < 1: that is, if participants do not find job opportunities before programmes are completed, or if they continue to have low probabilities of being employed on conclusion of the programme.[3]

---

[3] Caroleo and Pastore (2005) have detected the existence of a "training trap" for young unemployed persons in Italy, where participation in training programmes increases the probability of repeating this type of programme without improving the probability of finding a job.

Job-matching improvement facilitates the hiring process of firms and then lowers the cost of posting vacancies, as well as limiting wage settings. In our model, these effects can be synthesised by reductions in the reservation wage and reservation productivity.

Reservation productivity and the reservation wage are also affected by the effects on competition for jobs and productivity effects. It is self-evident that participation in ALMP (especially training programmes and job creation measures providing on-the-job training) increases the productivity of job-seekers, even if their reservation wages increase as well. The net effect is a matter for empirical investigation. Employment subsidies instead directly decrease labour costs for firms. ALMP participation may also have a positive effect on labour force participation, in that it increases the motivation to actively seek work and therefore increases the competition for the jobs available (Johansson 2001).

Finally, the desired effect of ALMP is a change in the allocation of the labour force among sectors, skills and regions (i.e. a reduced degree of mismatch in our model). If there is full employment among skilled workers, or in certain regions, or sectors, and if wages are flexible, employment subsidies or training programmes intended to increase the hiring probability of unskilled workers or workers employed in regions with high unemployment and wage rigidity have a positive effect on output and employment.

Likewise, a policy intended to reallocate workers from unskilled to skilled jobs, from low productivity sectors to high productivity sectors, or from low labour demand regions to high labour demand regions, also has a positive effect on gross output. As a consequence, if, for example, unskilled workers are retrained and become more skilled, the labour supply in the skilled sector augments, and if wages become more flexible, labour demand increases to the same extent. But the unskilled sector will be unaffected owing to wage rigidity (Layard 1999; Calmfors et al. 2002).

An unintentional side-effect is that ALMPs (especially subsidized employment schemes) may crowd out (*displacement effect*) regular labour demand. In fact, a *deadweight effect* occurs when the same person would have been hired even in the absence of such subsidies, and a *substitution effect* occurs when the subsidies induce employers to substitute one category of workers for another.[4]

An indirect crowding-out effect may come about to the extent that ALMPs improve the welfare of the unemployed through higher income rather than unemployment benefit for participants; a higher level of psychological well-being due to being employed; improvement in future labour market prospects; extension of income support beyond the maximum unemployment benefit period. In this case, the reservation wage is increased and the intensity of the job search is reduced. Wage pressure is increased.

---

[4] The *displacement effect* can have a positive employment effect to the extent that the employment of the long-term unemployed (outsiders) crowds out the employment of insiders, so that the latter group encounters more competition and moderates wage settings.

14.4   A macroeconomic evaluation of ALMP in Italy

For the foregoing reasons, the net employment effect of ALMP is an empirical issue. Consequently, as the EES stressed, it is important to monitor and evaluate these policies (Fay 1996). However, although monitoring now takes place in Italy (MLSP, various issues), evaluation to date has only been carried out using the conventional programme-oriented approach to policy evaluation.[5]

Empirical research on the effects of ALMP is of two types: microeconomic and macroeconomic. Microeconomic studies evaluate the effects of participation in ALMPs on the participating individuals, comparing their labour market outcomes to those that would have prevailed had they not participated in an active programme. Macroeconomic studies examine aggregate, general equilibrium effects. The issue addressed in what follows is whether ALMP represent a net gain for the economy as whole. There are two alternatives to consider: whether ALMP positively affect both unemployment and output, or whether the effect is simply distributional, that is, whether work is shifted from the old to the young or from a region to another, etc. (Bellmann and Jackman 1996). Studies on the matter concern themselves with evaluation of a Beveridge curve or a matching function, or a wage-setting function, and with evaluation of the direct, crowding-out effect or the effects of ALMP on labour force participation (Hujer and Caliendo 2001).

The method chosen to evaluate ALMPs in Italy is a reduced form which enables estimation of the net effects of ALMP participation on employment or unemployment in a regional framework (Hujer et al. 2002). This type of methodology has been used mainly by studies based on OECD data which explain the cross-country variation in unemployment rates by the cross-country variation in a number of labour market institutions; one of them being ALMP (Layard et al. 1991; Nickell 1997; Nickell and Layard 1999; Blanchard and Wolfers 2000).[6]

There are various drawbacks to a macroeconomic assessment of active labour market policies of the sort that we conduct below. Because we must work with aggregated data, the results tend to become vague and less robust. In many cases, we must deal with relatively crude data, making use of proxy variables when necessary. But the main problem is that of endogeneity or simultaneity. Given that

---

[5] For a comprehensive survey of the evaluation studies carried out in Italy, see Martini et al. 2003.

[6] The main difference between studies based on OECD data and our methodology is the ALMP measure. The former generally use expenditure (as a percentage of GDP) on ALMP, whilst we use participants in active policy programmes. The ALMP measure employed in a large number of studies using OECD data is: $\gamma = b_r r / u y$ (see the appendix in Calmfors et al. 2002), where r is the number of participants as a fraction of the labour force, u is the unemployment rate, y is GDP per capita, br is the expenditure on ALMP per programme participant. Consequently, the relation of the two measures is the following:

$$\rho = \gamma u (br / y) - 1$$

governments react to rising unemployment or other labour market problems with increased policy efforts, it becomes very difficult to distinguish the effect of policy on the labour market. Basically, expenditures on ALMPs may affect the unemployment rate, but it may be equally the case that the level of unemployment affects spending on ALMPs.

We use data on participation in active and passive labour policies furnished by MLPS (various issues) and reconstructed on a monthly basis from 1996:1 to 2002:6, and by region. The main active policies considered are: (a) mixed cause contracts; (b) subsidies for long-term or short-term employment; (c) incentives for the stabilization of short-term contracts, (d) incentives for self-employment. In contrast to the OECD's examination of ALMPs, the *Rapporto di Monitoraggio* restricts its analysis to measures targeted on young people and employment subsidies. Recently, however, it has also produced data on training measures and on public employment services, but without providing information on the time series.

Outcome variables are the labour market indices representing the main objectives of the EES: the employment rate, the unemployment rate, and the youth unemployment rate.

The period examined is 1996–2002, which corresponds to a marked positive cycle of increased employment. If we compare this period with a previous one similar to it (1985–1991), we observe that employment increased notwithstanding relative stagnation in economic growth.

	1996–2002	1985–1991
Δ Employment rate	1.2%	1.0%
Employed per year	271,000	224,000
Δ PIL	+1.7%	+2.7%
Employment/GDP elasticity	0.70	0.38

There are several explanations for this positive cycle: the introduction of more flexible forms of employment (atypical contracts), increased employment among women, employment creation in the services sector, and the wage restraint. Moreover, one of the potential explanations is the topic of our inquiry: a renewed impulse to ALMP due to the EES.

Figures 14.4 and 14.5 give a broad measure of the relationship between ALMP expenditures and passive labour market policy expenditures by the Italian regions. To be noted is that, in the period between 1996 and 2002, there was a general reduction in the percentage of passive policies over GDP.

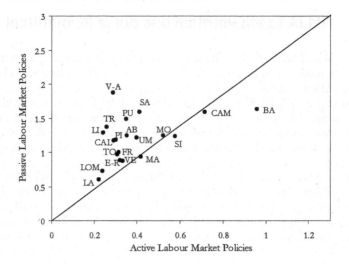

Fig. 14.4. ALMP and PLMP as percentages of GDP – 1996

Source: MPLS, Rapporto di Monitoraggio, various issues

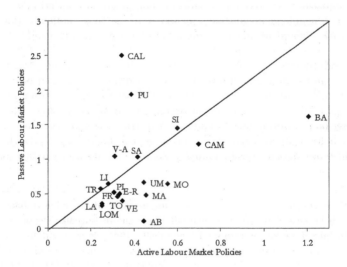

Fig. 14.5. ALMP and PLMP as percentages of GDP – 2000

Source: MPLS, Rapporto di Monitoraggio, various issues

14.5 Empirical models of labour market policies

The empirical analysis is based on two different econometric techniques: the first is the generalized method of moments (GMM); the second consists of applying the vector autoregression framework to panel data (P-VAR).

The aim of this analysis is to assess whether ALMP have different effects according to the particular region in which an programme is implemented. The study employs panel data for the 20 Italian regions. Each model is estimated for several dependent variables including employment rate, unemployment rate, and youth unemployment rate. The explanatory variables are a set of active labour market policies. Moreover, some variables enter the estimation as controls. These variables are GDP per capita, gross fixed investments, GDP per worker, and the school–attendance rate.

The data used for the empirical analysis were drawn from different sources: the monthly data on labour market policies from MLPS (various issues); the data on unemployment and employment from Istat publications.

The significant difference between the southern and the northern Italian labour markets makes it necessary to analyse the areas separately. There are eight cross-sections for Southern Italy, and twelve for Northern Italy.

14.5.1 The effectiveness of alternative ALMPs: a GMM model

The modern approach to the estimation of system instrumental variables is based on the principle of the generalized method of moment (GMM). In order to analyse the effects of ALMP on the unemployment rate, we estimate the following basic equation:

$$u_{i,t} = \alpha u_{i,t-1} + \gamma x_{it-1}^{MCC} + \varphi x_{it-1}^{SE} + \vartheta x_{it-1}^{JS} + D_{i,t} + \eta_{i,t} + \varepsilon_{i,t} \qquad (14.15)$$

with $i = 1,...., N$ and $t = 1,...., T$.

In Eq. (14.15) x_{it-1}^{MCC} represents the mixed cause contracts ratio; x_{it-1}^{SE} is the subsidized employment ratio; x_{it-1}^{JS} represents the job stabilization ratio; $D_{i,t}$ is a vector of time invariant region-specific effects; $\eta_{i,t}$ is a vector of region invariant time specific effects; and $\varepsilon_{i,t}$ is an i.i.d. vector of disturbances.

Each ratio has been constructed as the total number of participants in a programme in a particular region divided by the total working-age population in the same region. Then, the response coefficients γ, φ and ϑ measure the effect exerted by increase of participants in ALMP on unemployment dynamics.

Time and region dummies are very important components of the specification. Time dummies may reduce the reverse causality problem if the timing of adverse shocks is correlated between regions. Region fixed effects capture all time-invariant institutional and economic characteristics explaining why one region has a different-from-average unemployment rate.

The importance of these region-specific effects should not be underestimated. For example, since the mid-1990s, Abruzzo has spent, on average, a lower percentage of GDP on ALMP than Campania (4 per cent for Abruzzo and 7 per cent for Campania), yet Abruzzo had a higher business-sector employment rate in the sample period (35 per cent compared to 26 per cent for Campania). If only variables capturing institutional effects (which, in general, are not very precise) are used to control for region-specific effects, some of the differences in employment caused by other institutional factors will be wrongly attributed to ALMP spending.

The specification in Eq. (14.5) is a dynamic panel data model, where the dependent variable is also explained by its past value.

We now concentrate on the relative ability of alternative active policies to affect the unemployment rate, the employment rate, and the youth unemployment rate. The three policies we consider are mixed cause contracts (henceforth, MCC); subsidized employment (SE), which is the sum of subsidies for long-term or short-term hirings; and job stabilization (JS), that is, incentives for the stabilization of short-term contracts and incentives for self-employment.

The specified dynamic panel data model was estimated using three alternative methods. Table 14.1 reports the GMM estimator in first differences (GMM-DIF), the system estimator (GMM-SYS), and the OLS results.

Table 14.1 shows that, in the northern regions, an increase in MCC produces a larger response in terms of unemployment reaction, with a decrease of 35 basis points in the GMM-DIF model. The response is much smaller in the southern regions. An increase of 1 per cent in MCC induces a fall in the unemployment rate of 10 basis points.

While SE is more effective in the South (–0.44) than in the North (–0.14), an increase in JS produces a greater decrease in northern unemployment (–0.23) with respect to the fall in the southern unemployment rate (–0.12).

Table 14.2 presents the results of the GMM estimates for the model in which the employment rate is considered to be the dependent variable.

In this case, too, a 1 per cent increase in MCC induces a larger increase in the northern employment rate (0.30) than in southern employment (0.19). The opposite is the case of the other polices. In the South, an increase in SE generates a rise in the employment rate of 0.5 per cent, while in the North the effect is an increase of 0.33 per cent. The evidence from Table 14.2 thus corroborates the findings obtained with the unemployment rate model.

We finally look at the ability of the three active policy indicators to reduce the youth unemployment rate, finding in this case that the relative size of the coefficients observed above is not valid. In fact, Table 14.3 suggests a higher JS coefficient for the North as well as a lower MCC coefficient for the South. In general, the response coefficients for the southern regions are lower than the ones obtained for the northern ones.

Table 14.1. GMM estimates of the unemployment rate

South	GMM–DIF		GMM–SYS		OLS	
	Coeff.	Std.Error	Coeff.	Std.Error	Coeff.	Std.Error
Unemployment ($t-1$)	0.75	[0.05]	0.85	[0.03]	0.89	[0.02]
Mixed Cause Contracts ($t-1$)	−0.10	[0.30]	−0.17	[0.22]	−0.14	[0.06]
Subsidized Employment ($t-1$)	−0.44	[0.17]	−0.21	[0.05]	−0.23	[0.08]
Job Stabilization ($t-1$)	−0.12	[0.05]	−0.08	[0.04]	−0.09	[0.03]
	Statistic	p-value	Statistic	p-value		
Wald Test of Joint Significance	57.53	[0.000]	847.5	[0.000]		
Wald Test of Dummies Significance	1151	[0.000]	24430	[0.000]		
Sargan Test	87.25	[0.000]	56.47	[0.021]		
First-order serial correlation	−1.653	[0.098]	−1.774	[0.076]		
Second-order serial correlation	−1.762	[0.078]	−1.89	[0.047]		

North	GMM–DIF		GMM–SYS		OLS	
	Coeff.	Std.Error	Coeff.	Std.Error	Coeff.	Std.Error
Unemployment ($t-1$)	0.75	[0.02]	0.87	[0.28]	0.91	[0.01]
Mixed Cause Contracts ($t-1$)	−0.35	[0.09]	−0.32	[0.78]	−0.31	[0.11]
Subsidized Employment ($t-1$)	−0.14	[0.22]	−0.10	[0.08]	−0.19	[0.05]
Job Stabilization ($t-1$)	−0.23	[0.11]	−0.32	[0.15]	−0.79	[0.28]
	Statistic	p-value	Statistic	p-value		
Wald Test of Joint Significance	1325.0	[0.000]	507.2	[0.000]		
Wald Test of Dummies Significance	4535.0	[0.000]	157.2	[0.000]		
Sargan Test	59.3	[0.000]	61.8	[0.006]		
First-order serial correlation	−5.8	[0.000]	−1.9	[0.061]		
Second-order serial correlation	2.1	[0.021]	2.0	[0.01]		

Table 14.2. GMM estimates of the employment rate

South	GMM–DIF		GMM–SYS		OLS	
	Coeff.	Std.Error	Coeff.	Std.Error	Coeff.	Std.Error
Unemployment $(t-1)$	0.75	[0.03]	0.90	[0.04]	0.91	[0.02]
Mixed Cause Contracts $(t-1)$	0.19	[0.11]	0.22	[0.14]	0.17	[0.09]
Subsidized Employment $(t-1)$	0.50	[0.16]	0.42	[0.13]	0.37	[0.06]
Job Stabilization $(t-1)$	0.02	[0.03]	0.01	[0.05]	0.11	[0.02]
	Statistic	p-value	Statistic	p-value		
Wald Test of Joint Significance	275.5	[0.000]	179.3	[0.000]		
Wald Test of Dummies Significance	32890	[0.000]	1970	[0.000]		
Sargan Test	76.09	[0.000]	59.5	[0.000]		
First-order serial correlation	-2.041	[0.041]	-2.759	[0.006]		
Second-order serial correlation	-1.832	[0.067]	-2.445	[0.008]		

North	GMM-DIF		GMM-SYS		OLS	
	Coeff.	Std.Error	Coeff.	Std.Error	Coeff.	Std.Error
Unemployment $(t-1)$	0.80	[0.02]	0.89	[0.01]	0.90	[0.01]
Mixed Cause Contracts $(t-1)$	0.30	[0.11]	0.32	[0.07]	0.33	[0.06]
Subsidized Employment $(t-1)$	0.33	[0.12]	0.21	[0.12]	0.21	[0.13]
Job Stabilization $(t-1)$	0.36	[0.17]	0.37	[0.15]	0.63	[0.32]
	Statistic	p-value	Statistic	p-value		
Wald Test of Joint Significance	1386.0	[0.000]	4514.0	[0.000]		
Wald Test of Dummies Significance	1837.0	[0.000]	800.0	[0.000]		
Sargan Test	75.2	[0.000]	115.8	[0.000]		
First-order serial correlation	-2.8	[0.006]	-2.6	[0.009]		
Second-order serial correlation	-1.7	[0.084]	1.8	[0.070]		

Table 14.3. GMM estimates of the youth unemployment rate

South	GMM–DIF		GMM–SYS		OLS	
	Coeff.	Std.Error	Coeff.	Std.Error	Coeff.	Std.Error
Unemployment ($t-1$)	0.90	[0.03]	0.87	[0.03]	0.91	[0.02]
Mixed Cause Contracts ($t-1$)	−0.25	[0.13]	−0.23	[0.15]	−0.10	[0.49]
Subsidized Employment ($t-1$)	−0.31	[0.11]	−0.43	[0.16]	−0.41	[0.18]
Job Stabilization ($t-1$)	−0.13	[0.26]	−0.13	[0.16]	−0.27	[0.13]
	Statistic	p-value	Statistic	p-value		
Wald Test of Joint Significance	2206	[0.000]	579.6	[0.000]		
Wald Test of Dummies Significance	388	[0.000]	13990	[0.000]		
Sargan Test	79.32	[0.000]	65.9	[0.002]		
First-order serial correlation	−1.923	[0.054]	−1.951	[0.051]		
Second-order serial correlation	−1.58	[0.114]	0.1764	[0.860]		

North	GMM–DIF		GMM–SYS		OLS	
	Coeff.	Std.Error	Coeff.	Std.Error	Coeff.	Std.Error
Unemployment ($t-1$)	0.69	[0.03]	0.81	[0.02]	0.78	[0.01]
Mixed Cause Contracts ($t-1$)	−0.38	[0.62]	−0.38	[0.29]	−0.46	[0.52]
Subsidized Employment ($t-1$)	−0.80	[1.68]	−0.83	[1.15]	−0.68	[0.30]
Job Stabilization ($t-1$)	−0.52	[2.39]	−0.47	[1.68]	−0.21	[2.51]
	Statistic	p-value	Statistic	p-value		
Wald Test of Joint Significance	32.4	[0.000]	350.0	[0.000]		
Wald Test of Dummies Significance	5056.0	[0.000]	283.7	[0.000]		
Sargan Test	98.2	[0.000]	61.5	[0.007]		
First-order serial correlation	−6.0	[0.000]	−2.6	[0.009]		
Second-order serial correlation	−1.0	[0.314]	0.8	[0.451]		

14.5.2 Unemployment, ALMP and atypical contracts: a P-VAR model

There has been a growing interest in the use of panel VAR models for applied labour policy analysis. Problems concerning the evaluation of the effect of regional policies lend themselves naturally to study in this framework. Vector autoregression (VAR) models are widely used in econometric studies and in a broad variety of fields. The extension to panel data is an interesting challenge given the possible presence of cross-sectional heterogeneity.

In particular, we estimate a second order VAR using a four variable system comprising the unemployment rate, participation rate, a ratio of atypical contracts over the total of employees, and ALMP. We include atypical contracts in the estimated model because, in recent years, a significant change has taken place in the structure of employment. This structural change has resulted in a decrease in permanent, full-time 'typical' employment and an increase in the so-called 'atypical', 'contingent' or 'non-standard' employment.

We start with a panel structural dynamic linear model taking the form:

$$A \begin{bmatrix} u_{i,t} \\ P_{i,t} \\ AC_{i,t} \\ ALMP_{i,t} \end{bmatrix} = D_{i,t} + C(L) \begin{bmatrix} u_{i,t-1} \\ P_{i,t-1} \\ AC_{i,t-1} \\ ALMP_{i,t-1} \end{bmatrix} + B \begin{bmatrix} \varepsilon_{i,t}^{u} \\ \varepsilon_{i,t}^{P} \\ \varepsilon_{i,t}^{AC} \\ \varepsilon_{i,t}^{ALMP} \end{bmatrix} \quad (14.16)$$

where u_t is the unemployment rate; $P_{i,t}$ represent the participation ratio; $AC_{i,t}$ is a ratio of atypical contracts; and $ALMP_t$ is the active labour market policy rate as constructed above; $C(L)$ is a finite-order lag polynomial matrix. The region-fixed effects, i.e. the vector D, account for institutional differences as well as other region-specific unobserved influences on unemployment. This means that the system allows for different region-specific constant terms in each equation, since some regions may have higher average unemployment rates and more active labour policies than others, for reasons that are not captured by the explanatory variables. In the specified model, the four variables are assumed to be stationary. The structure of this system incorporates a feedback relationship between u_t and $ALMP_t$. This means that the two variables are allowed to affect each other contemporaneously. The contemporaneous relations among the variables are described in the A matrix.

The structural model has a VAR representation:

$$\begin{bmatrix} u_{i,t} \\ P_{i,t} \\ AC_{i,t} \\ ALMP_{i,t} \end{bmatrix} = \Gamma + A^{-1}C(L) \begin{bmatrix} u_{i,t-1} \\ P_{i,t-1} \\ AC_{i,t-1} \\ ALMP_{i,t-1} \end{bmatrix} + \begin{bmatrix} e_{i,t}^{u} \\ e_{i,t}^{P} \\ e_{i,t}^{AC} \\ e_{i,t}^{ALMP} \end{bmatrix} \quad (14.17)$$

with $E\left(e_t e_t'\right) = \Sigma$.

The structural parameters are identified by imposing linear restriction on the elements of A and B, taking into account the following relation between VAR innovations and structural disturbances:

$$A \begin{bmatrix} e_{i,t}^{u} \\ e_{i,t}^{P} \\ e_{i,t}^{AC} \\ e_{i,t}^{ALMP} \end{bmatrix} = B \begin{bmatrix} \varepsilon_{i,t}^{u} \\ \varepsilon_{i,t}^{P} \\ \varepsilon_{i,t}^{AC} \\ \varepsilon_{i,t}^{ALMP} \end{bmatrix}$$

Starting from the $n(n+1)/2$ free elements of $\hat{\Sigma}$, the lack of identification emerges from estimation of $n^2 + n^2$ parameters contained in A and B.

The identification problem is solved by restricting the contemporaneous relation matrix to a lower triangular form. This solution imposes a recursive structure on the economy, giving rise to a particular causal ordering of the variables in the system. In particular, we impose the following restrictions:

$$
\begin{bmatrix}
1 & 0 & 0 & 0 \\
a_{21} & 1 & 0 & 0 \\
a_{31} & a_{32} & 1 & 0 \\
a_{41} & a_{42} & a_{43} & 1
\end{bmatrix}
\begin{bmatrix}
e_{i,t}^{u} \\
e_{i,t}^{P} \\
e_{i,t}^{AC} \\
e_{i,t}^{ALMP}
\end{bmatrix}
=
\begin{bmatrix}
b_{11} & 0 & 0 & 0 \\
0 & b_{22} & 0 & 0 \\
0 & 0 & b_{33} & 0 \\
0 & 0 & 0 & b_{44}
\end{bmatrix}
\begin{bmatrix}
\varepsilon_{i,t}^{u} \\
\varepsilon_{i,t}^{P} \\
\varepsilon_{i,t}^{AC} \\
\varepsilon_{i,t}^{ALMP}
\end{bmatrix}
$$

The assumption $(a_{14} = 0)$ means that $ALMP_t$ does not have a contemporaneous effect on u_t. In other words, both ε_t^{u} and ε_t^{ALMP} shocks affect the contemporaneous value of $ALMP_t$, but only ε_t^{u} shocks affect the contemporaneous value of u_t.

The timing of the model can be summarized as follows: a shock to $ALMP$ in period t affects the unemployment rate at time $t + 1$. In fact, at time t the unemployment rate is predetermined, and hence cannot be influenced by any policy instrument. For example, an increase in active labour policy increases labour force participation, thereby facilitating a decrease in the unemployment rate.

The model just outlined was estimated separately for the South and North. Moreover, two different models were estimated for each macro area: in Model 1 the variable AC consisted of the ratio between part-time workers and total employees, while in Model 2 AC was the ratio between fixed-term workers and total dependent employees.

The four different specifications (Model 1 and Model 2 for South and North) were estimated in order to assess possible asymmetries between northern and southern regional unemployment levels in response to a shock to AC and $ALMP$.

14.5.3 Results of the impulse-response analysis

This section presents the estimated dynamic effects of AC and $ALMP$ shocks on unemployment examining in particular the similarity of unemployment responses in each area. This is accomplished by using impulse response functions with a structural decomposition of the variance covariance matrix explained above. A 20-quarter horizon is considered.

The estimated responses to a 1 per cent increase in unemployment and $ALMP$ are reported in Figs 14.6, 14.7, 14.8 and 14.9. Each response is provided with the associated asymptotic confidence bands.

The impulse responses for the southern regions are significantly larger than those for the northern ones. The patterns of the responses are qualitatively similar in the two areas. However, the results also suggest that the unemployment rate in the selected regions responds to identical labour policy shocks with different speeds and movements, as well as with different magnitudes of the effects.

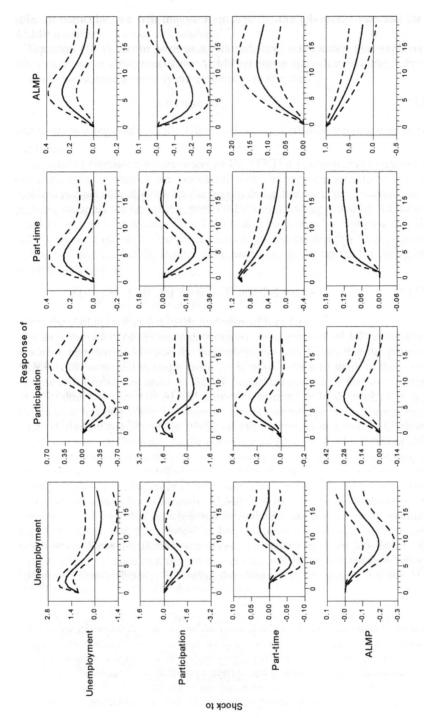

Fig. 14.6. Impulse-Response Analysis for the South: Model 1

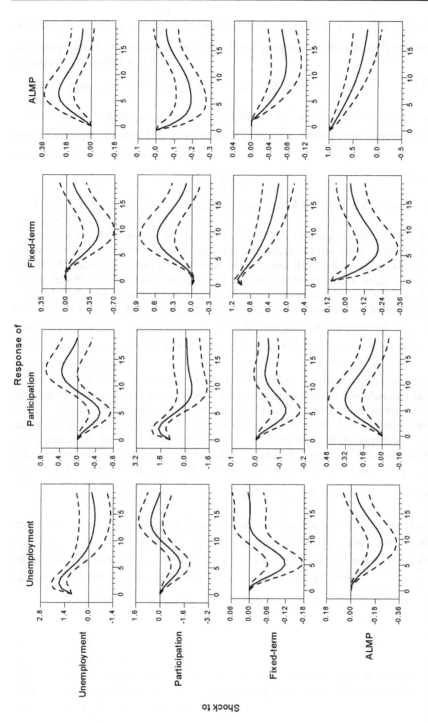

Fig. 14.7. Impulse-Response Analysis for the South: Model 2

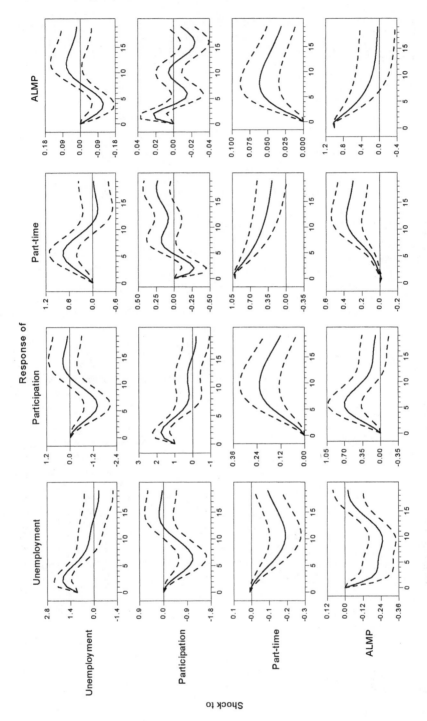

Fig. 14.8. Impulse-Response Analysis for the North: Model 1

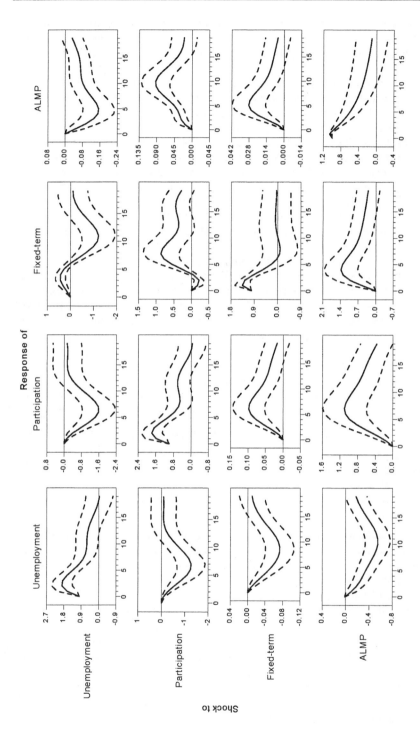

Fig. 14.9. Impulse-Response Analysis for the North: Model 2

In fact, a positive *ALMP* shock decreases unemployment. Moreover, after an initial delay, the response function displays a hump-shaped pattern that reaches maximum decline after roughly two years in the North and three years in the South.

The different adjustment speeds of the unemployment rates to *ALMP* shocks for the two selected areas can be partly explained by the existence of a higher degree of labour market rigidity in the South. This finding suggests that the 'efficiency' of the labour market should be improved.

On the other hand, the different magnitudes of the effect can be explained by considering the existing differences in both the number of vacancies and the number of unemployed in the two areas. Whilst the northern regions are characterized by a large number of vacancies and a small number of unemployed workers (the upper part of the Beveridge curve), southern regions have a small number of vacancies and a large number of unemployed (the lower part of the Beveridge curve). It follows that an identical increase in *ALMP* has a smaller effect on the southern unemployment rate.

The average response and the maximum impact of an expansionary labour policy shock are shown in Table 14.4. Table 14.4 outlines some key characteristics of the estimated response functions. In particular, it gives information about the maximum impact and the average responses of the unemployment rate to *ALMP* and *AC* structural shocks. The table also considers the time that a shock takes to exert its maximum effect on unemployment, as well as the time that it takes to die out.

Table 14.4. Estimated response function features

	South				North			
	Model 1		Model 2		Model 1		Model 2	
	Part-time	Almp	Fixed-term	Almp	Part-time	Almp	Fixed-term	Almp
Average Effect	-0.01	-0.09	-0.04	-0.12	-0.13	-0.14	-0.04	-0.34
Maximum Effect	-0.06	-0.19	-0.12	-0.23	-0.20	-0.24	-0.07	-0.53
Time to maximum	6	10	10	10	12	9	10	11
Time to die out	16	20	24	22	22	20	20	24

Despite some qualitative similarities, the table seems to suggest the existence of different quantitative responses across regions. In both areas, an ALMP shock produces a decline in the unemployment rate. However, the magnitudes of the effect are quite dissimilar. Whilst in the South the unemployment rate decreases by more than 20 basis points (Model 2 – South), an ALMP shock in the North reduces the unemployment rate by 53 basis points (Model 2 – North). The maximum impact of fixed-term contracts is observed in the southern regions: –12 basis points. Moreover, the effect of fixed-term shock reaches its maximum later than in the North, so that in the Southern regions, the unemployment rate appears to be more greatly influenced by the changes in the number of fixed-term contracts. Finally, there are no large differences across regions in the time that the shock takes to die out. A fixed-term shock lasts longer in southern regions, but an ALMP shock seems to be more persistent in the north.

Asymmetries are also detected in the response of the unemployment rate to an exogenous part-time shock. Again, the largest responses are observed in the North: in particular, the response of unemployment in the northern regions reaches a maximum of twenty basis points after 12 months, while the reaction of the southern Italian regions is smaller and more rapid: six basis points after 6 months.

14.5.4 Results of forecast error variance decomposition (FEVD)

An important tool developed in the *S-VAR* framework is the forecast error variance decomposition. The main strength of this type of analysis is its ability to capture the weight of different variable innovations on a given variable forecast error variance decomposition.

In other words, it yields information on the percentage of variation in the forecast error of a variable explained by its own innovation and the proportion explained by innovations in other variables at different horizons.

Table 14.5 depicts the forecast error variance decomposition of the unemployment rate in the four models estimated above, and up to a two-year horizon, due to the four structural shocks.

Table 14.5. Fraction of the unemployment rate that FEVD attributed to the four structural shocks

	South							
Horizon	Model 1				Model 2			
	Unemp.	Partic.	Part-time	Almp	Unemp.	Partic.	Fixed-term	Almp
1	100	0	0	0	100	0	0	0
6	95.4	0.8	0.3	3.2	91.0	0.5	2.3	6.5
12	83.1	2.3	0.8	13.4	79.2	1.6	9.9	9.7
18	80.6	3.4	1.3	14.7	76.7	2.3	10.9	10.2
24	79.6	3.6	1.7	15.1	75.7	2.5	11.3	10.6

	North							
Horizon	Model 1				Model 2			
	Unemp.	Partic.	Part-time	Almp	Unemp.	Partic.	Fixed-term	Almp
1	100	0	0	0	100	0	0	0
6	83.1	6.3	3.8	6.7	83.5	6.4	5.4	4.7
12	65.4	8.8	17.3	8.5	71.1	9.6	10.1	9.3
18	56.9	8.4	25.4	9.3	68.8	9.1	10.7	11.4
24	54.9	8.6	27.2	9.3	67.5	9.4	11.1	12.0

The above table furnishes useful information on the relative capacities of *ALMP* and *AC* to affect unemployment dynamics at different horizons.

Hence, according to the variance decomposition at short horizons, ALMP innovations do not play a major role in the monthly fluctuations of the unemployment rate. The dynamics of unemployment are largely dominated by its own shocks, and they indicate that short-run fluctuations in the unemployment rate display no association with active labour market programmes or with the dynamics of atypical contracts. For long horizons, we find that both ALMP and atypical contracts exert a certain influence in determining unemployment dynamics. This influence varies across the regions.

In the southern regions, unemployment is essentially driven by its own shocks. The fixed-term ratio, although greater than the part-time variable, does not significantly affect movements in the unemployment rate: after two years, it explains 11 per cent of the unemployment change. Nor do the ALMP shocks seem to explain more than 15 per cent of unemployment change.

In the northern regions, by contrast, unemployment dynamics seem to be partially explained by the increase in atypical contracts: in particular, movements in the part-time ratio after two years account for almost 30 per cent of unemployment variation.

We may conclude that there are different explanations for unemployment dynamics in the two areas. In the South neither *ALMP* nor *AC* seems to account for changes in the unemployment rate: the unemployment is driven by its own shocks. By contrast, in the northern regions, the unemployment dynamics is significantly explained by part-time work dynamics.

14.6 Conclusions

The paper has been concerned with theoretical and empirical measurement of the ability of ALMPs to reduce regional unemployment. The importance of the issues addressed springs from the possible asymmetries the differences in the economic structure of the Italian regions may arise concerning the effectiveness of alternative labour market programs.

The econometric methodologies implemented have been the generalized method of moment (GMM) and the panel vector autoregression (P-VAR). As regards the former, we estimated a single equation dynamic panel data model for several dependent variables including employment rate, unemployment rate, and youth unemployment rate. The evidence furnished by this model suggested that the effects of different ALMPs on unemployment are dissimilar across the Italian regions. Some programmes are likely to have a greater effect in the South than in the North. The second methodology was based on the P-VAR framework, and it was used to estimate four different models, the purpose being to outline the effects that the total ALMP/labour force ratio and atypical contracts exert on unemployment dynamics.

The impulse-response analysis highlighted the presence of significant differences across the Italian regions. Importantly, the results suggest that the unemployment rate in the regions selected responds to identical labour policy shocks with different speeds and movements, and also with different magnitudes of effects. The same applies to the response of the unemployment rate to AC shocks.

Finally, the forecast error variance decomposition yielded information on the extent to which various structural shocks affect the behaviour of each variable at different horizons. We conclude from this analysis that there are different explanations for unemployment dynamics in the two areas. In the South neither $ALMP$ nor AC seem to be responsible for changes in the unemployment rate: unemployment is driven by its own shocks. In the North, by contrast, unemployment dynamics are significantly explained by part-time work dynamics.

References

Bellmann L, Jackman R (1996), Aggregate impact analysis. In: Schmid G, O'Relly J and Schomann K (eds) International handbook of labour market policy and evaluation. Edward Elgar, London, pp. 143–162.

Blanchard O, Wolfers J (2000) The role of shocks and institutions in the rise of European unemployment: the aggregate evidence. Economic Journal 110: C1–C33.

Scarpetta S (1996) Addressing the role of labor market policies and institutional settings on unemployment: a cross-country study. OECD Economic Studies 26: 44–98.

Calmfors L (1994) Active labour market policy and unemployment – a framework for the analysis of crucial design features. OECD Economic Studies 22: 7–47.

Calmfors L, Lang H. (1995) Macroeconomic effects of active labour market programmes in a union wage-setting model. Economic Journal 105: 601–619.

Calmfors L, Forslund A, Hemström M (2001) Does active labour market policies work? lessons from the Swedish experiences. Swedish Economic Policy Review 8: 61–124.

Caroleo FE, Pastore F (2005) La disoccupazione giovanile in Italia. La riforma dei sistemi d'istruzione e della formazione professionale come alternativa alla flessibilità numerica per accrescere l'occupabilità. Economia & Lavoro. Forthcoming.

Christl J (1992) The unemployment/vacancy curve: theoretical foundation and empirical relevance. Physica, Heidelberg.

European Commission (2003), The future of the European Employment Strategy (EES): a strategy for full employment and better jobs for all, European Commission, Brussels.

Fay RG (1996) Enhancing the effectiveness of active labour market policies: evidence from programme evaluations in OECD countries. OECD Labour Market and Social Policy Occasional Paper 18. OECD, Paris.

Frisch H (1984), Theories of inflation. Cambridge University Press, Cambridge.

Hall RE (1977) An aspect of the economic role of unemployment. In: Harcourt GC (ed.) Microeconomic foundations of macroeconomics. McMillan, London, pp 354–372.

Heckman J, La Londe R, Smith J (1999) The economics and econometrics of active labor market programs. In: Ashenfelter O, Card D, Handbook of labor economics, vol 3. Elsevier, Amsterdam, pp 1865–2097.

Hujer R, Caliendo M (2001) Evaluation of active labour market policy – Methodological concepts and empirical estimates. In: Becker I, Ott N, Rolf G (eds) Soziale Sicherung in einer dynamischen Gesellschaft. Campus, Frankfurt, pp 583–617.

Jackman R, Pissarides C, Savouri S (1990) Labour market policies and unemployment in the OECD. Economic Policy 5: 450–490.

Johansson K (2001) Do labor market programs affect labor force participation?. Swedish Economic Policy Review 8: 215–234.

Layard R (1999), Tackling unemployment. MacMillan Press, London.

Layard R, Nickell S, Jackman R (1991), Unemployment: macroeconomic performance and the labour market. Oxford University Press, Oxford.

Martin JP, Grubb D (2001), What works and for whom: a review of OECD countries' experiences with active labour market policies. Swedish Economic Policy Review 8: 9–56.

Martini A, Rettore E, Trivellato U (2003) La valutazione delle politiche del lavoro in presenza di selezione: migliorare la teoria, i metodi o i dati?. Politica Economica, 3: 301–342.

McCall JJ (1970) Economics of information and job search. Quarterly Journal of Economics 84: 113–126.

MLPS (various issues), Rapporto di monitoraggio sulle politiche occupazionali e del lavoro, Ministero del Lavoro e delle Politiche Sociali, Roma.

Mortensen DT (1970) Job search, duration of unemployment and the Phillips curve. American Economic Review 60:847–862.

Nickell S (1997) Unemployment and labor market rigidities: Europe versus North America. Journal of Economic Perspectives 11: 55–74.

Nickell S, Layard R (1997) Labour market institutions and economic performance. In: Ashenfelter O, Card D, Handbook of labor economics, vol 3. Elsevier, Amsterdam, pp 3029–3085.

OECD (1994), The OECD jobs study. OECD, Paris.

OECD (1996), The OECD jobs strategy: enhancing the effectiveness of active labour market. OECD, Paris.

Petrongolo B, Pissarides CA (2001) Looking into the black box: a survey of the matching function. Journal of Economic Literature, 39: 390–441.

Pissarides CA (1990), Equilibrium unemployment theory. Blackwell, Oxford.

List of Contributors

Altavilla, Carlo, Professor
  Department of Economics, University of Naples "Parthenope'
  Via Medina, 40, I-80133 Napoli
  Italy

Amendola, Adalgiso, Professor
  CELPE, University of Salerno
  Via Ponte Don Melillo, I-84084 Fisciano (SA)
  Italy

Blien, Uwe, Research Director
  Institute for Employment Research (IAB)
  Weddigenstrasse 20-22, D-90478 Nürnberg
  Germany

Caliendo, Marco, Senior Research Associate
  German Institute for Economic Research (DIW)
  Königin-Luise-Strasse 5, D-14195 Berlin
  Germany

Caroleo, Floro Ernesto, Professor
  CELPE, University of Salerno
  Via Ponte Don Melillo, I-84084 Fisciano (SA)
  Italy

Coppola, Gianluigi, Assistant Professor
  CELPE, University of Salerno
  Via Ponte Don Melillo, I-84084 Fisciano (SA)
  Italy

Destefanis, Sergio, Professor
  CELPE, University of Salerno
  Via Ponte Don Melillo, I-84084 Fisciano (SA)
  Italy

Domadenik, Polona, Assistant Professor
  Economics Faculty, University of Ljubljana
  Kardeljeva ploščad 17, SI-1000 Ljubljana
  Slovenia

Ferragina, Anna Maria, Research Fellow
ISSM-CNR
Via Pietro Castellino 111, I-80131 Napoli
Italy

Fernández, Melchor, Professor
Department of Economic Analysis, University of Santiago de Compostela
Avda do Burgo dos Nacións s/n, E-15782 Santiago de Compostela
Spain

Fonseca, Raquel, Research Fellow
CSEF, University of Salerno
Via Ponte Don Melillo, I-84084 Fisciano (SA)
Italy

Gambarotto, Francesca, Professor
'Marco Fanno' Department of Economics, University of Padova
Via del Santo 33, I-35123 Padova
Italy

García, Inmaculada, Professor
Department of Economic Analysis, University of Zaragoza
Gran Via 2, E-50005 Zaragoza
Spain

Hujer, Reinhard, Professor
Department of Economics, University of Frankfurt
Mertonstrasse 17, D-60054 Frankfurt/Main
Germany

Limosani, Michele, Professor
Department of Economics, University of Messina
Via T. Cannizzaro 278, I-98122 Messina
Italy

Maggioni, Mario A., Professor
DISEIS, Catholic University of 'Sacro Cuore', Milan
Via Necchi 5, I-2123 Milano
Italy

Marelli, Enrico, Professor
Department of Economics, University of Brescia
Via San Faustino 74/B, I-25122 Brescia
Italy

Monastiriotis, Vassilis, Lecturer
   European Institute and Hellenic Observatory, London School of Economics
   Houghton Street, London WC2A 2AE
   United Kingdom

Montuenga, Victor, Professor
   Department of Economics and Business Studies, University of La Rioja
   Edificio Quintiliano, c/La Cigüeña 60, E-26004 Logroño
   Spain

Newell, Andrew, Professor
   Department of Economics, University of Sussex
   Falmer, Brighton BN1 9QN
   United Kingdom

Pastore, Francesco, Assistant Professor
   Faculty of Law, University of Naples II
   Via Mazzocchi 5, I-81055 Santa Maria Capua Vetere (CE)
   Italy

Sena, Vania, Senior Lecturer
   Aston Business School, Aston University
   Birmingham B4 7EF
   United Kingdom

Südekum, Jens, Assistant Professor
   Department of Economics, University of Konstanz
   Fach D132, D-78457 Konstanz
   Germany

Vehovec, Maja, Professor
   School of Economics, University of Rijeka
   Filipovičeva 4, HR-51000 Rijeka,
   Croatia

Zeiss, Christopher, Research Assistent
   Department of Economics, University of Frankfurt
   Mertonstrasse 17, D-60054 Frankfurt/Main
   Germany